LIVING·ROOM

LIVING·ROOM
↑
MATSUNAGA·SAN

4

Keiko Iwashita

MATSUNAGA
SAN

LIVING-ROOM

Contents

Story

Family circumstances have wrested Meeko from an ordinary family life to her uncle's boarding house, where she must learn to live with rather unusual adult housemates. What's more, the oldest of the bunch, Matsunaga-san, is a little scary. However, contrary to his appearance, he watches out for Meeko and helps her get used to her new life, and Meeko finds herself increasingly drawn to him. Swept up in the moment after an accidental kiss, Meeko confesses her feelings! She manages to cover it up, but her love for him only grows ♡. As her most recent escapade, Meeko starts a part-time job to prepare for Matsunaga-san's upcoming birthday. On his special day, everyone at the boarding house gathers for a grand party atop the roof. But right at the height of the festivities, Matsunaga-san suddenly tells her something unbelievable...!!!

MATSUNAGA-SAN

Let's introduce the people living at my boarding house!

Uncle   Sabako   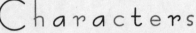Characters

Miko Sonoda

A 17-year-old high school girl.
Only knows how to cook curry.
Pining for Matsunaga-san.

Jun Matsunaga

A designer who works from home.
28 years old.
Sharp-tongued but caring.

Kentaro Suzuki
A bartender.
Girl-crazy (?)

Asako Onuki
A nail artist.
Like a big sister.

Ryo Hojo
A quiet
college student.
Doesn't have a
girlfriend.

Akane Hattori
An enigma.
Actually has
a boyfriend.

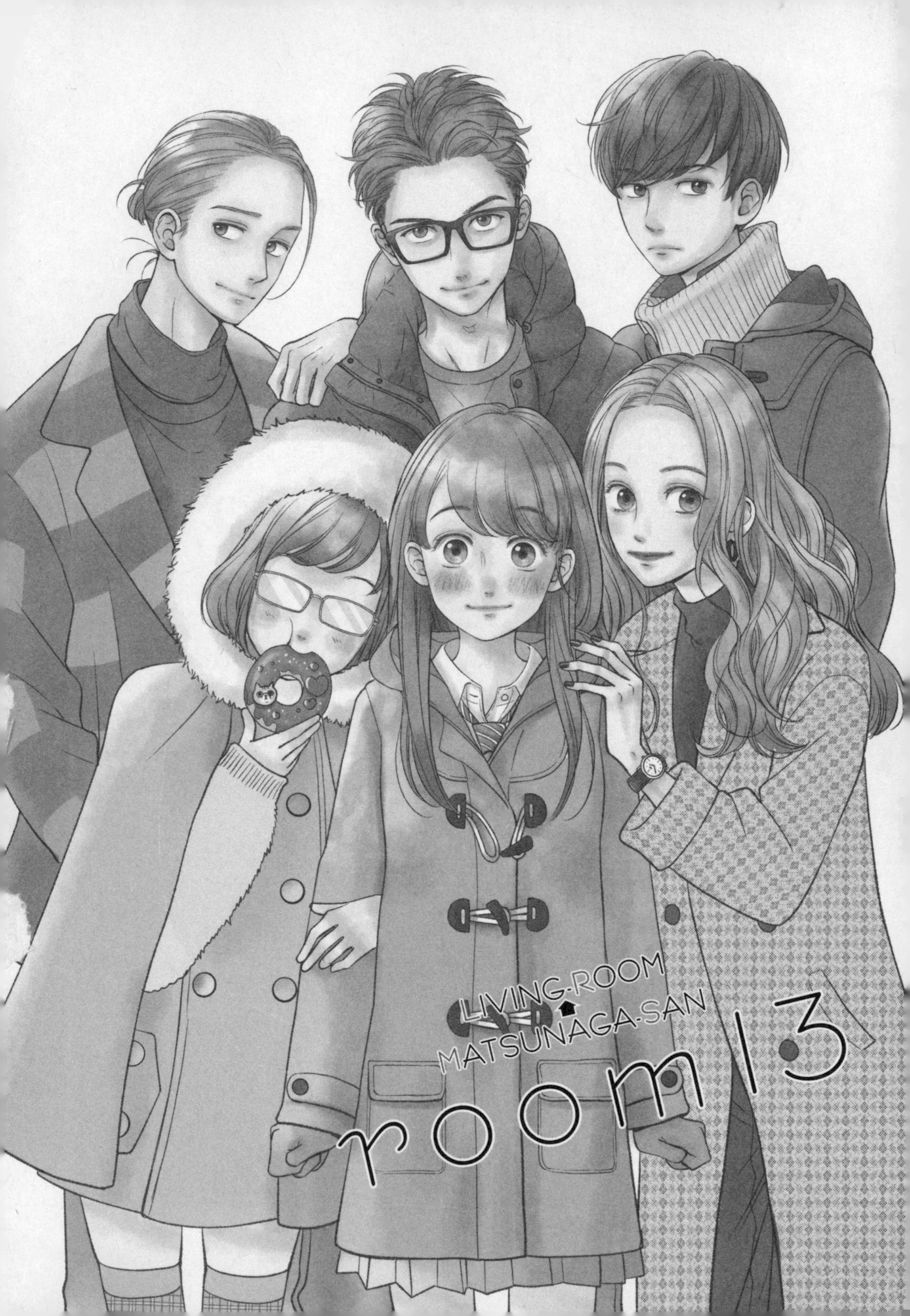
LIVING-ROOM MATSUNAGA-SAN
room 13

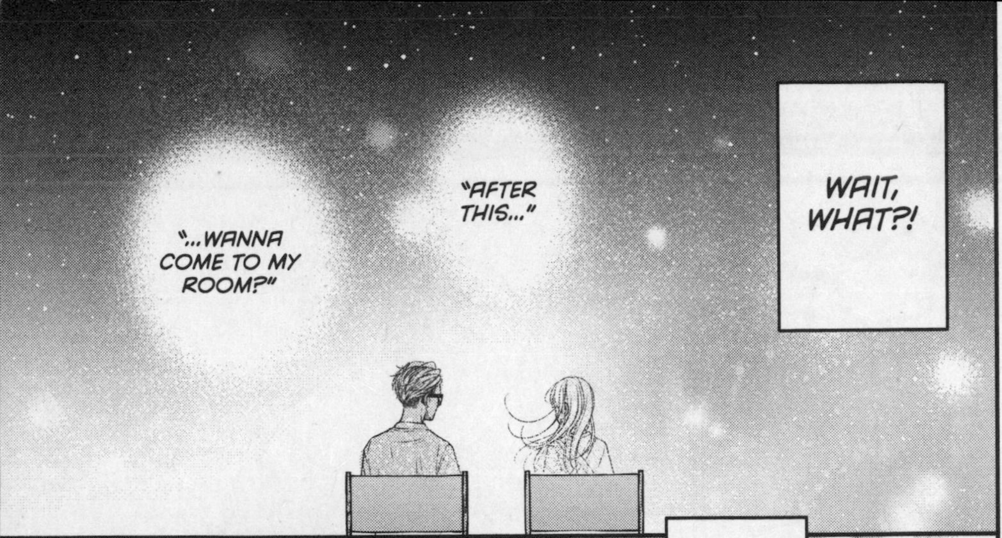
WAIT, WHAT?!
"AFTER THIS..."
"...WANNA COME TO MY ROOM?"

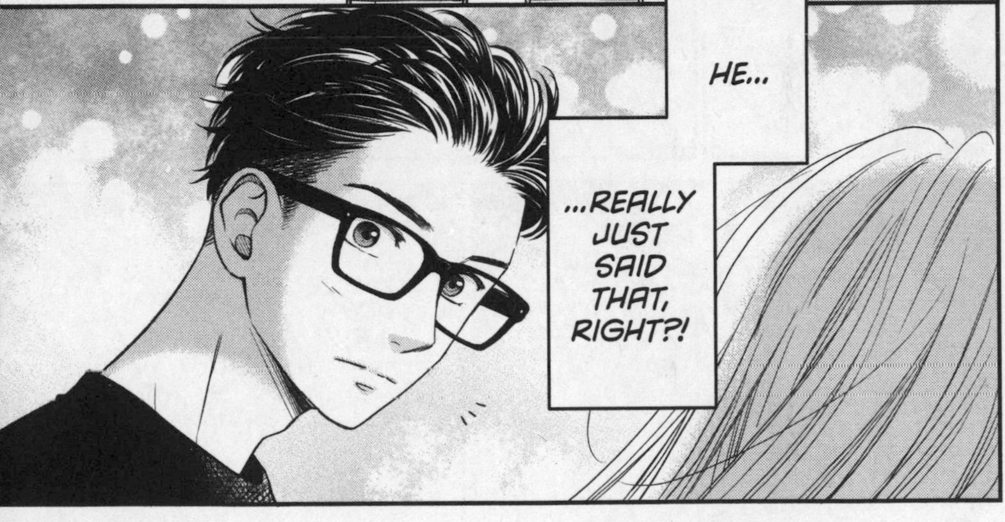
HE...
...REALLY JUST SAID THAT, RIGHT?!

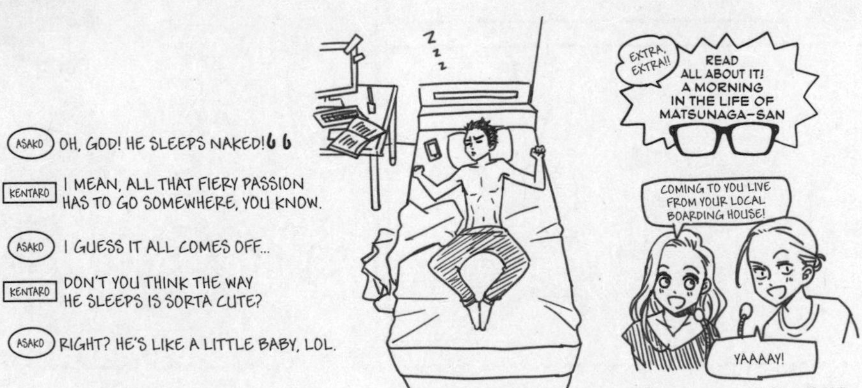
EXTRA, EXTRA!!
READ ALL ABOUT IT! A MORNING IN THE LIFE OF MATSUNAGA-SAN
COMING TO YOU LIVE FROM YOUR LOCAL BOARDING HOUSE!
YAAAAY!
ASAKO & KENTARO
Z Z Z
ASAKO OH, GOD! HE SLEEPS NAKED!
KENTARO I MEAN, ALL THAT FIERY PASSION HAS TO GO SOMEWHERE, YOU KNOW.
ASAKO I GUESS IT ALL COMES OFF...
KENTARO DON'T YOU THINK THE WAY HE SLEEPS IS SORTA CUTE?
ASAKO RIGHT? HE'S LIKE A LITTLE BABY, LOL.

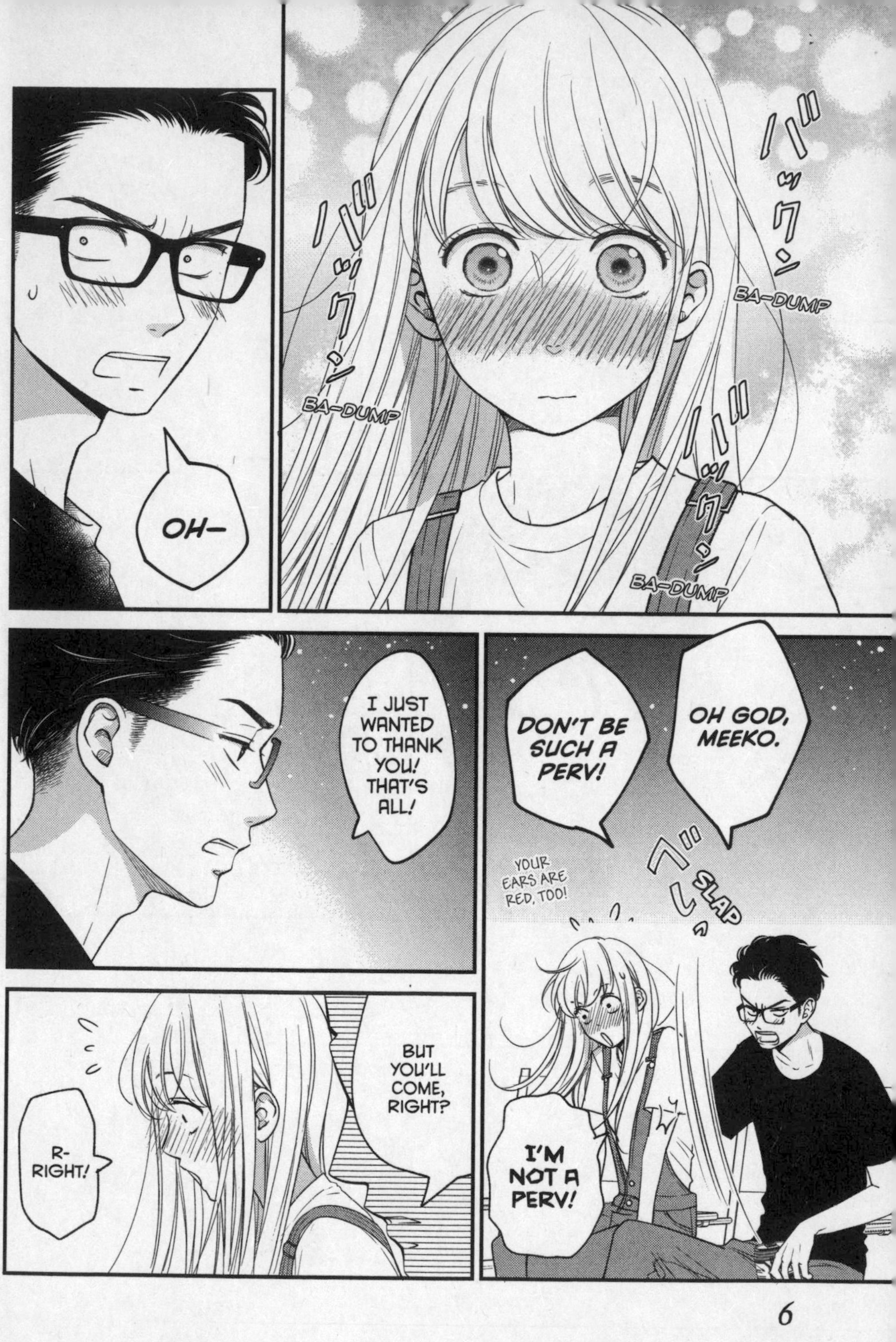
バックン
BA-DUMP
バックン
BA-DUMP
バックン
BA-DUMP
OH—
OH GOD, MEEKO.
DON'T BE SUCH A PERV!
へし
SLAP
YOUR EARS ARE RED, TOO!
I'M NOT A PERV!
I JUST WANTED TO THANK YOU! THAT'S ALL!
BUT YOU'LL COME, RIGHT?
R-RIGHT!

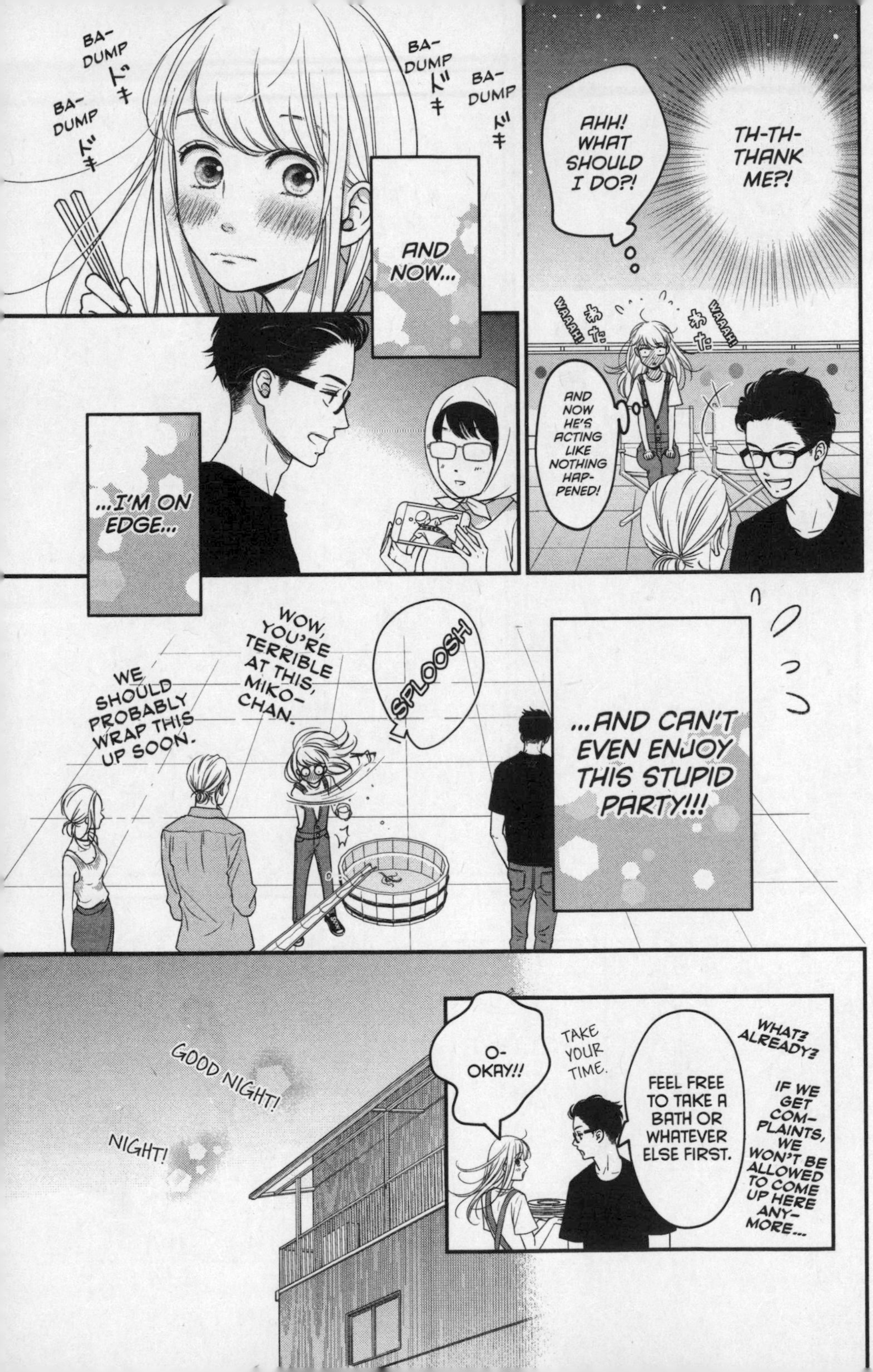
TH-TH-THANK ME?!
AHH! WHAT SHOULD I DO?!
WAAAH! わた
WAAAH! わた
AND NOW HE'S ACTING LIKE NOTHING HAP-PENED!
BA-DUMP ドキ
BA-DUMP ドキ
BA-DUMP ドキ
BA-DUMP ドキ
AND NOW...
...I'M ON EDGE...
...AND CAN'T EVEN ENJOY THIS STUPID PARTY!!!
SPLOOSH
WOW, YOU'RE TERRIBLE AT THIS, MIKO-CHAN.
WE SHOULD PROBABLY WRAP THIS UP SOON.
WHAT? ALREADY?
IF WE GET COM-PLAINTS, WE WON'T BE ALLOWED TO COME UP HERE ANY-MORE...
FEEL FREE TO TAKE A BATH OR WHATEVER ELSE FIRST.
TAKE YOUR TIME.
O-OKAY!!
GOOD NIGHT!
NIGHT!

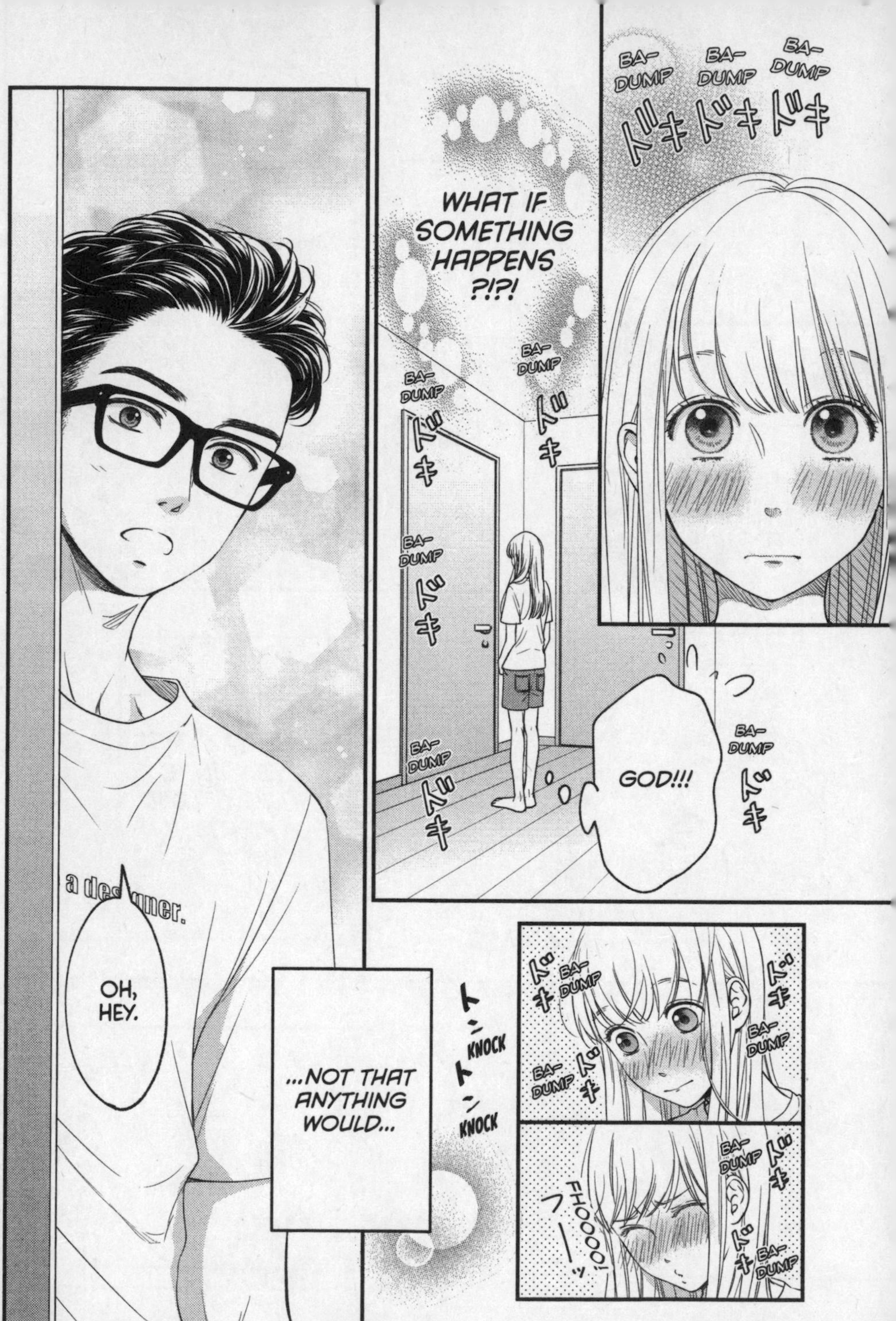

BA-DUMP
BA-DUMP
BA-DUMP
BA-DUMP
WHAT IF SOMETHING HAPPENS ?!?!
BA-DUMP
BA-DUMP
BA-DUMP
BA-DUMP
GOD!!!
BA-DUMP
BA-DUMP
BA-DUMP
BA-DUMP
BA-DUMP
FHOOOO!
BA-DUMP
KNOCK
KNOCK
...NOT THAT ANYTHING WOULD...
OH, HEY.

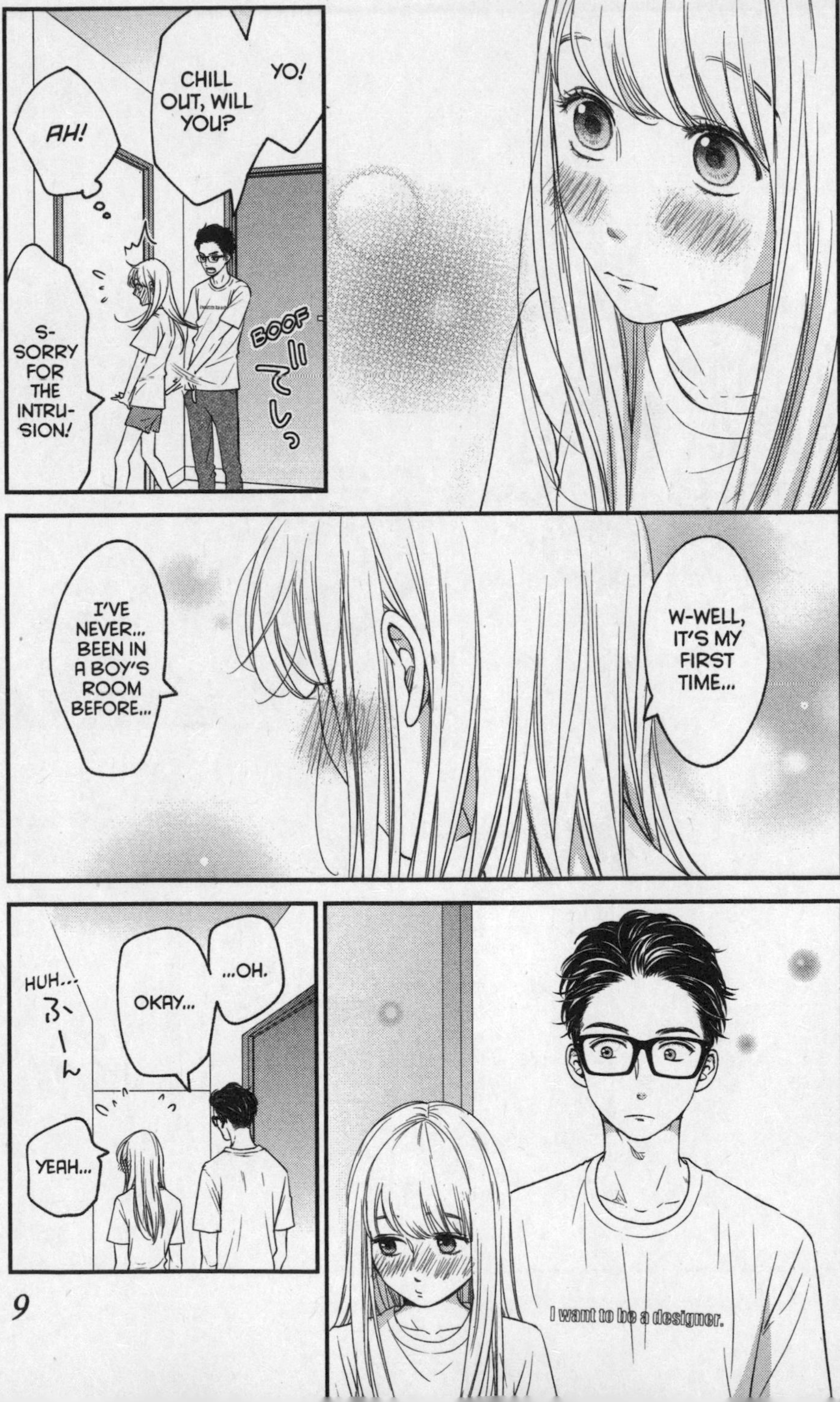
YO!
CHILL OUT, WILL YOU?
AH!
BOOF
でしっ
S-SORRY FOR THE INTRUSION!
W-WELL, IT'S MY FIRST TIME...
I'VE NEVER... BEEN IN A BOY'S ROOM BEFORE...
I want to be a designer.
...OH.
OKAY...
HUH...
ふーん
YEAH...

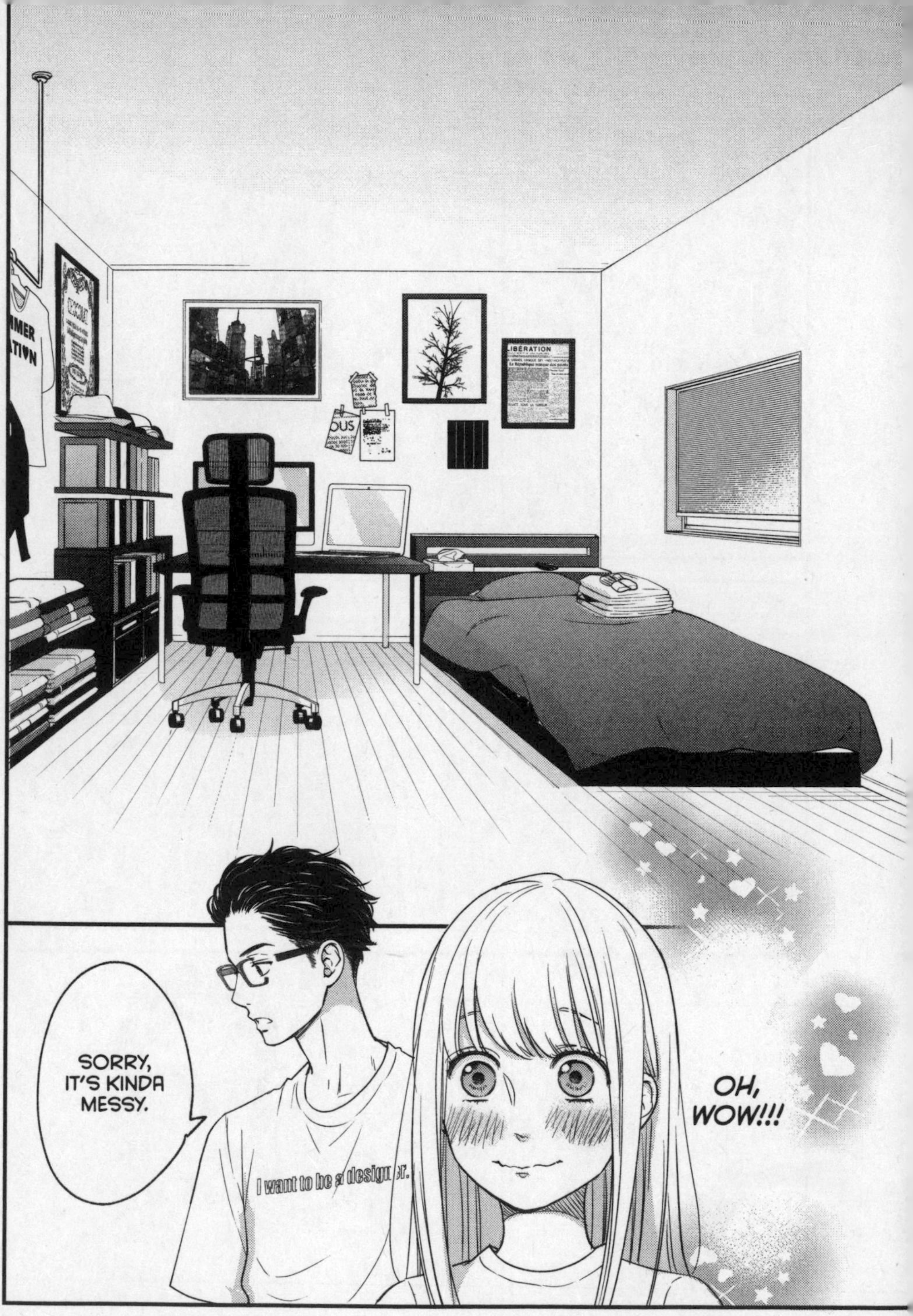
LIBÉRATION
OH, WOW!!!
SORRY, IT'S KINDA MESSY.

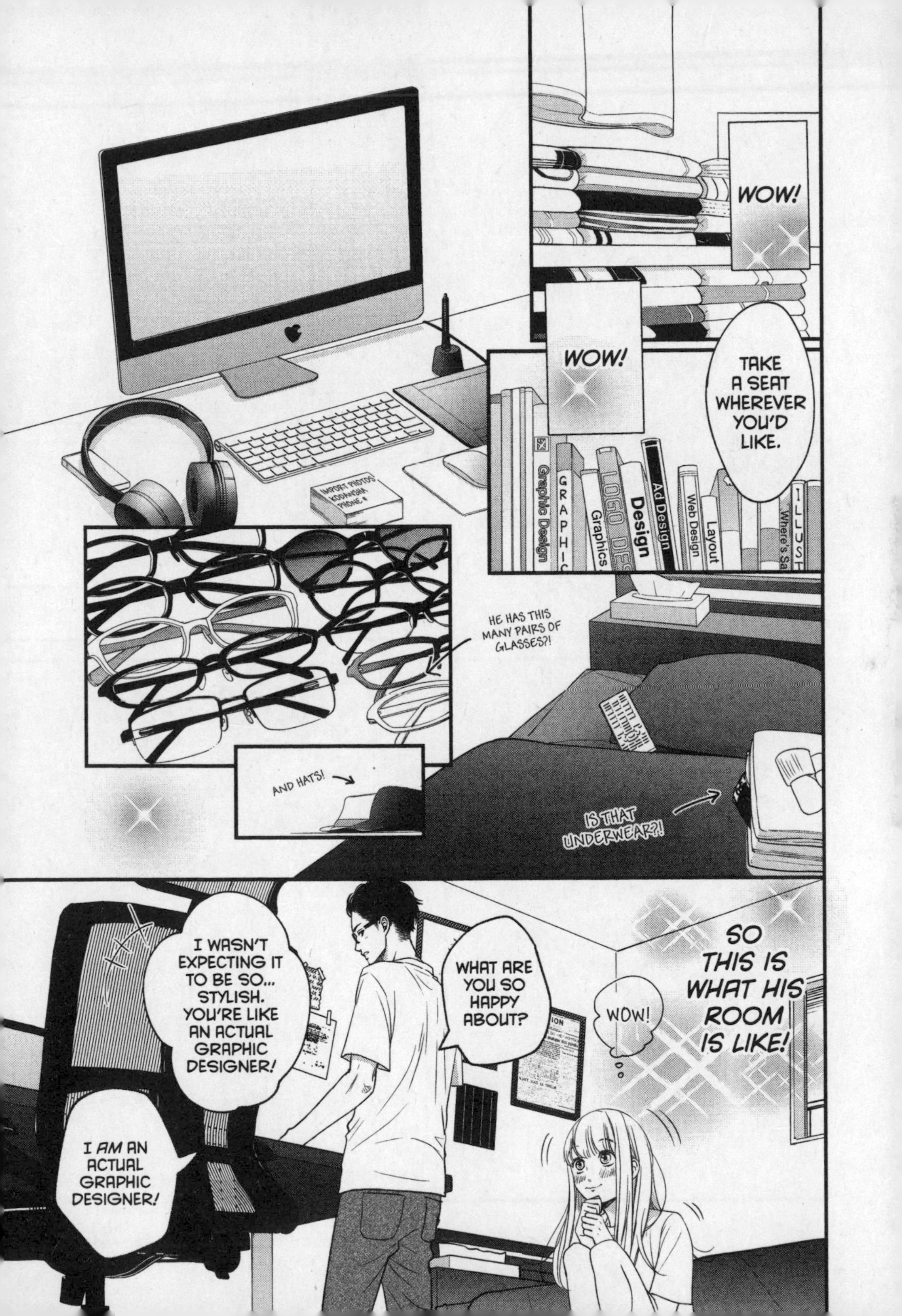
WOW!
WOW!
TAKE A SEAT WHEREVER YOU'D LIKE.
Graphic Design
GRAPHIC
LOGO DES
Graphics
Design
Ad Design
Web Design
Layout
Where's Sa
ILLUST
IMPORT PHOTOS KODANSHA PHONE #
HE HAS THIS MANY PAIRS OF GLASSES?!
AND HATS!
IS THAT UNDERWEAR?!
SO THIS IS WHAT HIS ROOM IS LIKE!
WOW!
WHAT ARE YOU SO HAPPY ABOUT?
I WASN'T EXPECTING IT TO BE SO... STYLISH. YOU'RE LIKE AN ACTUAL GRAPHIC DESIGNER!
I AM AN ACTUAL GRAPHIC DESIGNER!

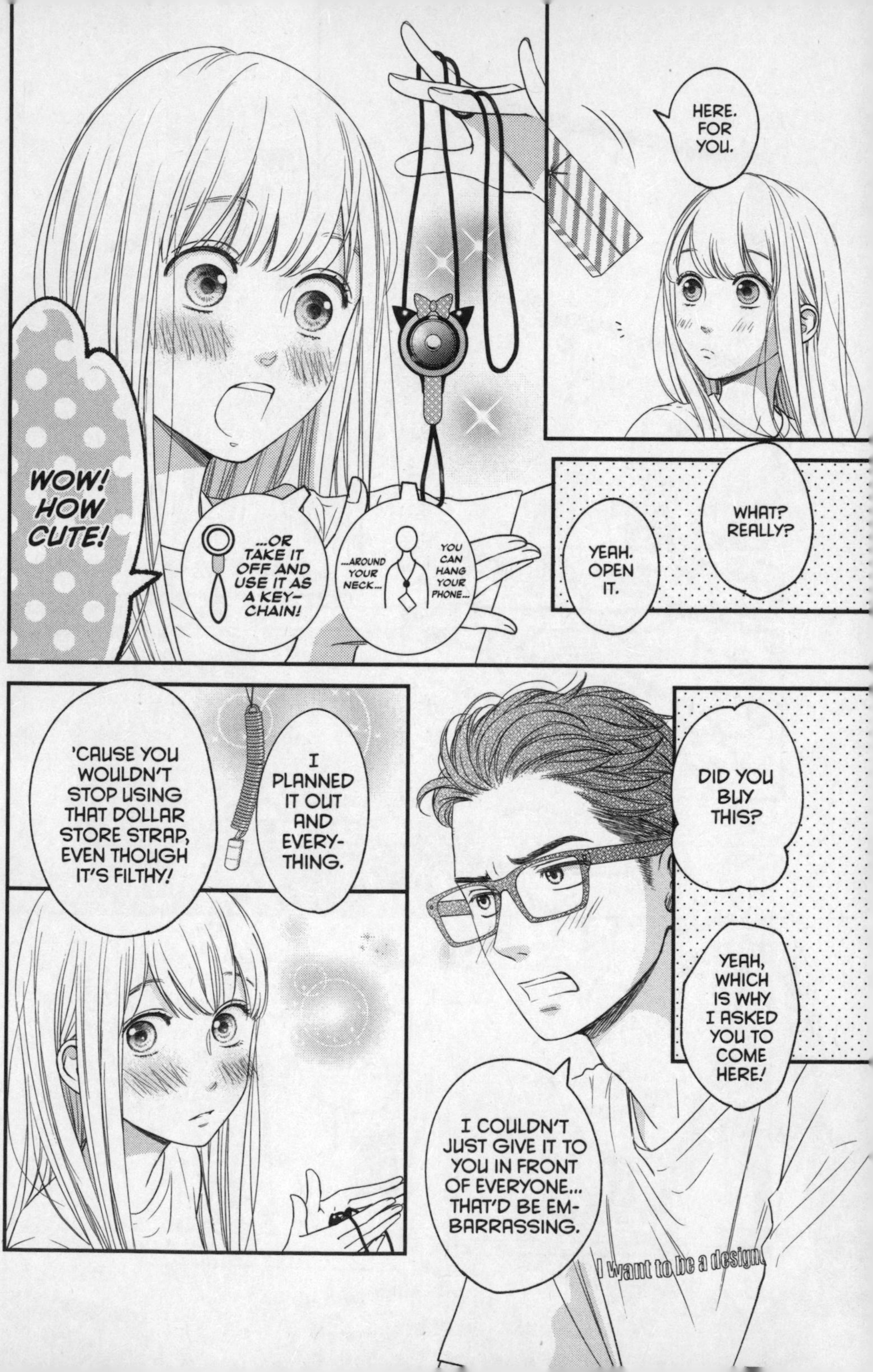
HERE. FOR YOU.
WHAT? REALLY?
YEAH. OPEN IT.
WOW! HOW CUTE!
YOU CAN HANG YOUR PHONE...
...AROUND YOUR NECK...
...OR TAKE IT OFF AND USE IT AS A KEY-CHAIN!
DID YOU BUY THIS?
YEAH, WHICH IS WHY I ASKED YOU TO COME HERE!
I COULDN'T JUST GIVE IT TO YOU IN FRONT OF EVERYONE... THAT'D BE EM-BARRASSING.
I want to be a design
I PLANNED IT OUT AND EVERY-THING.
'CAUSE YOU WOULDN'T STOP USING THAT DOLLAR STORE STRAP, EVEN THOUGH IT'S FILTHY!

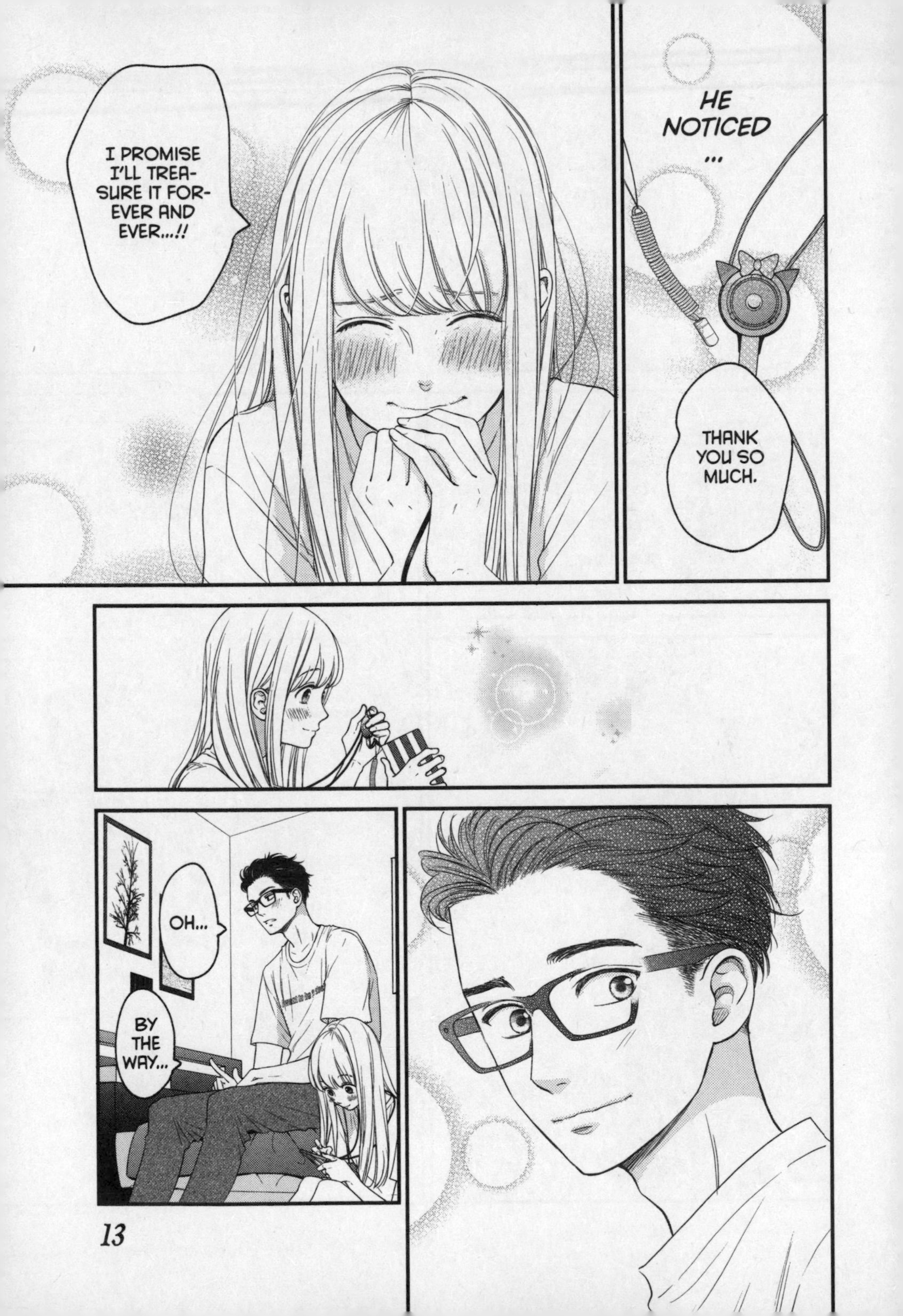
HE NOTICED ...
THANK YOU SO MUCH.
I PROMISE I'LL TREA-SURE IT FOR-EVER AND EVER...!!
OH...
BY THE WAY...

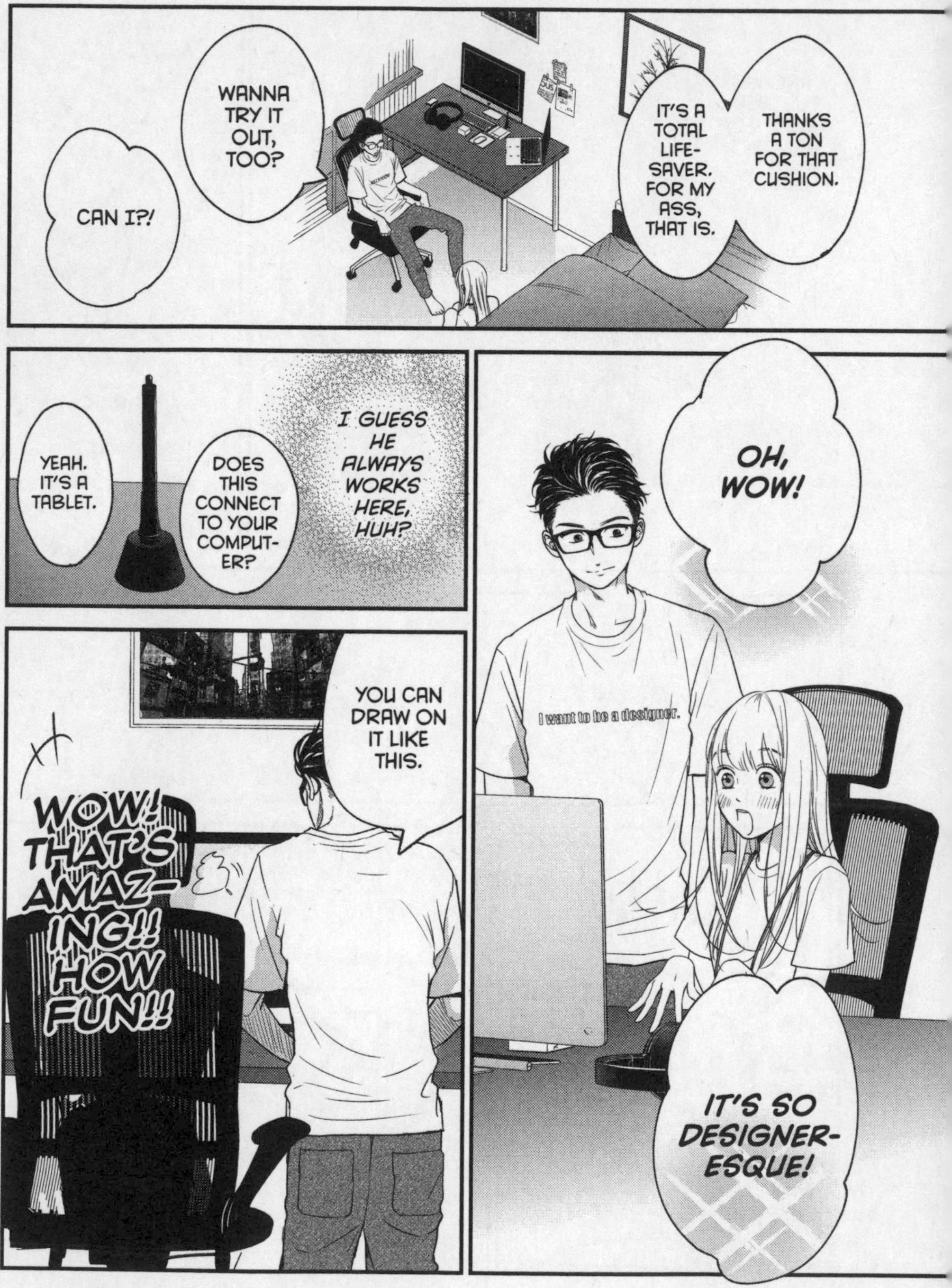
THANKS A TON FOR THAT CUSHION.
IT'S A TOTAL LIFE-SAVER. FOR MY ASS, THAT IS.
WANNA TRY IT OUT, TOO?
CAN I?!
OH, WOW!
I want to be a designer.
IT'S SO DESIGNER-ESQUE!
I GUESS HE ALWAYS WORKS HERE, HUH?
DOES THIS CONNECT TO YOUR COMPUTER?
YEAH. IT'S A TABLET.
YOU CAN DRAW ON IT LIKE THIS.
WOW! THAT'S AMAZ-ING!! HOW FUN!!

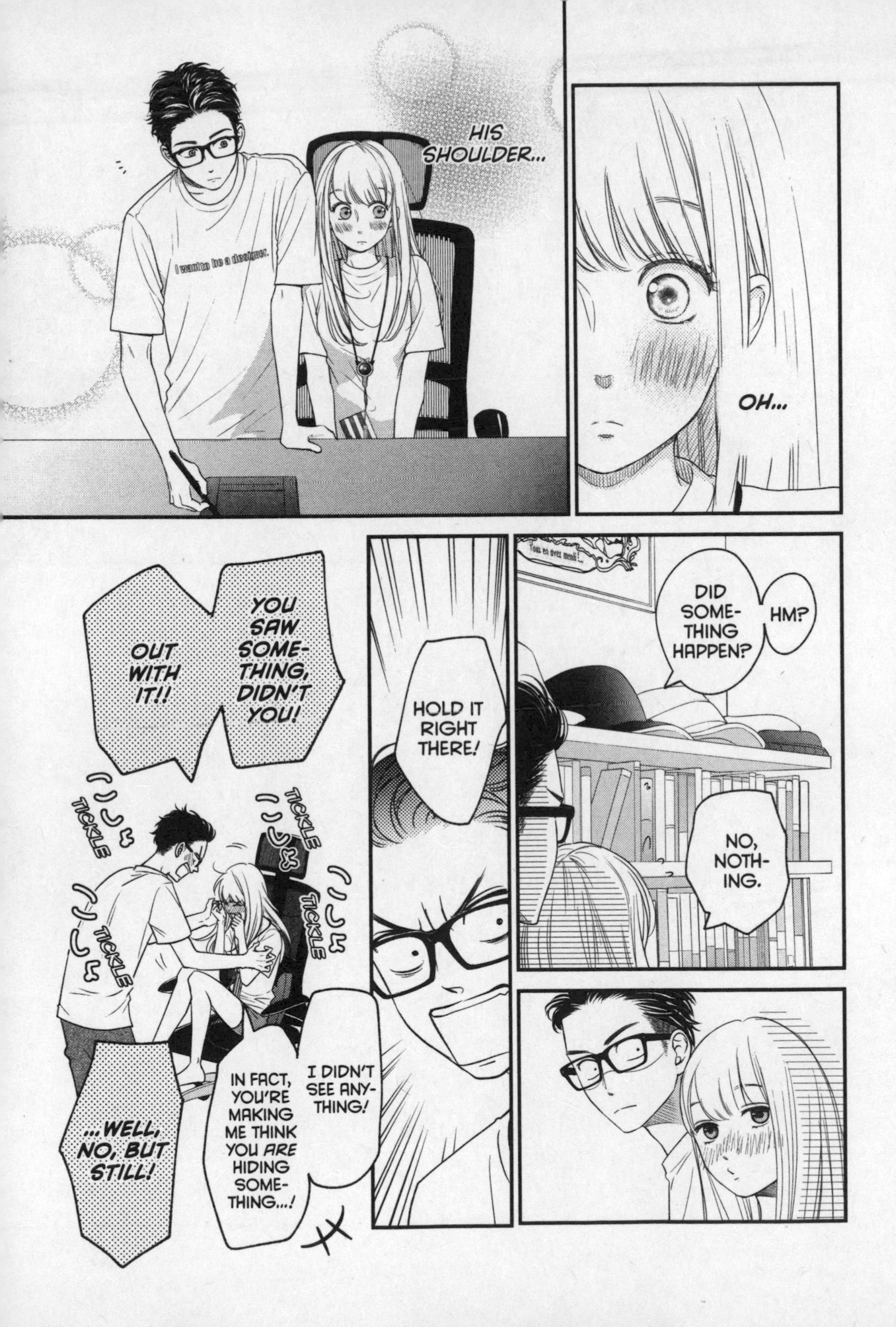
OH...
HIS SHOULDER...
I want to be a designer.
HM?
DID SOME-THING HAPPEN?
NO, NOTH-ING.
HOLD IT RIGHT THERE!
I DIDN'T SEE ANY-THING!
IN FACT, YOU'RE MAKING ME THINK YOU *ARE* HIDING SOME-THING...!
YOU SAW SOME-THING, DIDN'T YOU!
OUT WITH IT!!
TICKLE
TICKLE
TICKLE
TICKLE
...WELL, NO, BUT STILL!

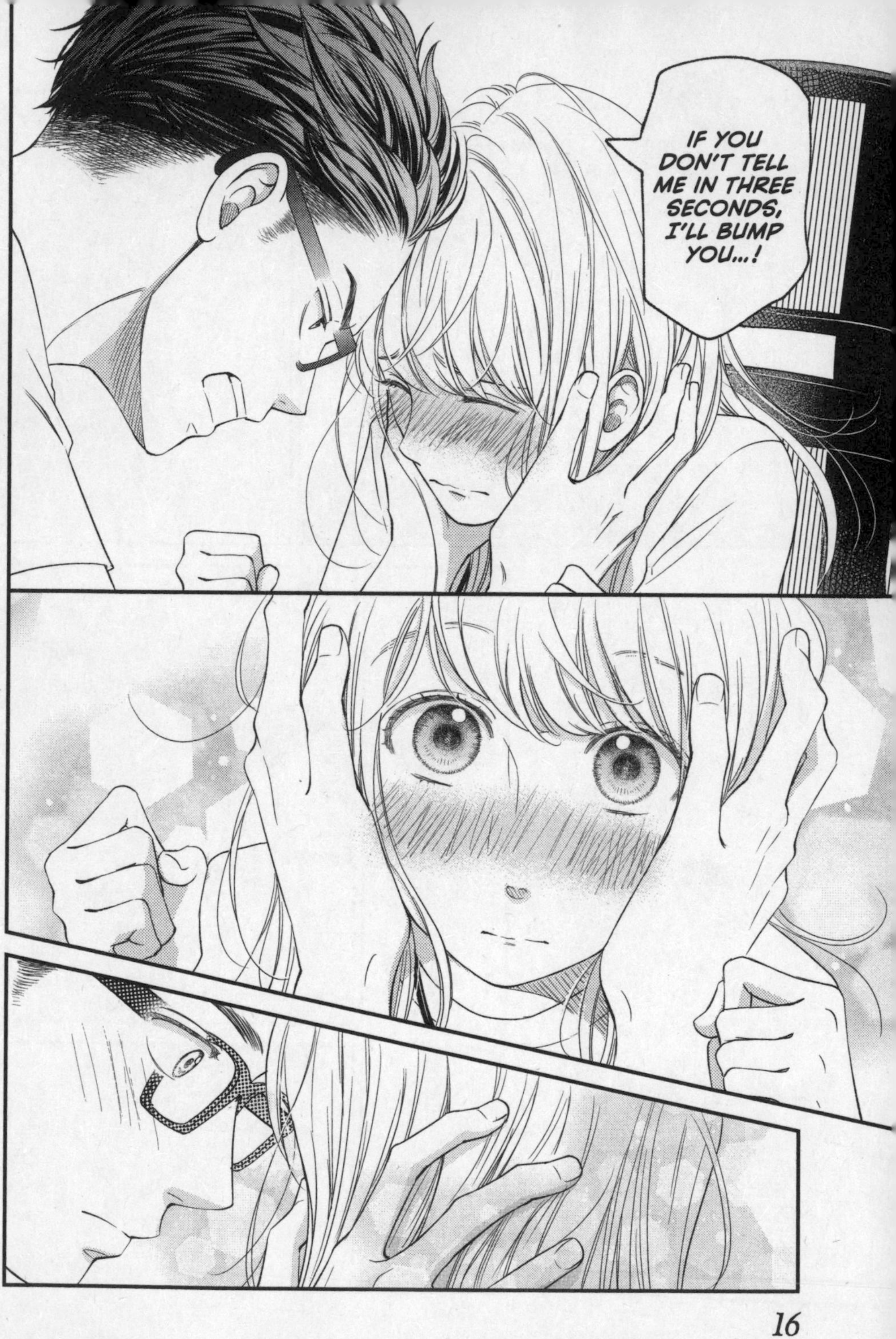
IF YOU DON'T TELL ME IN THREE SECONDS, I'LL BUMP YOU...!

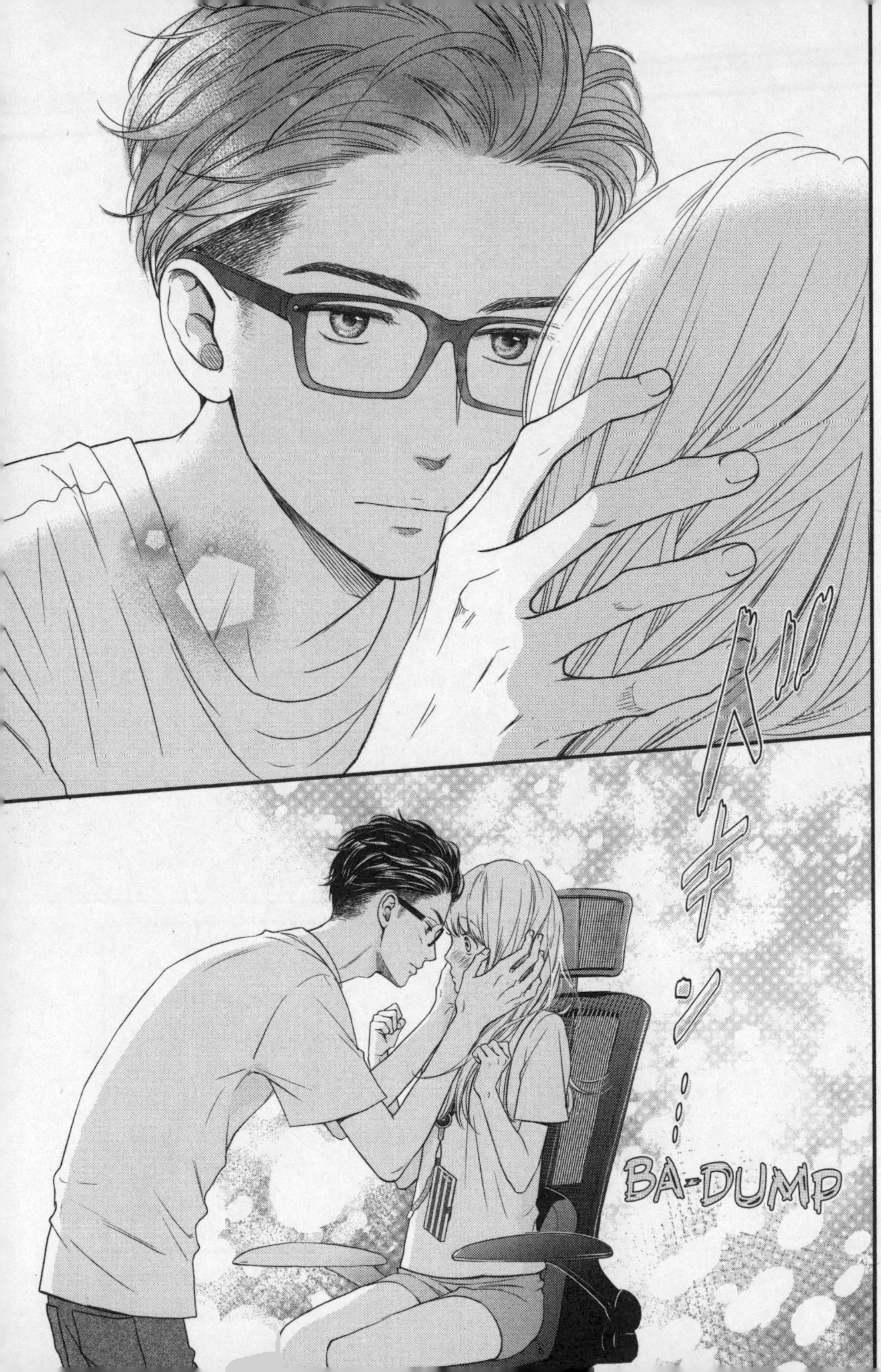
ドキン…
BA-DUMP

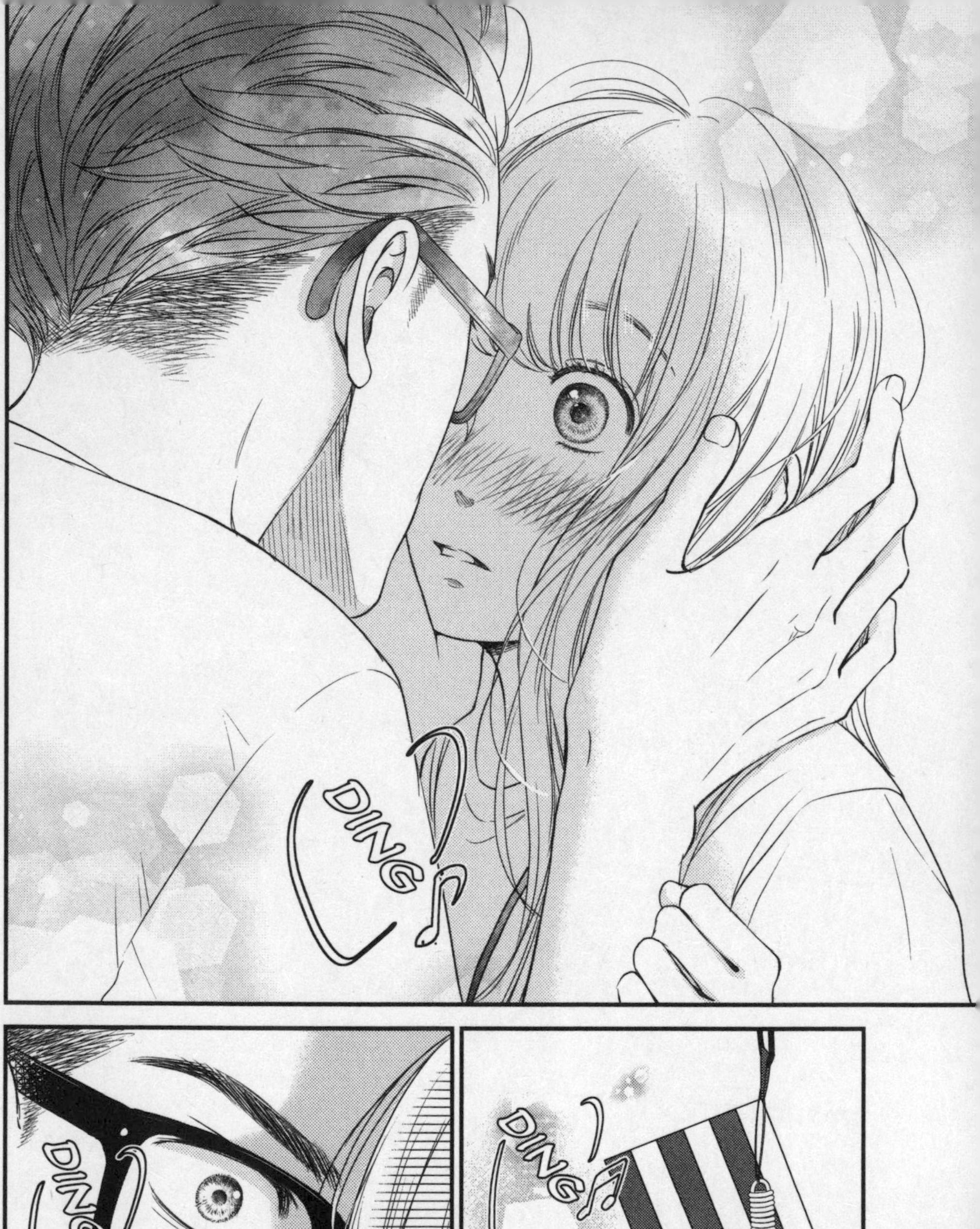
DING♪
DING♪
DING♪

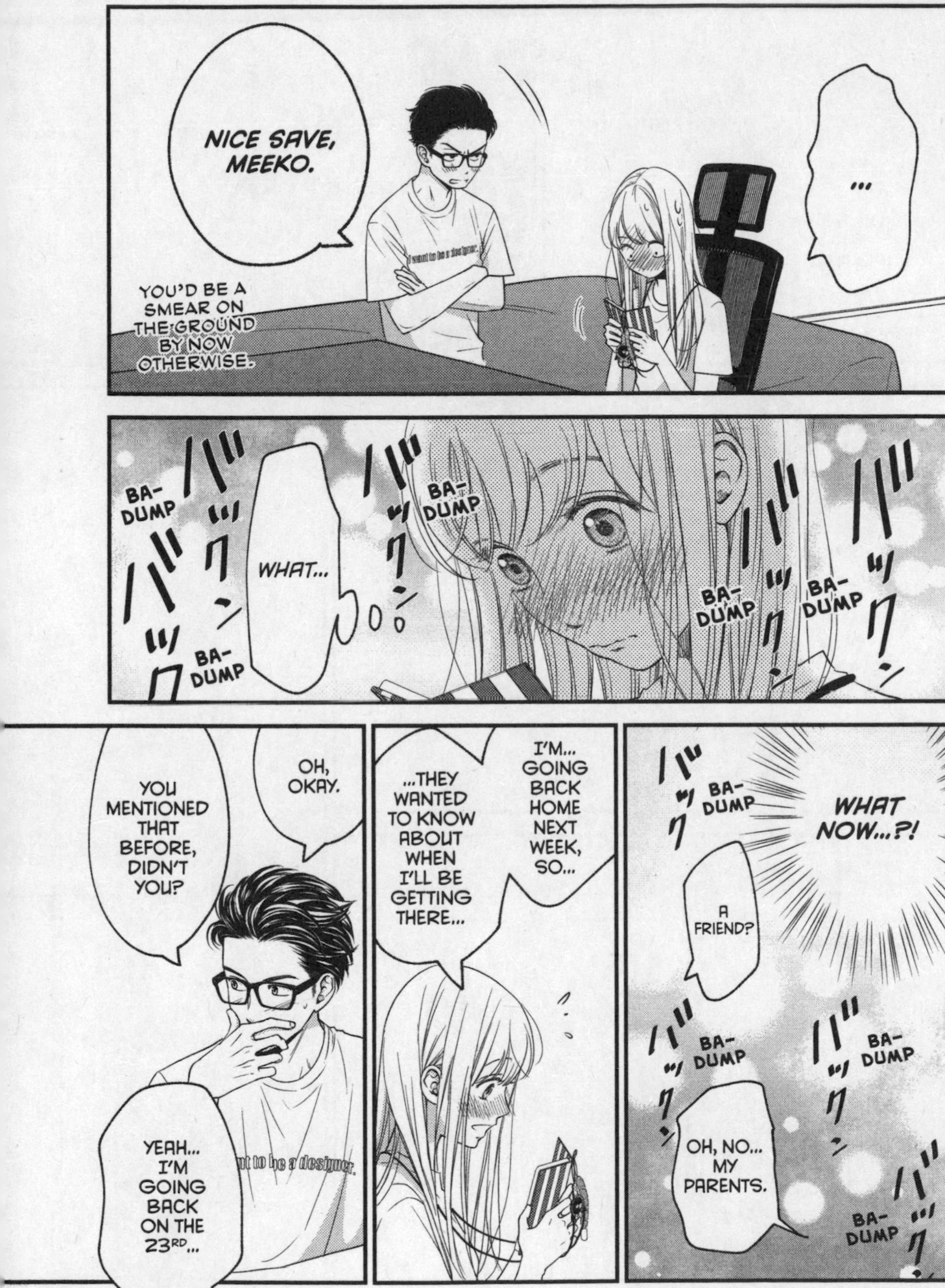
...
NICE SAVE, MEEKO.
YOU'D BE A SMEAR ON THE GROUND BY NOW OTHERWISE.
BA-DUMP
BA-DUMP
BA-DUMP
WHAT...
BA-DUMP
BA-DUMP
BA-DUMP
WHAT NOW...?!
A FRIEND?
BA-DUMP
BA-DUMP
OH, NO... MY PARENTS.
BA-DUMP
I'M... GOING BACK HOME NEXT WEEK, SO...
...THEY WANTED TO KNOW ABOUT WHEN I'LL BE GETTING THERE...
OH, OKAY.
YOU MENTIONED THAT BEFORE, DIDN'T YOU?
YEAH... I'M GOING BACK ON THE 23RD...

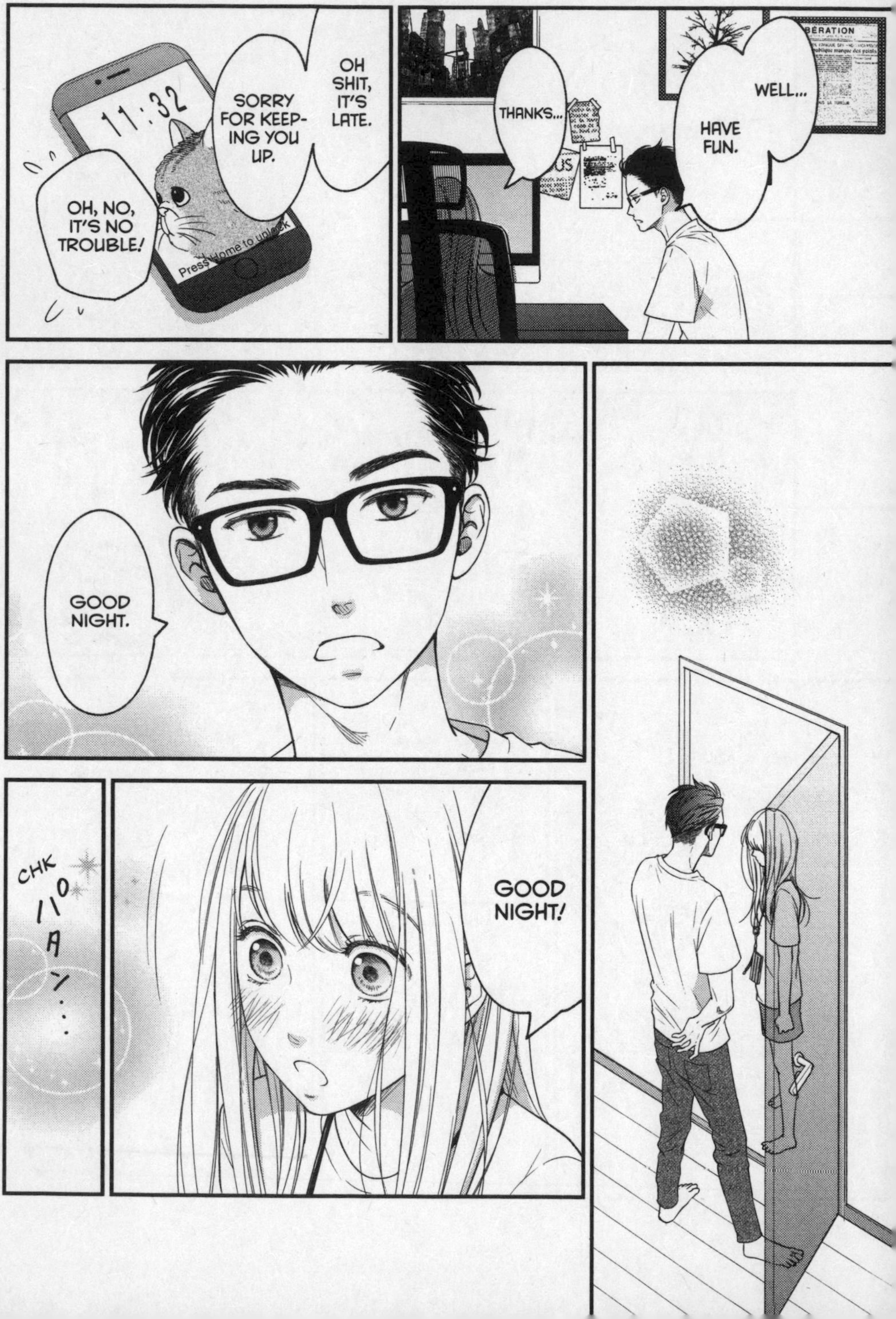
WELL... HAVE FUN.
THANKS...
OH SHIT, IT'S LATE.
SORRY FOR KEEP-ING YOU UP.
11:32
OH, NO, IT'S NO TROUBLE!
Press Home to unlock
GOOD NIGHT.
GOOD NIGHT!
CHK
パタン…

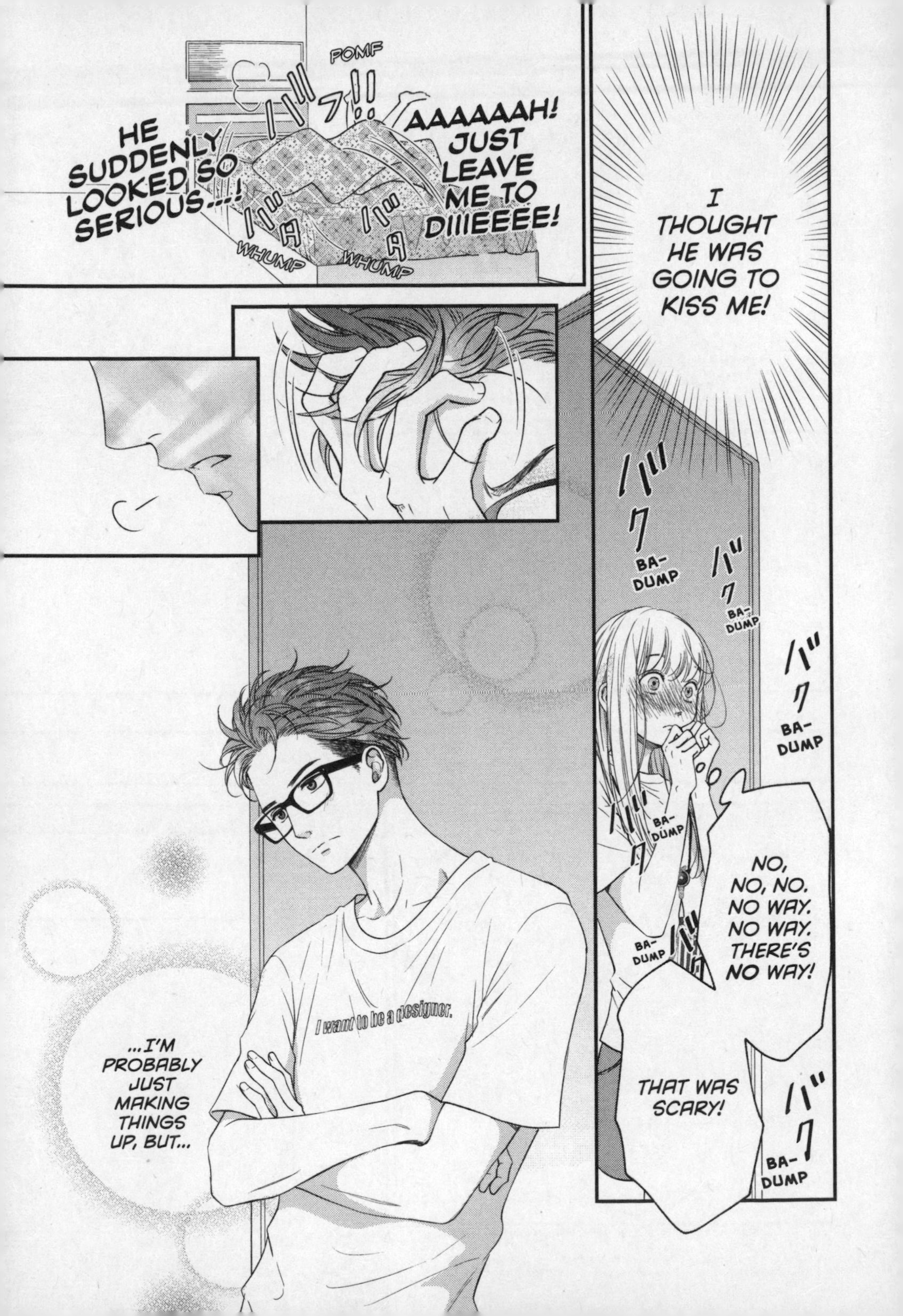
I THOUGHT HE WAS GOING TO KISS ME!
バク
BA-DUMP
バク
BA-DUMP
バク
BA-DUMP
BA-DUMP
BA-DUMP
NO, NO, NO. NO WAY. NO WAY. THERE'S NO WAY!
THAT WAS SCARY!
バク
BA-DUMP
POMF
AAAAAAH! JUST LEAVE ME TO DIIIEEEE!
HE SUDDENLY LOOKED SO SERIOUS...!
WHUMP
WHUMP
...I'M PROBABLY JUST MAKING THINGS UP, BUT...
I want to be a designer.

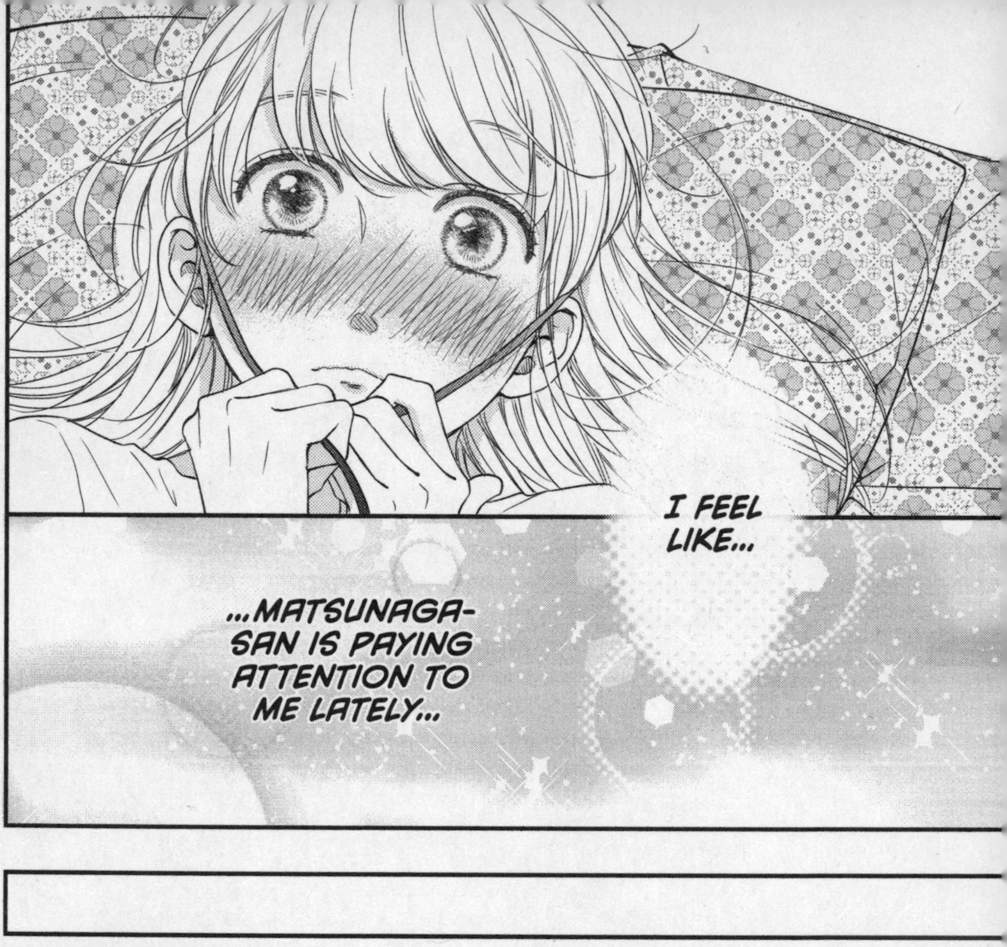
I FEEL LIKE...
...MATSUNAGA-SAN IS PAYING ATTENTION TO ME LATELY...

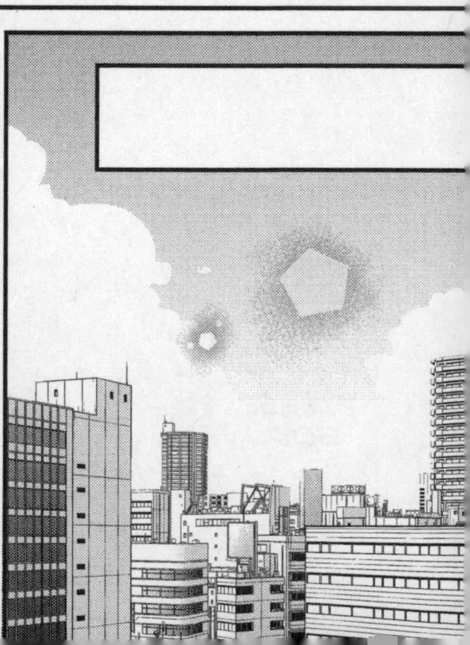

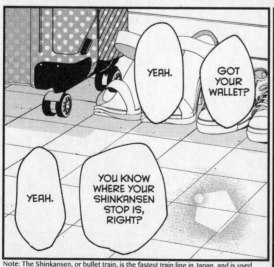

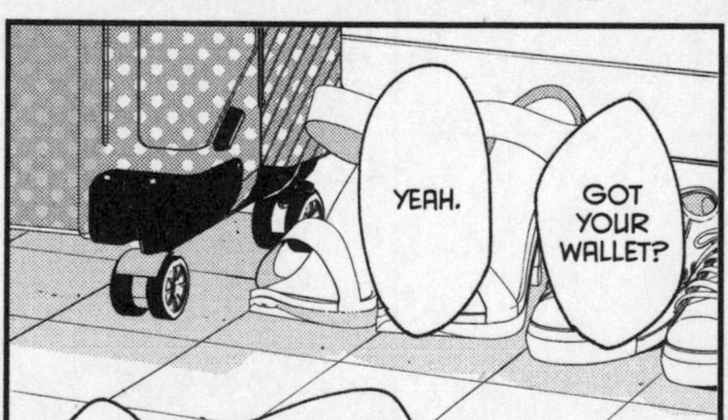
GOT YOUR WALLET?
YEAH.
YOU KNOW WHERE YOUR SHINKANSEN STOP IS, RIGHT?
YEAH.

Note: The Shinkansen, or bullet train, is the fastest train line in Japan, and is used to travel to major cities across the country. To travel from Tokyo to Nagoya, where Meeko is traveling, would take approximately one hour and forty-five minutes on the fastest shinkansen line, or three hours on the slowest shinkansen line.

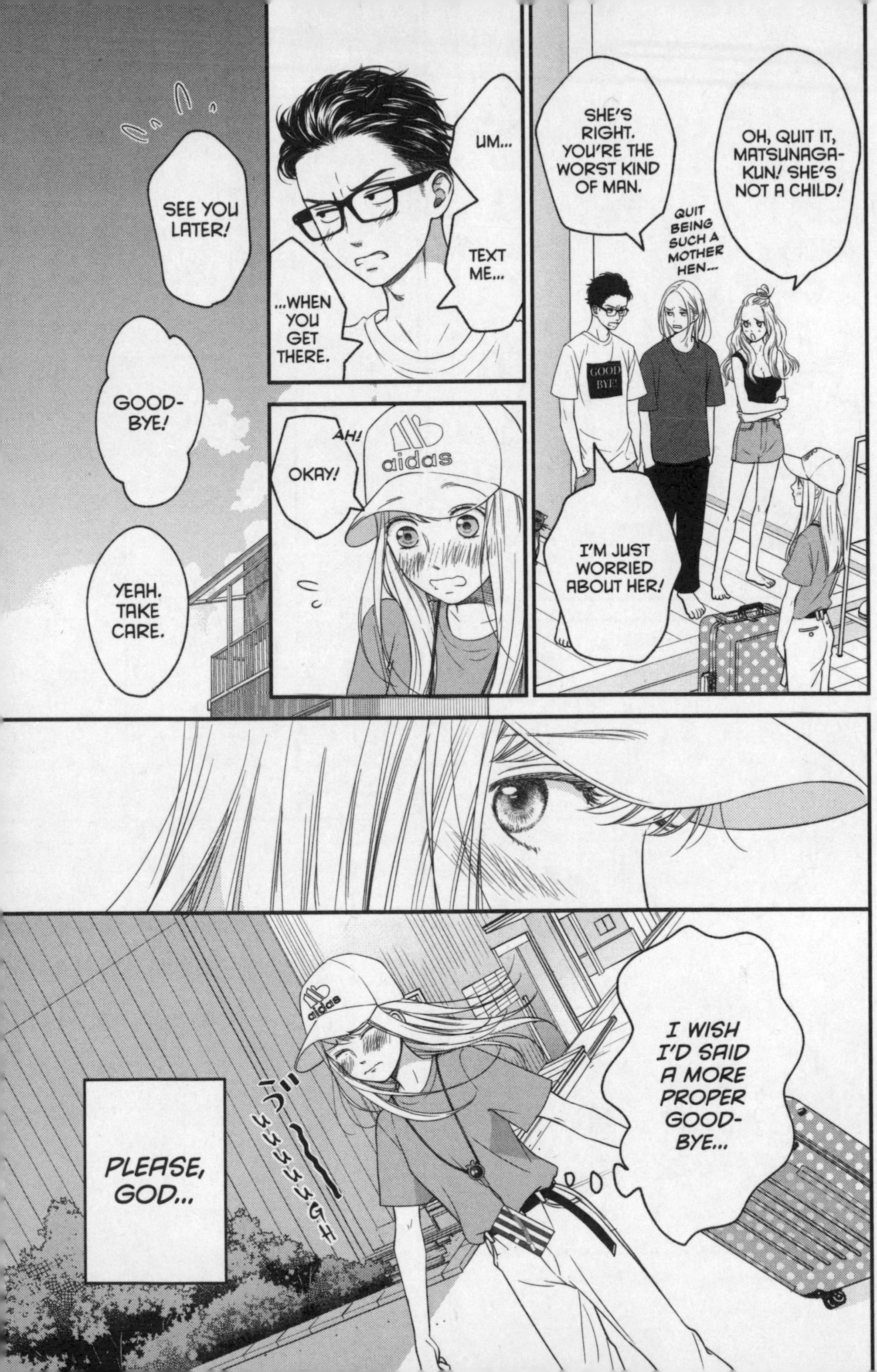
OH, QUIT IT, MATSUNAGA-KUN! SHE'S NOT A CHILD!
QUIT BEING SUCH A MOTHER HEN...
SHE'S RIGHT. YOU'RE THE WORST KIND OF MAN.
I'M JUST WORRIED ABOUT HER!
UM...
TEXT ME...
...WHEN YOU GET THERE.
AH!
OKAY!
SEE YOU LATER!
GOOD-BYE!
YEAH. TAKE CARE.
I WISH I'D SAID A MORE PROPER GOOD-BYE...
UUUUUUGH
PLEASE, GOD...

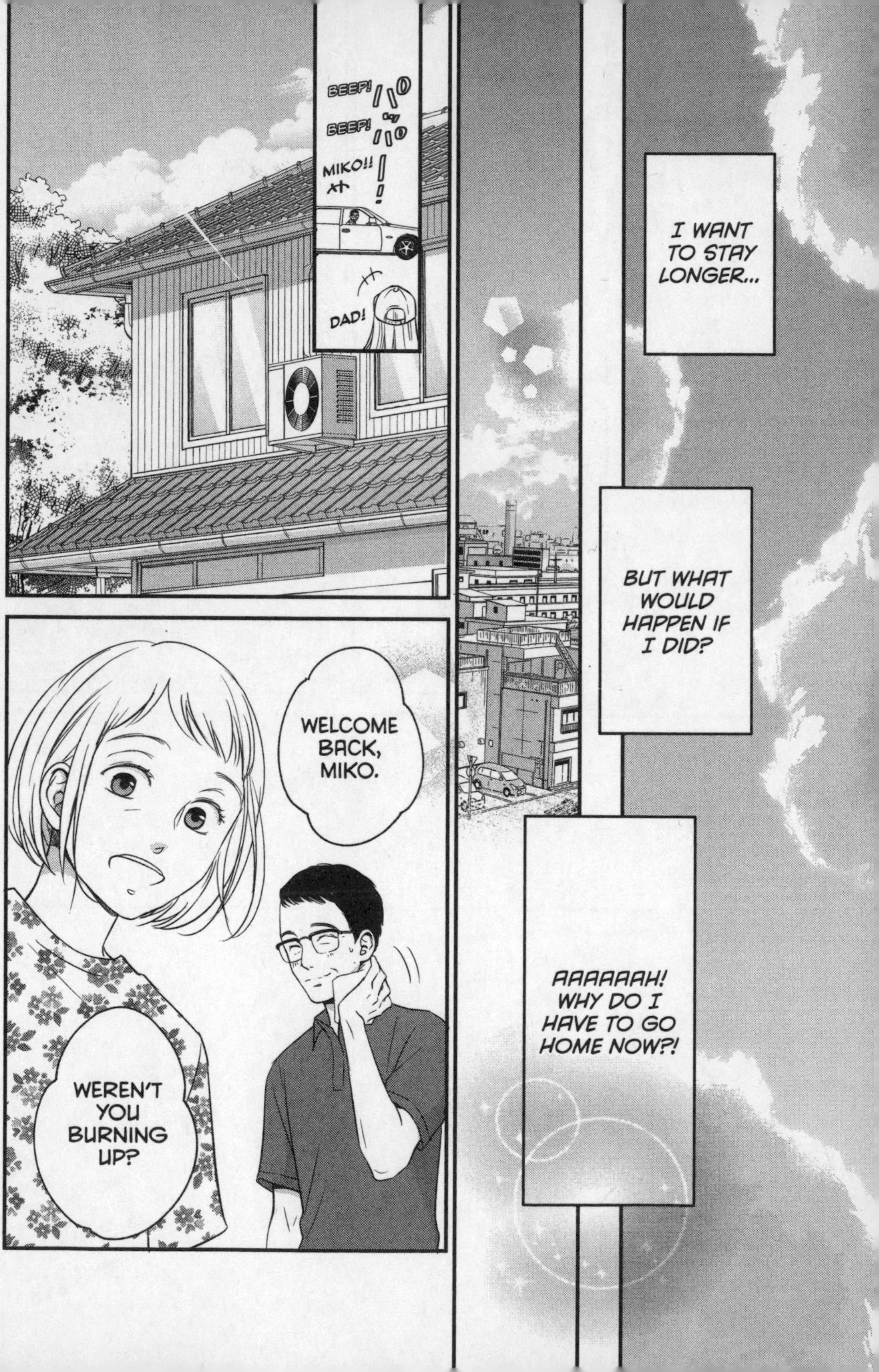
I WANT TO STAY LONGER...
BUT WHAT WOULD HAPPEN IF I DID?
AAAAAAH! WHY DO I HAVE TO GO HOME NOW?!
BEEP!
BEEP!
MIKO!!
DAD!
WELCOME BACK, MIKO.
WEREN'T YOU BURNING UP?

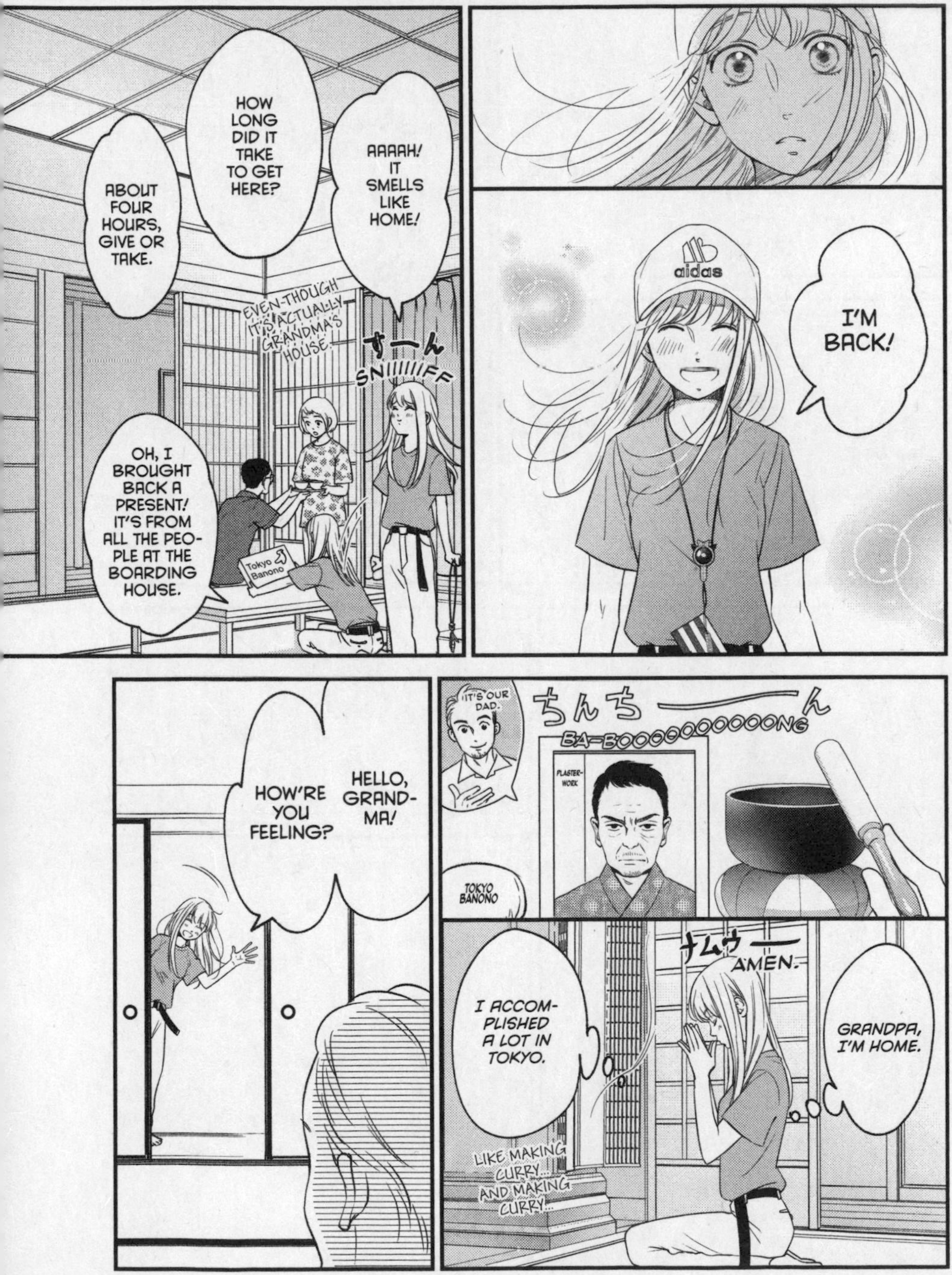
I'M BACK!
AAAAH! IT SMELLS LIKE HOME!
HOW LONG DID IT TAKE TO GET HERE?
ABOUT FOUR HOURS, GIVE OR TAKE.
すーん
SNIIIIIIFF
EVEN-THOUGH IT'S ACTUALLY GRANDMA'S HOUSE.
OH, I BROUGHT BACK A PRESENT! IT'S FROM ALL THE PEO-PLE AT THE BOARDING HOUSE.
Tokyo Banono
ちんち――ん
BA-BOOOOOOOOOOONG
IT'S OUR DAD.
PLASTER-WORK
TOKYO BANONO
ナムウ―
AMEN.
GRANDPA, I'M HOME.
I ACCOM-PLISHED A LOT IN TOKYO.
LIKE MAKING CURRY... AND MAKING CURRY...
HELLO, GRAND-MA!
HOW'RE YOU FEELING?

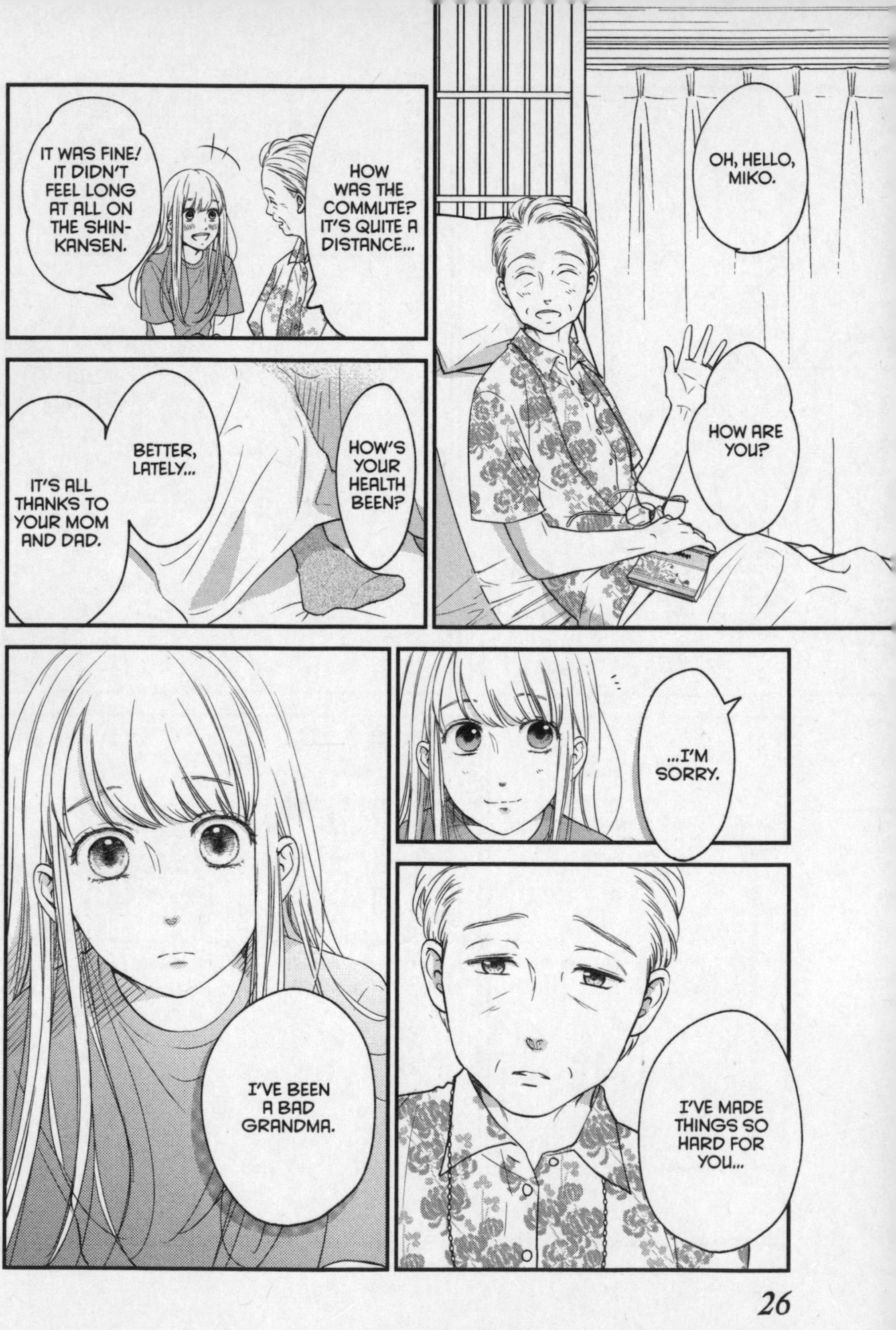
OH, HELLO, MIKO.
HOW ARE YOU?
HOW WAS THE COMMUTE? IT'S QUITE A DISTANCE...
IT WAS FINE! IT DIDN'T FEEL LONG AT ALL ON THE SHIN-KANSEN.
HOW'S YOUR HEALTH BEEN?
BETTER, LATELY...
IT'S ALL THANKS TO YOUR MOM AND DAD.
...I'M SORRY.
I'VE MADE THINGS SO HARD FOR YOU...
I'VE BEEN A BAD GRANDMA.

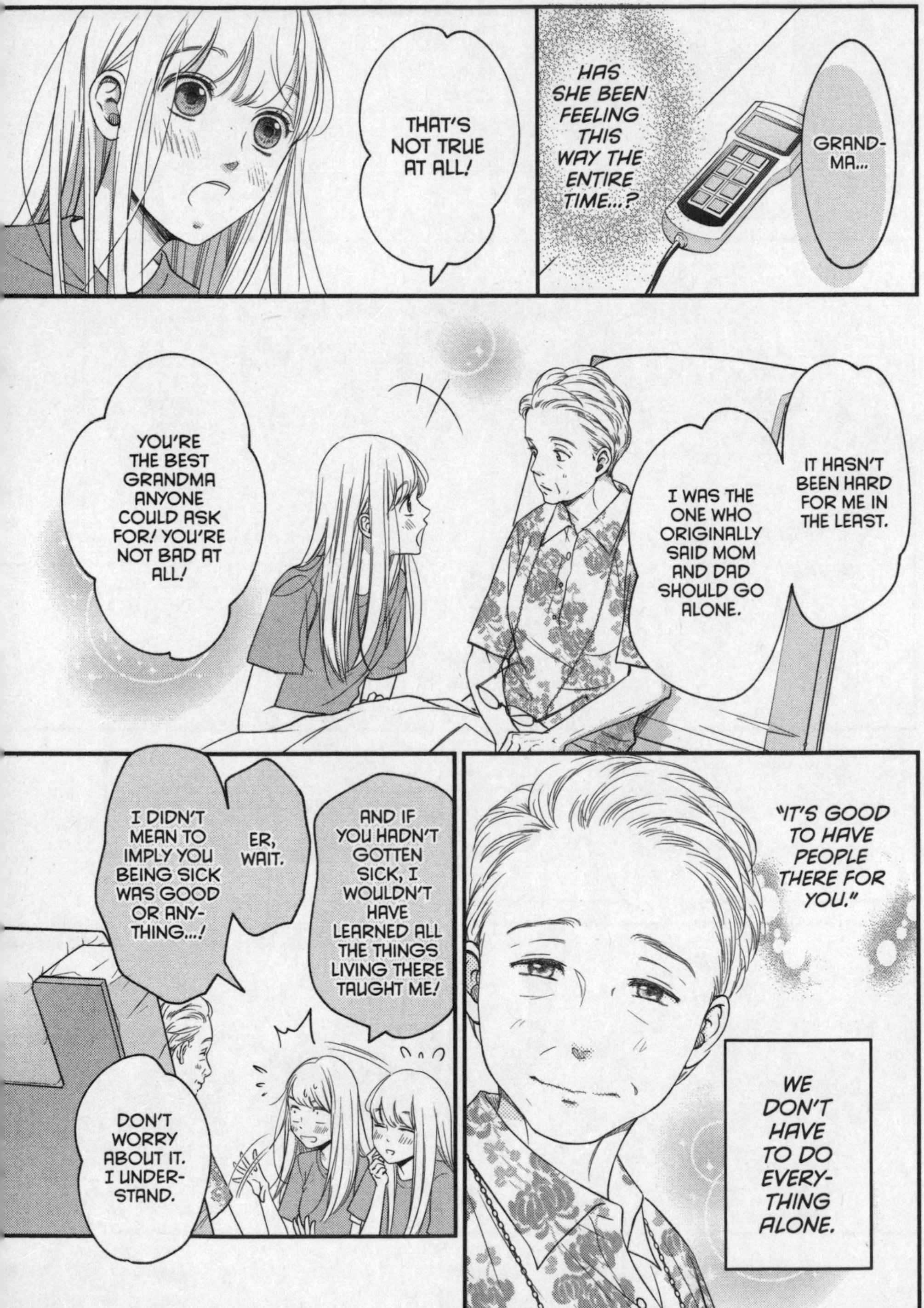
GRAND-MA...
HAS SHE BEEN FEELING THIS WAY THE ENTIRE TIME...?
THAT'S NOT TRUE AT ALL!
IT HASN'T BEEN HARD FOR ME IN THE LEAST.
I WAS THE ONE WHO ORIGINALLY SAID MOM AND DAD SHOULD GO ALONE.
YOU'RE THE BEST GRANDMA ANYONE COULD ASK FOR! YOU'RE NOT BAD AT ALL!
"IT'S GOOD TO HAVE PEOPLE THERE FOR YOU."
WE DON'T HAVE TO DO EVERY-THING ALONE.
AND IF YOU HADN'T GOTTEN SICK, I WOULDN'T HAVE LEARNED ALL THE THINGS LIVING THERE TAUGHT ME!
ER, WAIT.
I DIDN'T MEAN TO IMPLY YOU BEING SICK WAS GOOD OR ANY-THING...!
DON'T WORRY ABOUT IT. I UNDER-STAND.

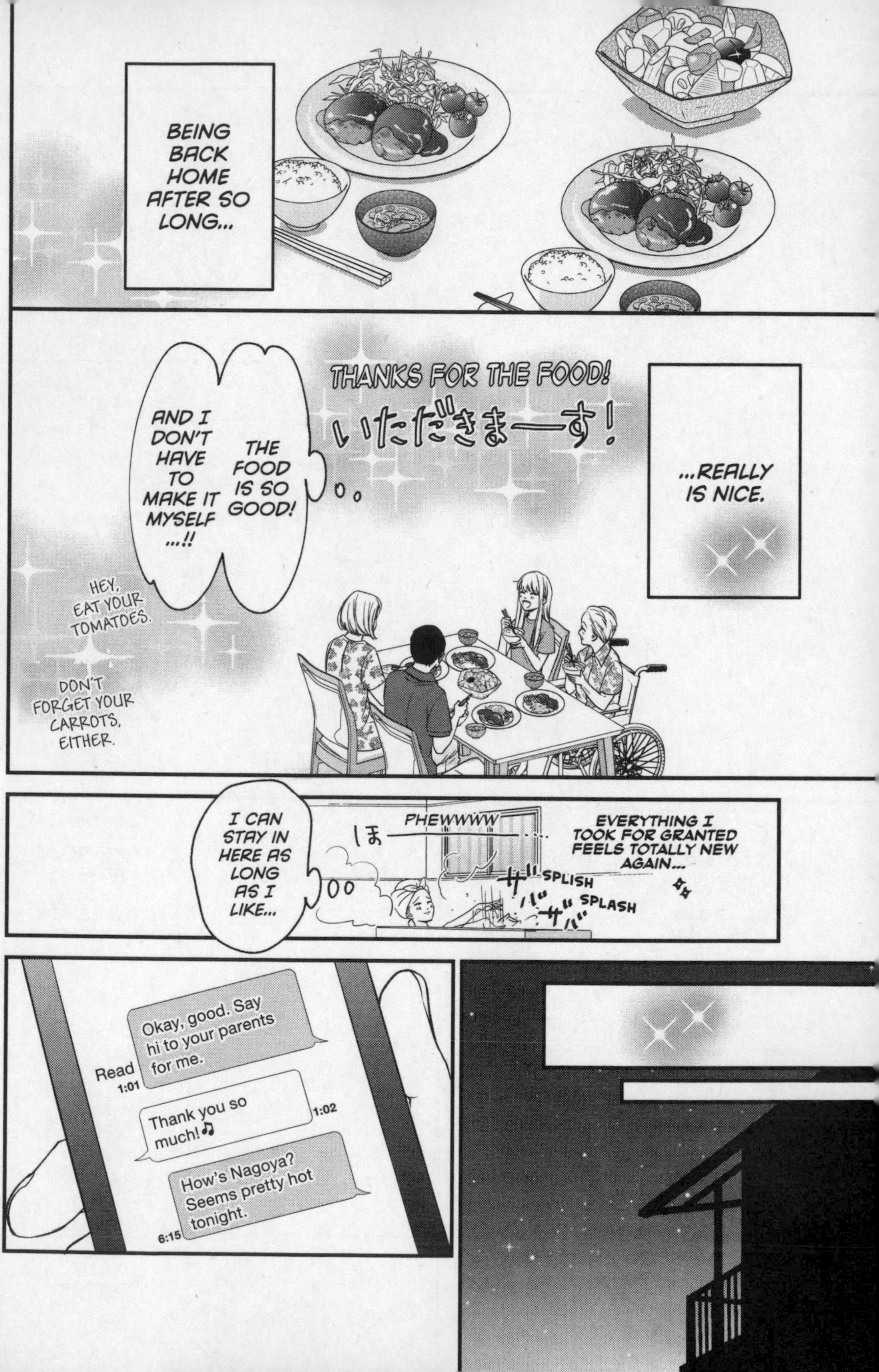
BEING BACK HOME AFTER SO LONG...
...REALLY IS NICE.
THANKS FOR THE FOOD!
いただきまーす!
THE FOOD IS SO GOOD!
AND I DON'T HAVE TO MAKE IT MYSELF ...!!
HEY, EAT YOUR TOMATOES.
DON'T FORGET YOUR CARROTS, EITHER.
EVERYTHING I TOOK FOR GRANTED FEELS TOTALLY NEW AGAIN...
ザバ SPLISH
ザバ SPLASH
ほー PHEWWWW
I CAN STAY IN HERE AS LONG AS I LIKE...
Okay, good. Say hi to your parents for me.
Read 1:01
Thank you so much!♫
1:02
How's Nagoya? Seems pretty hot tonight.
6:15

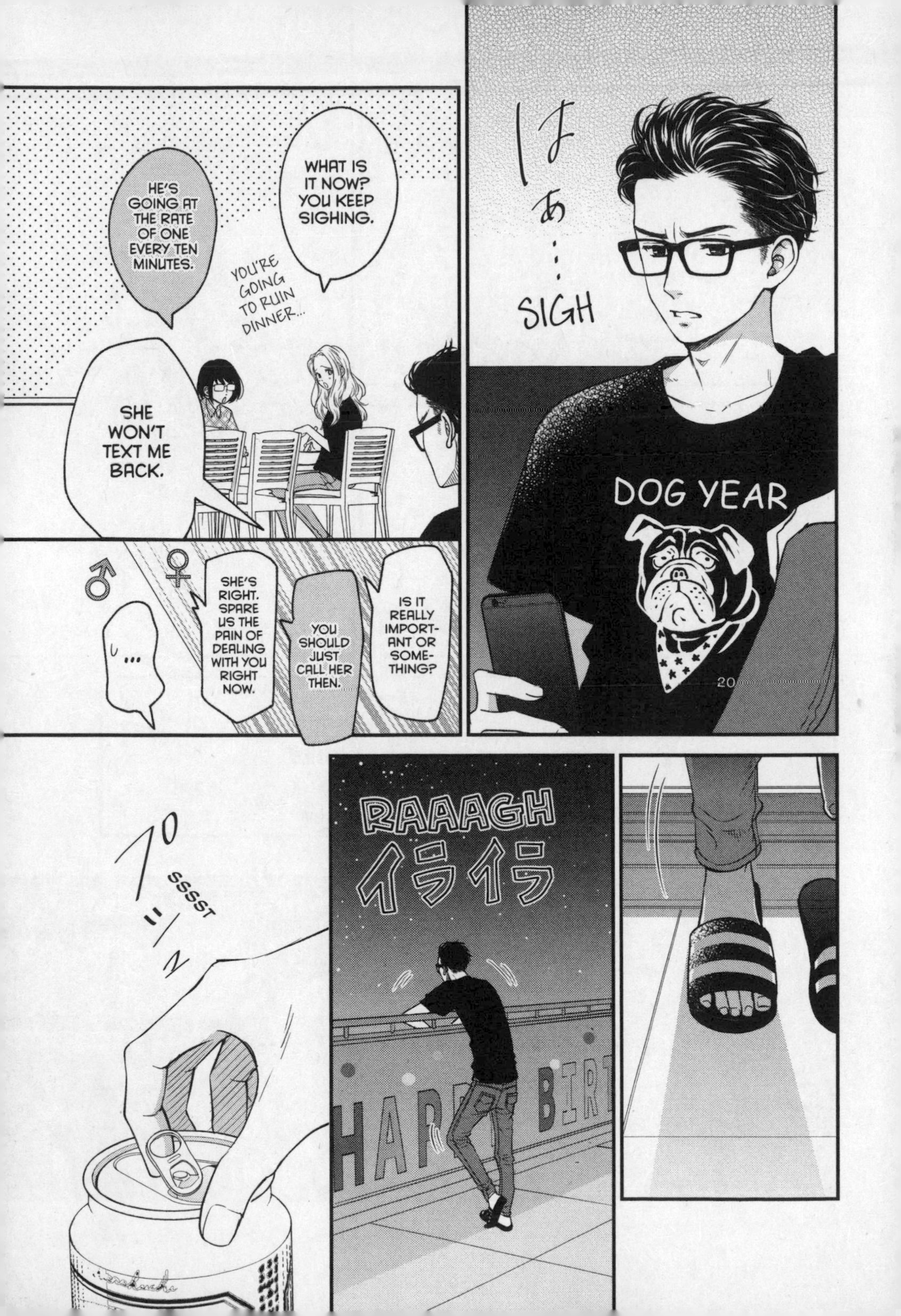
はあ…
SIGH
DOG YEAR
WHAT IS IT NOW? YOU KEEP SIGHING.
HE'S GOING AT THE RATE OF ONE EVERY TEN MINUTES.
YOU'RE GOING TO RUIN DINNER...
SHE WON'T TEXT ME BACK.
IS IT REALLY IMPORT-ANT OR SOME-THING?
YOU SHOULD JUST CALL HER THEN.
SHE'S RIGHT. SPARE US THE PAIN OF DEALING WITH YOU RIGHT NOW.
♀
♂
RAAAGH
イライラ
HAPP BIRT
SSSST

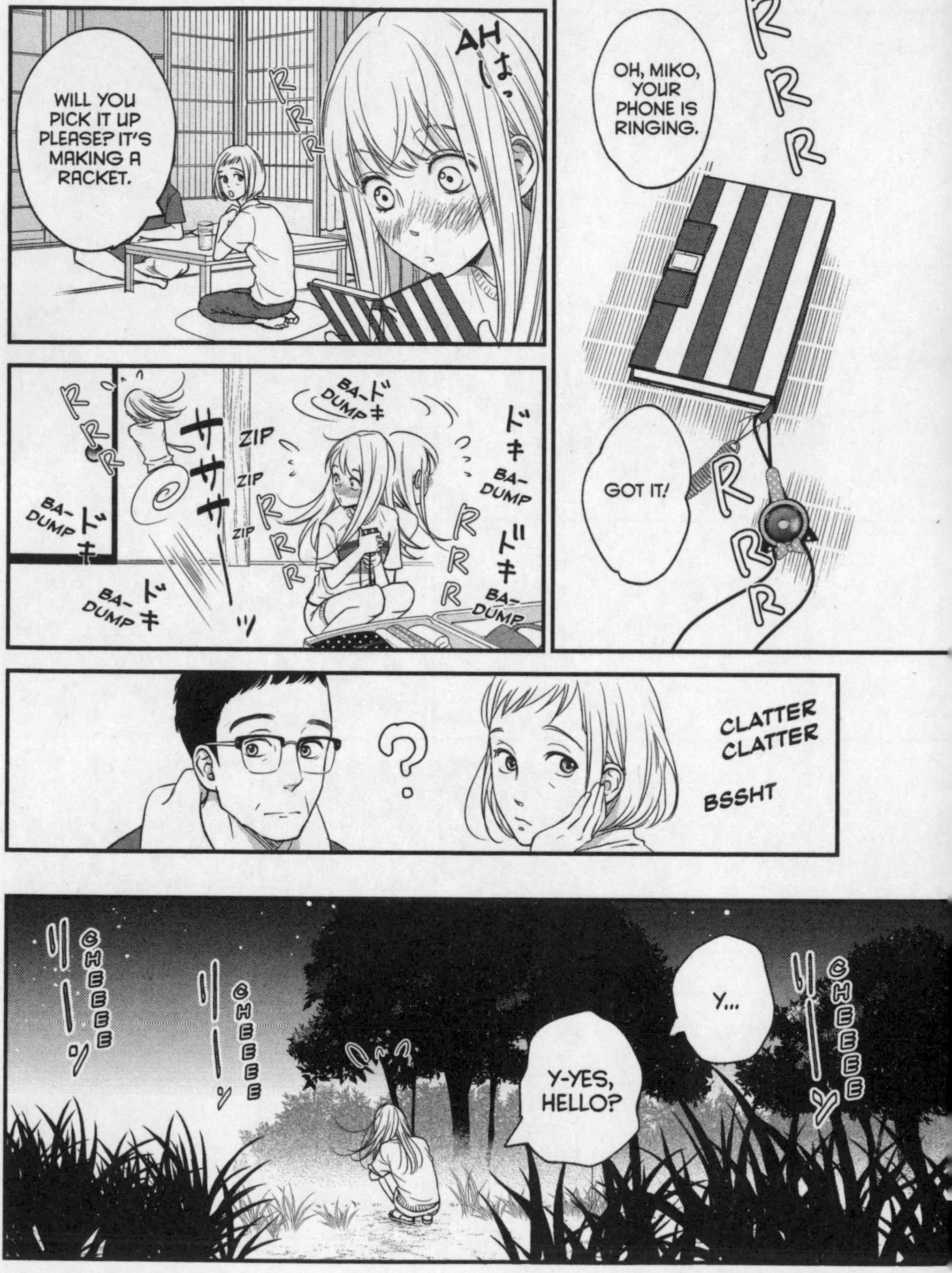
RRR
OH, MIKO, YOUR PHONE IS RINGING.
GOT IT!
RRRR
AH はっ
RRR
WILL YOU PICK IT UP PLEASE? IT'S MAKING A RACKET.
BA-ドDUMPキ
ドキ BA-DUMP
ドキ BA-DUMP
RRR
RRR
ZIP
ZIP
ZIP
ササーッ
RRR
BA-DUMP ドキ
BA-DUMP ドキ
CLATTER CLATTER
BSSHT
?
CHEEEE リーーy
Y...
Y-YES, HELLO?
CHEEEE リーーッ
CHEEEE リーーッ

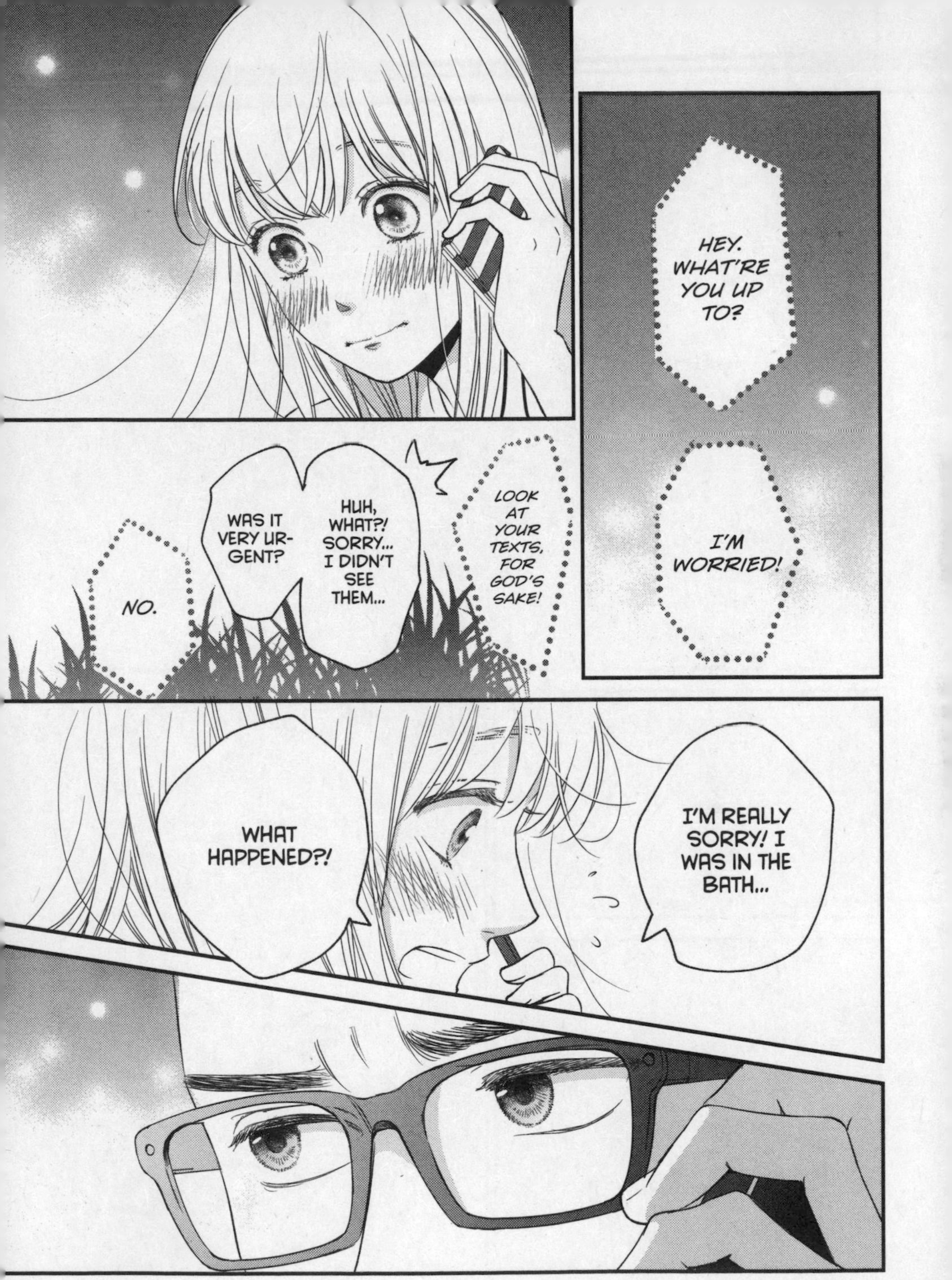
HEY. WHAT'RE YOU UP TO?
I'M WORRIED!
LOOK AT YOUR TEXTS, FOR GOD'S SAKE!
HUH, WHAT?! SORRY... I DIDN'T SEE THEM...
WAS IT VERY UR-GENT?
NO.
I'M REALLY SORRY! I WAS IN THE BATH...
WHAT HAPPENED?!

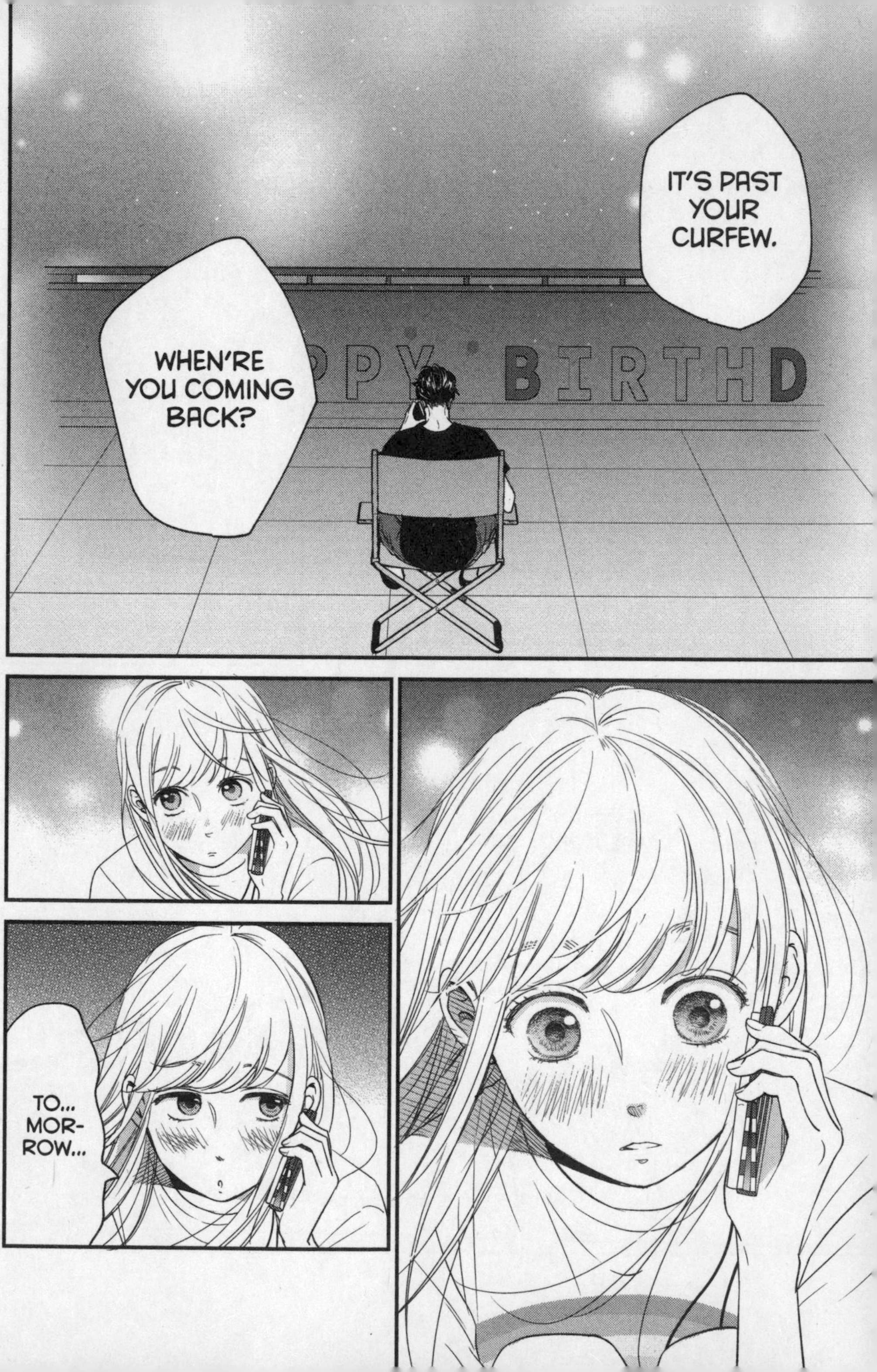
IT'S PAST YOUR CURFEW.
WHEN'RE YOU COMING BACK?
TO... MOR-ROW...

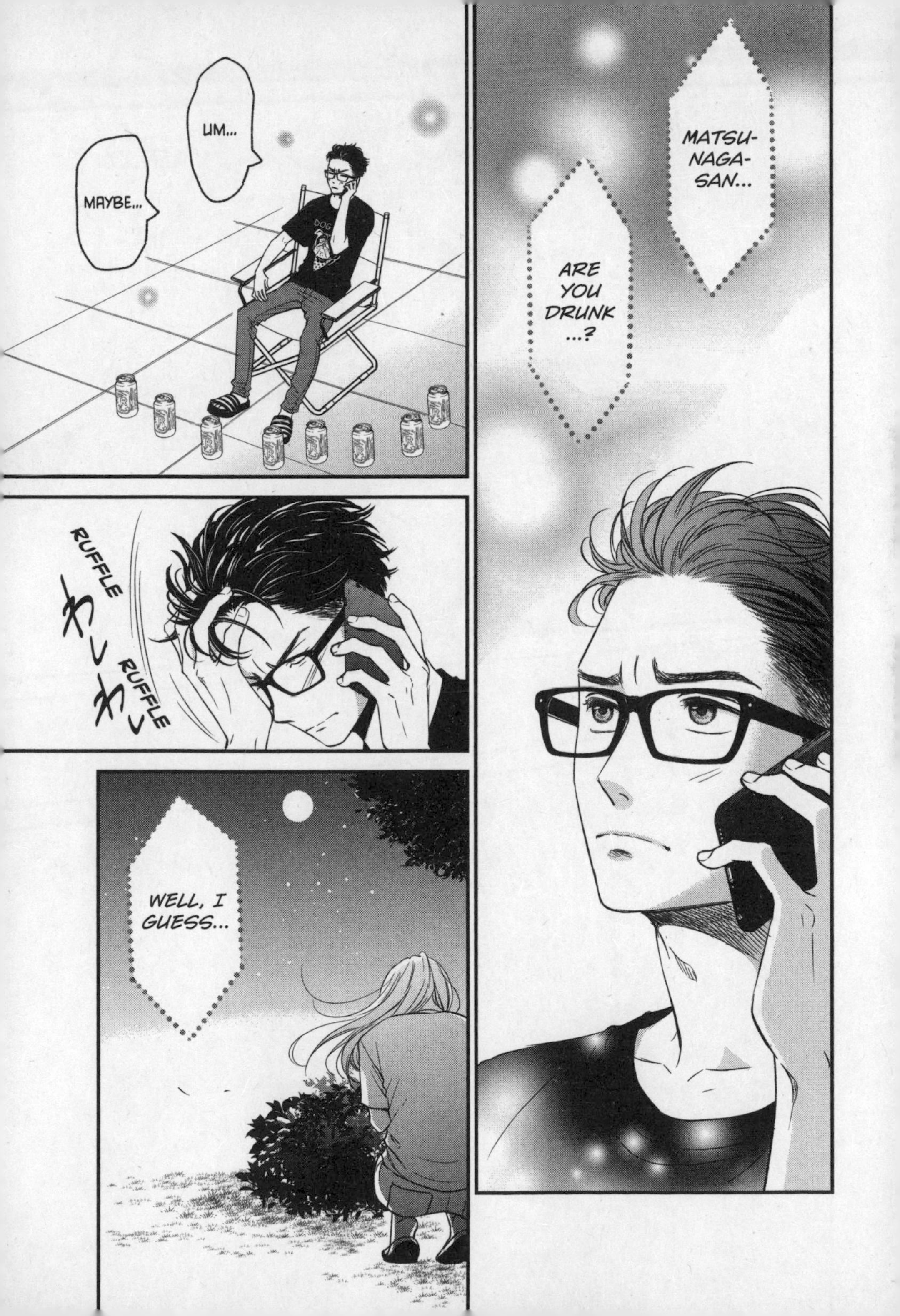
MATSU-NAGA-SAN...
ARE YOU DRUNK ...?
UM...
MAYBE...
RUFFLE RUFFLE
わしわし
WELL, I GUESS...

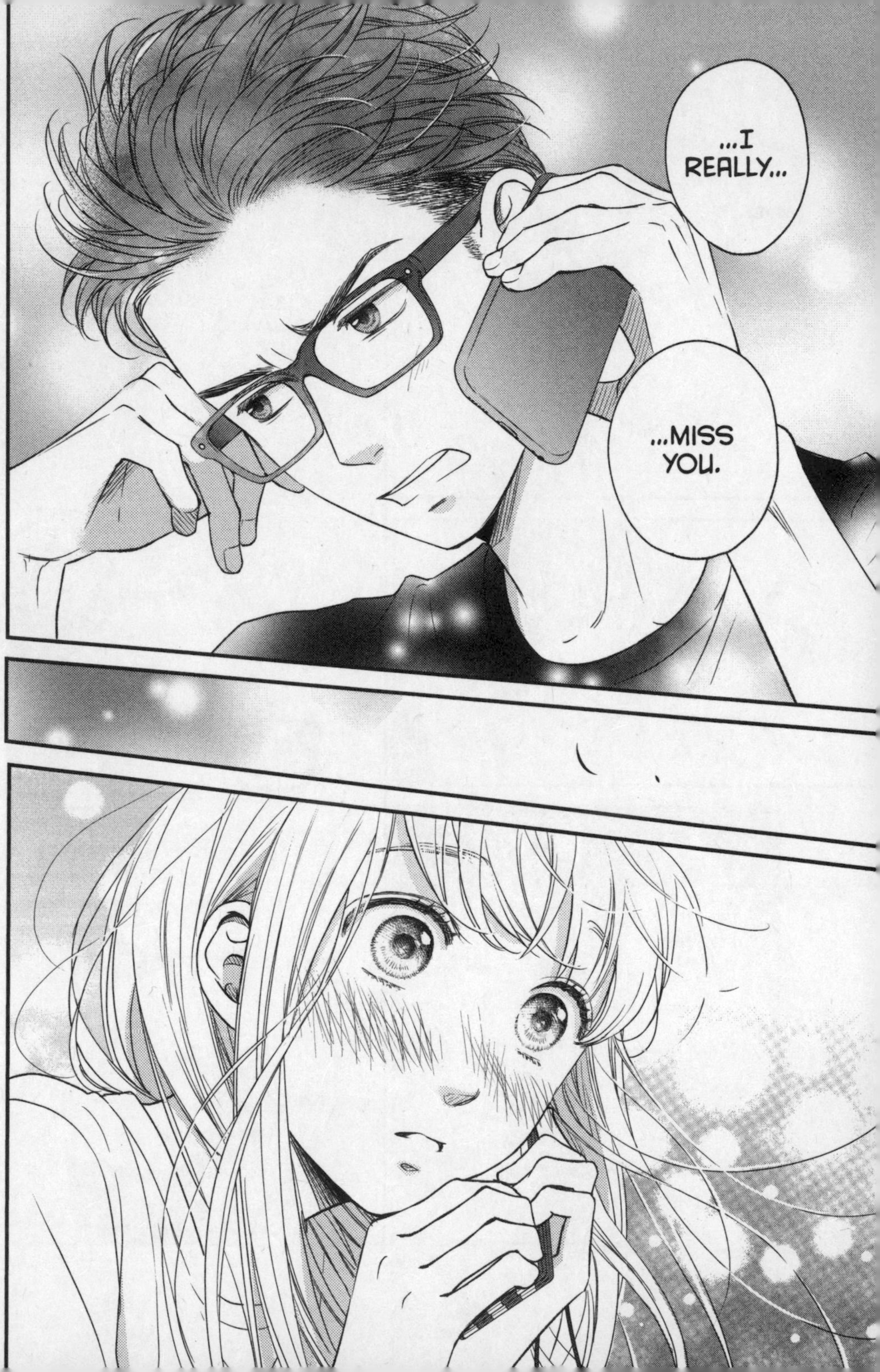
...I REALLY...
...MISS YOU.

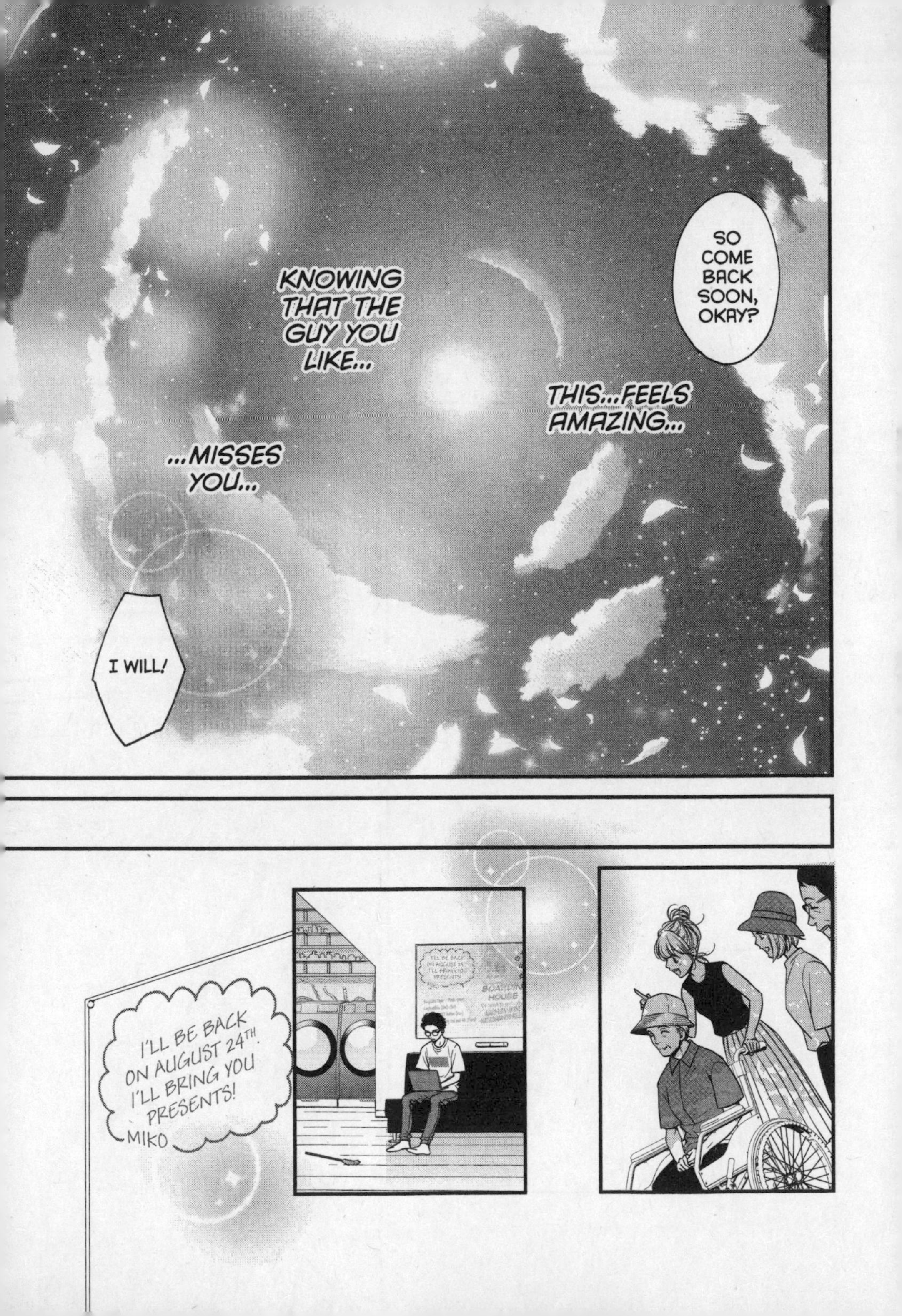
SO COME BACK SOON, OKAY?
KNOWING THAT THE GUY YOU LIKE...
...MISSES YOU...
THIS...FEELS AMAZING...
I WILL!
I'LL BE BACK ON AUGUST 24TH. I'LL BRING YOU PRESENTS! MIKO

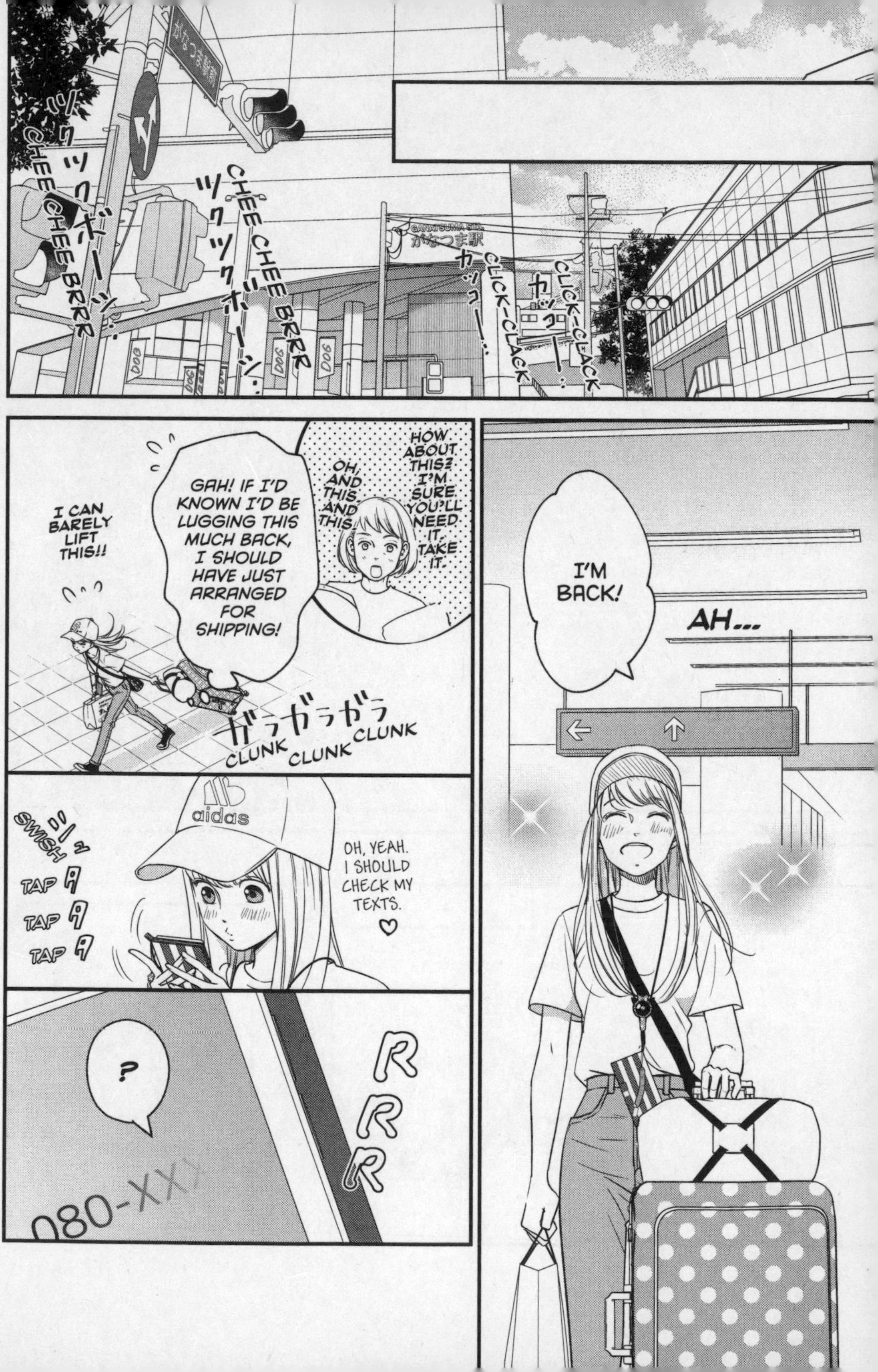
がなつま駅前
GANATSUMA STA.
がなつま駅
カッコー…
CLICK-CLACK
カッコー…
CLICK-CLACK
ツクツクボーシ…
CHEE CHEE BRRR
ツクツクボーシ…
CHEE CHEE BRRR
I'M BACK!
AH...
HOW ABOUT THIS? I'M SURE YOU'LL NEED IT. TAKE IT.
OH, AND THIS. AND THIS.
GAH! IF I'D KNOWN I'D BE LUGGING THIS MUCH BACK, I SHOULD HAVE JUST ARRANGED FOR SHIPPING!
I CAN BARELY LIFT THIS!!
ガラガラガラ
CLUNK CLUNK CLUNK
aidas
OH, YEAH. I SHOULD CHECK MY TEXTS.
シュ
SWISH
タ TAP
タ TAP
タ TAP
R R R
?
080-XX

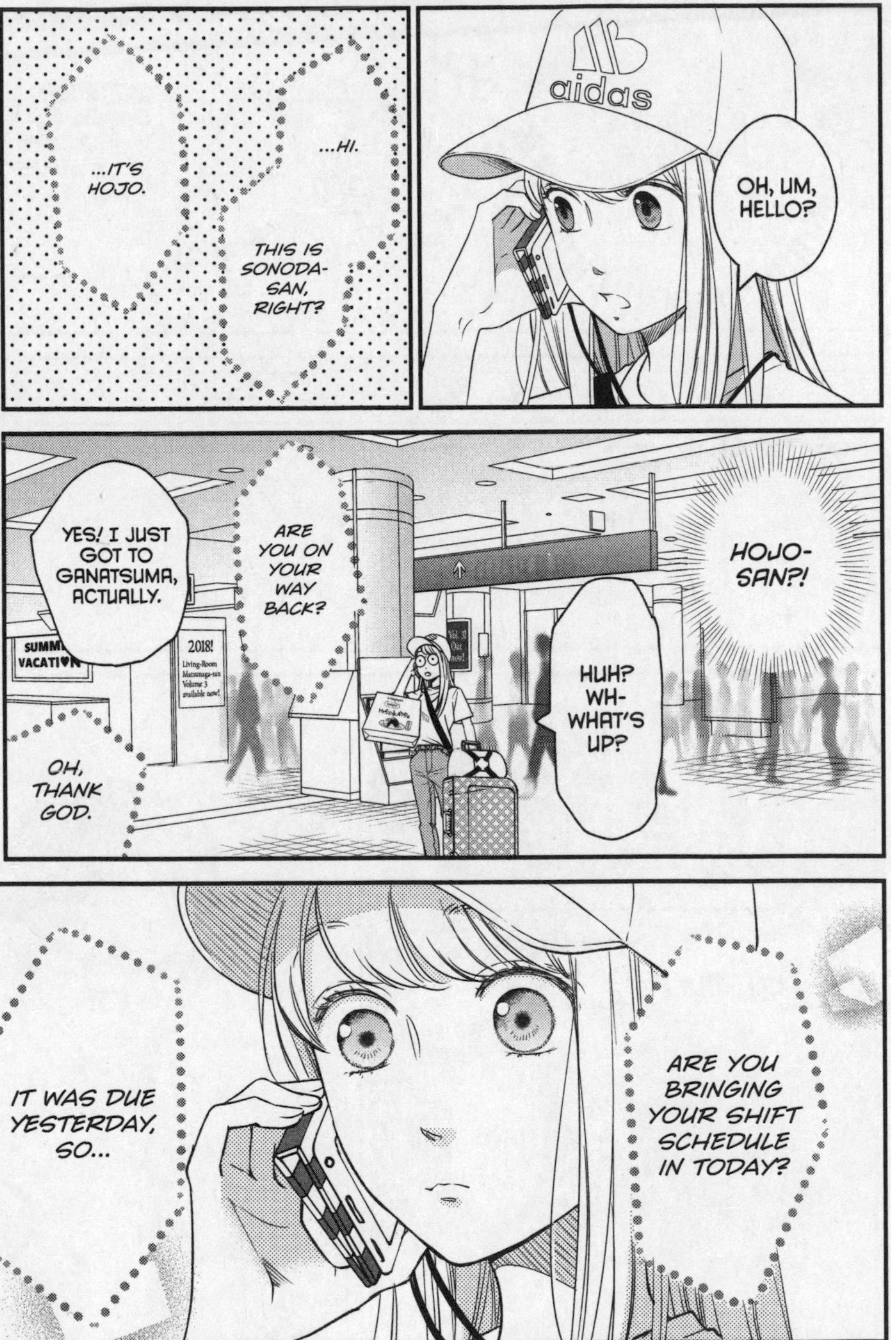
OH, UM, HELLO?
...HI.
...IT'S HOJO.
THIS IS SONODA-SAN, RIGHT?
HOJO-SAN?!
HUH? WH-WHAT'S UP?
ARE YOU ON YOUR WAY BACK?
YES! I JUST GOT TO GANATSUMA, ACTUALLY.
2018! Living-Room Matsunaga-san Volume 3 available now!
OH, THANK GOD.
ARE YOU BRINGING YOUR SHIFT SCHEDULE IN TODAY?
IT WAS DUE YESTERDAY, SO...

*It is typical in Japan for employees to inform their employers of their schedules by handing in shift sheets.

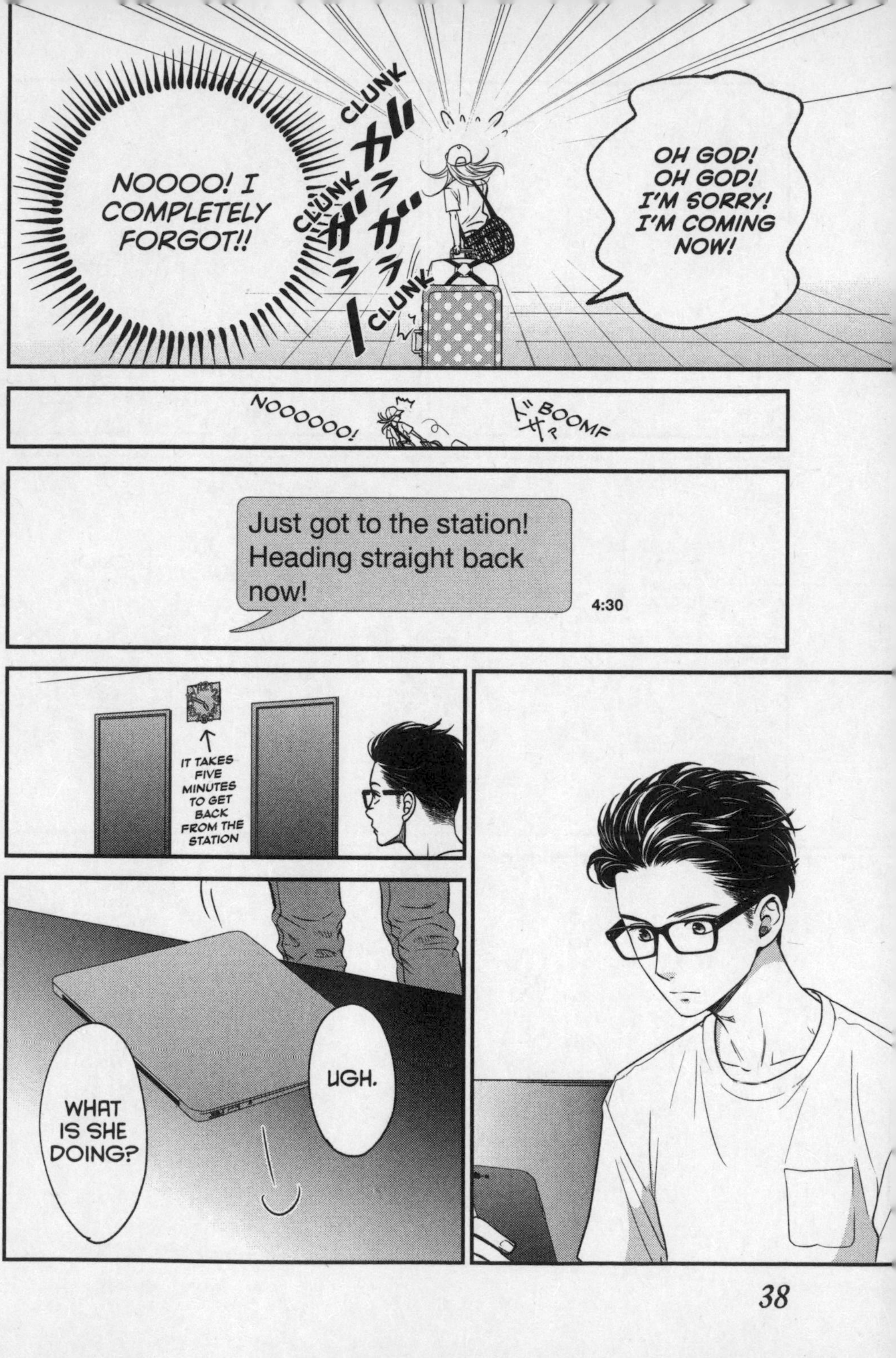
OH GOD! OH GOD! I'M SORRY! I'M COMING NOW!
CLUNK
CLUNK
CLUNK
CLUNK
NOOOO! I COMPLETELY FORGOT!!
BOOMF
NOOOOOO!
Just got to the station! Heading straight back now!
4:30
IT TAKES FIVE MINUTES TO GET BACK FROM THE STATION
UGH.
WHAT IS SHE DOING?

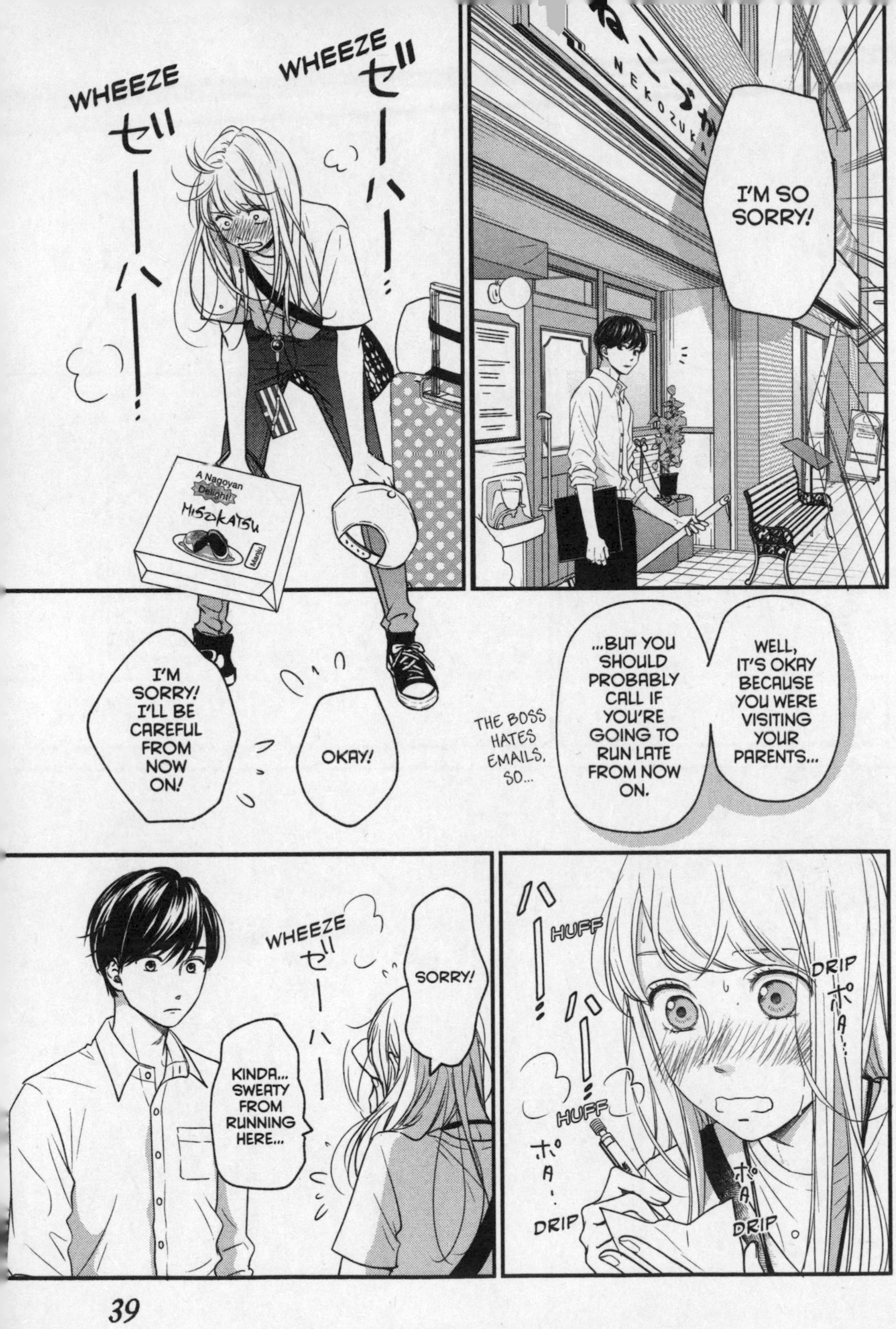
NEKOZUKA
I'M SO SORRY!
WHEEZE
ゼーハー!!
WHEEZE
ゼーハー!
A Nagoyan Delight!
MISOKATSU
Manju
WELL, IT'S OKAY BECAUSE YOU WERE VISITING YOUR PARENTS...
...BUT YOU SHOULD PROBABLY CALL IF YOU'RE GOING TO RUN LATE FROM NOW ON.
THE BOSS HATES EMAILS, SO...
OKAY!
I'M SORRY! I'LL BE CAREFUL FROM NOW ON!
HUFF
ハー!!
HUFF
ハー!!
DRIP
ポタ...
DRIP
ポタ
DRIP
ポタ...
SORRY!
WHEEZE
ゼーハー
KINDA... SWEATY FROM RUNNING HERE...

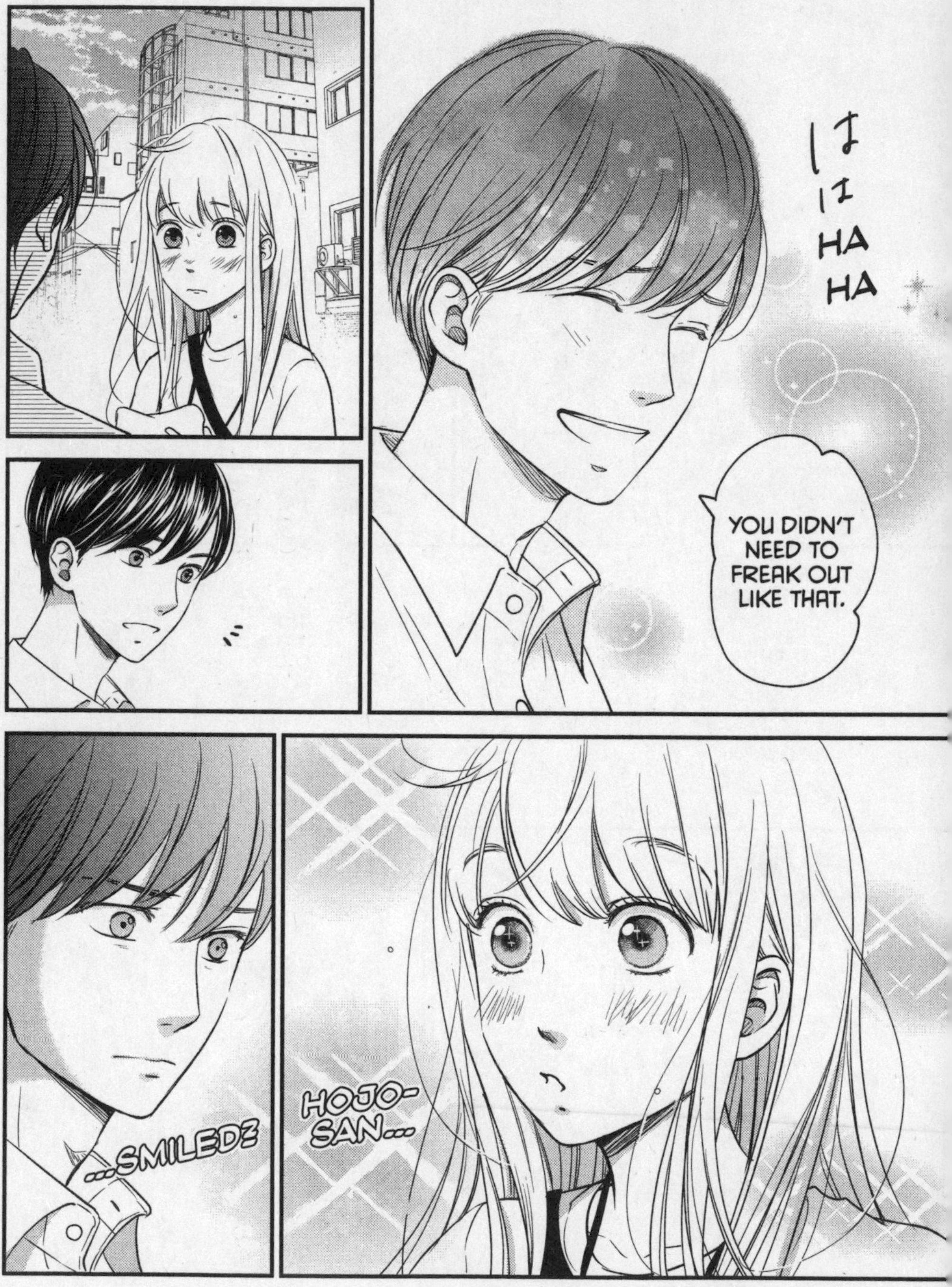
はは
HA HA
YOU DIDN'T NEED TO FREAK OUT LIKE THAT.
HOJO-SAN...
...SMILED?

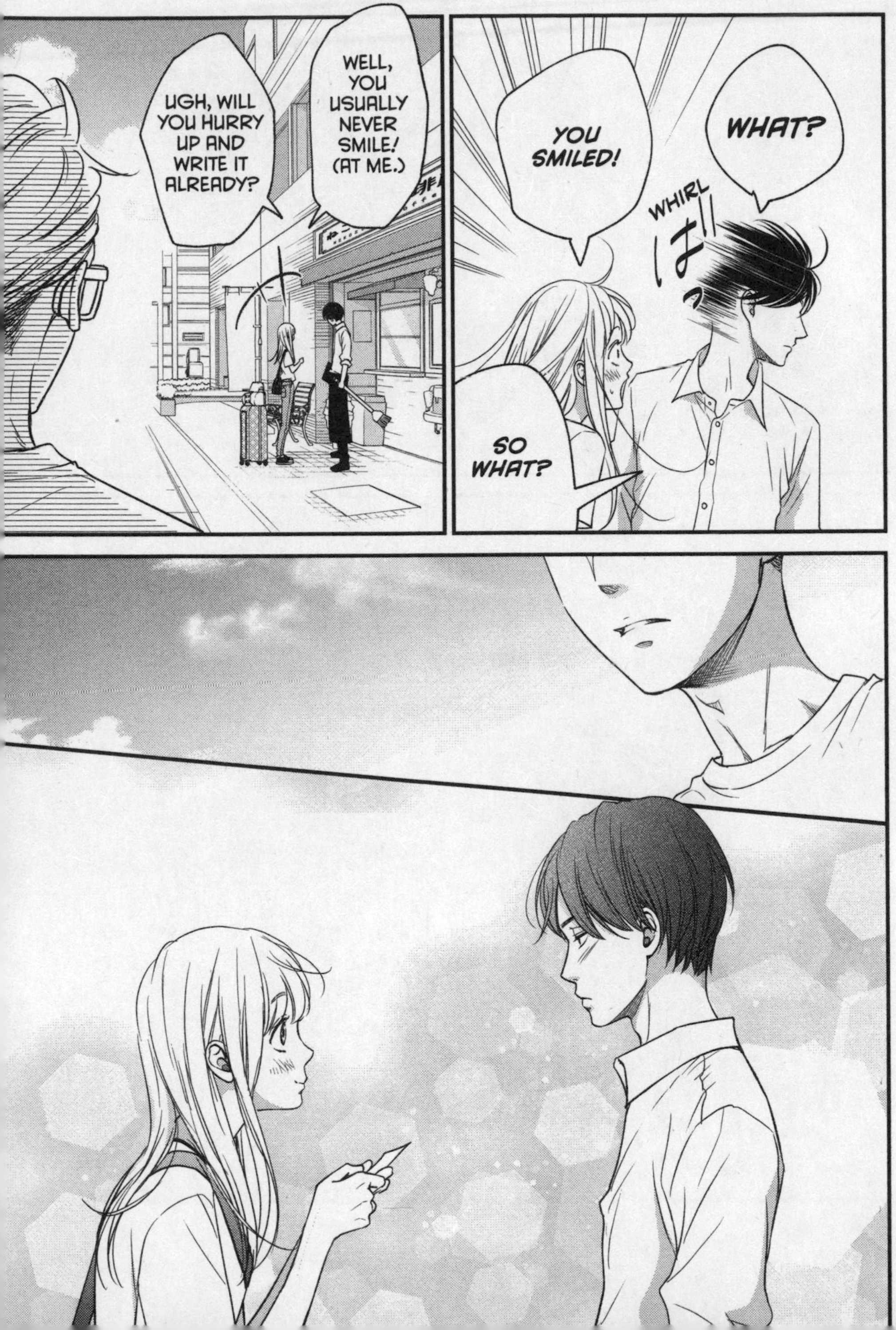
WHAT?
WHIRL
YOU SMILED!
SO WHAT?
WELL, YOU USUALLY NEVER SMILE! (AT ME.)
UGH, WILL YOU HURRY UP AND WRITE IT ALREADY?

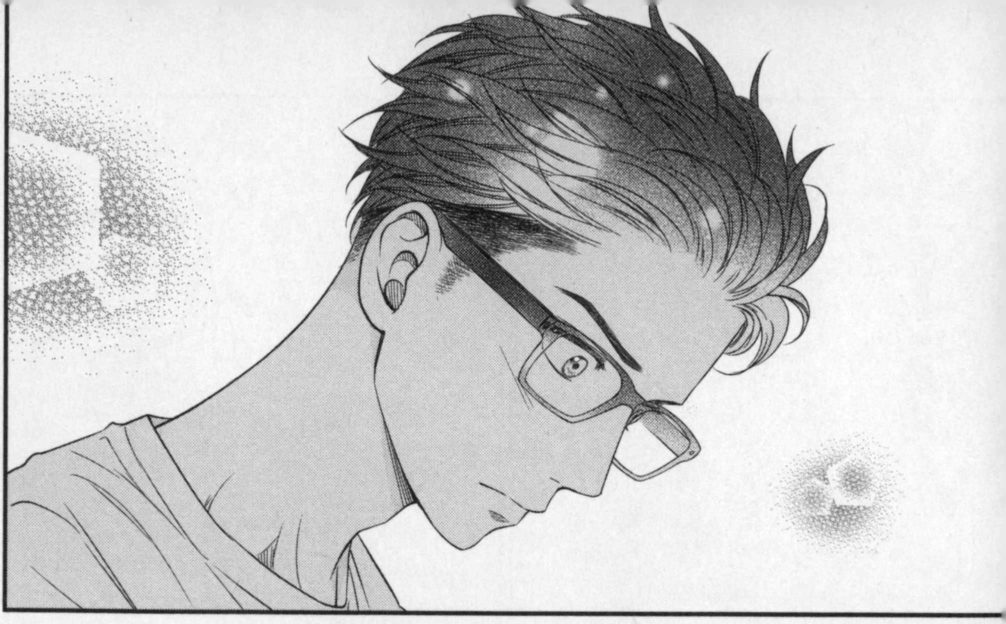

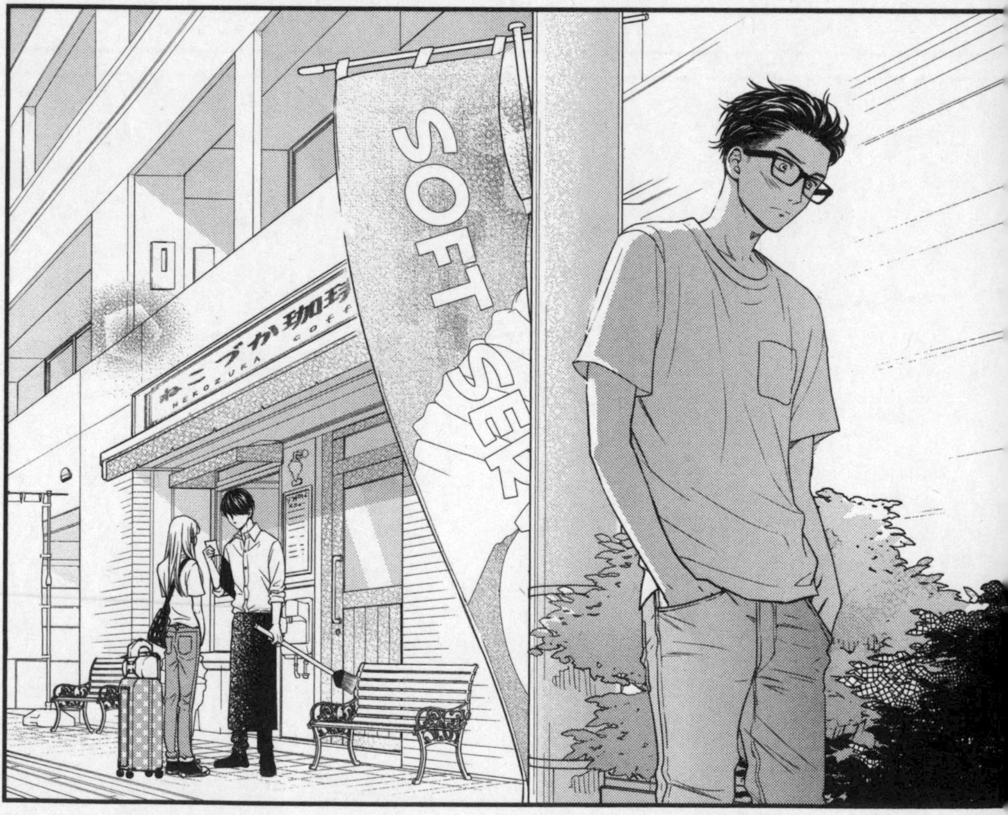
SOFT SER
ねこづか珈琲
NEKOZUKA COFF

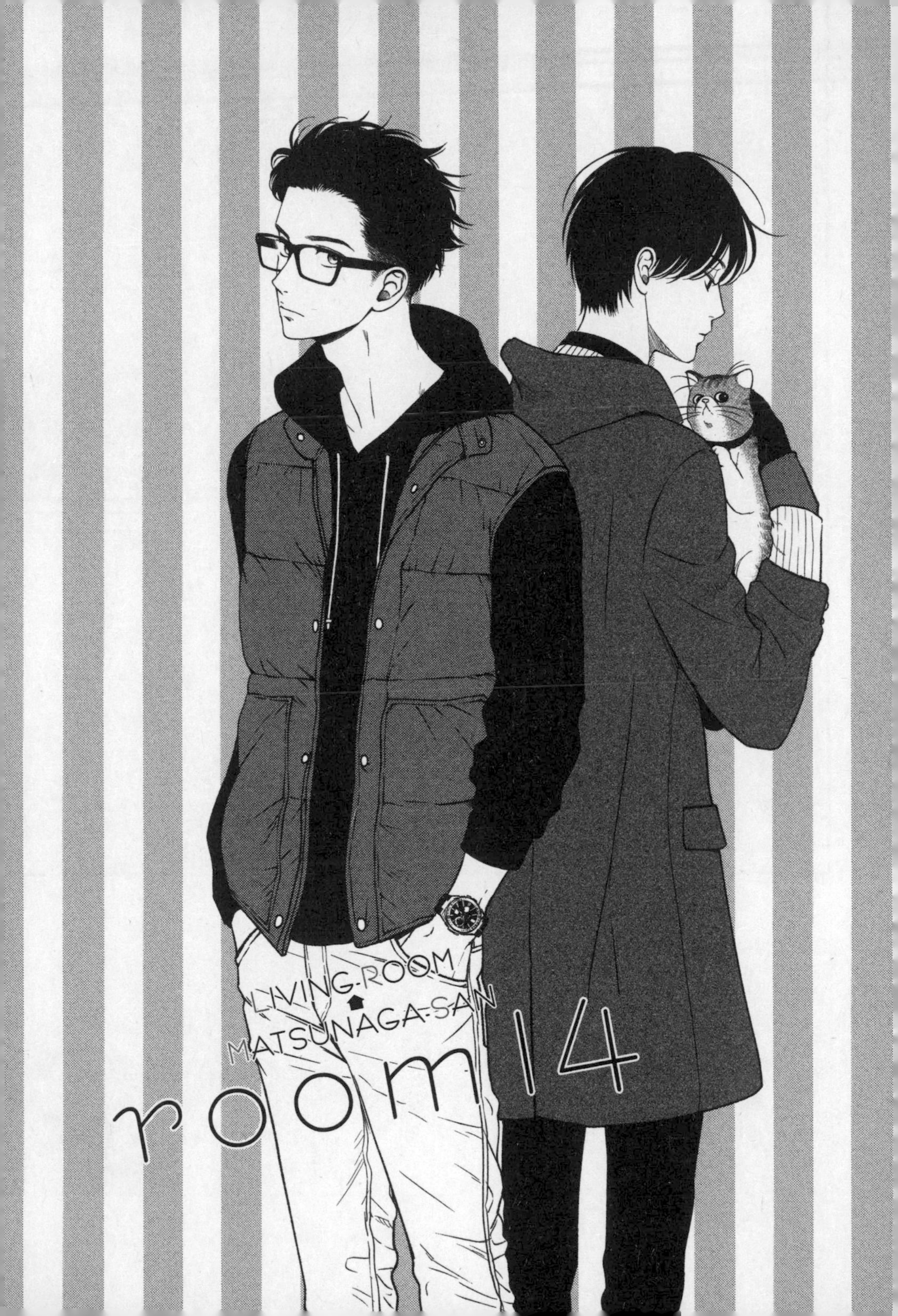
LIVING-ROOM
MATSUNAGA-SAN
room 14

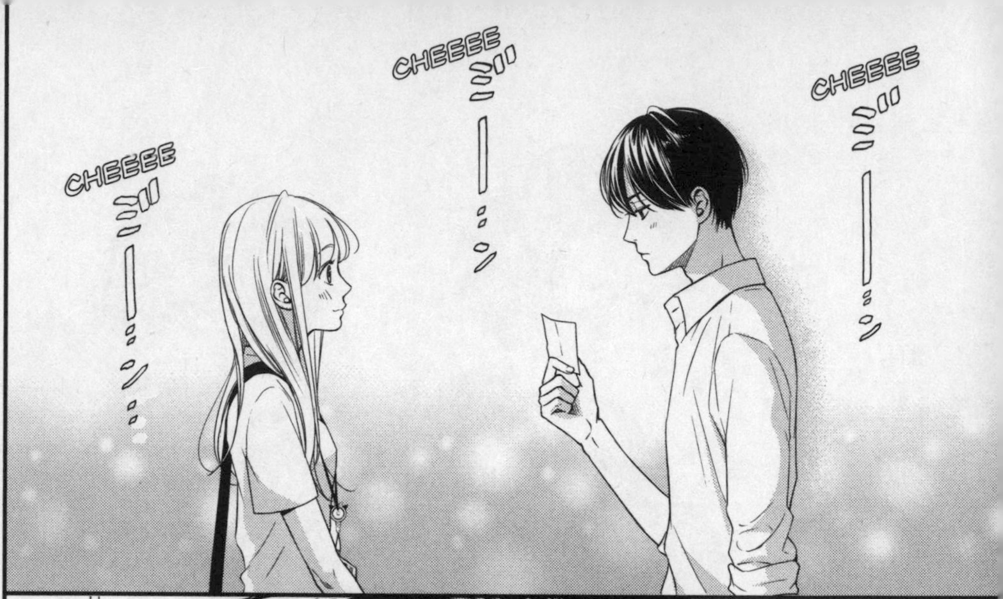
CHEEEE
CHEEEE
CHEEEE

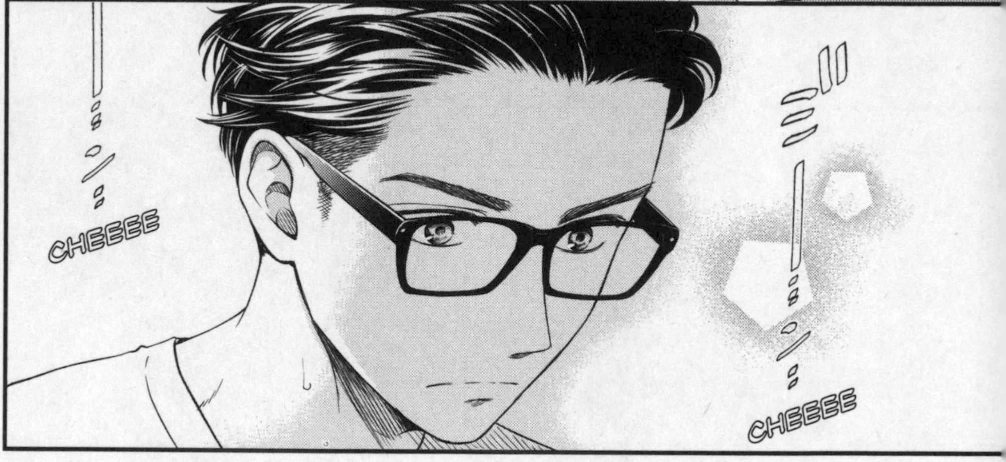
CHEEEE
CHEEEE

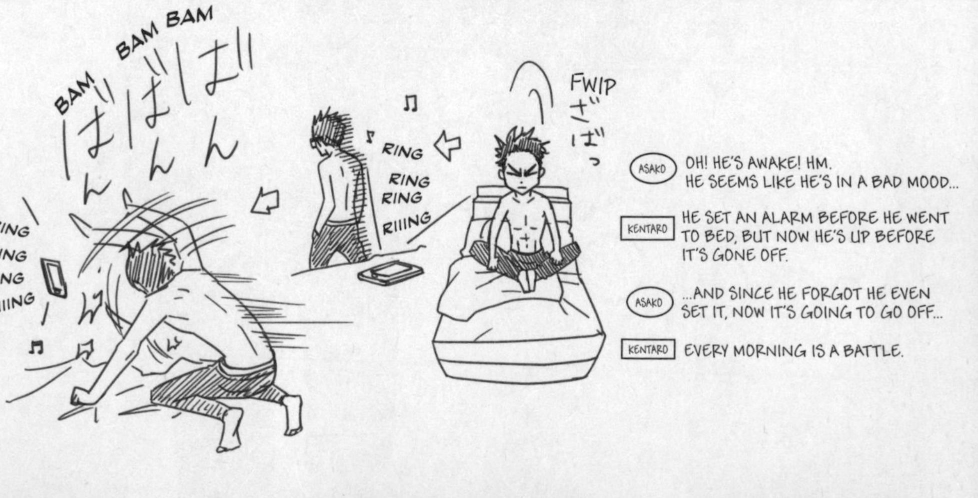
ASAKO
OH! HE'S AWAKE! HM.
HE SEEMS LIKE HE'S IN A BAD MOOD...
KENTARO
HE SET AN ALARM BEFORE HE WENT TO BED, BUT NOW HE'S UP BEFORE IT'S GONE OFF.
ASAKO
...AND SINCE HE FORGOT HE EVEN SET IT, NOW IT'S GOING TO GO OFF...
KENTARO
EVERY MORNING IS A BATTLE.
FWIP
ざばっ
RING
RING
RING
RIIING
BAM
BAM BAM
ばばばんんん
RING
RING
RING
RIIING

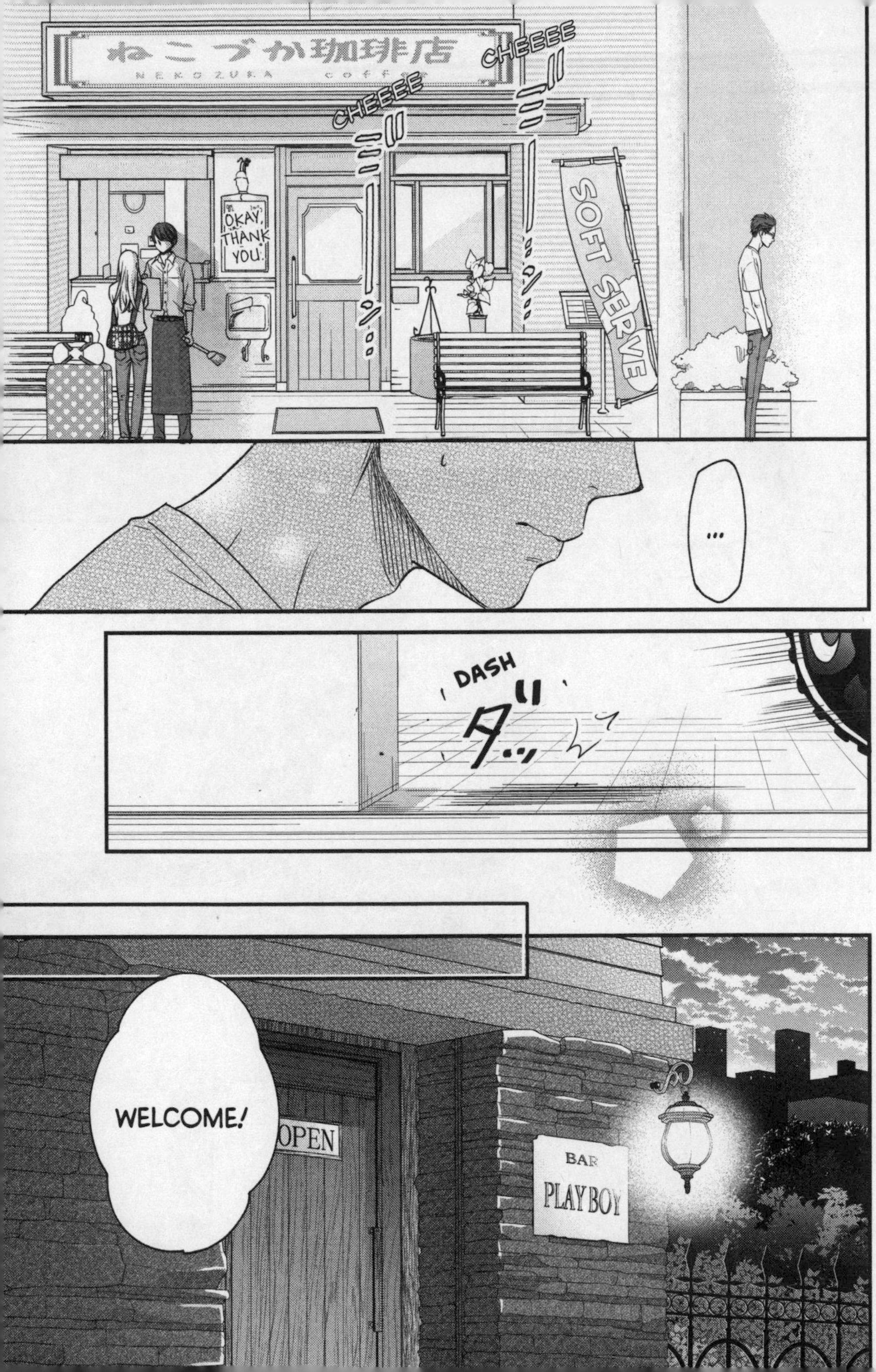
ねこづか珈琲店
CHEEEE
CHEEEE
OKAY, THANK YOU.
...
DASH
ダッ
WELCOME!
OPEN
BAR PLAYBOY

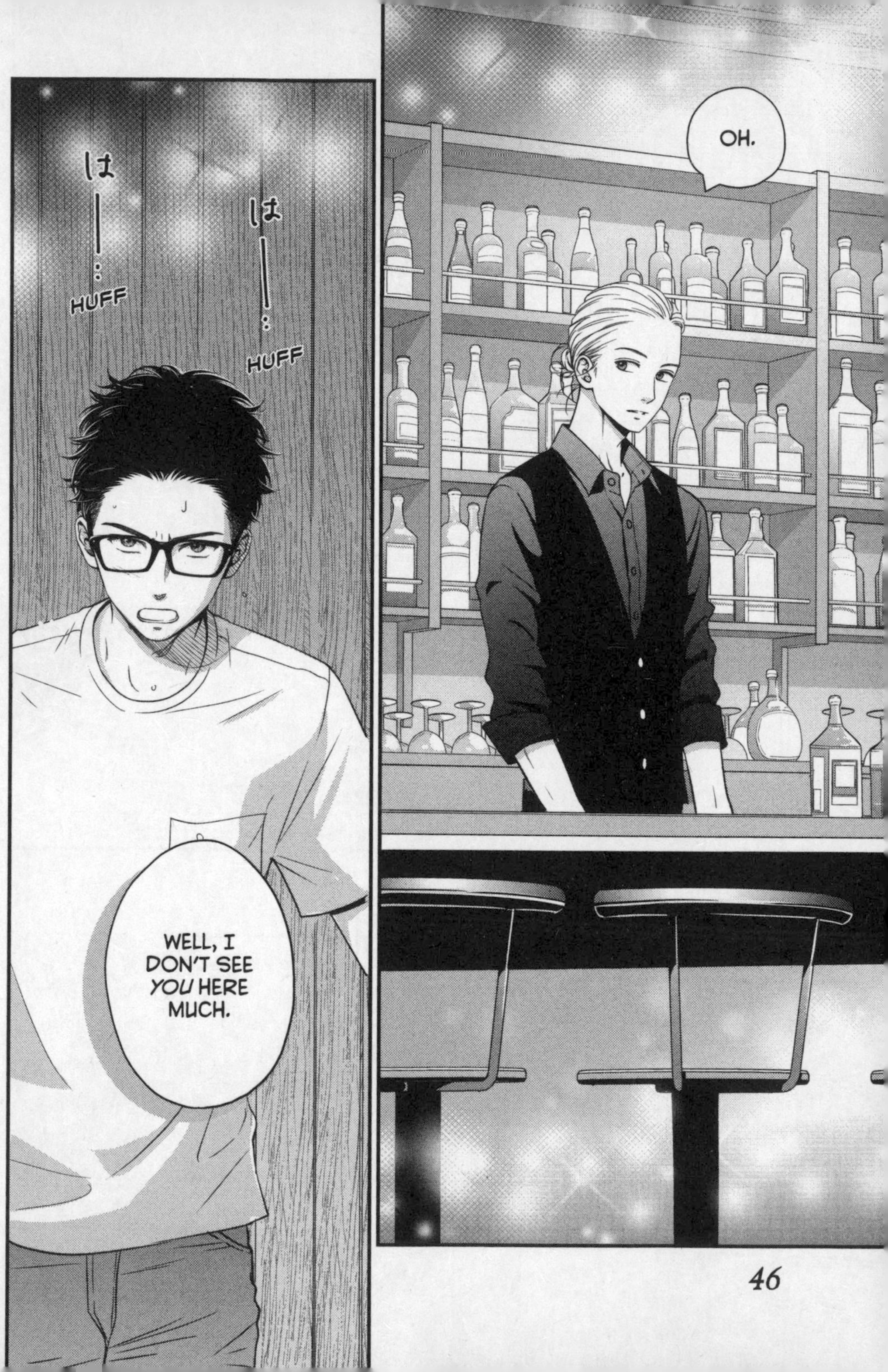
OH.
は――…
HUFF
は――…
HUFF
WELL, I DON'T SEE *YOU* HERE MUCH.

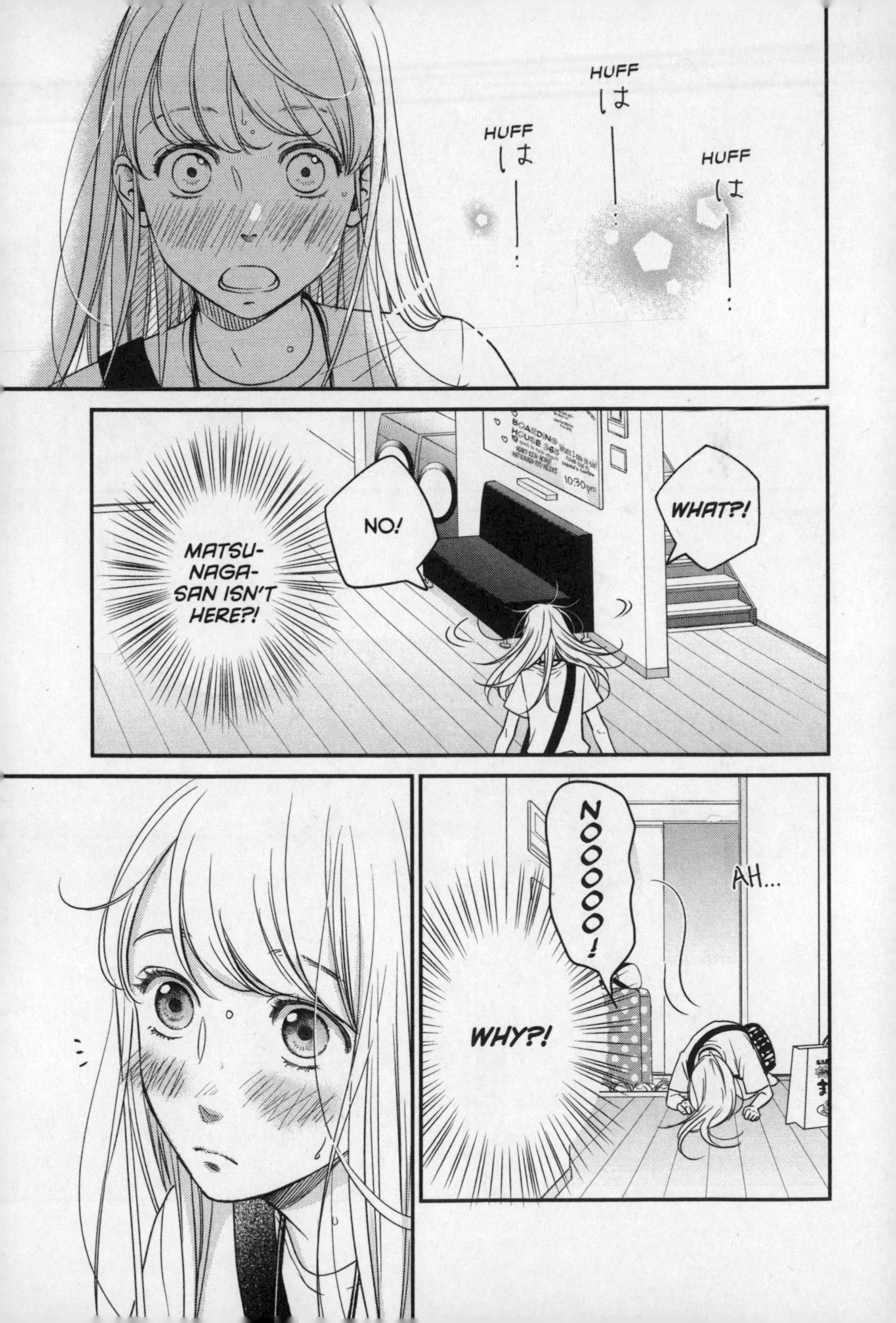
HUFF
は―…
HUFF
は―…
HUFF
は―…
WHAT?!
NO!
MATSU-NAGA-SAN ISN'T HERE?!
AH...
NOOOOO!
WHY?!

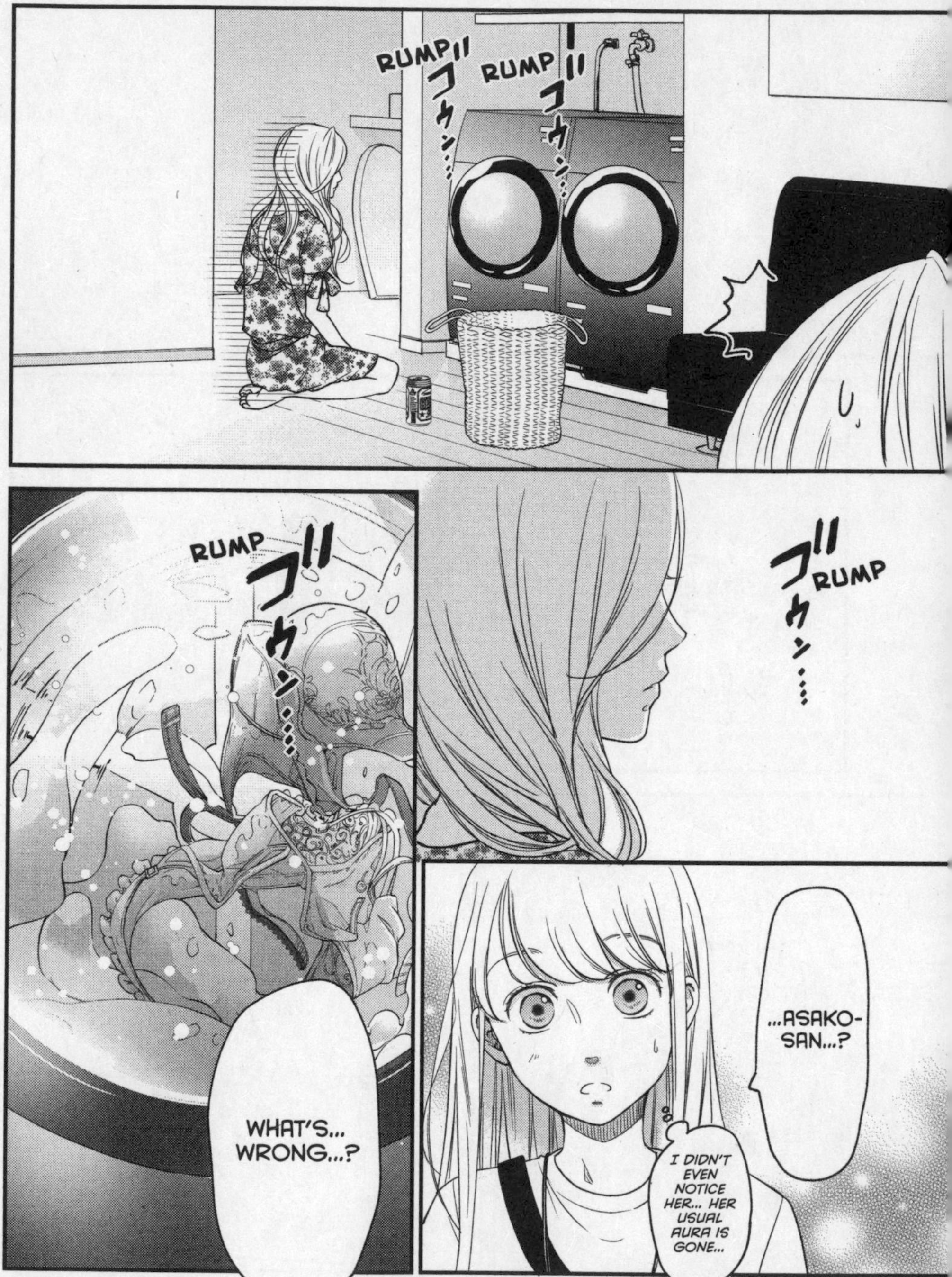
RUMP
ゴウン…
RUMP
ゴウン…
ブウン…
RUMP
...ASAKO-SAN...?
I DIDN'T EVEN NOTICE HER... HER USUAL AURA IS GONE...
RUMP
ブウン…
WHAT'S... WRONG...?

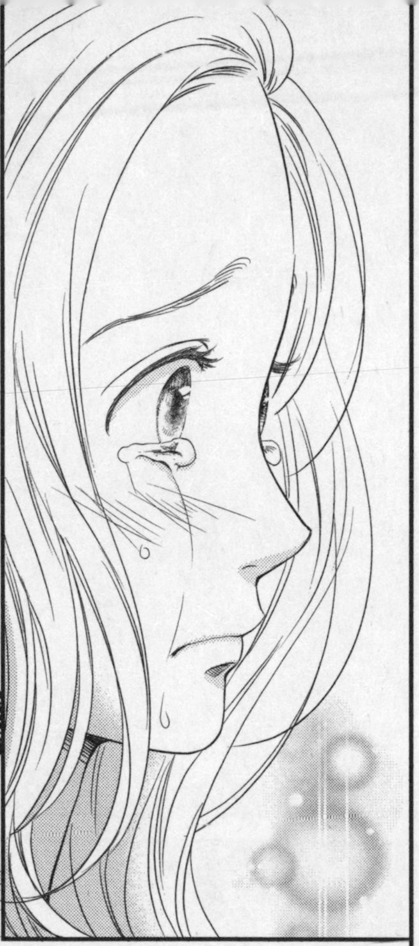

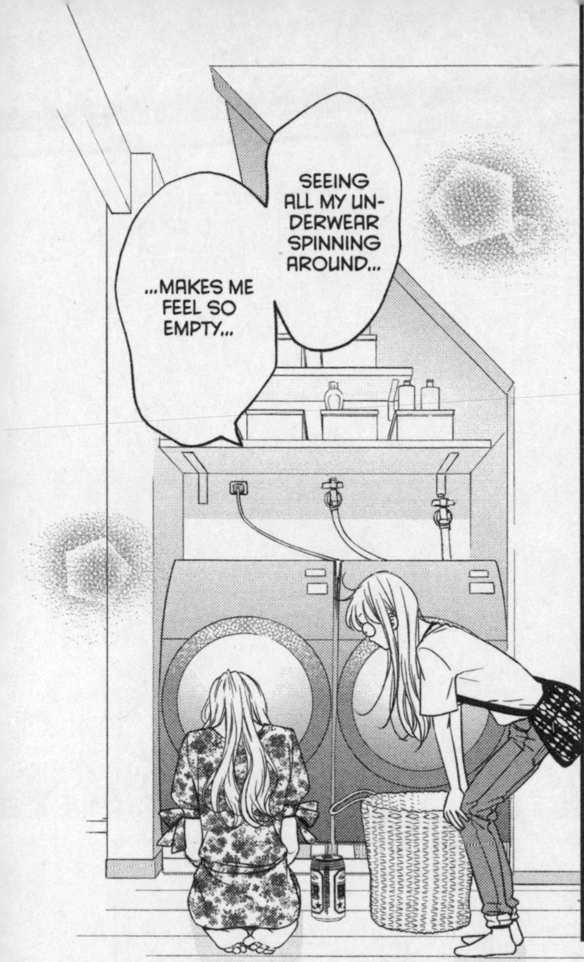
SEEING ALL MY UNDERWEAR SPINNING AROUND...
...MAKES ME FEEL SO EMPTY...

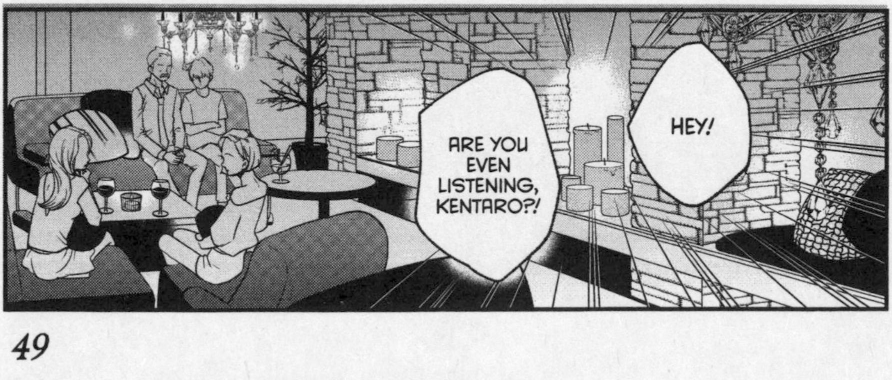
HEY!
ARE YOU EVEN LISTENING, KENTARO?!

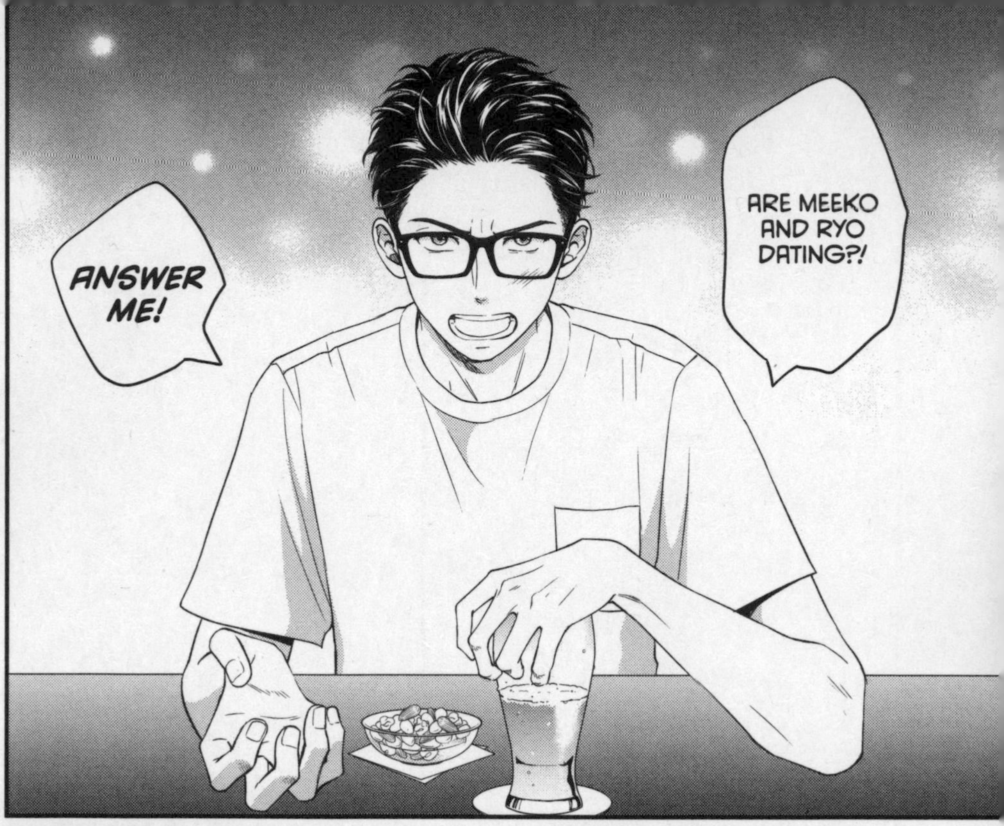
ARE MEEKO AND RYO DATING?!
ANSWER ME!

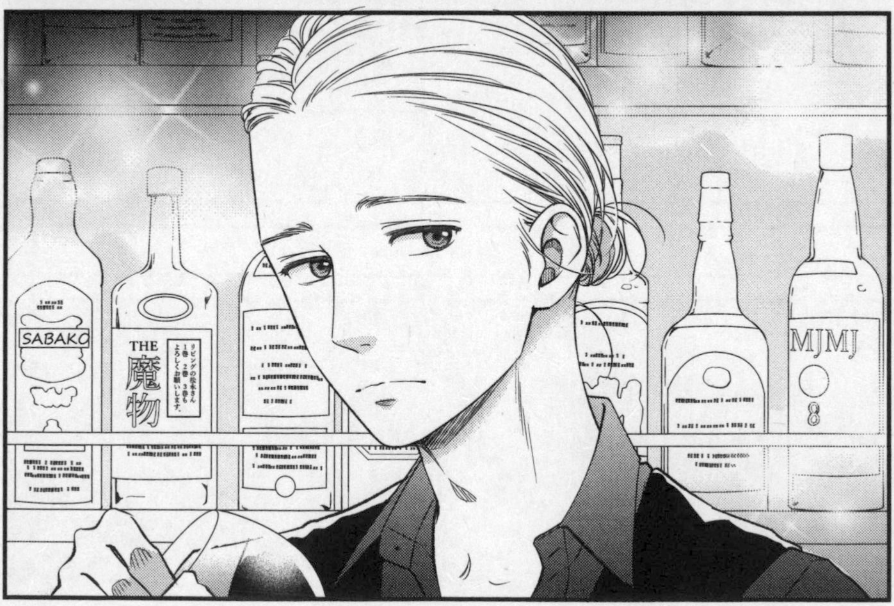
SABAKO
THE 魔物
リビングの松永さん 1巻 2巻 3巻も よろしくお願いします。
MJMJ
8

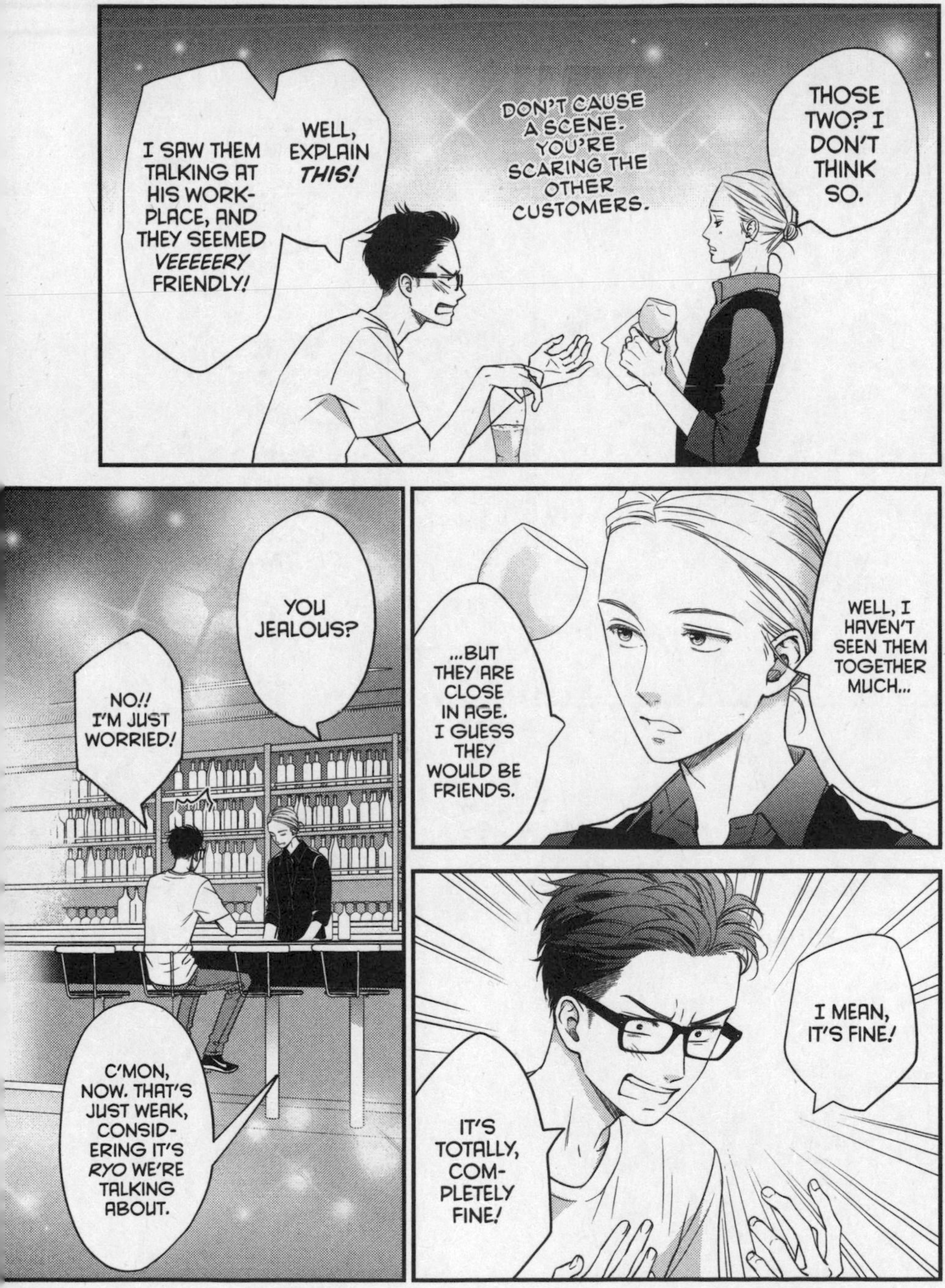
THOSE TWO? I DON'T THINK SO.
DON'T CAUSE A SCENE. YOU'RE SCARING THE OTHER CUSTOMERS.
WELL, EXPLAIN *THIS!*
I SAW THEM TALKING AT HIS WORK-PLACE, AND THEY SEEMED *VEEEEERY* FRIENDLY!
WELL, I HAVEN'T SEEN THEM TOGETHER MUCH...
...BUT THEY ARE CLOSE IN AGE. I GUESS THEY WOULD BE FRIENDS.
I MEAN, IT'S FINE!
IT'S TOTALLY, COM-PLETELY FINE!
YOU JEALOUS?
NO!! I'M JUST WORRIED!
C'MON, NOW. THAT'S JUST WEAK, CONSID-ERING IT'S *RYO* WE'RE TALKING ABOUT.

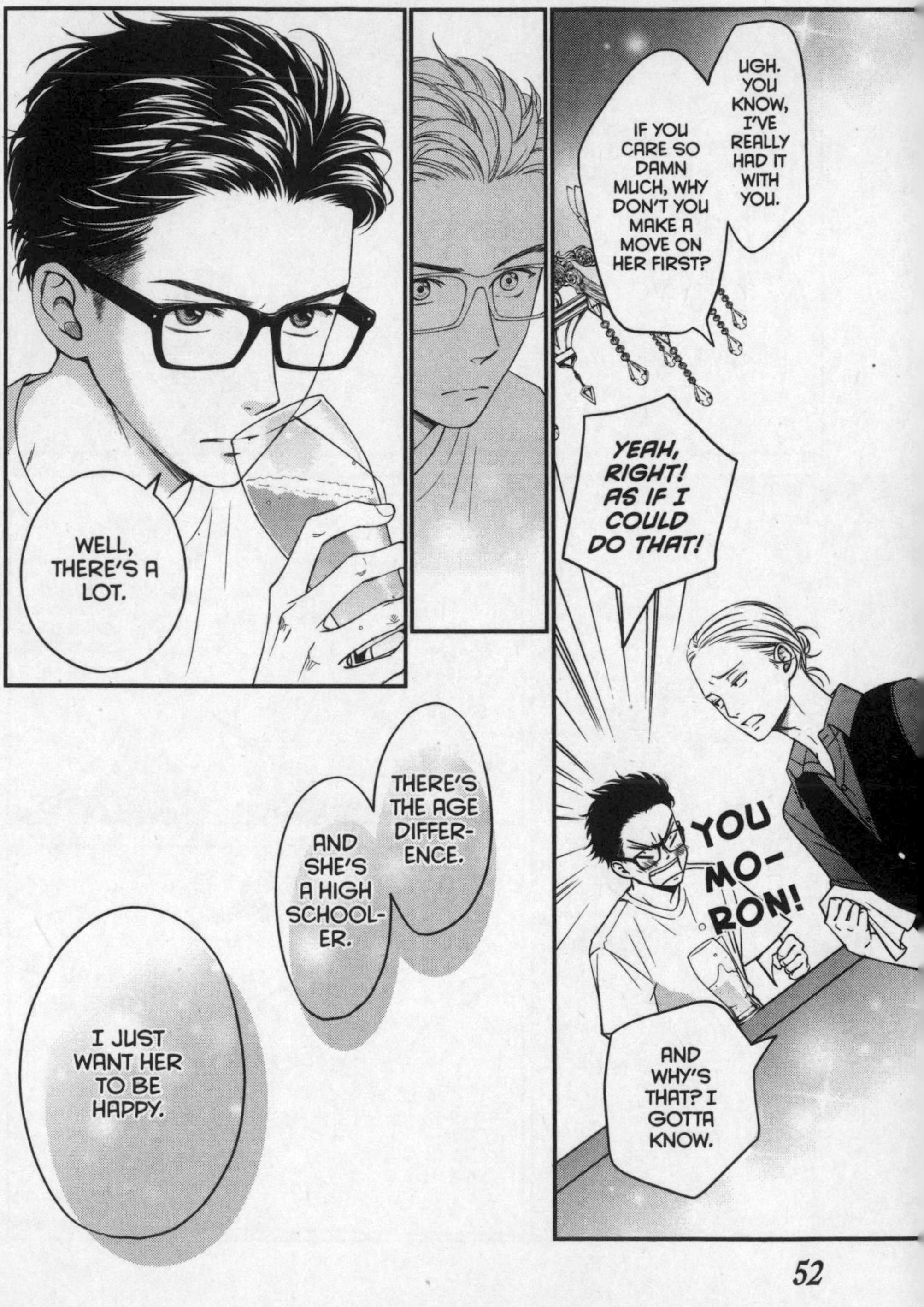
UGH. YOU KNOW, I'VE REALLY HAD IT WITH YOU.
IF YOU CARE SO DAMN MUCH, WHY DON'T YOU MAKE A MOVE ON HER FIRST?
YEAH, RIGHT! AS IF I COULD DO THAT!
YOU MORON!
AND WHY'S THAT? I GOTTA KNOW.
WELL, THERE'S A LOT.
THERE'S THE AGE DIFFERENCE.
AND SHE'S A HIGH SCHOOLER.
I JUST WANT HER TO BE HAPPY.

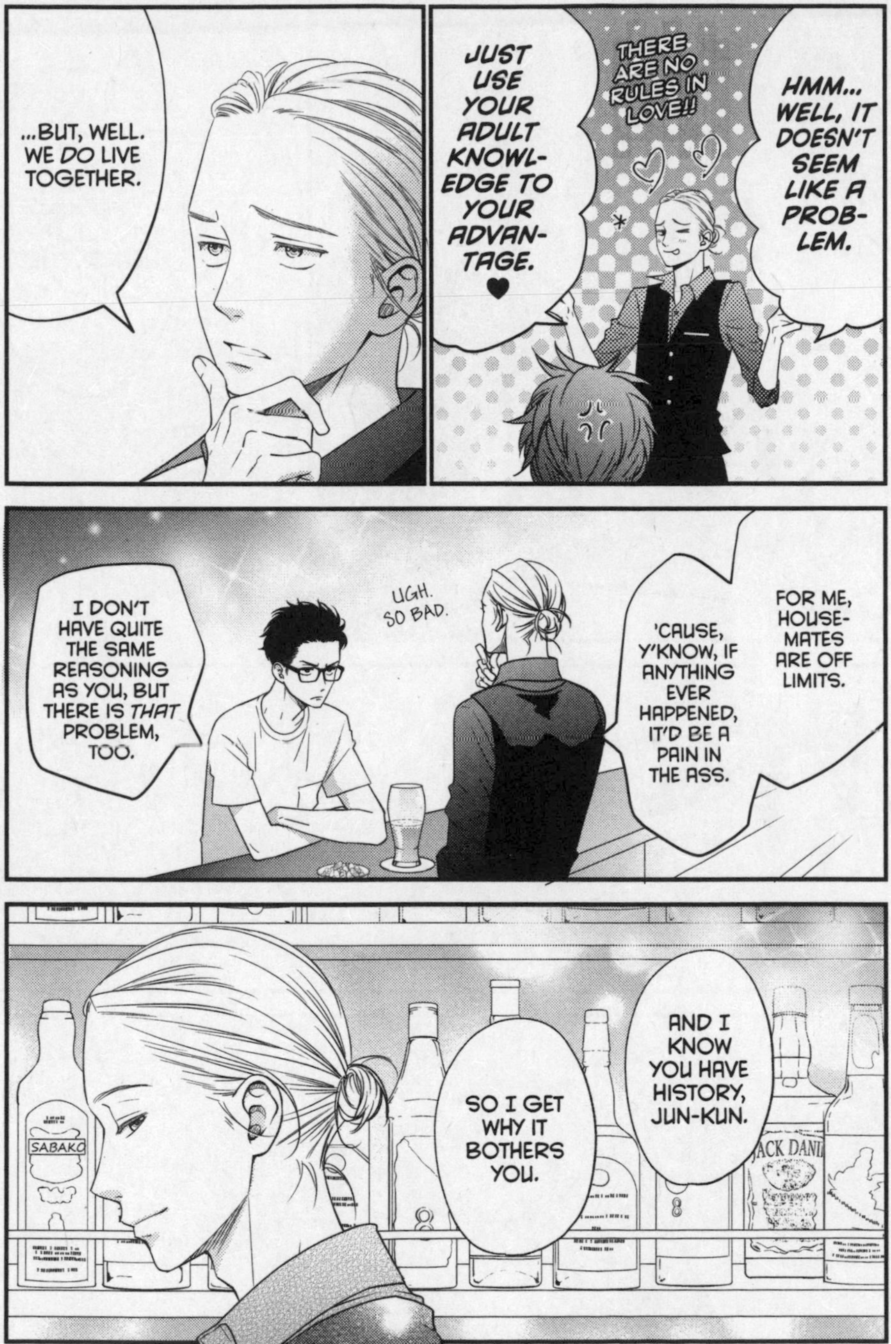
HMM... WELL, IT DOESN'T SEEM LIKE A PROB-LEM.
THERE ARE NO RULES IN LOVE!!
JUST USE YOUR ADULT KNOWL-EDGE TO YOUR ADVAN-TAGE. ♥
...BUT, WELL. WE *DO* LIVE TOGETHER.
FOR ME, HOUSE-MATES ARE OFF LIMITS.
'CAUSE, Y'KNOW, IF ANYTHING EVER HAPPENED, IT'D BE A PAIN IN THE ASS.
UGH. SO BAD.
I DON'T HAVE QUITE THE SAME REASONING AS YOU, BUT THERE IS *THAT* PROBLEM, TOO.
AND I KNOW YOU HAVE HISTORY, JUN-KUN.
SO I GET WHY IT BOTHERS YOU.
SABAKO
JACK DANI

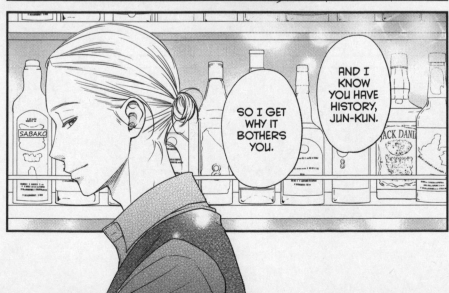

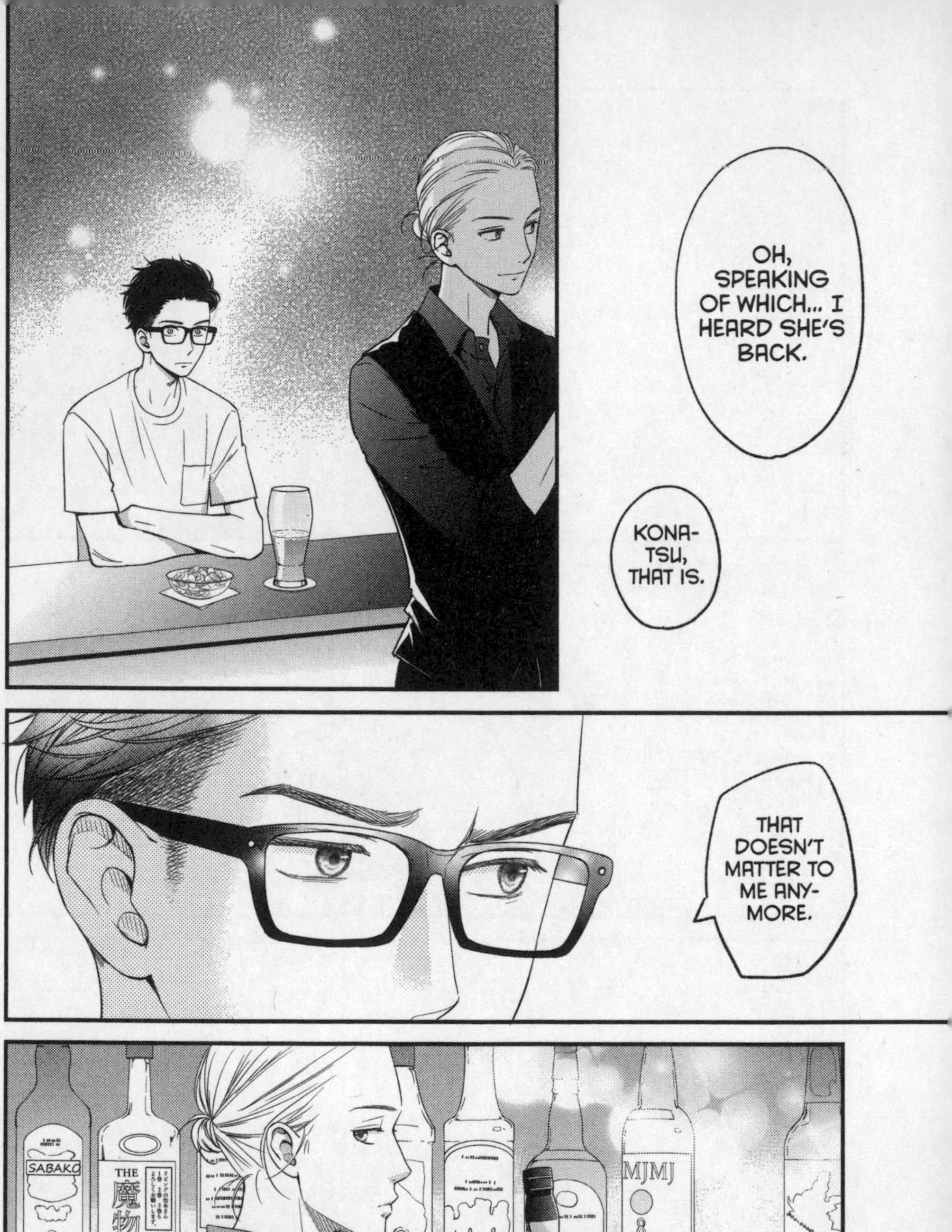
OH, SPEAKING OF WHICH... I HEARD SHE'S BACK.
KONA-TSU, THAT IS.
THAT DOESN'T MATTER TO ME ANY-MORE.
SABAKO
THE 魔物
MJMJ

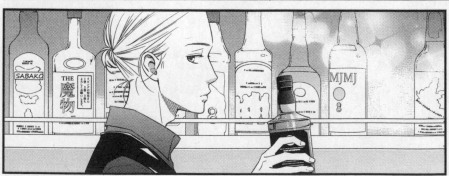

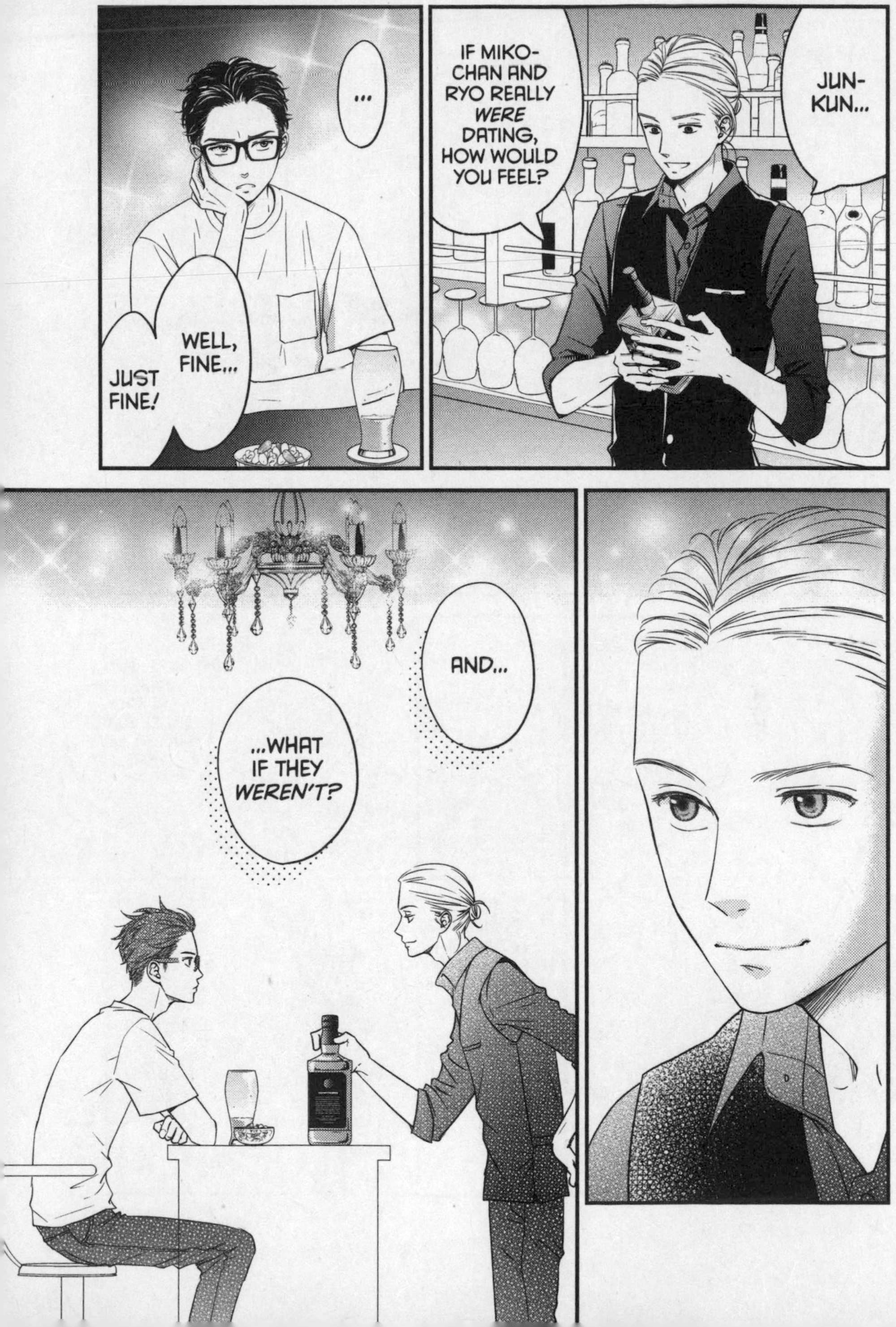
JUN-KUN...
IF MIKO-CHAN AND RYO REALLY *WERE* DATING, HOW WOULD YOU FEEL?
...
WELL, FINE...
JUST FINE!
AND...
...WHAT IF THEY *WEREN'T*?

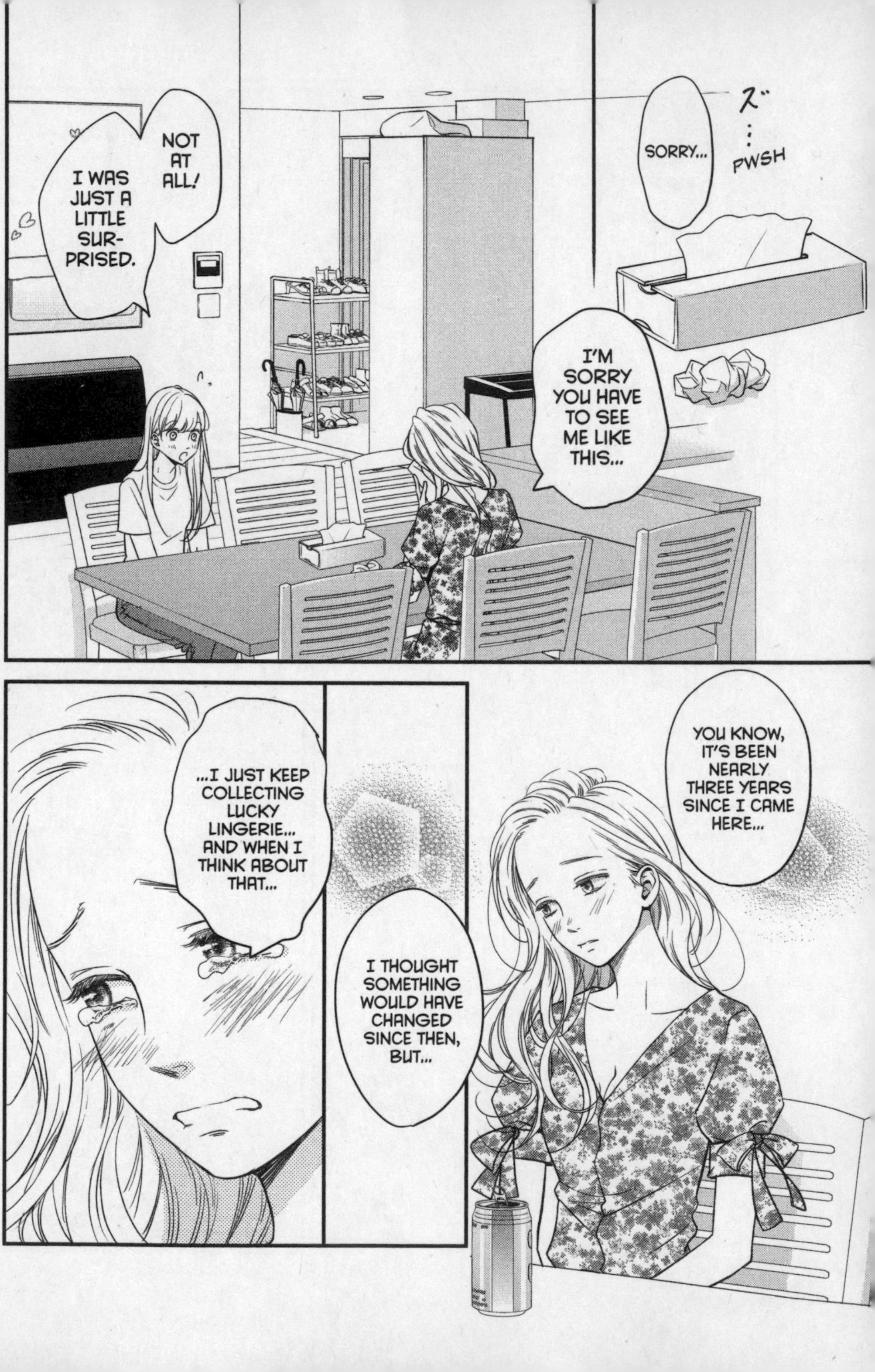
SORRY...
ズ
PWSH
I'M SORRY YOU HAVE TO SEE ME LIKE THIS...
NOT AT ALL!
I WAS JUST A LITTLE SUR-PRISED.
YOU KNOW, IT'S BEEN NEARLY THREE YEARS SINCE I CAME HERE...
I THOUGHT SOMETHING WOULD HAVE CHANGED SINCE THEN, BUT...
...I JUST KEEP COLLECTING LUCKY LINGERIE... AND WHEN I THINK ABOUT THAT...

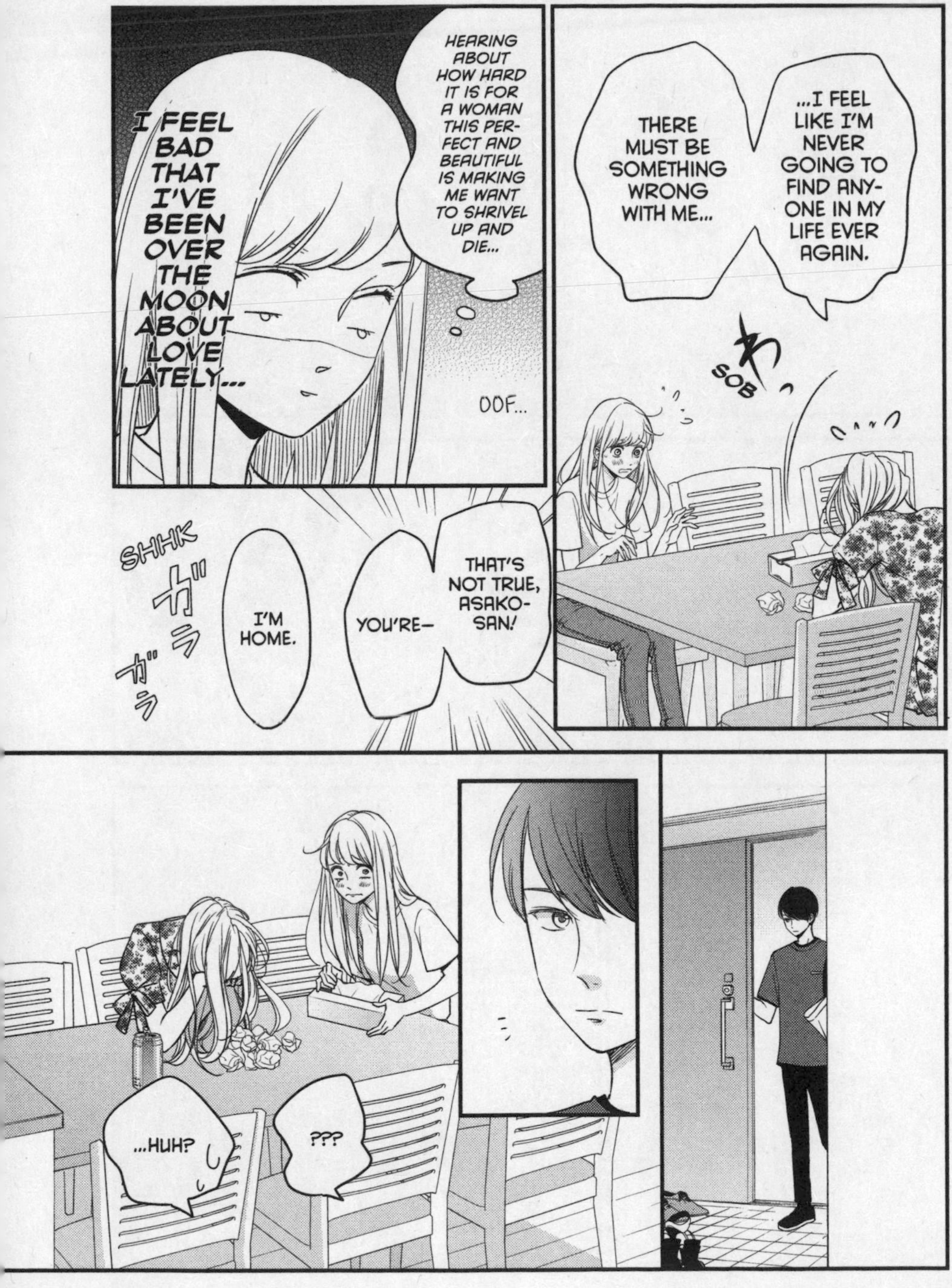
THERE MUST BE SOMETHING WRONG WITH ME...
...I FEEL LIKE I'M NEVER GOING TO FIND ANYONE IN MY LIFE EVER AGAIN.
SOB
HEARING ABOUT HOW HARD IT IS FOR A WOMAN THIS PERFECT AND BEAUTIFUL IS MAKING ME WANT TO SHRIVEL UP AND DIE...
I FEEL BAD THAT I'VE BEEN OVER THE MOON ABOUT LOVE LATELY...
OOF...
THAT'S NOT TRUE, ASAKO-SAN!
YOU'RE—
I'M HOME.
SHHK
???
...HUH?

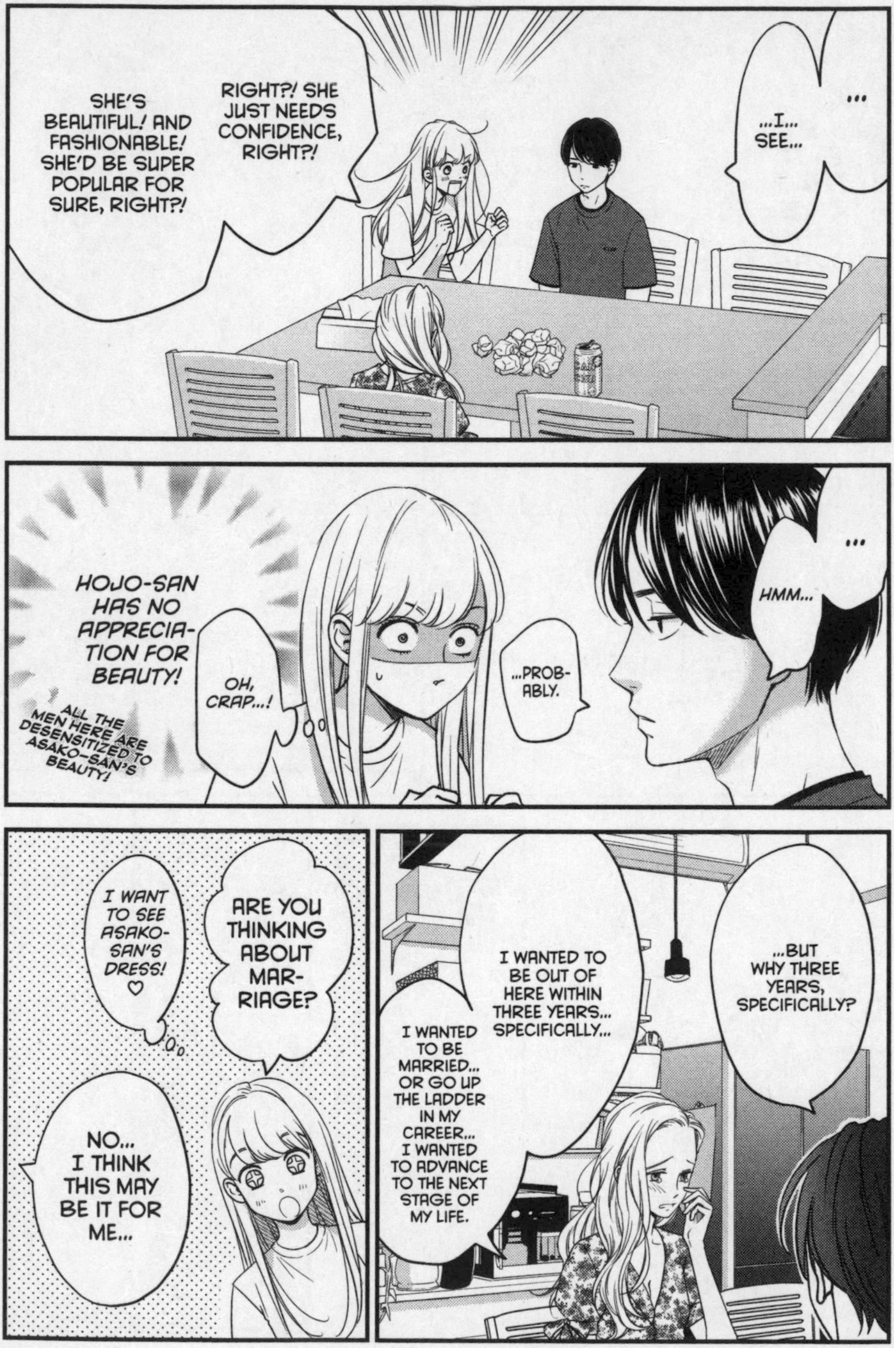
...
...I... SEE...
RIGHT?! SHE JUST NEEDS CONFIDENCE, RIGHT?!
SHE'S BEAUTIFUL! AND FASHIONABLE! SHE'D BE SUPER POPULAR FOR SURE, RIGHT?!
...
HMM...
...PROB-ABLY.
OH, CRAP...!
HOJO-SAN HAS NO APPRECIA-TION FOR BEAUTY!
ALL THE MEN HERE ARE DESENSITIZED TO ASAKO-SAN'S BEAUTY!
...BUT WHY THREE YEARS, SPECIFICALLY?
I WANTED TO BE OUT OF HERE WITHIN THREE YEARS... SPECIFICALLY...
I WANTED TO BE MARRIED... OR GO UP THE LADDER IN MY CAREER... I WANTED TO ADVANCE TO THE NEXT STAGE OF MY LIFE.
ARE YOU THINKING ABOUT MAR-RIAGE?
I WANT TO SEE ASAKO-SAN'S DRESS! ♡
NO... I THINK THIS MAY BE IT FOR ME...

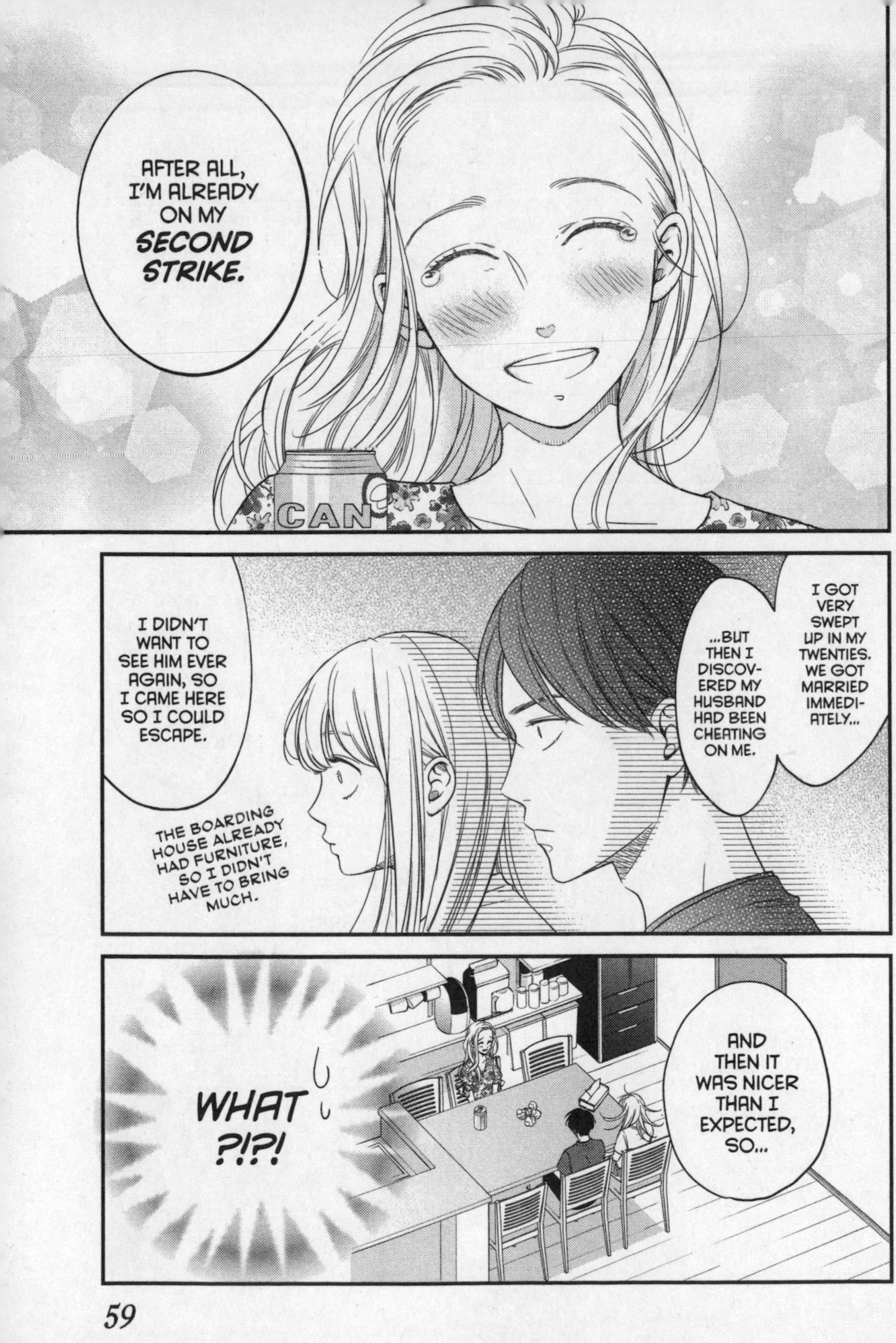
AFTER ALL, I'M ALREADY ON MY SECOND STRIKE.
CAN
I GOT VERY SWEPT UP IN MY TWENTIES. WE GOT MARRIED IMMEDIATELY...
...BUT THEN I DISCOVERED MY HUSBAND HAD BEEN CHEATING ON ME.
I DIDN'T WANT TO SEE HIM EVER AGAIN, SO I CAME HERE SO I COULD ESCAPE.
THE BOARDING HOUSE ALREADY HAD FURNITURE, SO I DIDN'T HAVE TO BRING MUCH.
AND THEN IT WAS NICER THAN I EXPECTED, SO...
WHAT ?!?!

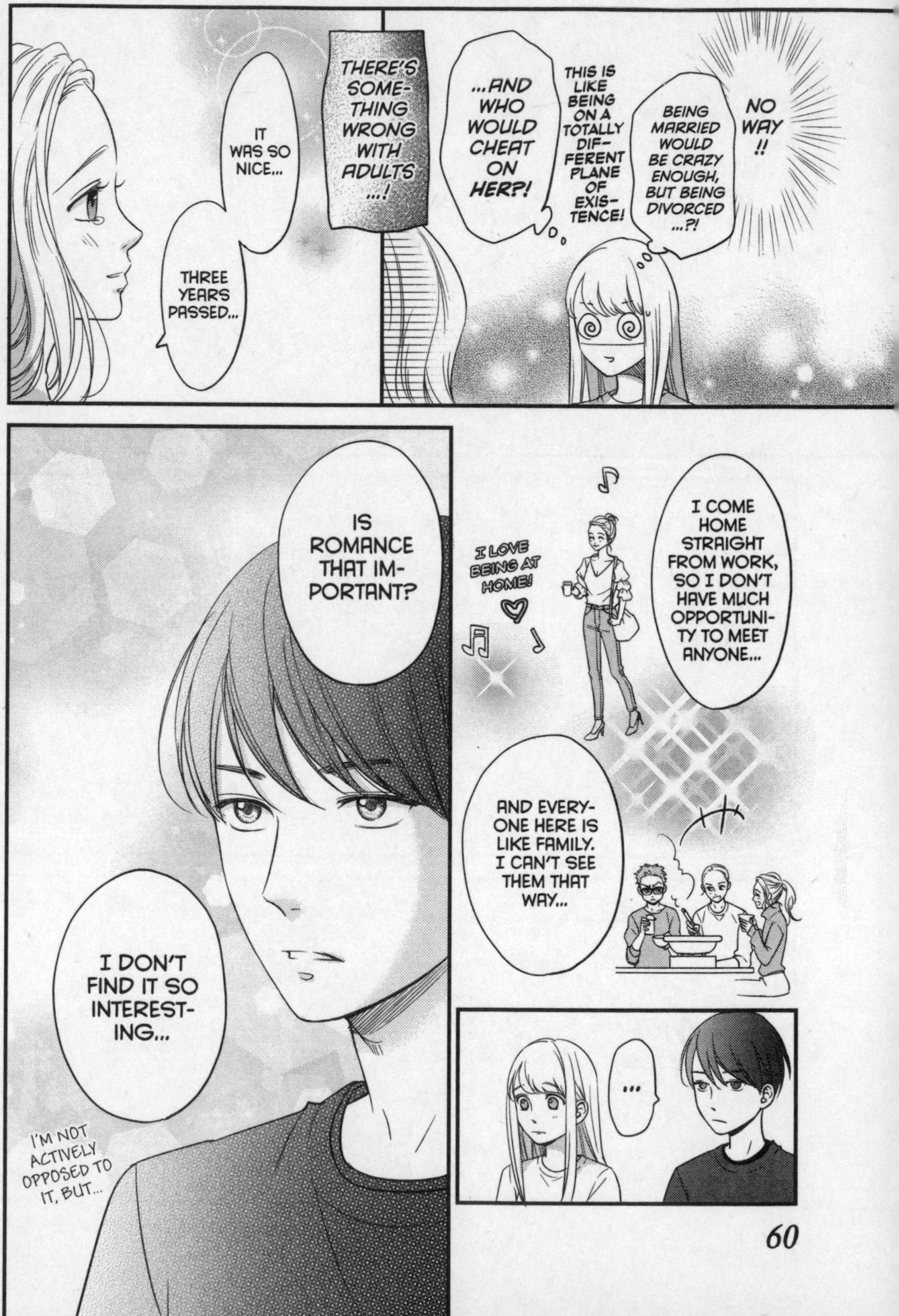
NO WAY!!
BEING MARRIED WOULD BE CRAZY ENOUGH, BUT BEING DIVORCED ...?!
THIS IS LIKE BEING ON A TOTALLY DIFFERENT PLANE OF EXISTENCE!
...AND WHO WOULD CHEAT ON HER?!
THERE'S SOMETHING WRONG WITH ADULTS ...!
IT WAS SO NICE...
THREE YEARS PASSED...
I COME HOME STRAIGHT FROM WORK, SO I DON'T HAVE MUCH OPPORTUNITY TO MEET ANYONE...
I LOVE BEING AT HOME!
AND EVERYONE HERE IS LIKE FAMILY. I CAN'T SEE THEM THAT WAY...
...
IS ROMANCE THAT IMPORTANT?
I DON'T FIND IT SO INTERESTING...
I'M NOT ACTIVELY OPPOSED TO IT, BUT...

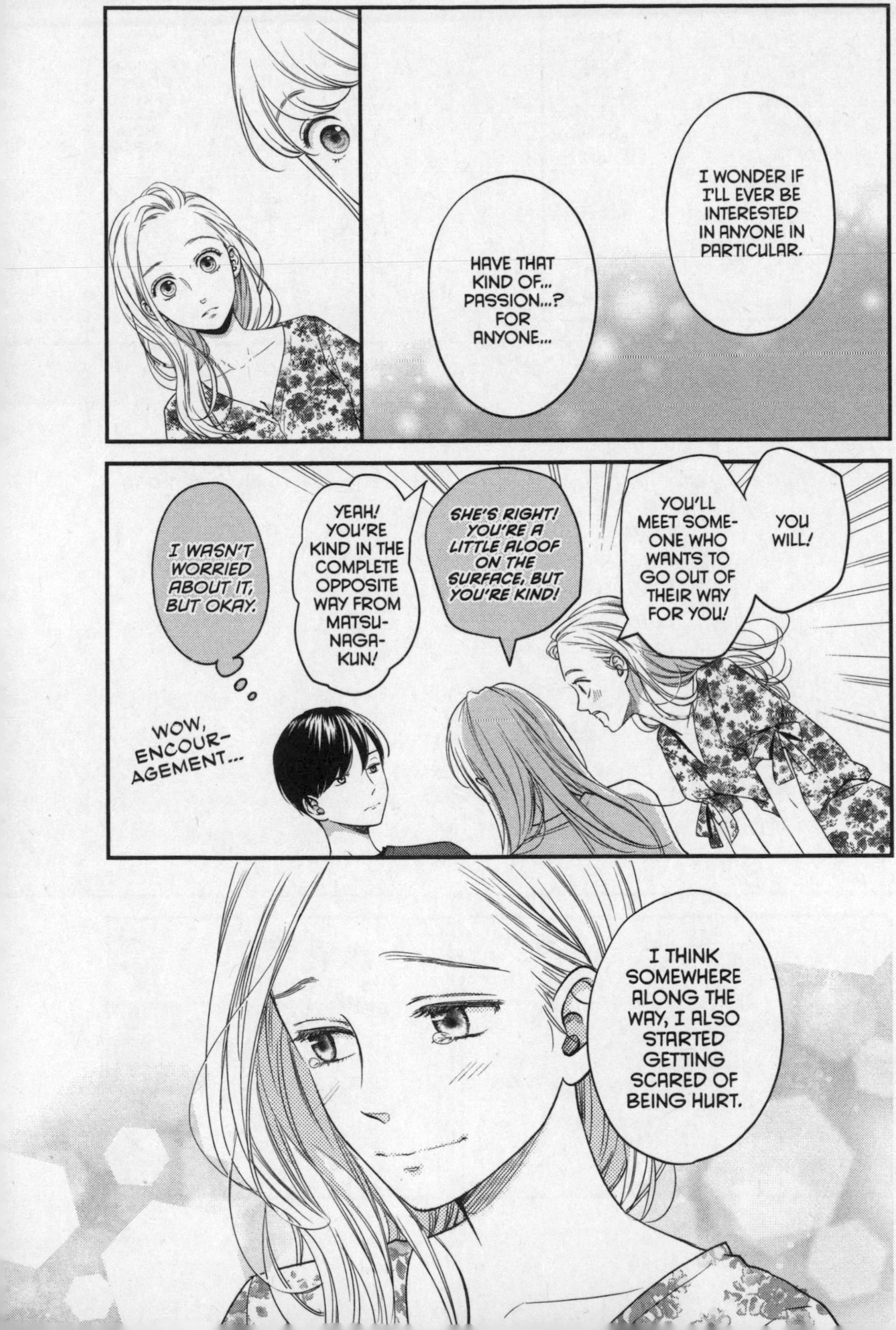
I WONDER IF I'LL EVER BE INTERESTED IN ANYONE IN PARTICULAR.
HAVE THAT KIND OF... PASSION...? FOR ANYONE...
YOU WILL!
YOU'LL MEET SOME-ONE WHO WANTS TO GO OUT OF THEIR WAY FOR YOU!
SHE'S RIGHT! YOU'RE A LITTLE ALOOF ON THE SURFACE, BUT YOU'RE KIND!
YEAH! YOU'RE KIND IN THE COMPLETE OPPOSITE WAY FROM MATSU-NAGA-KUN!
I WASN'T WORRIED ABOUT IT, BUT OKAY.
WOW, ENCOUR-AGEMENT...
I THINK SOMEWHERE ALONG THE WAY, I ALSO STARTED GETTING SCARED OF BEING HURT.

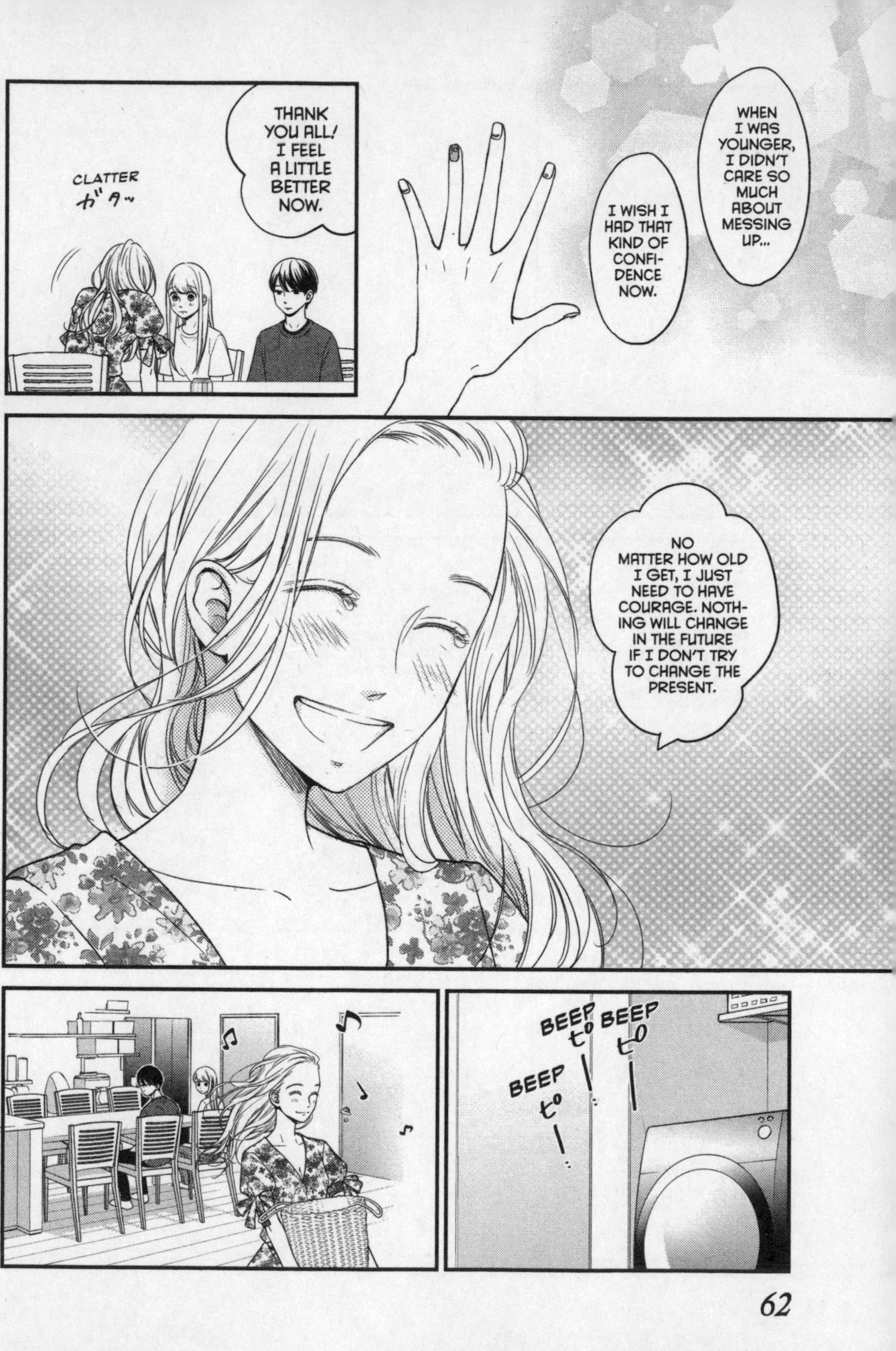
WHEN I WAS YOUNGER, I DIDN'T CARE SO MUCH ABOUT MESSING UP...
I WISH I HAD THAT KIND OF CONFI-DENCE NOW.
THANK YOU ALL! I FEEL A LITTLE BETTER NOW.
CLATTER
ガタッ
NO MATTER HOW OLD I GET, I JUST NEED TO HAVE COURAGE. NOTH-ING WILL CHANGE IN THE FUTURE IF I DON'T TRY TO CHANGE THE PRESENT.
BEEP
ピー
BEEP
ピー
BEEP
ピー

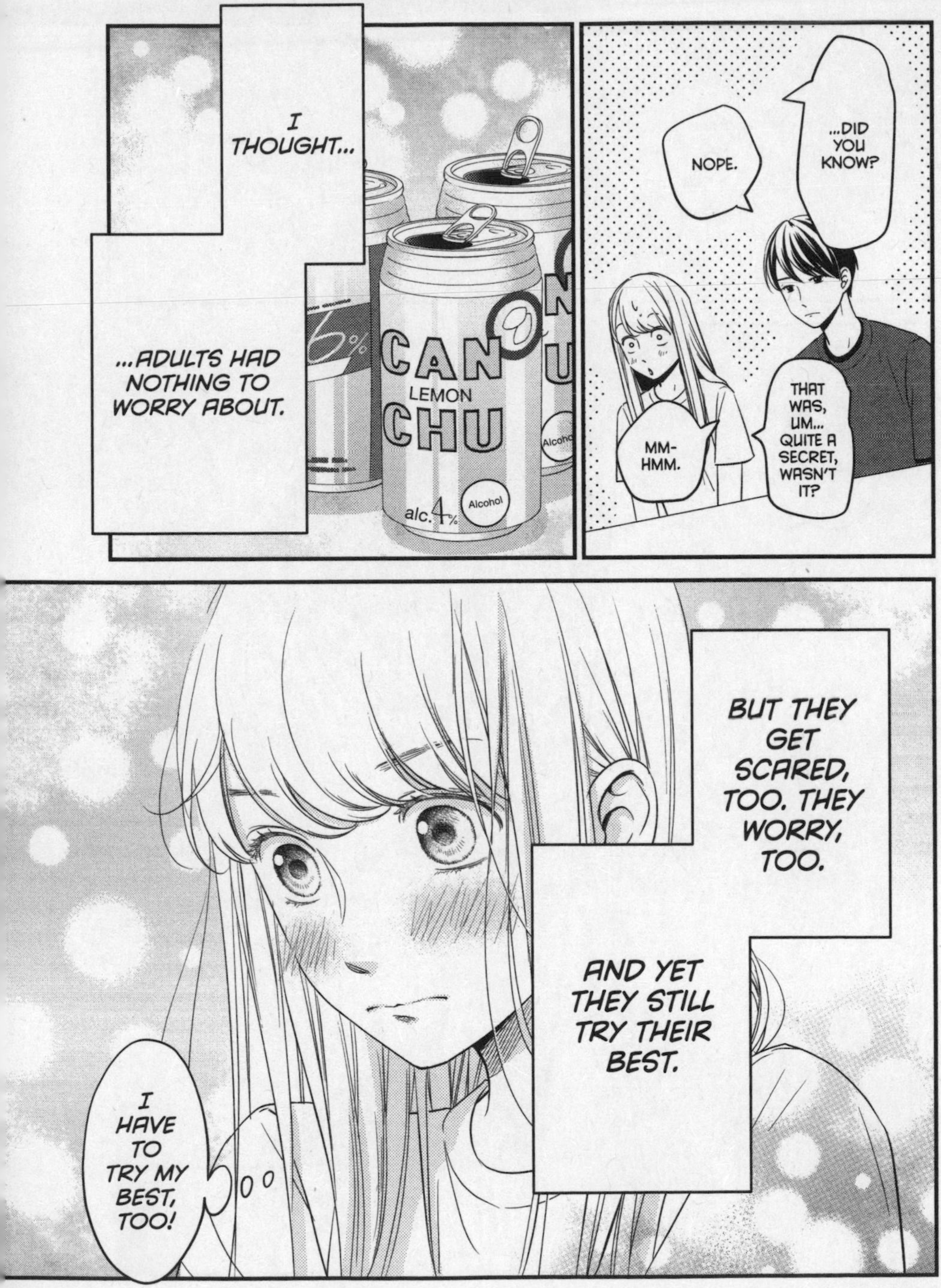
...DID YOU KNOW?
NOPE.
THAT WAS, UM... QUITE A SECRET, WASN'T IT?
MM-HMM.
I THOUGHT...
...ADULTS HAD NOTHING TO WORRY ABOUT.
CAN CHU
LEMON
Alcohol
alc.4%
Alcohol
BUT THEY GET SCARED, TOO. THEY WORRY, TOO.
AND YET THEY STILL TRY THEIR BEST.
I HAVE TO TRY MY BEST, TOO!

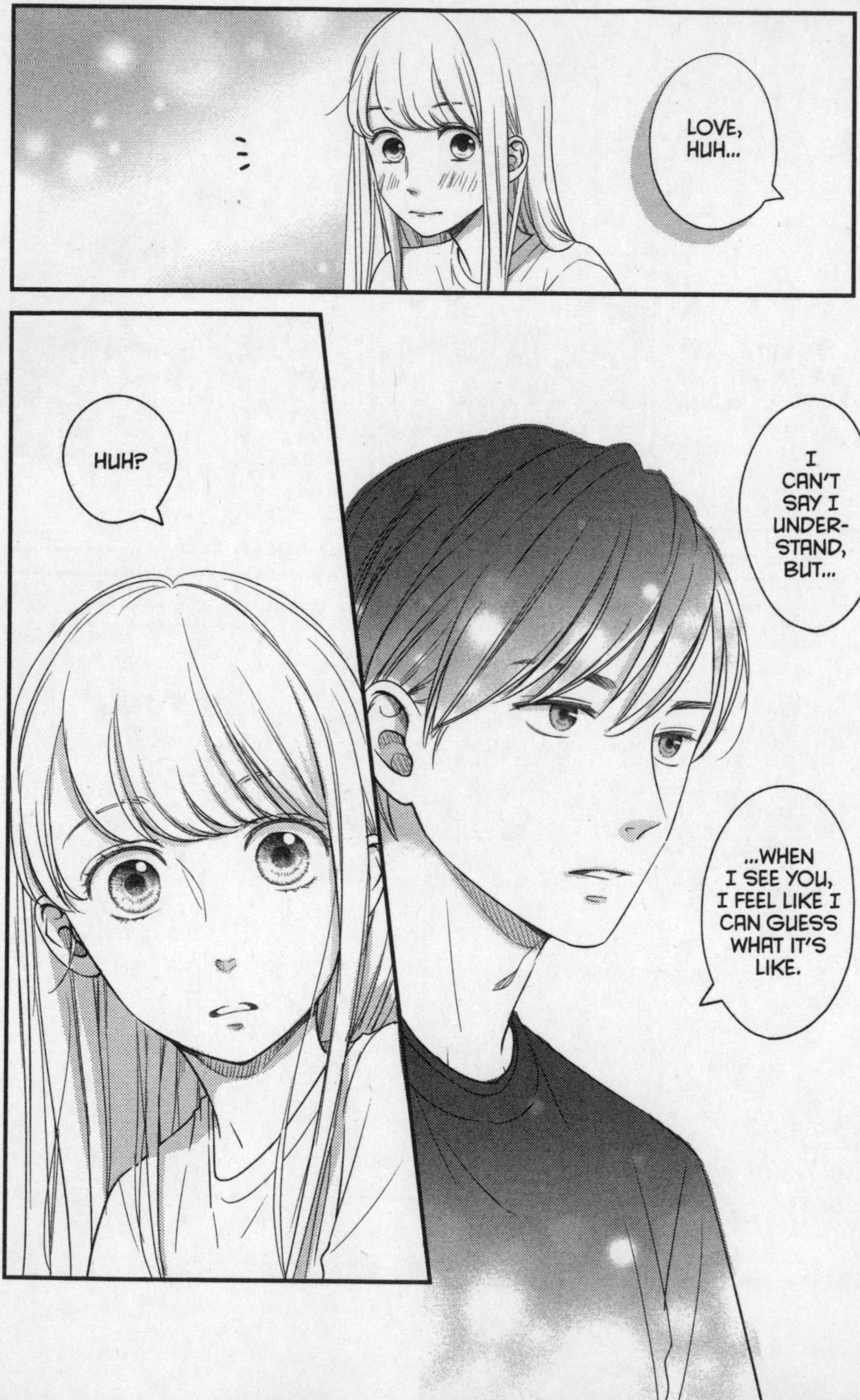
LOVE, HUH...
I CAN'T SAY I UNDER-STAND, BUT...
HUH?
...WHEN I SEE YOU, I FEEL LIKE I CAN GUESS WHAT IT'S LIKE.

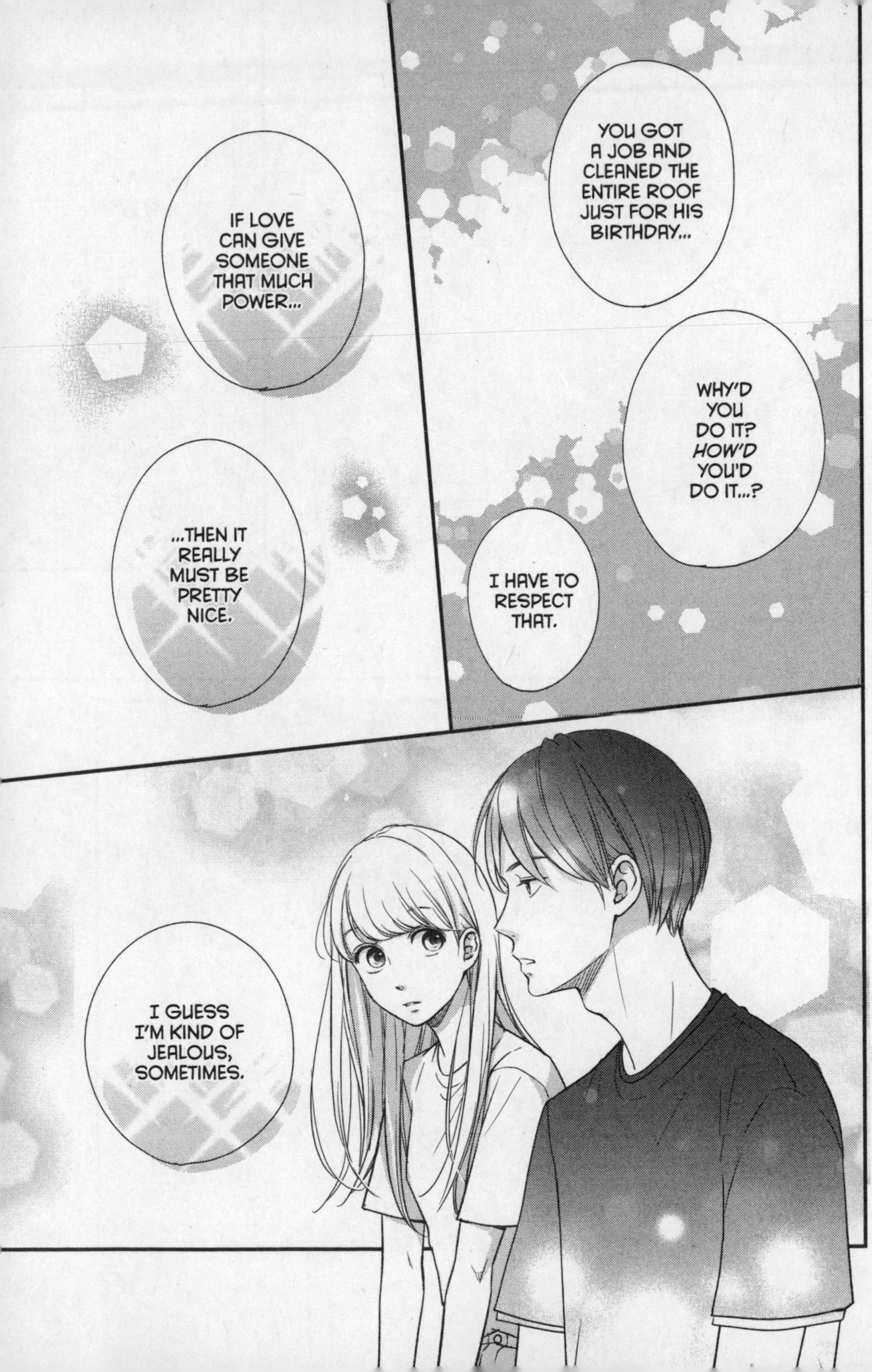
YOU GOT A JOB AND CLEANED THE ENTIRE ROOF JUST FOR HIS BIRTHDAY...
WHY'D YOU DO IT? *HOW'D* YOU'D DO IT...?
I HAVE TO RESPECT THAT.
IF LOVE CAN GIVE SOMEONE THAT MUCH POWER...
...THEN IT REALLY MUST BE PRETTY NICE.
I GUESS I'M KIND OF JEALOUS, SOMETIMES.

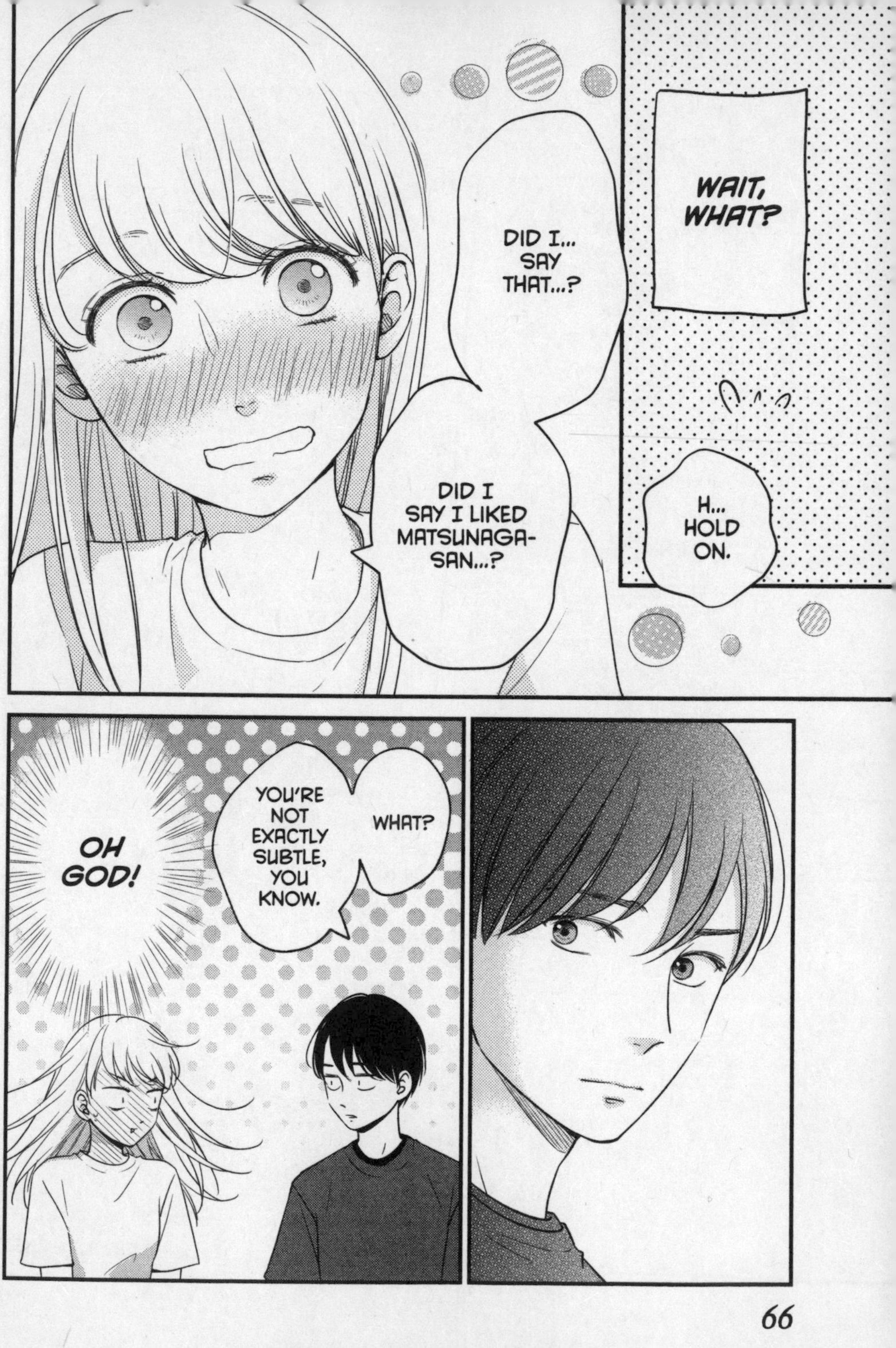
WAIT, WHAT?
H... HOLD ON.
DID I... SAY THAT...?
DID I SAY I LIKED MATSUNAGA-SAN...?
WHAT?
YOU'RE NOT EXACTLY SUBTLE, YOU KNOW.
OH GOD!

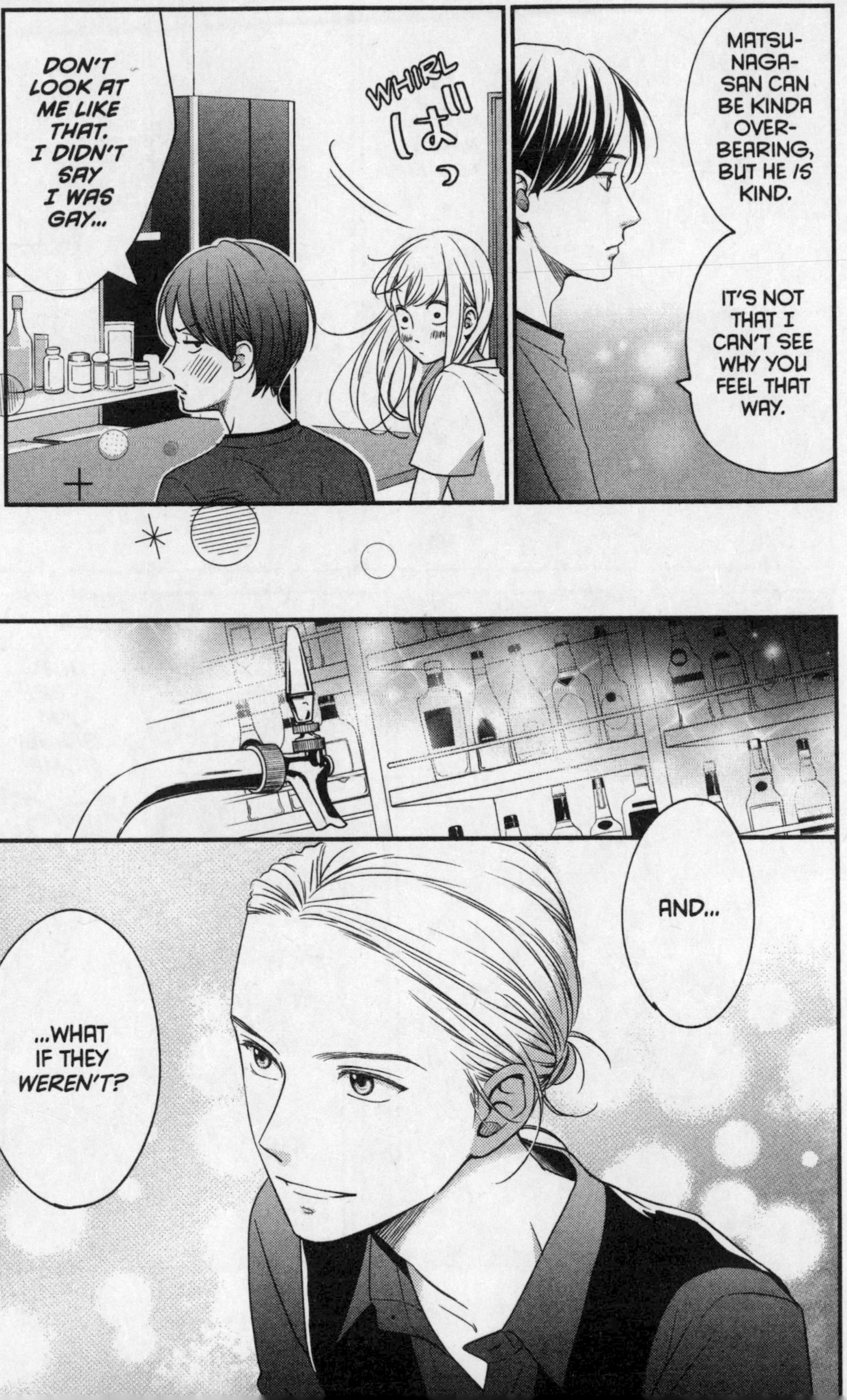
MATSU-NAGA-SAN CAN BE KINDA OVER-BEARING, BUT HE *IS* KIND.
IT'S NOT THAT I CAN'T SEE WHY YOU FEEL THAT WAY.
DON'T LOOK AT ME LIKE THAT. I DIDN'T SAY I WAS GAY...
WHIRL
ぱっ
AND...
...WHAT IF THEY WEREN'T?

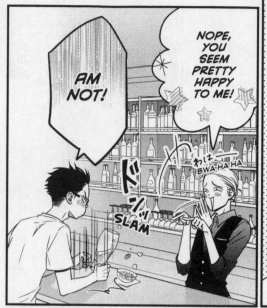

I WOULDN'T CARE.
NOPE, YOU SEEM PRETTY HAPPY TO ME!
AM NOT!
わは―
BWA-HA HA
ドンッ
SLAM
WHAT-EVER! I'M GOING HOME!
AND WHO WAS THE ONE WHO FORGOT THEIR WALLET AND STILL STUCK AROUND FOR A THOUSAND DRINKS?
ME!
JUST PUT IT ON MY TAB.
HEY, JUN-KUN.
DO YOU REALLY NOT KNOW?

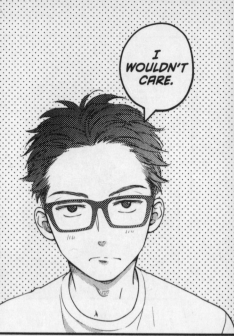

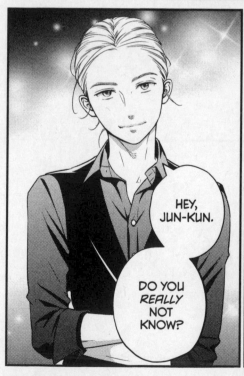

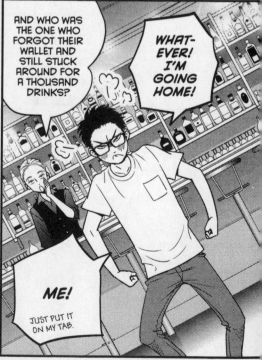

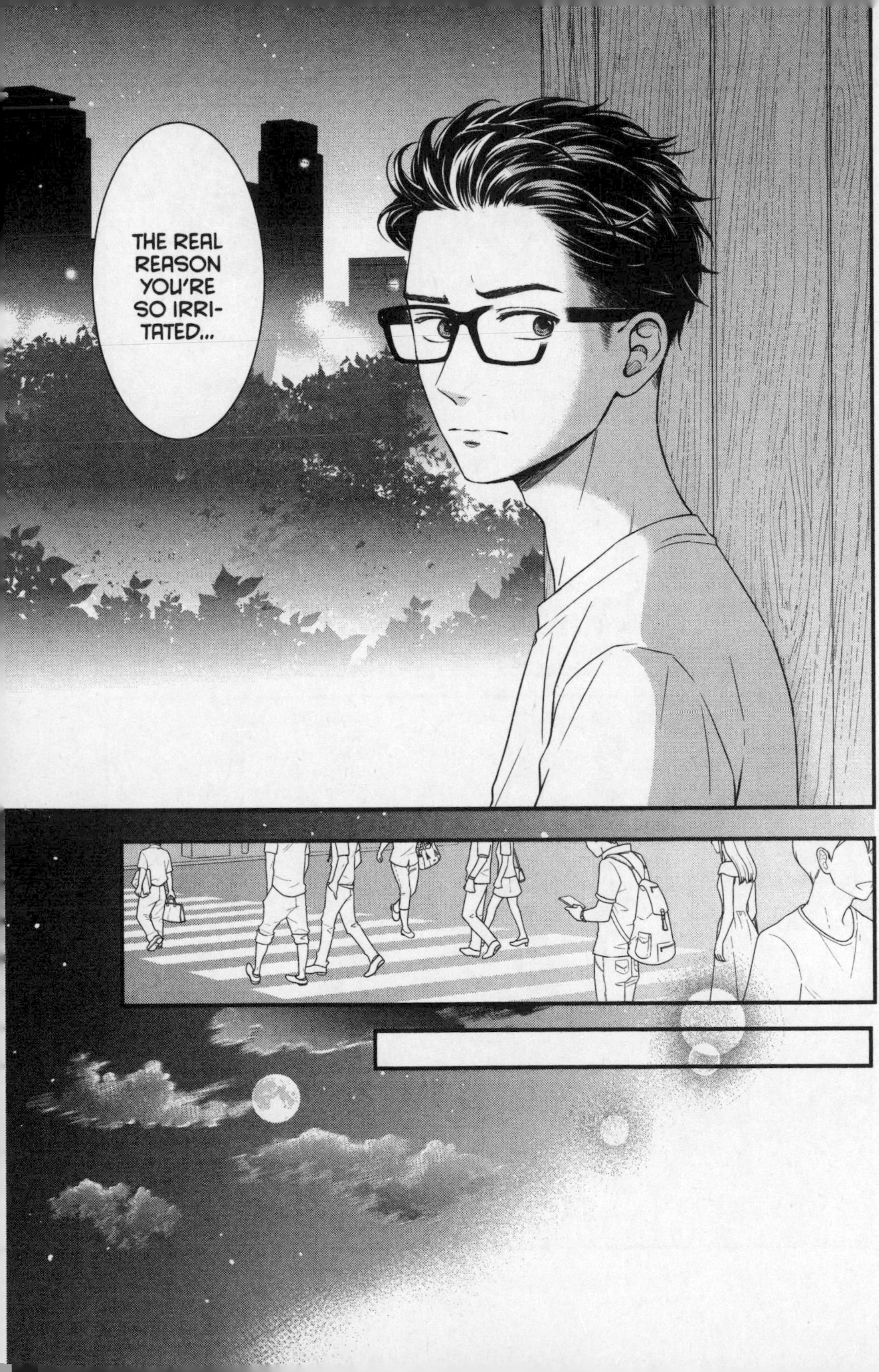
THE REAL REASON YOU'RE SO IRRI-TATED...

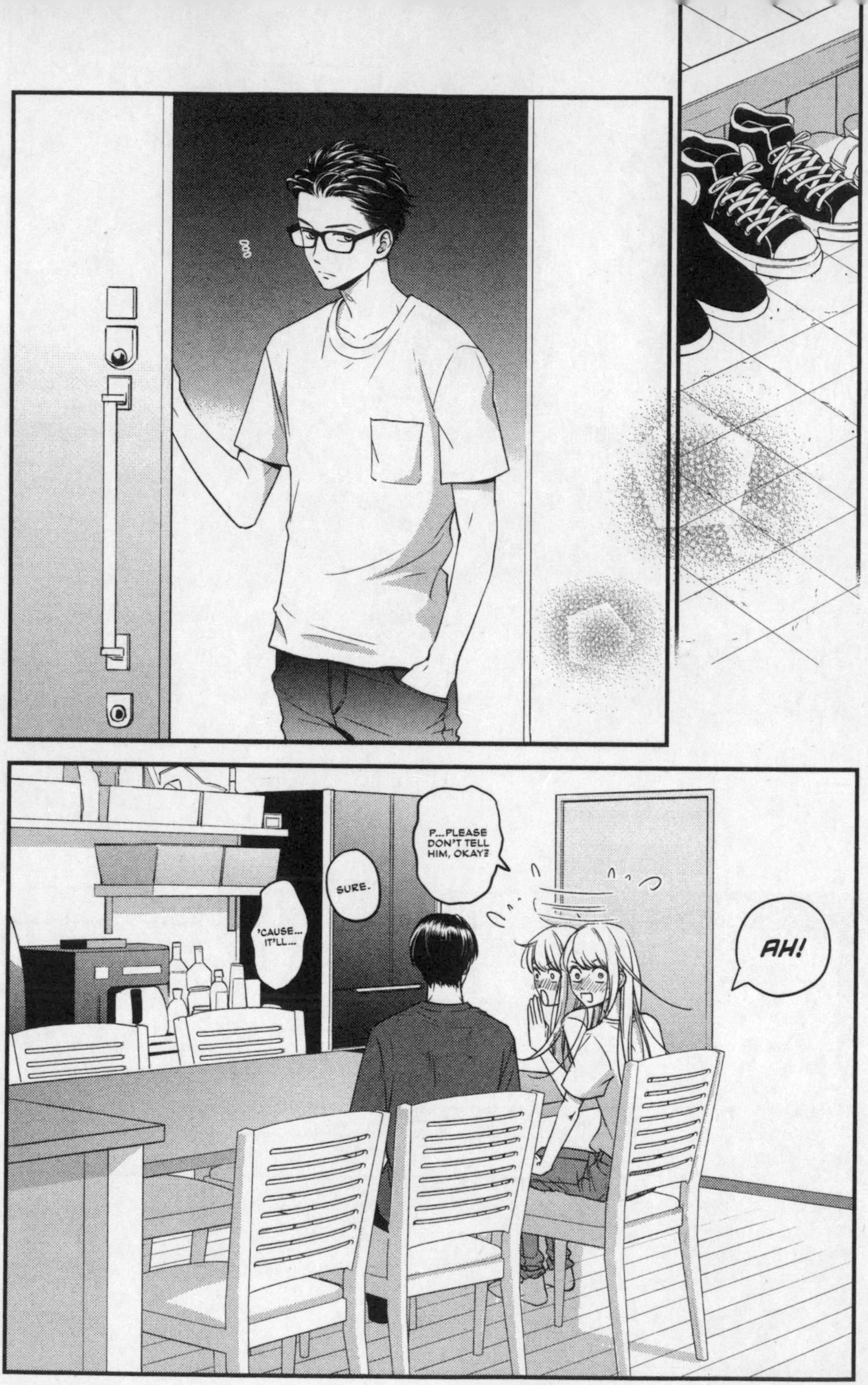
AH!
P...PLEASE DON'T TELL HIM, OKAY?
SURE.
'CAUSE... IT'LL...

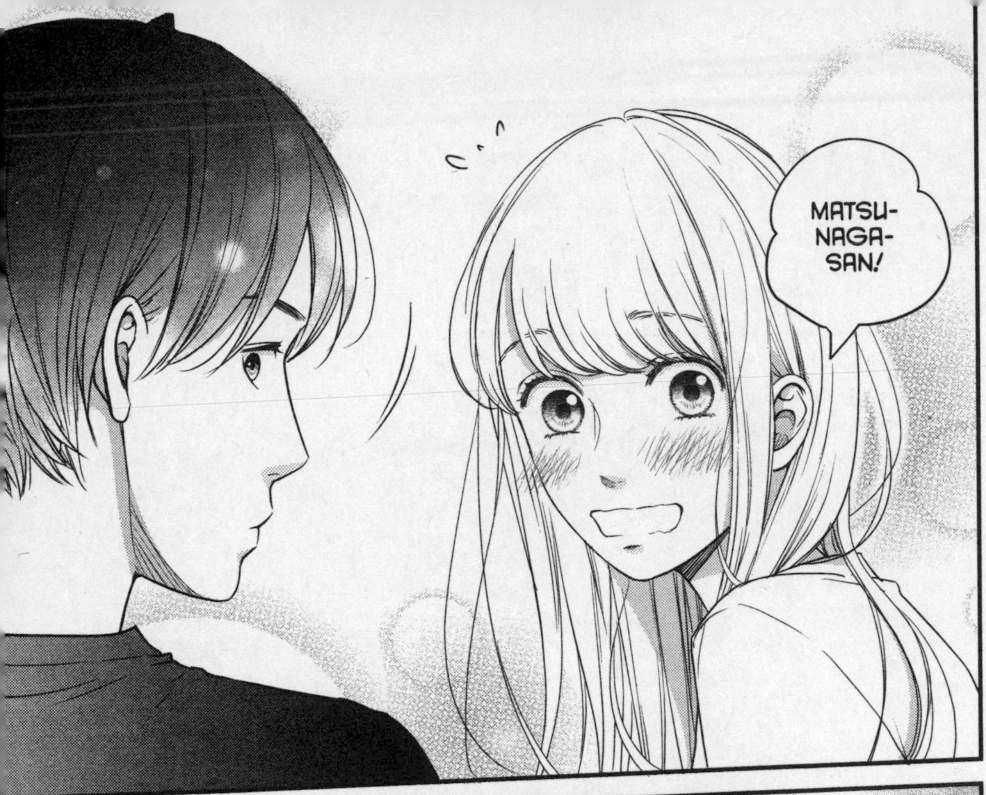
MATSU-
NAGA-
SAN!
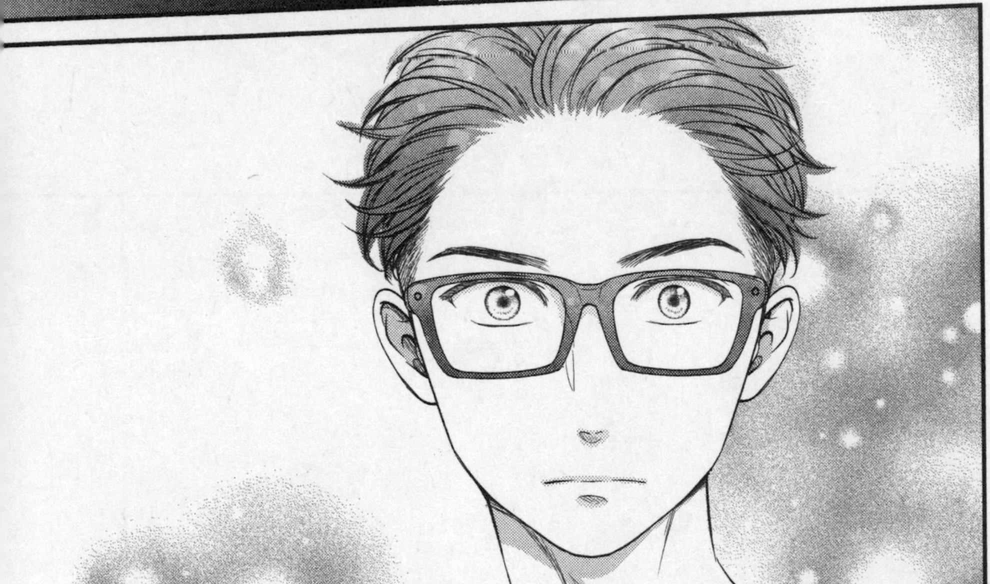

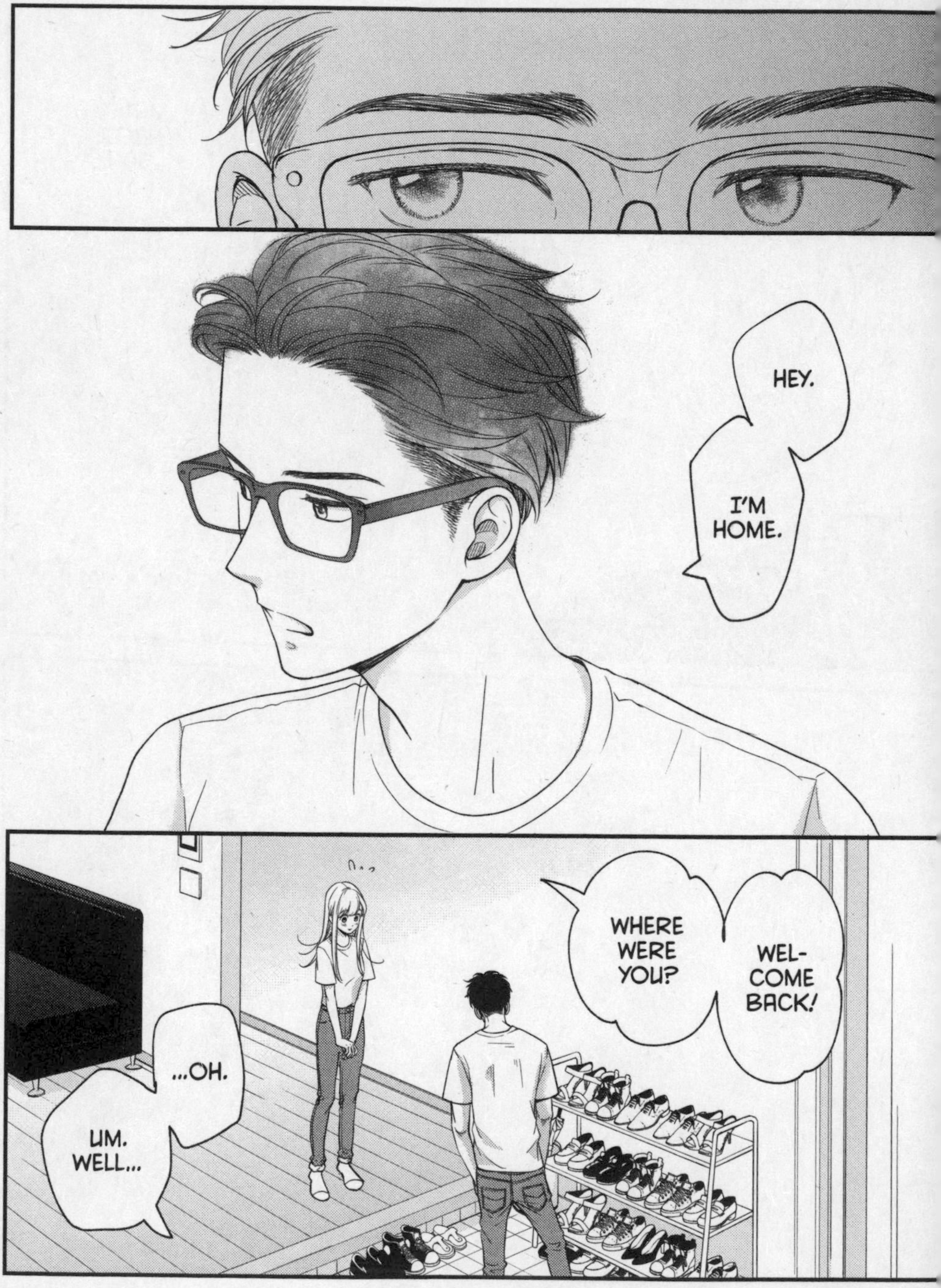
HEY. I'M HOME.
WEL- COME BACK!
WHERE WERE YOU?
...OH.
UM. WELL...

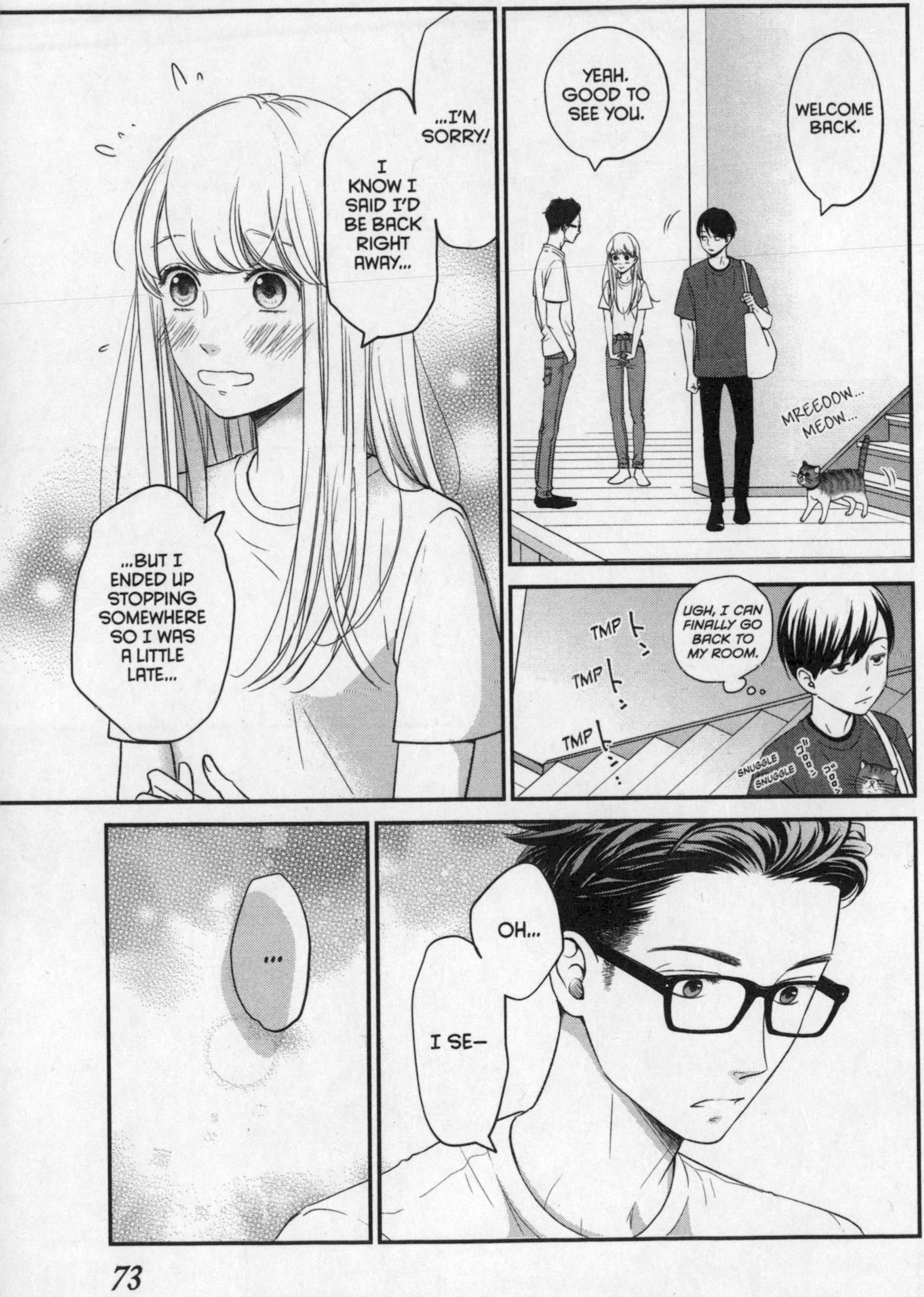
WELCOME BACK.
YEAH. GOOD TO SEE YOU.
MREEOOW... MEOW...
UGH, I CAN FINALLY GO BACK TO MY ROOM.
TMP
TMP
TMP
SNUGGLE
SNUGGLE
...I'M SORRY!
I KNOW I SAID I'D BE BACK RIGHT AWAY...
...BUT I ENDED UP STOPPING SOMEWHERE SO I WAS A LITTLE LATE...
OH...
I SE—
...

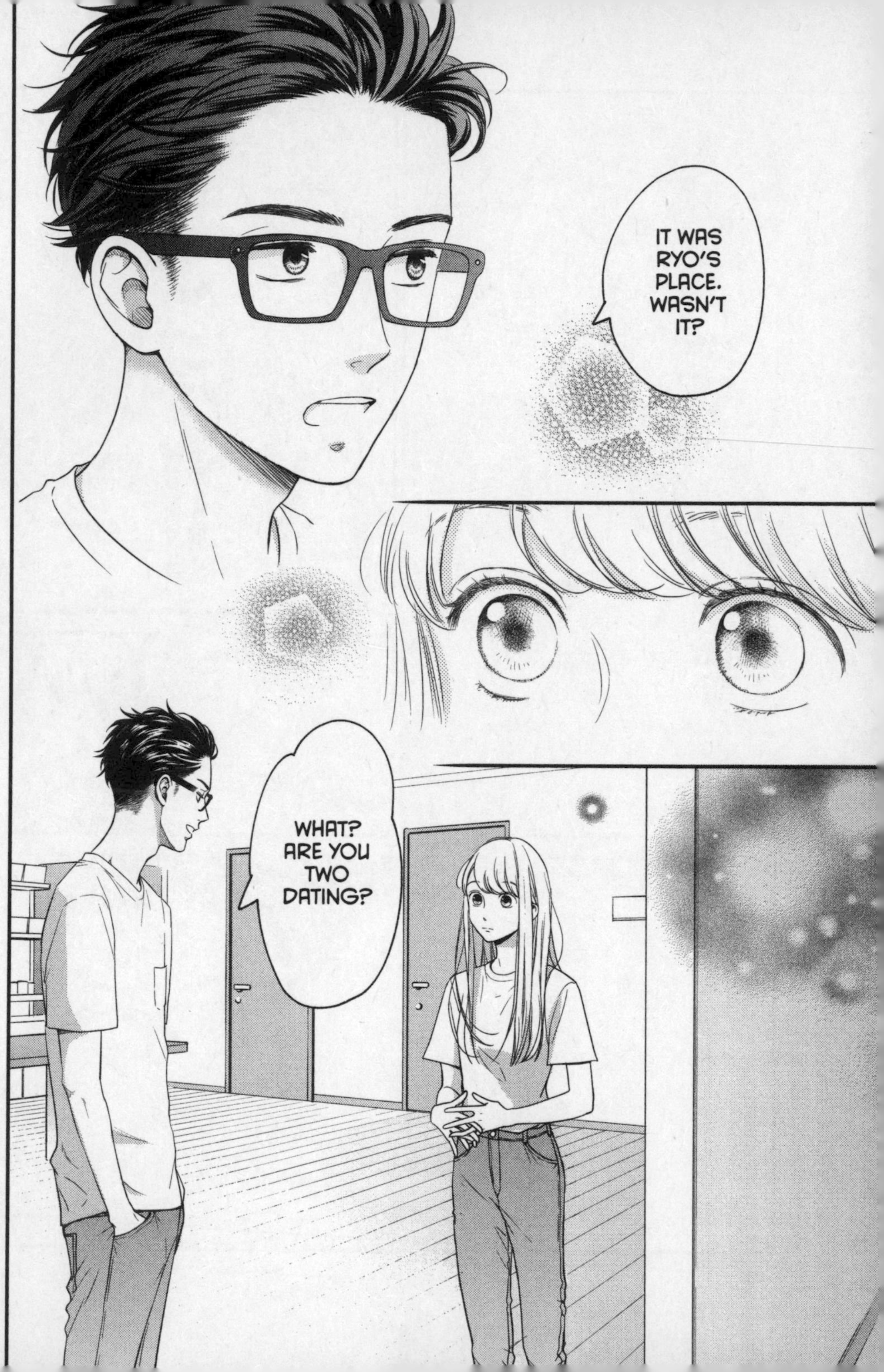
IT WAS RYO'S PLACE. WASN'T IT?
WHAT? ARE YOU TWO DATING?

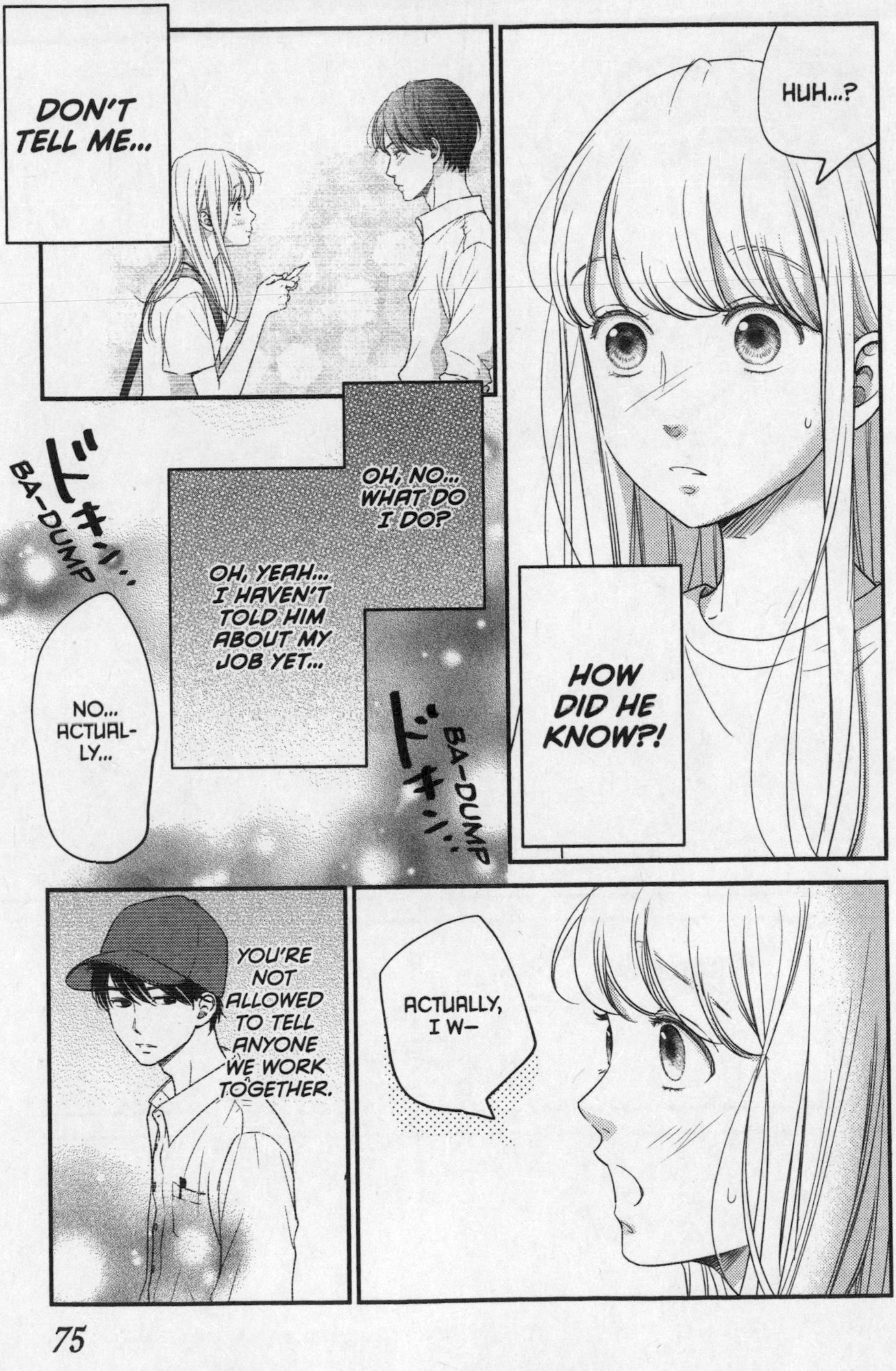
HUH...?
HOW DID HE KNOW?!
DON'T TELL ME...
OH, NO... WHAT DO I DO?
OH, YEAH... I HAVEN'T TOLD HIM ABOUT MY JOB YET...
ドキン BA-DUMP
ドキン BA-DUMP
NO... ACTUAL-LY...
ACTUALLY, I W—
YOU'RE NOT ALLOWED TO TELL ANYONE WE WORK TOGETHER.

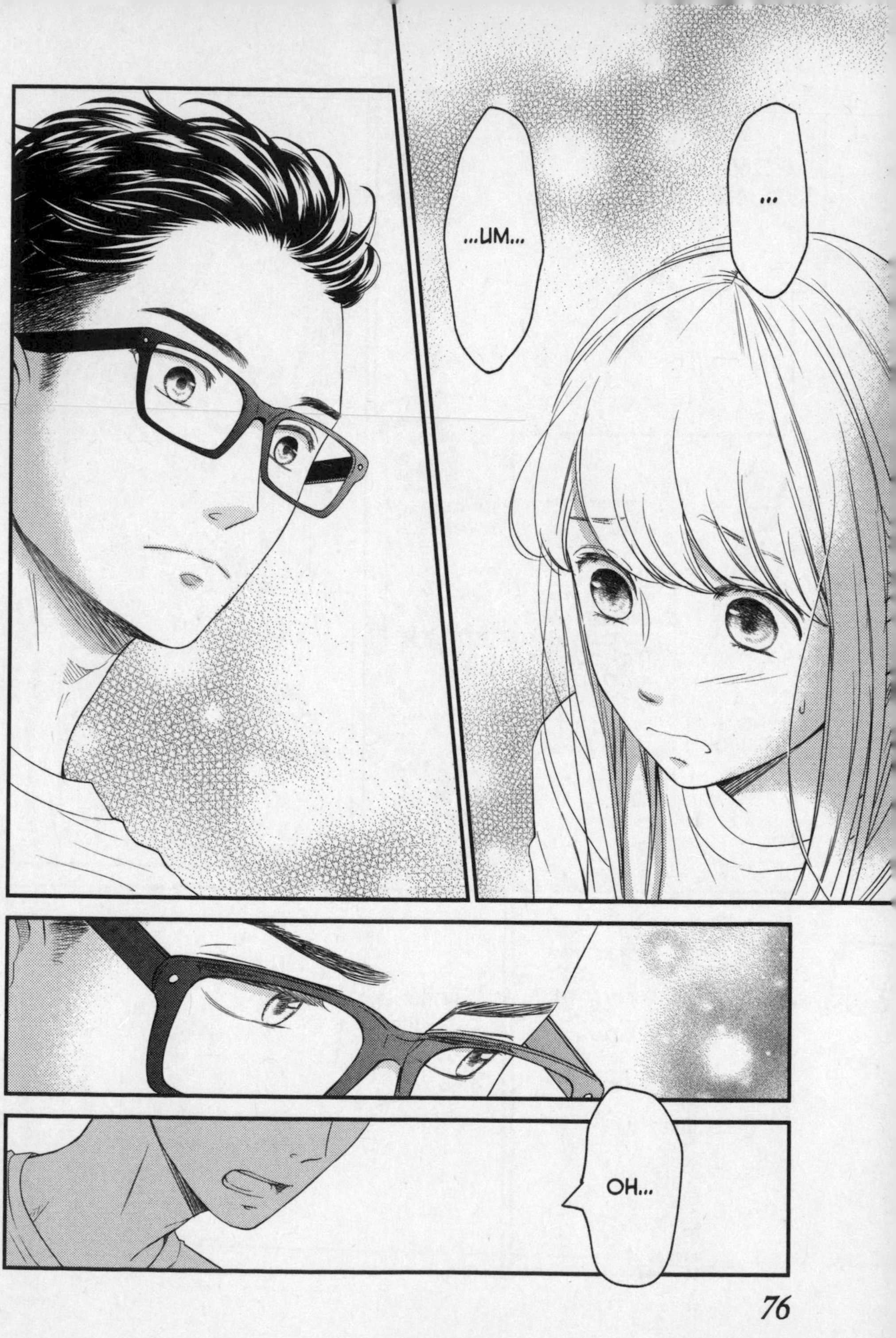
...
...UM...
OH...

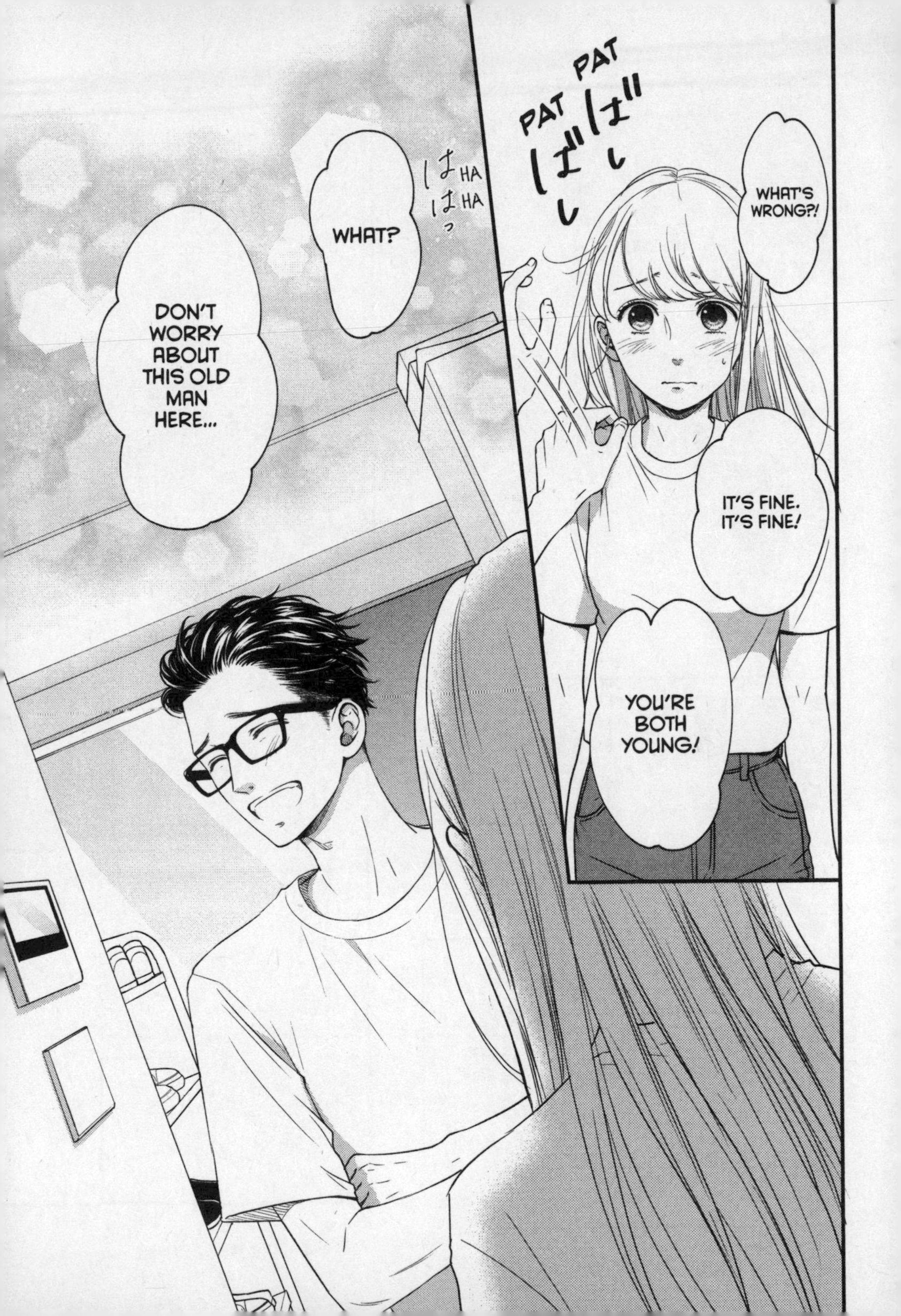
PAT PAT
WHAT'S WRONG?!
IT'S FINE. IT'S FINE!
YOU'RE BOTH YOUNG!
ははっ HA HA
WHAT?
DON'T WORRY ABOUT THIS OLD MAN HERE...

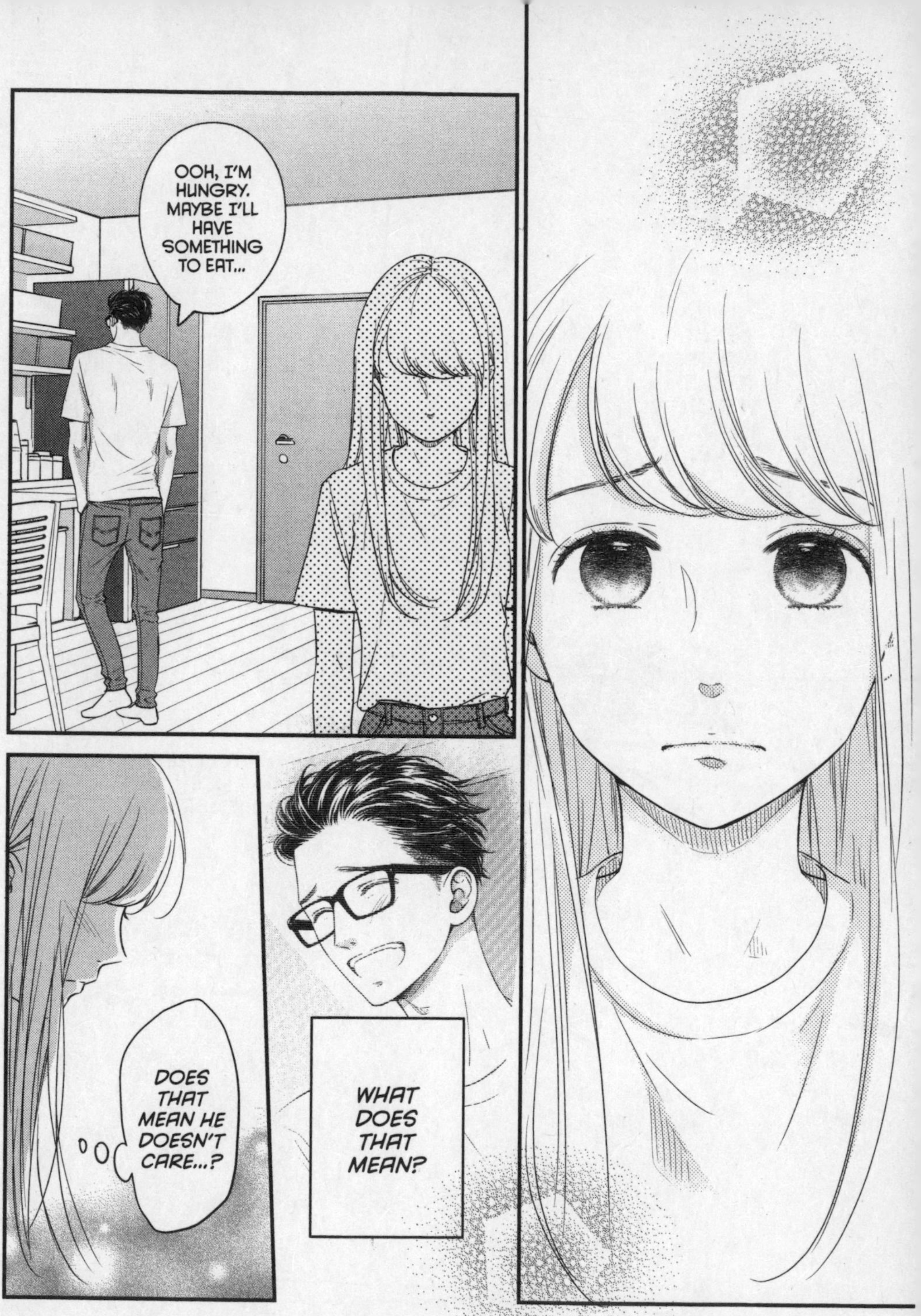
OOH, I'M HUNGRY. MAYBE I'LL HAVE SOMETHING TO EAT...
WHAT DOES THAT MEAN?
DOES THAT MEAN HE DOESN'T CARE...?

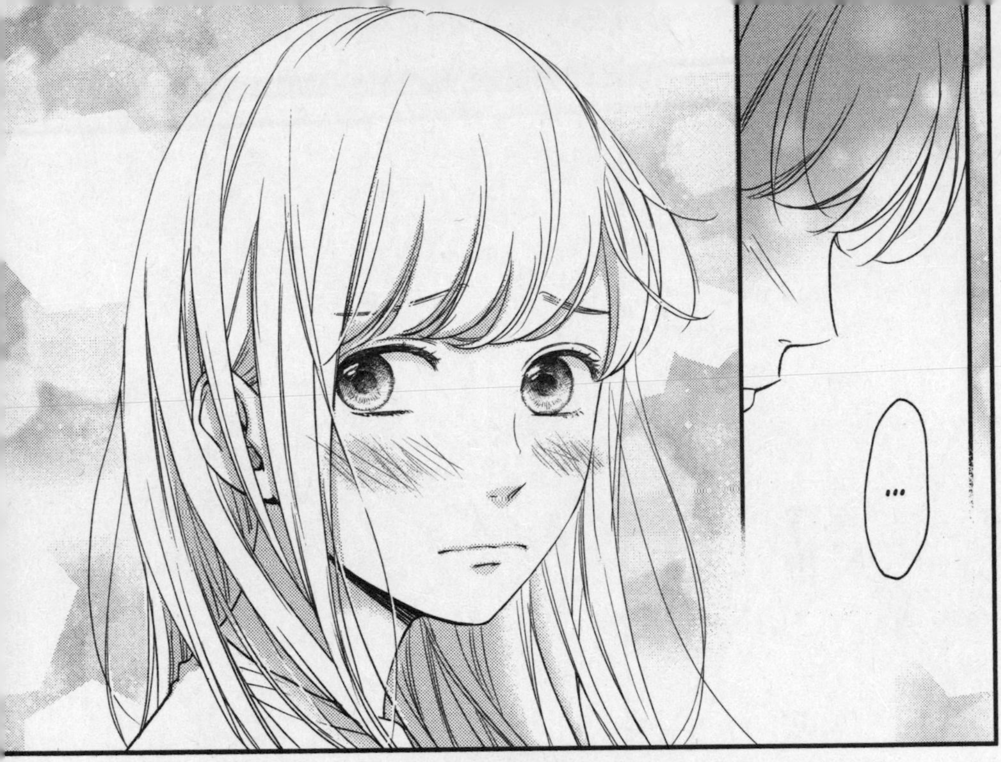
...
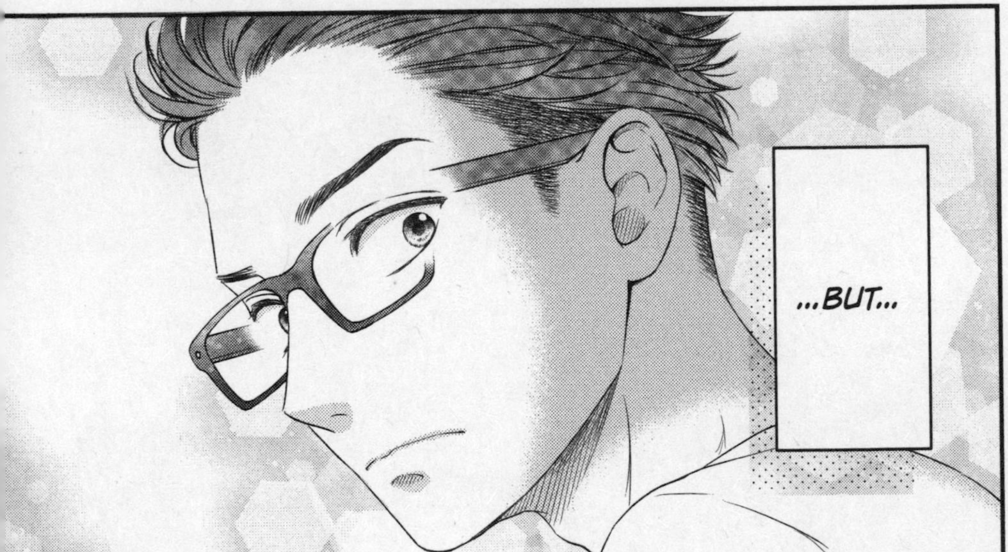
...BUT...

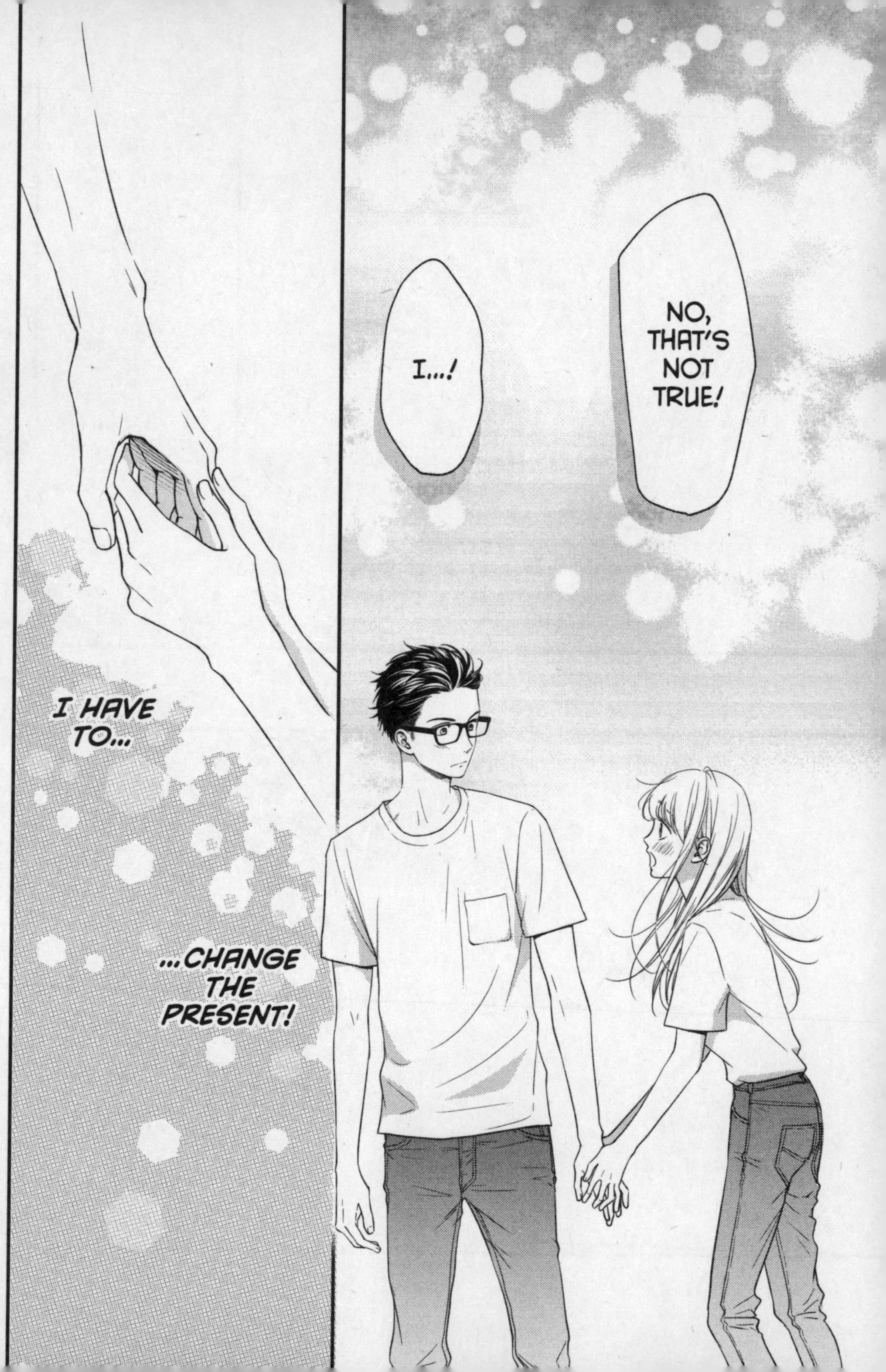
NO, THAT'S NOT TRUE!
I...!
I HAVE TO...
...CHANGE THE PRESENT!

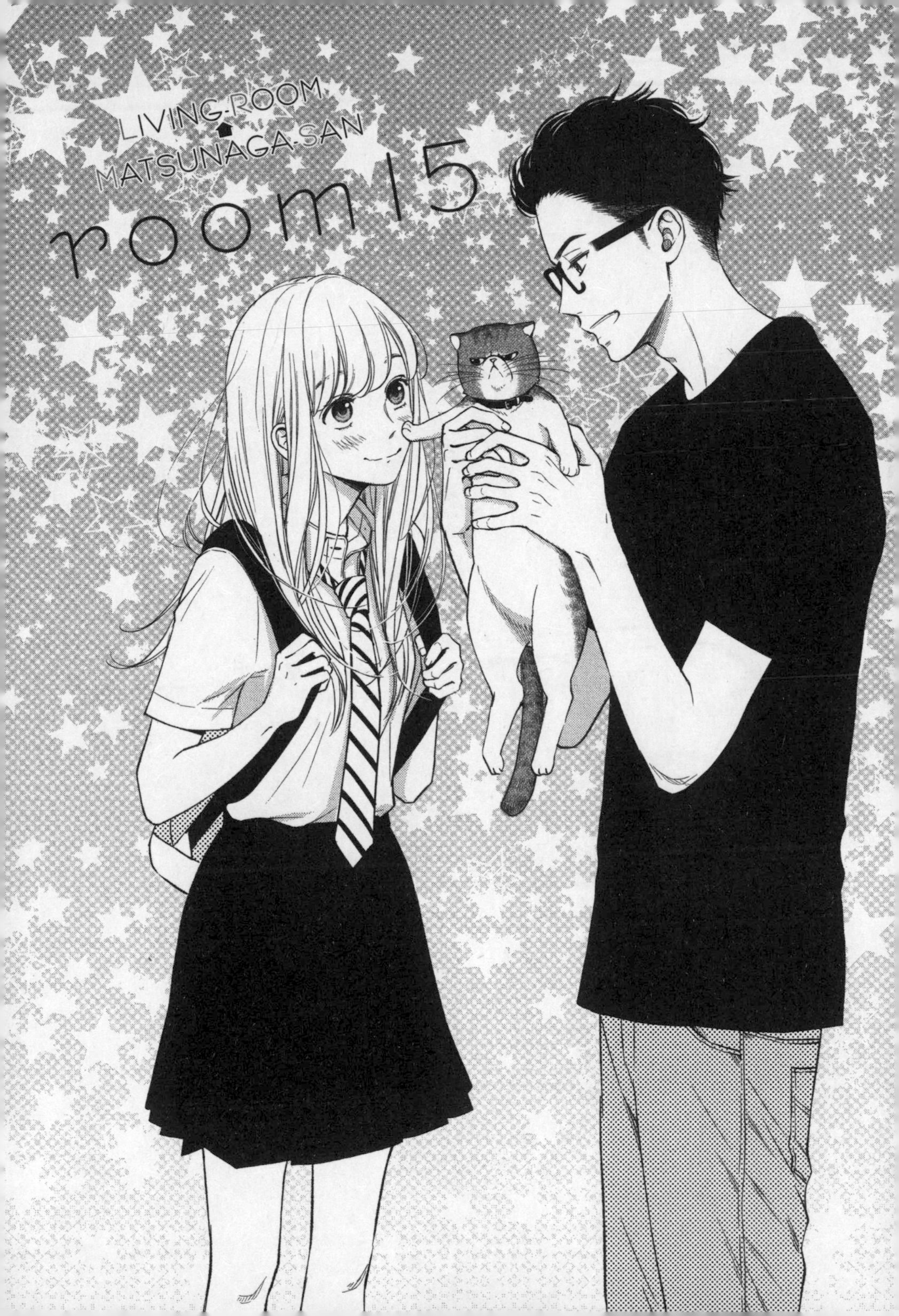
LIVING-ROOM
MATSUNAGA-SAN
room 15

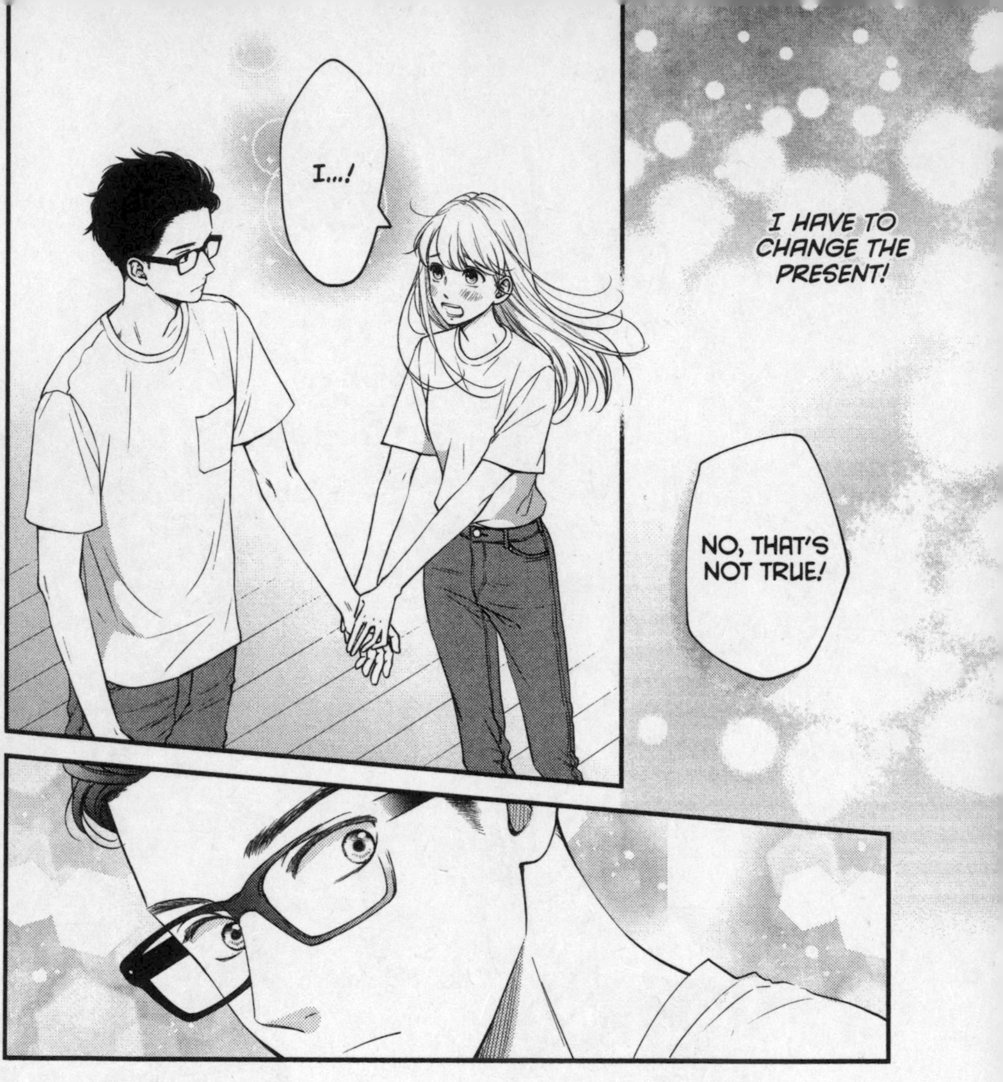
I HAVE TO CHANGE THE PRESENT!
NO, THAT'S NOT TRUE!
I...!

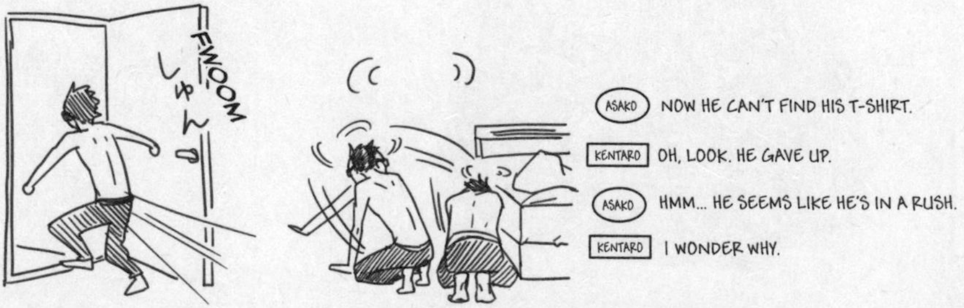
FWOOM
しゅん
ASAKO NOW HE CAN'T FIND HIS T-SHIRT.
KENTARO OH, LOOK. HE GAVE UP.
ASAKO HMM... HE SEEMS LIKE HE'S IN A RUSH.
KENTARO I WONDER WHY.

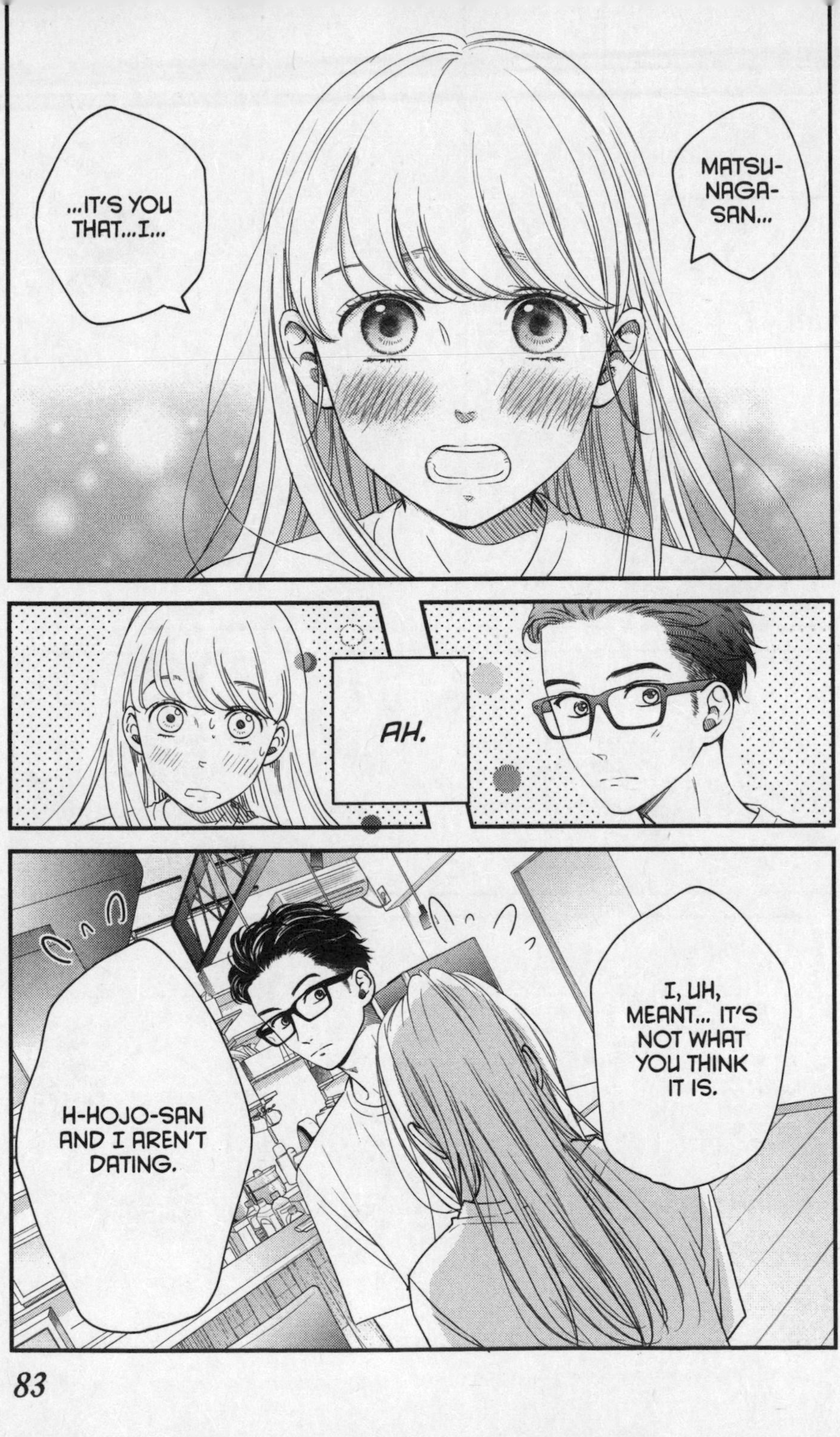
MATSU-NAGA-SAN...
...IT'S YOU THAT...I...
AH.
I, UH, MEANT... IT'S NOT WHAT YOU THINK IT IS.
H-HOJO-SAN AND I AREN'T DATING.

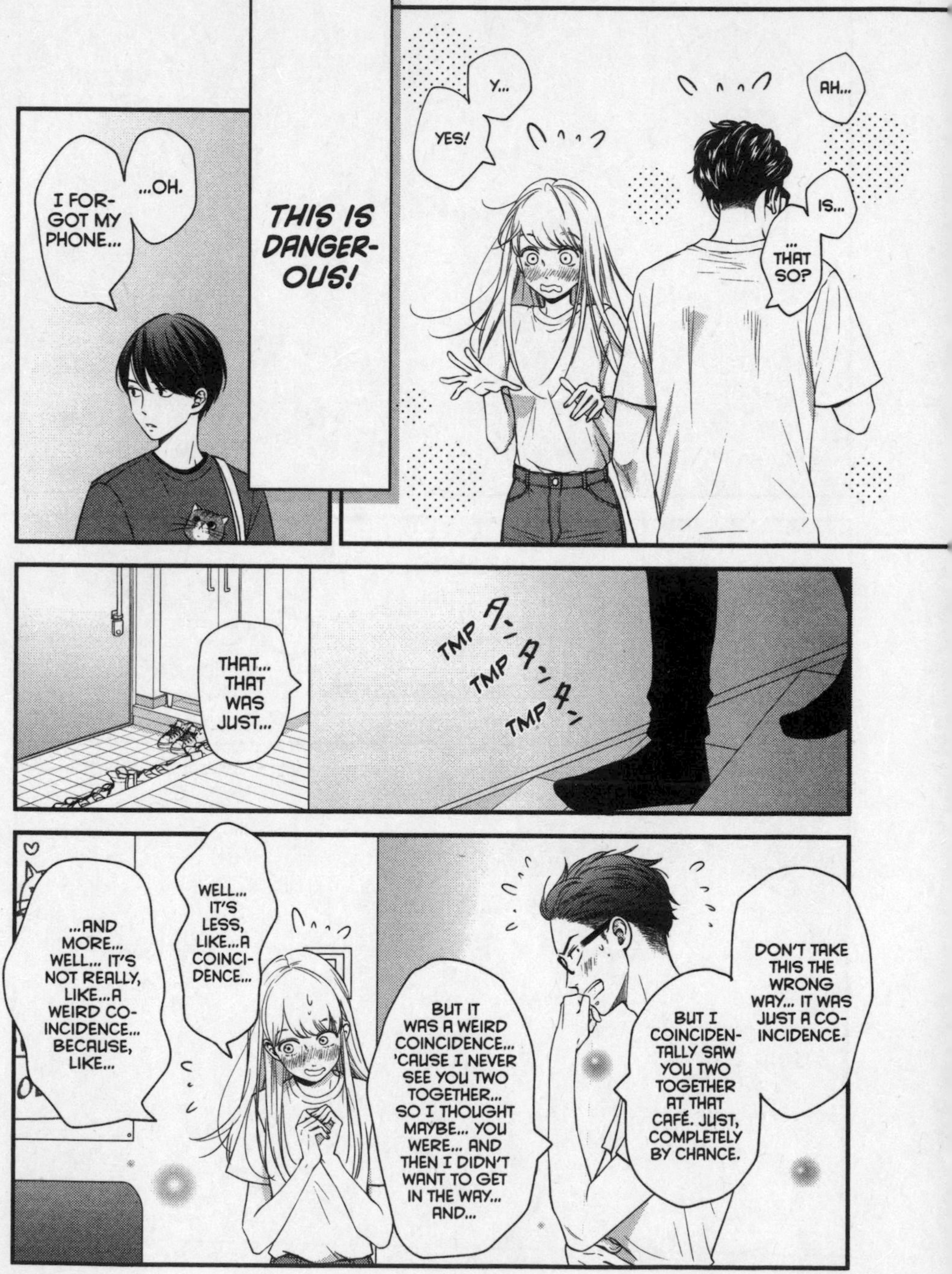
AH...
Y... YES!
IS... ...THAT SO?
THIS IS DANGEROUS!
...OH.
I FORGOT MY PHONE...
TMP TMP TMP
THAT... THAT WAS JUST...
DON'T TAKE THIS THE WRONG WAY... IT WAS JUST A COINCIDENCE.
BUT I COINCIDENTALLY SAW YOU TWO TOGETHER AT THAT CAFÉ. JUST, COMPLETELY BY CHANCE.
BUT IT WAS A WEIRD COINCIDENCE... 'CAUSE I NEVER SEE YOU TWO TOGETHER... SO I THOUGHT MAYBE... YOU WERE... AND THEN I DIDN'T WANT TO GET IN THE WAY... AND...
WELL... IT'S LESS, LIKE...A COINCIDENCE...
...AND MORE... WELL... IT'S NOT REALLY, LIKE...A WEIRD COINCIDENCE... BECAUSE, LIKE...

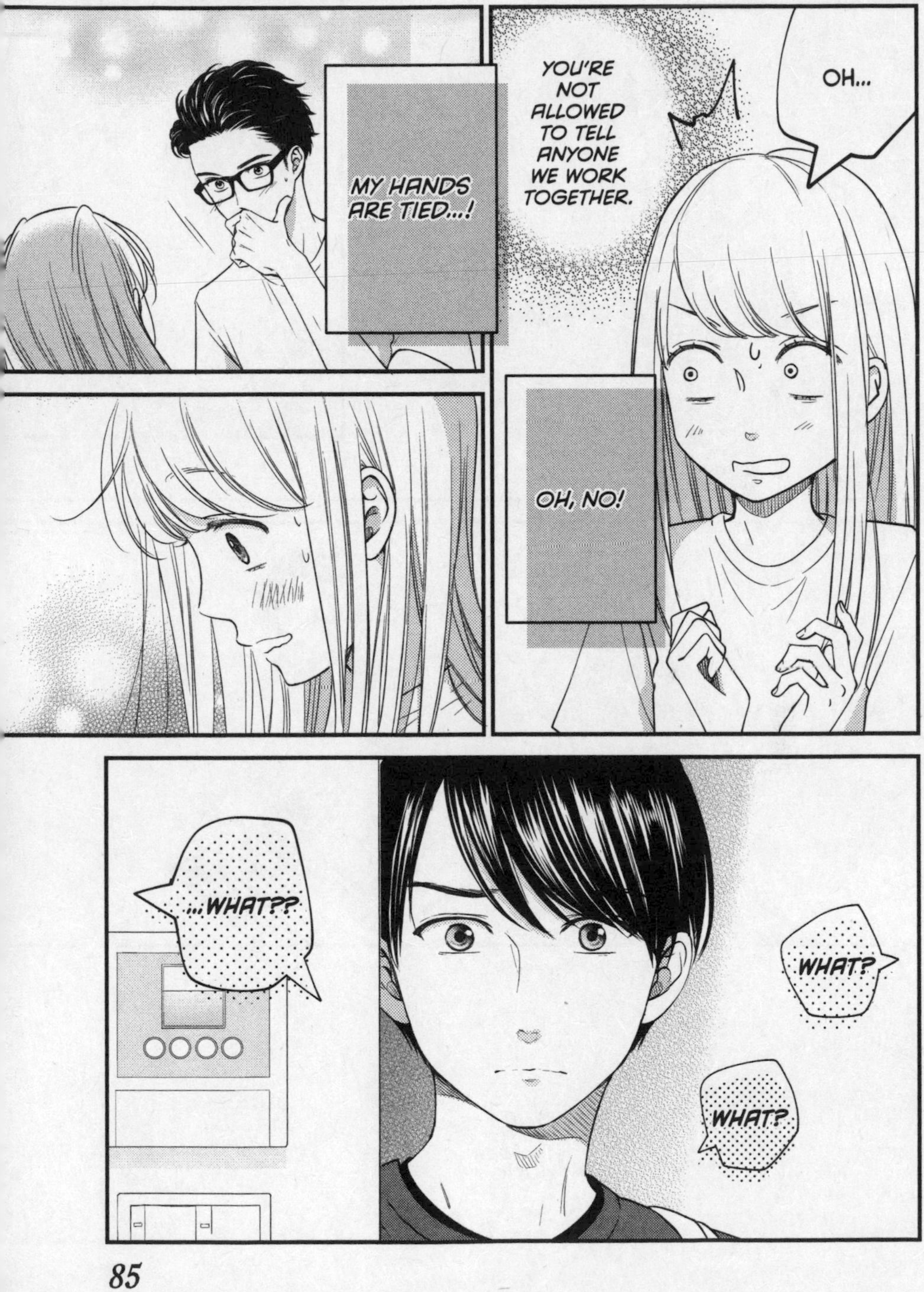
OH...
YOU'RE NOT ALLOWED TO TELL ANYONE WE WORK TOGETHER.
OH, NO!
MY HANDS ARE TIED...!
WHAT?
WHAT?
...WHAT??

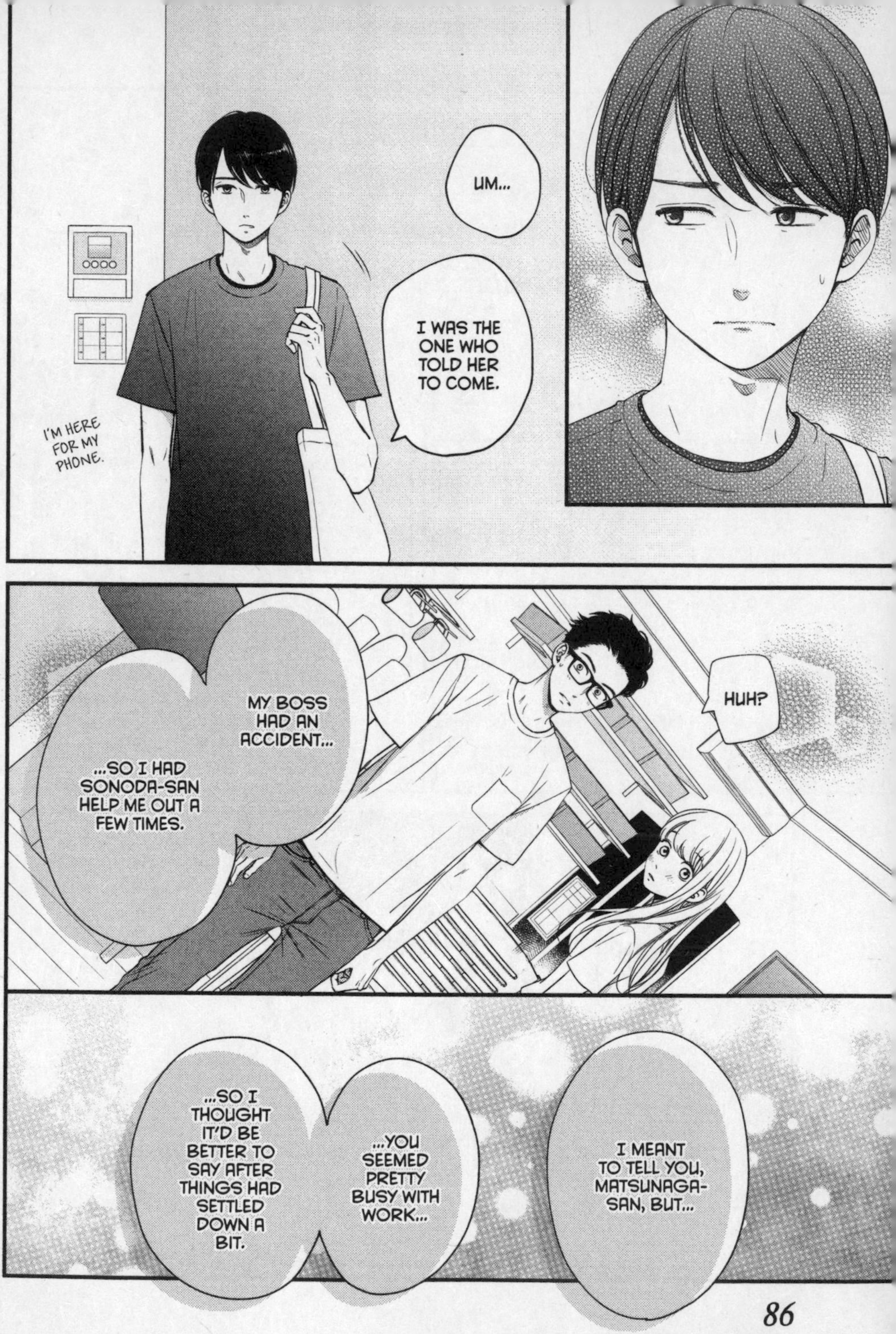
UM...
I WAS THE ONE WHO TOLD HER TO COME.
I'M HERE FOR MY PHONE.
HUH?
MY BOSS HAD AN ACCIDENT...
...SO I HAD SONODA-SAN HELP ME OUT A FEW TIMES.
I MEANT TO TELL YOU, MATSUNAGA-SAN, BUT...
...YOU SEEMED PRETTY BUSY WITH WORK...
...SO I THOUGHT IT'D BE BETTER TO SAY AFTER THINGS HAD SETTLED DOWN A BIT.

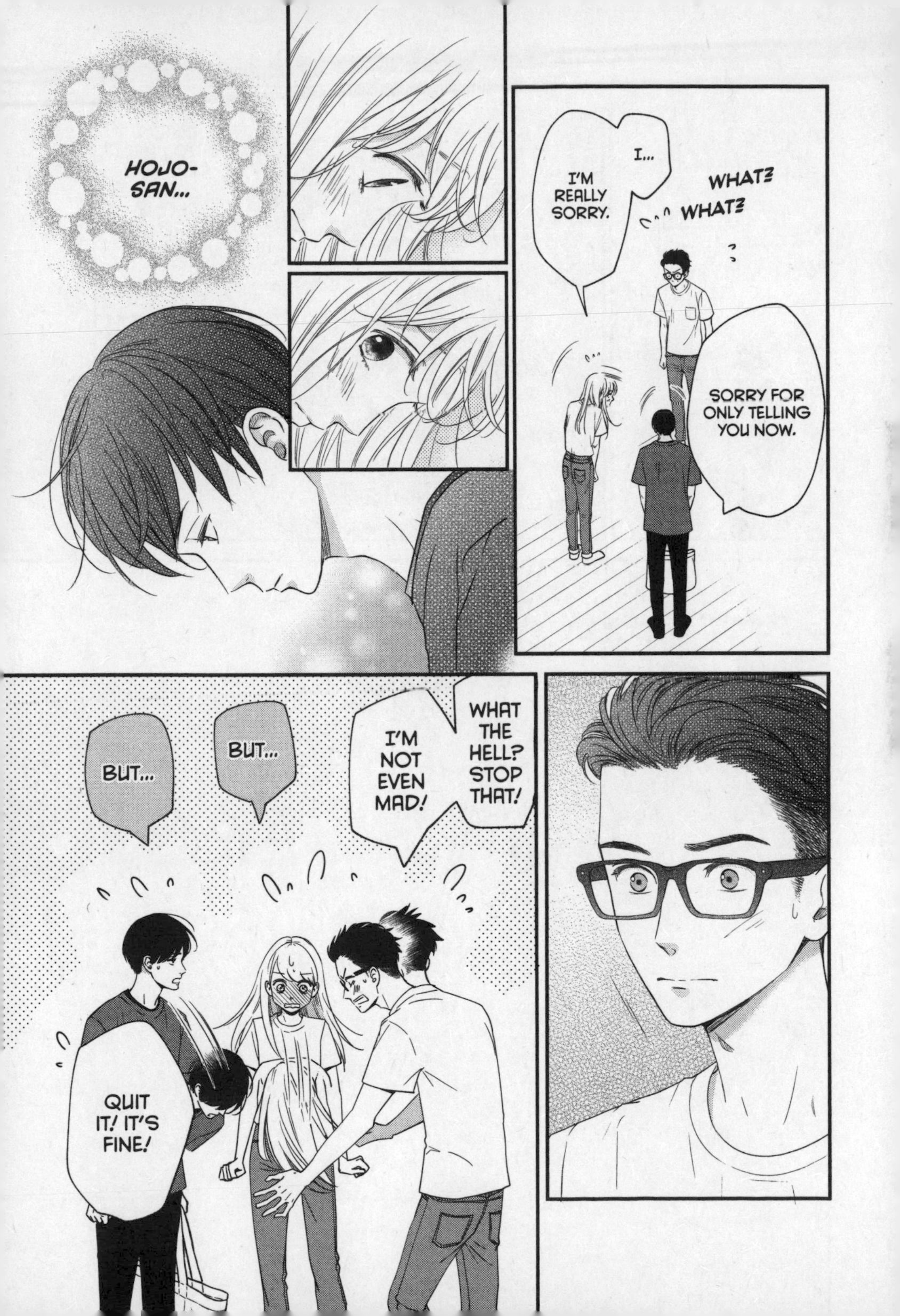
I...
I'M REALLY SORRY.
WHAT?!
WHAT?!
SORRY FOR ONLY TELLING YOU NOW.
HOJO-SAN...
WHAT THE HELL? STOP THAT!
I'M NOT EVEN MAD!
BUT...
BUT...
QUIT IT! IT'S FINE!

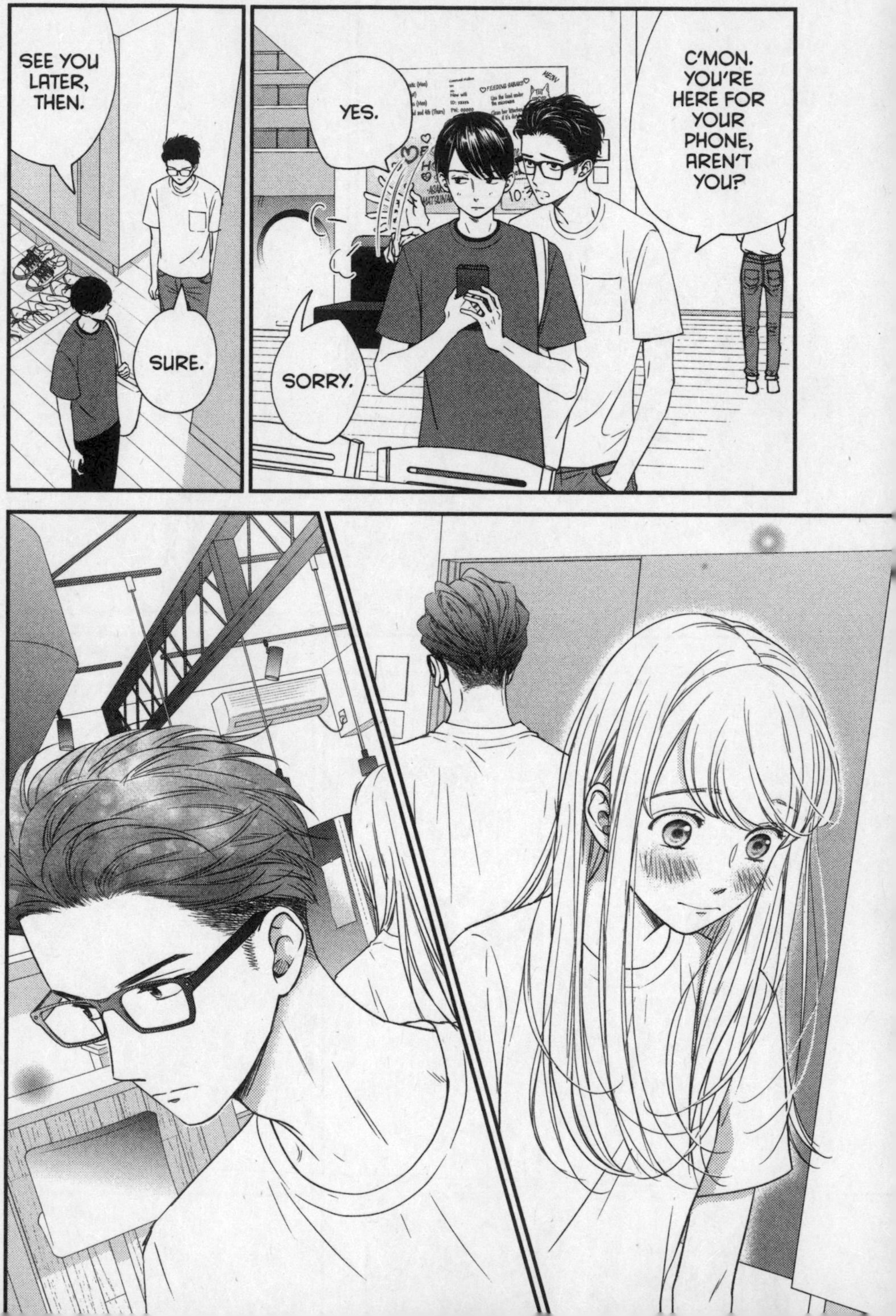
C'MON. YOU'RE HERE FOR YOUR PHONE, AREN'T YOU?
YES.
SORRY.
SEE YOU LATER, THEN.
SURE.

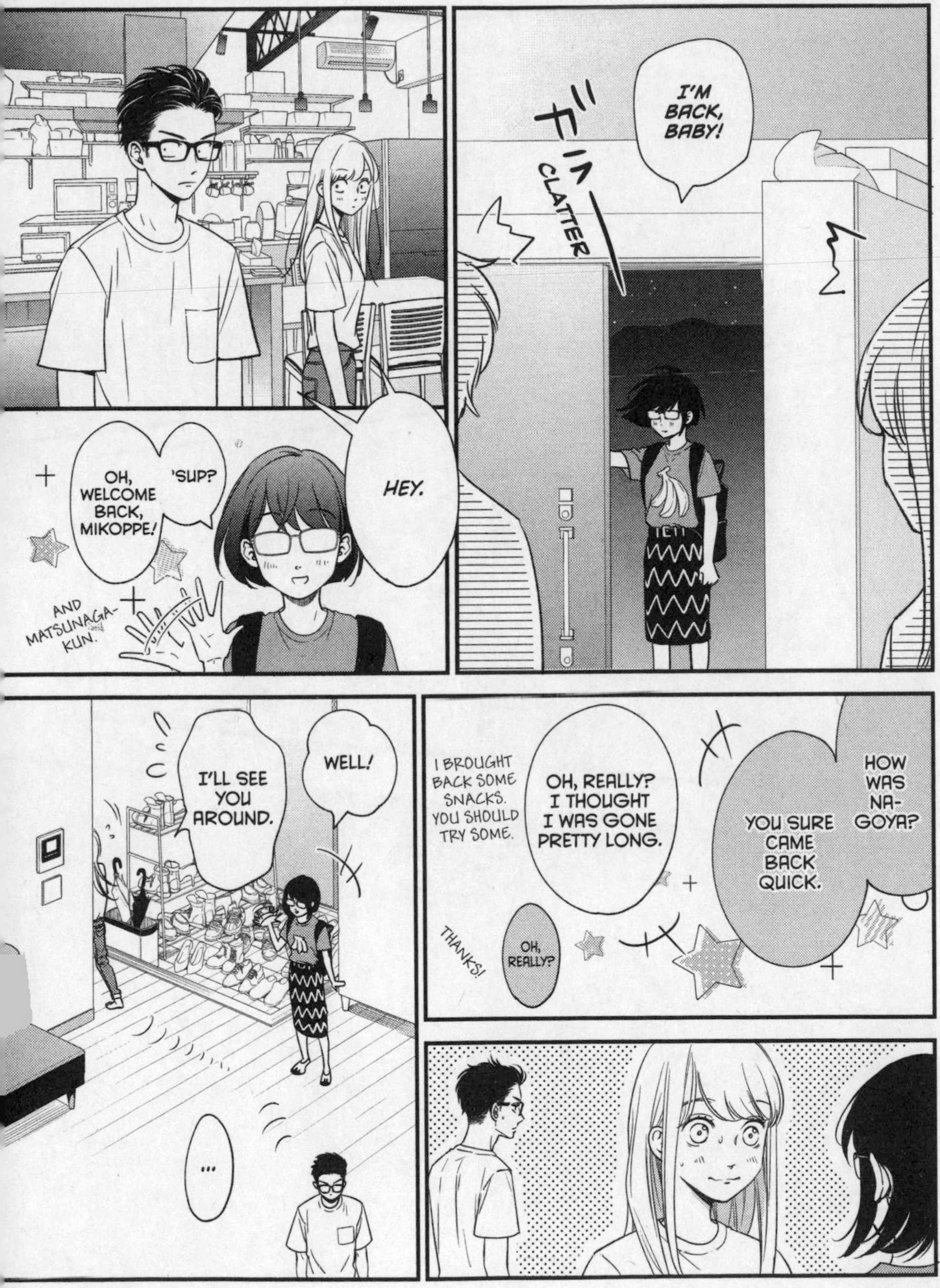
I'M BACK, BABY!
ガラ
CLATTER
HEY.
'SUP?
OH, WELCOME BACK, MIKOPPE!
AND MATSUNAGA-KUN.
HOW WAS NA-GOYA?
YOU SURE CAME BACK QUICK.
OH, REALLY? I THOUGHT I WAS GONE PRETTY LONG.
I BROUGHT BACK SOME SNACKS. YOU SHOULD TRY SOME.
OH, REALLY?
THANKS!
WELL!
I'LL SEE YOU AROUND.
...

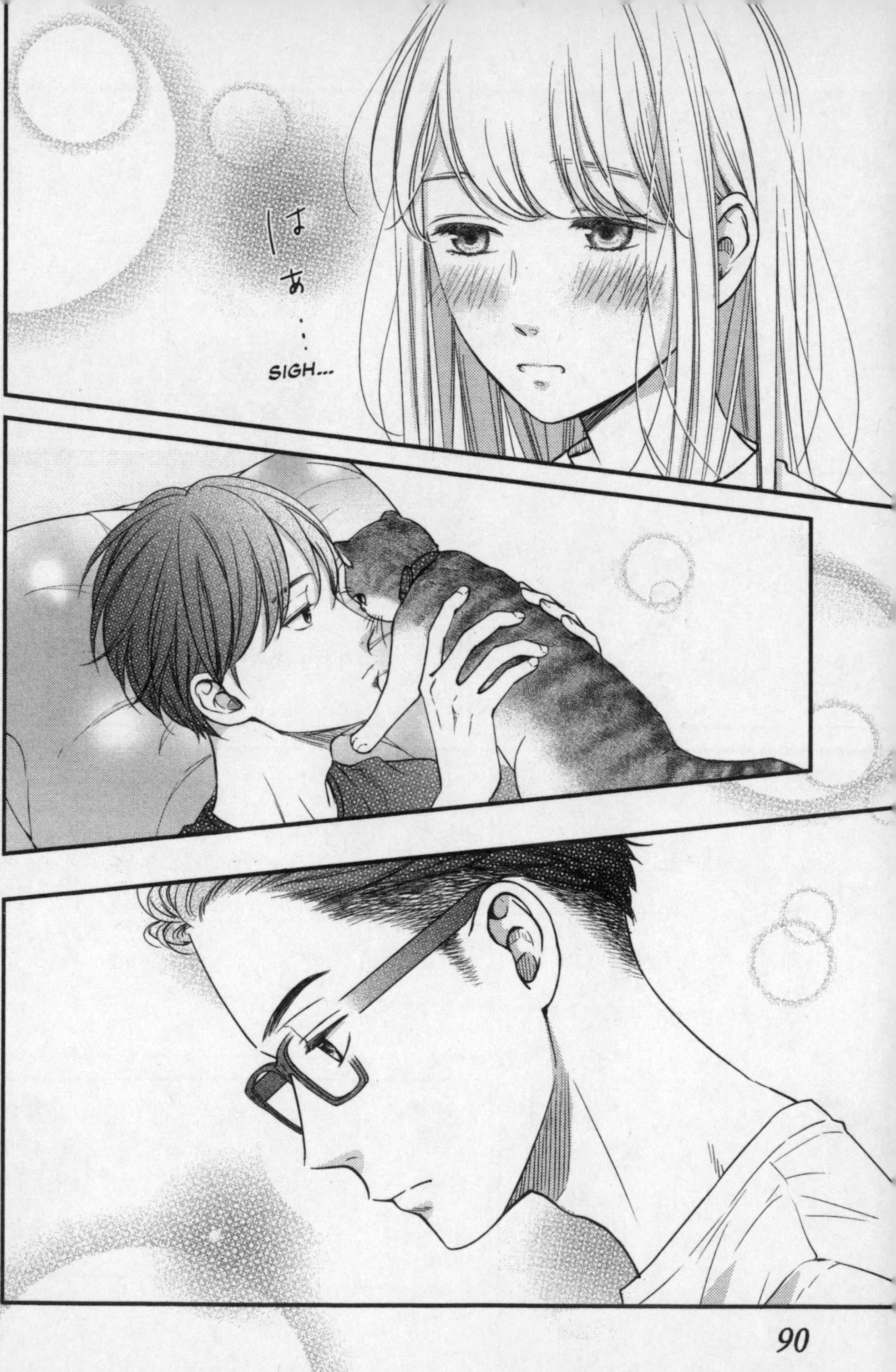
はあ…
SIGH...

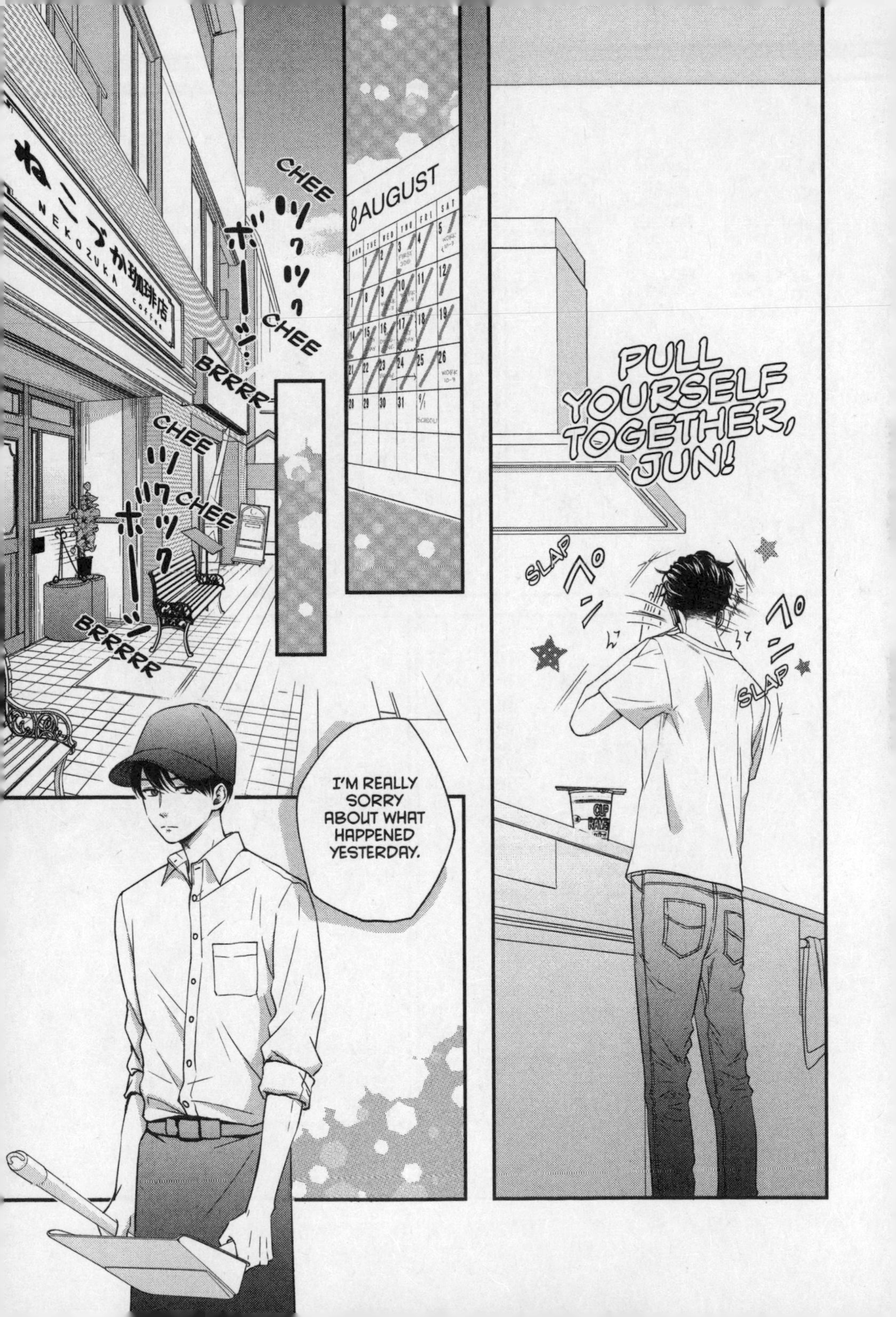
PULL YOURSELF TOGETHER, JUN!
SLAP
SLAP
8 AUGUST
ねこづか珈琲店
NEKOZUKA COFFEE
CHEE
CHEE
BRRRRR
CHEE
CHEE
BRRRRR
I'M REALLY SORRY ABOUT WHAT HAPPENED YESTERDAY.

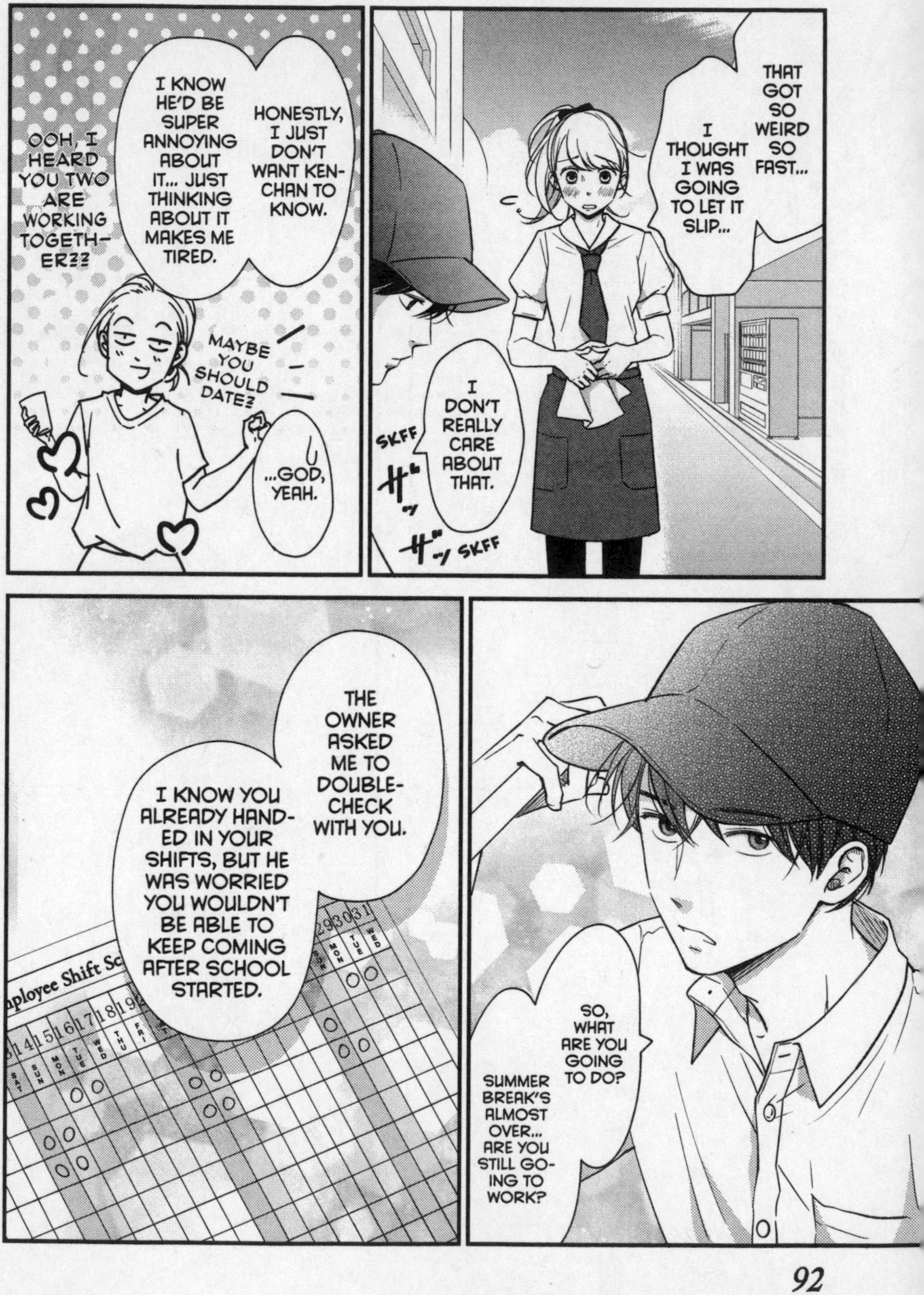
THAT GOT SO WEIRD SO FAST...
I THOUGHT I WAS GOING TO LET IT SLIP...
I DON'T REALLY CARE ABOUT THAT.
SKFF
SKFF
HONESTLY, I JUST DON'T WANT KEN-CHAN TO KNOW.
I KNOW HE'D BE SUPER ANNOYING ABOUT IT... JUST THINKING ABOUT IT MAKES ME TIRED.
OOH, I HEARD YOU TWO ARE WORKING TOGETHER??
MAYBE YOU SHOULD DATE?
...GOD, YEAH.
SO, WHAT ARE YOU GOING TO DO?
SUMMER BREAK'S ALMOST OVER... ARE YOU STILL GOING TO WORK?
THE OWNER ASKED ME TO DOUBLE-CHECK WITH YOU.
I KNOW YOU ALREADY HANDED IN YOUR SHIFTS, BUT HE WAS WORRIED YOU WOULDN'T BE ABLE TO KEEP COMING AFTER SCHOOL STARTED.

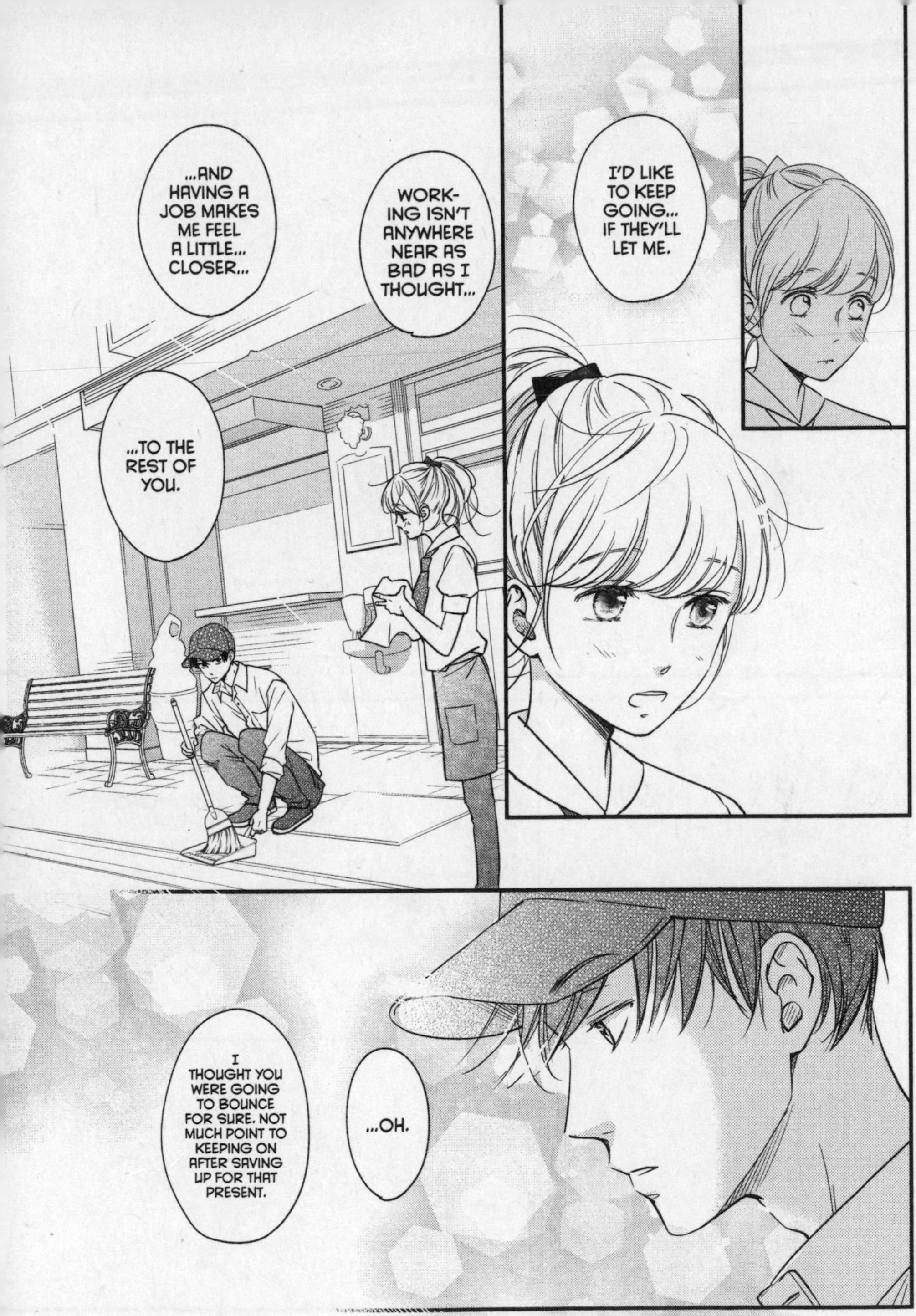
I'D LIKE TO KEEP GOING... IF THEY'LL LET ME.
WORKING ISN'T ANYWHERE NEAR AS BAD AS I THOUGHT...
...AND HAVING A JOB MAKES ME FEEL A LITTLE... CLOSER...
...TO THE REST OF YOU.
...OH.
I THOUGHT YOU WERE GOING TO BOUNCE FOR SURE. NOT MUCH POINT TO KEEPING ON AFTER SAVING UP FOR THAT PRESENT.

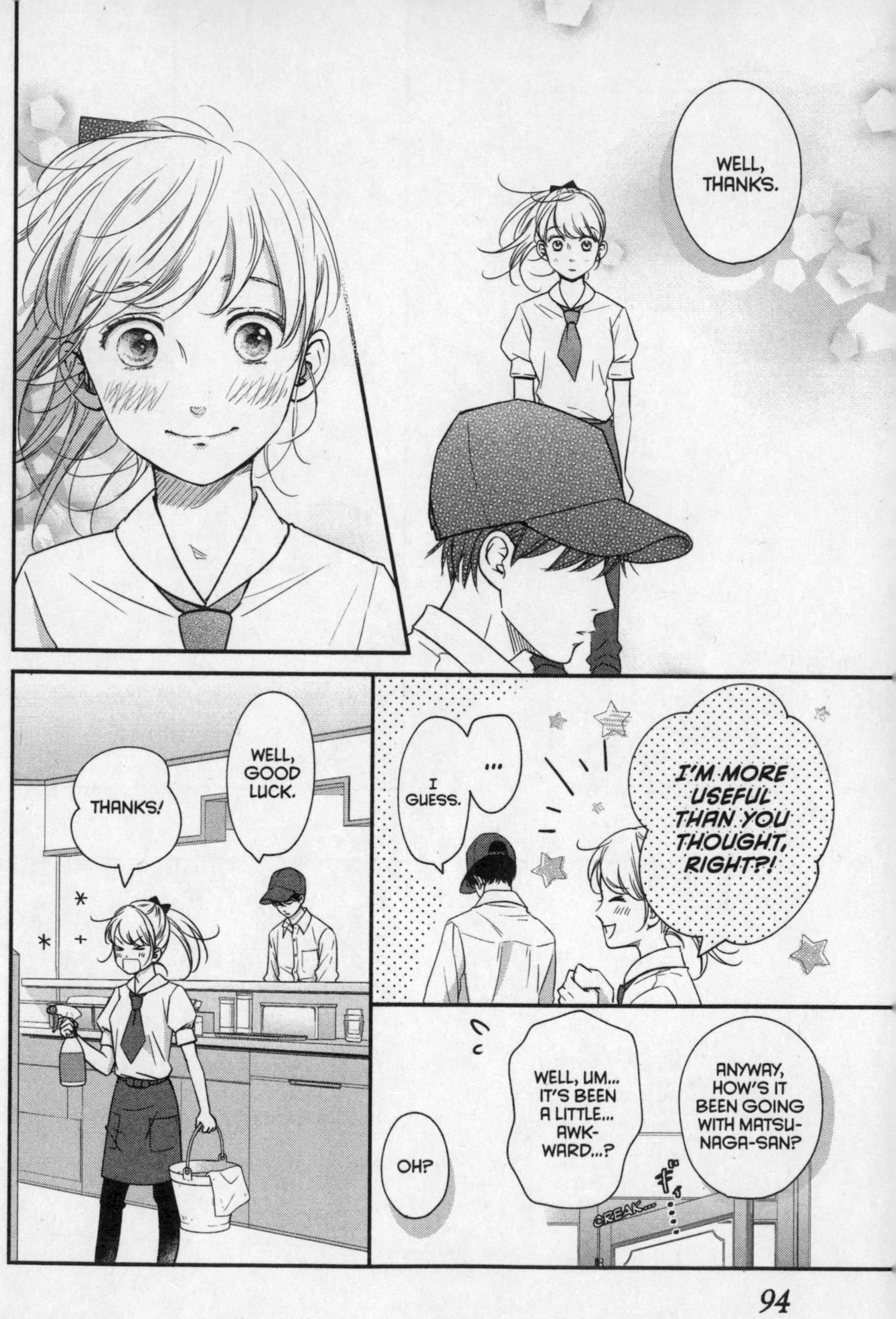
WELL, THANKS.
I'M MORE USEFUL THAN YOU THOUGHT, RIGHT?!
... I GUESS.
ANYWAY, HOW'S IT BEEN GOING WITH MATSU-NAGA-SAN?
WELL, UM... IT'S BEEN A LITTLE... AWK-WARD...?
OH?
CREAK...
WELL, GOOD LUCK.
THANKS!

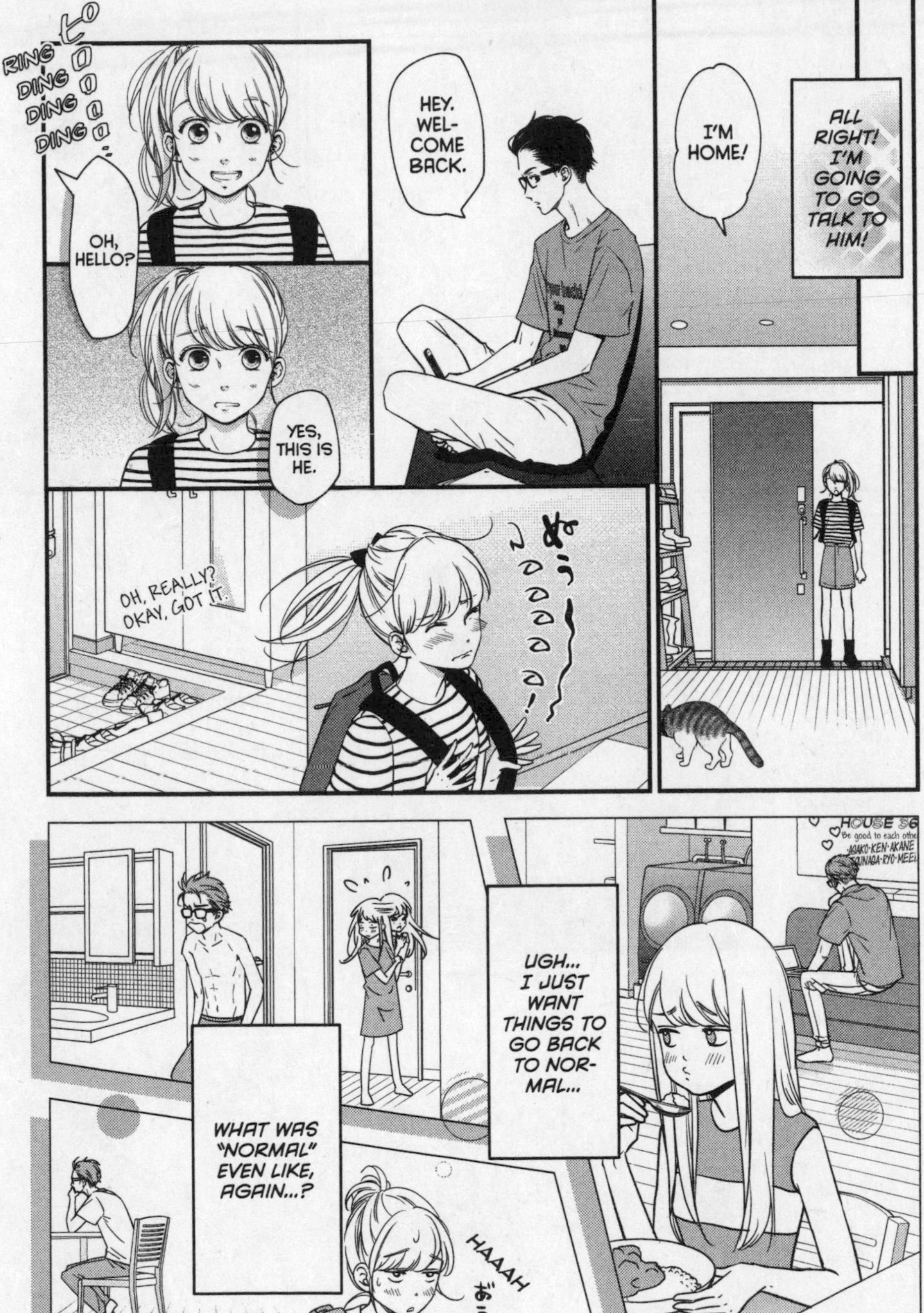
ALL RIGHT! I'M GOING TO GO TALK TO HIM!
I'M HOME!
HEY. WELCOME BACK.
RING DING DING DING
ピロロロロ
OH, HELLO?
YES, THIS IS HE.
ぬぅ〜〜〜〜〜〜!
OH, REALLY? OKAY, GOT IT.
HOUSE 36
Be good to each other
UGH... I JUST WANT THINGS TO GO BACK TO NORMAL...
WHAT WAS "NORMAL" EVEN LIKE, AGAIN...?
HAAAH
はぁ〜

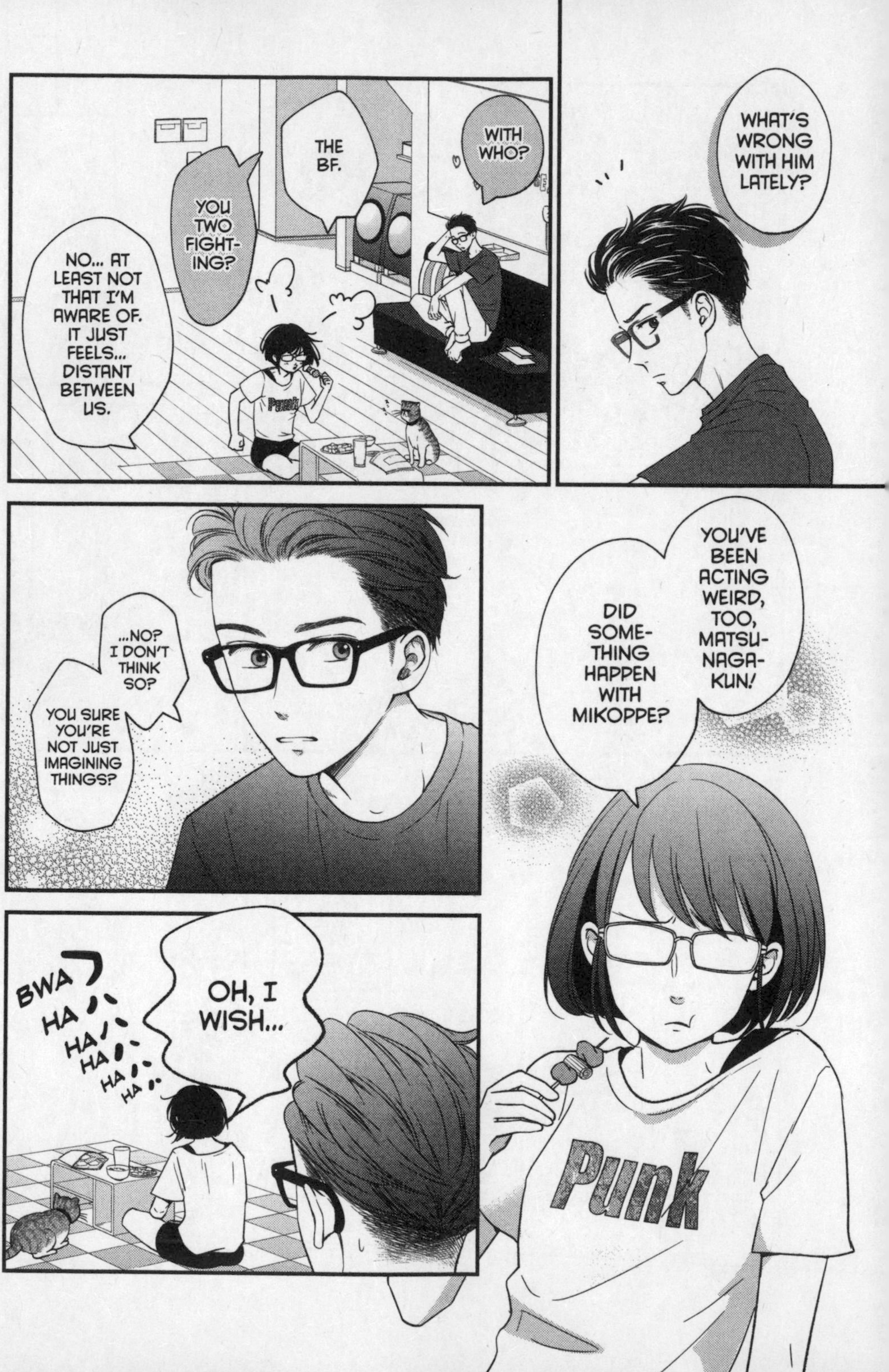
WHAT'S WRONG WITH HIM LATELY?
WITH WHO?
THE BF.
YOU TWO FIGHT-ING?
NO... AT LEAST NOT THAT I'M AWARE OF. IT JUST FEELS... DISTANT BETWEEN US.
YOU'VE BEEN ACTING WEIRD, TOO, MATSU-NAGA-KUN!
DID SOME-THING HAPPEN WITH MIKOPPE?
...NO? I DON'T THINK SO?
YOU SURE YOU'RE NOT JUST IMAGINING THINGS?
OH, I WISH...
BWA HA HA HA HA HA

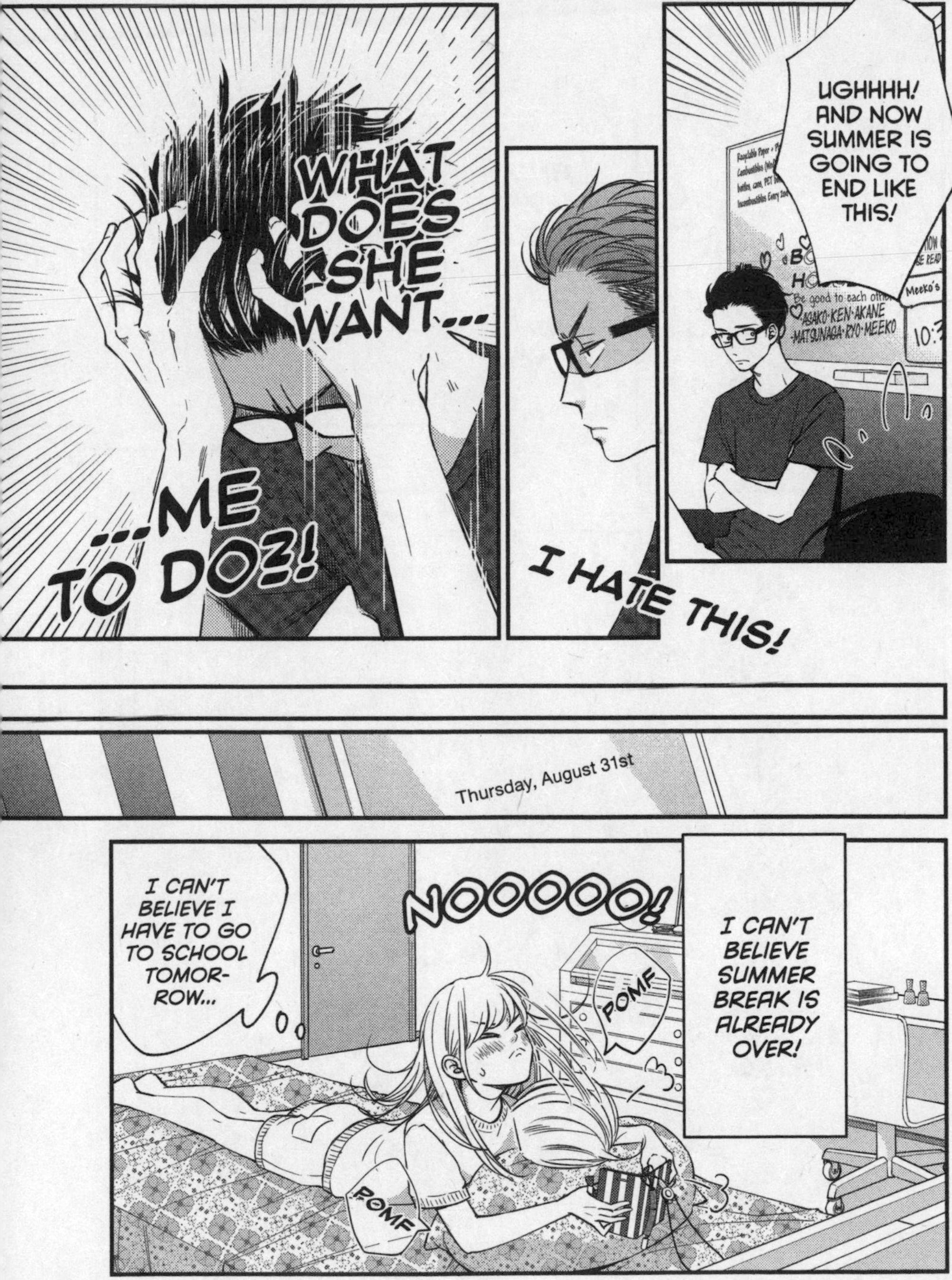
UGHHHH! AND NOW SUMMER IS GOING TO END LIKE THIS!
Be good to each other
ASAKO·KEN·AKANE·MATSUNAGA·RYO·MEEKO
Meeko's
I HATE THIS!
WHAT DOES SHE WANT...
...ME TO DO?!
Thursday, August 31st
I CAN'T BELIEVE SUMMER BREAK IS ALREADY OVER!
NOOOOO!
POMF
I CAN'T BELIEVE I HAVE TO GO TO SCHOOL TOMOR-ROW...
POMF

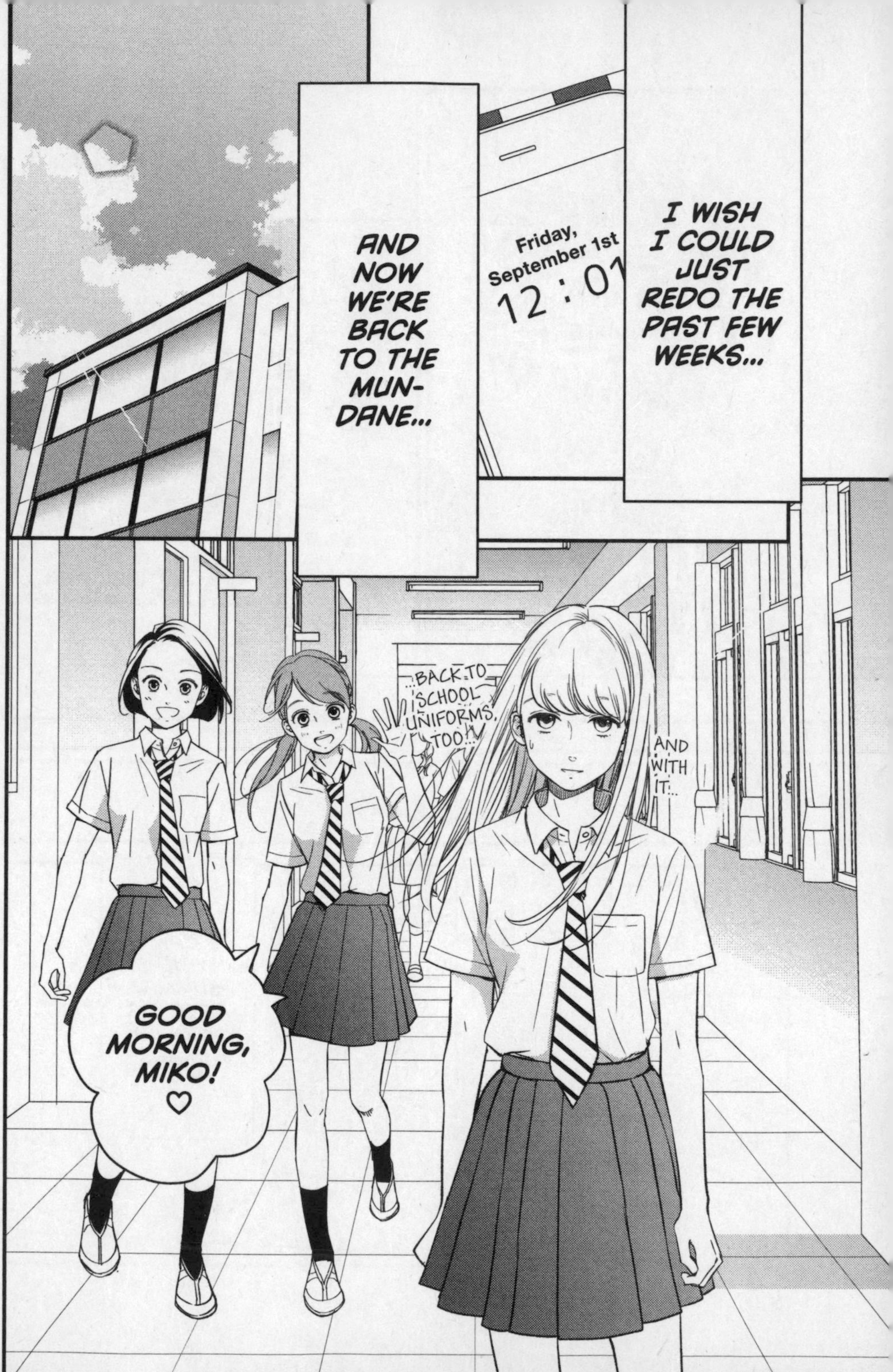
Friday, September 1st
12 : 01
I WISH I COULD JUST REDO THE PAST FEW WEEKS...
AND NOW WE'RE BACK TO THE MUN-DANE...
AND WITH IT...
...BACK TO SCHOOL UNIFORMS, TOO!
GOOD MORNING, MIKO! ♡

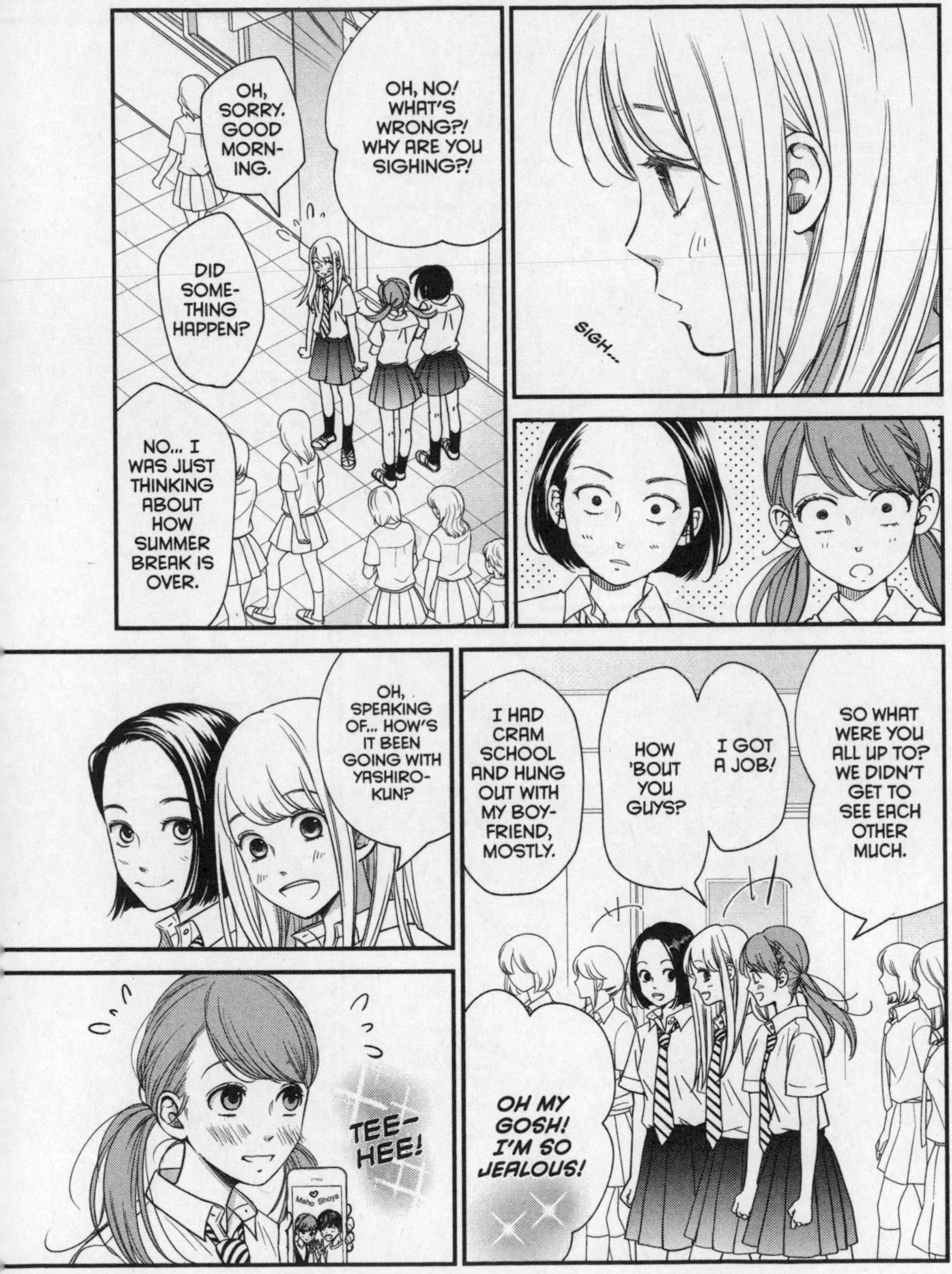
SIGH...
OH, NO! WHAT'S WRONG?! WHY ARE YOU SIGHING?!
OH, SORRY. GOOD MORN-ING.
DID SOME-THING HAPPEN?
NO... I WAS JUST THINKING ABOUT HOW SUMMER BREAK IS OVER.
SO WHAT WERE YOU ALL UP TO? WE DIDN'T GET TO SEE EACH OTHER MUCH.
I GOT A JOB!
HOW 'BOUT YOU GUYS?
I HAD CRAM SCHOOL AND HUNG OUT WITH MY BOY-FRIEND, MOSTLY.
OH MY GOSH! I'M SO JEALOUS!
OH, SPEAKING OF... HOW'S IT BEEN GOING WITH YASHIRO-KUN?
TEE-HEE!
Maho Shoya

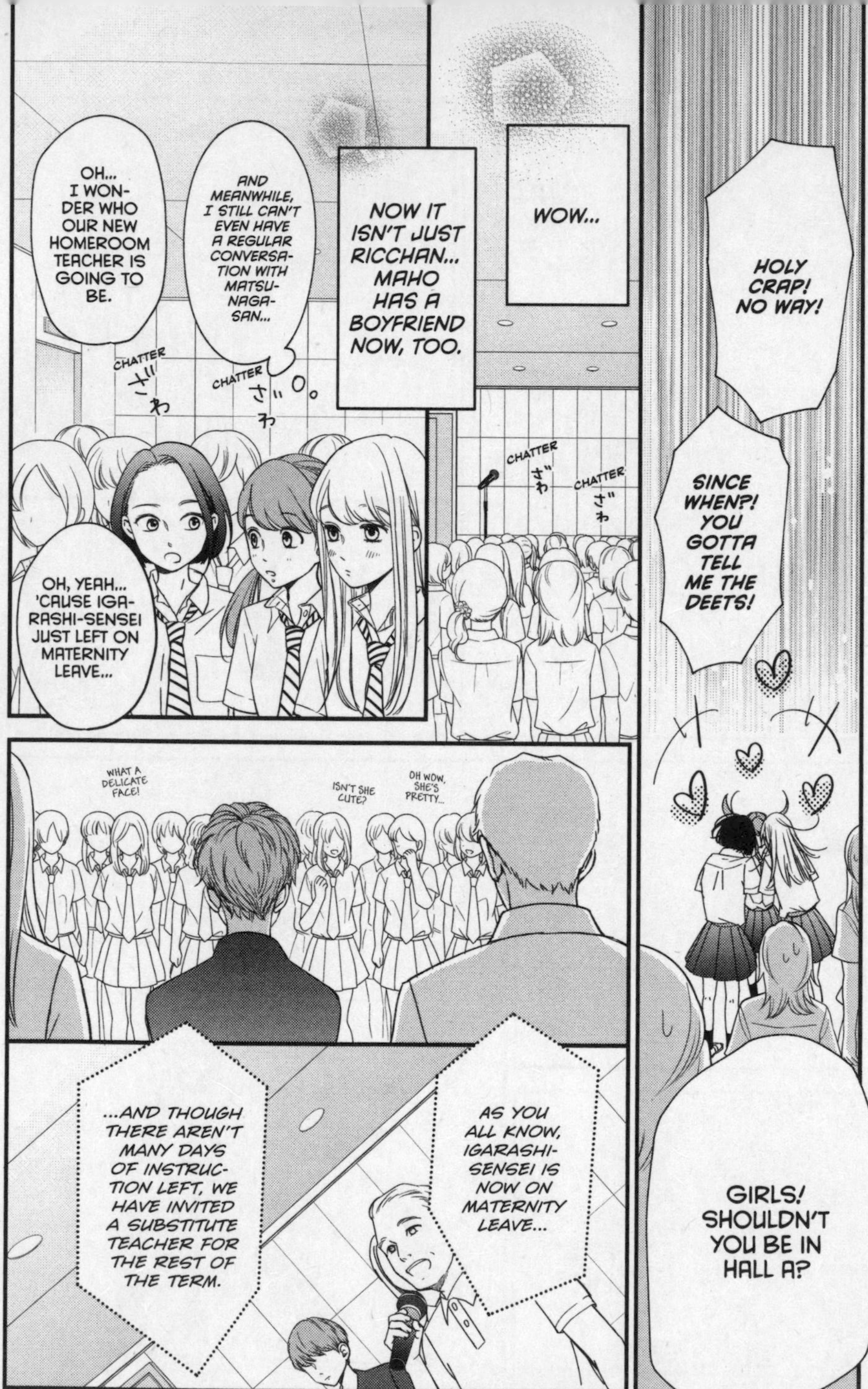
HOLY CRAP! NO WAY!
SINCE WHEN?! YOU GOTTA TELL ME THE DEETS!
GIRLS! SHOULDN'T YOU BE IN HALL A?
WOW...
NOW IT ISN'T JUST RICCHAN... MAHO HAS A BOYFRIEND NOW, TOO.
AND MEANWHILE, I STILL CAN'T EVEN HAVE A REGULAR CONVERSATION WITH MATSUNAGA-SAN...
OH... I WONDER WHO OUR NEW HOMEROOM TEACHER IS GOING TO BE.
CHATTER
CHATTER
CHATTER
CHATTER
OH, YEAH... 'CAUSE IGARASHI-SENSEI JUST LEFT ON MATERNITY LEAVE...
OH WOW, SHE'S PRETTY...
ISN'T SHE CUTE?
WHAT A DELICATE FACE!
AS YOU ALL KNOW, IGARASHI-SENSEI IS NOW ON MATERNITY LEAVE...
...AND THOUGH THERE AREN'T MANY DAYS OF INSTRUCTION LEFT, WE HAVE INVITED A SUBSTITUTE TEACHER FOR THE REST OF THE TERM.

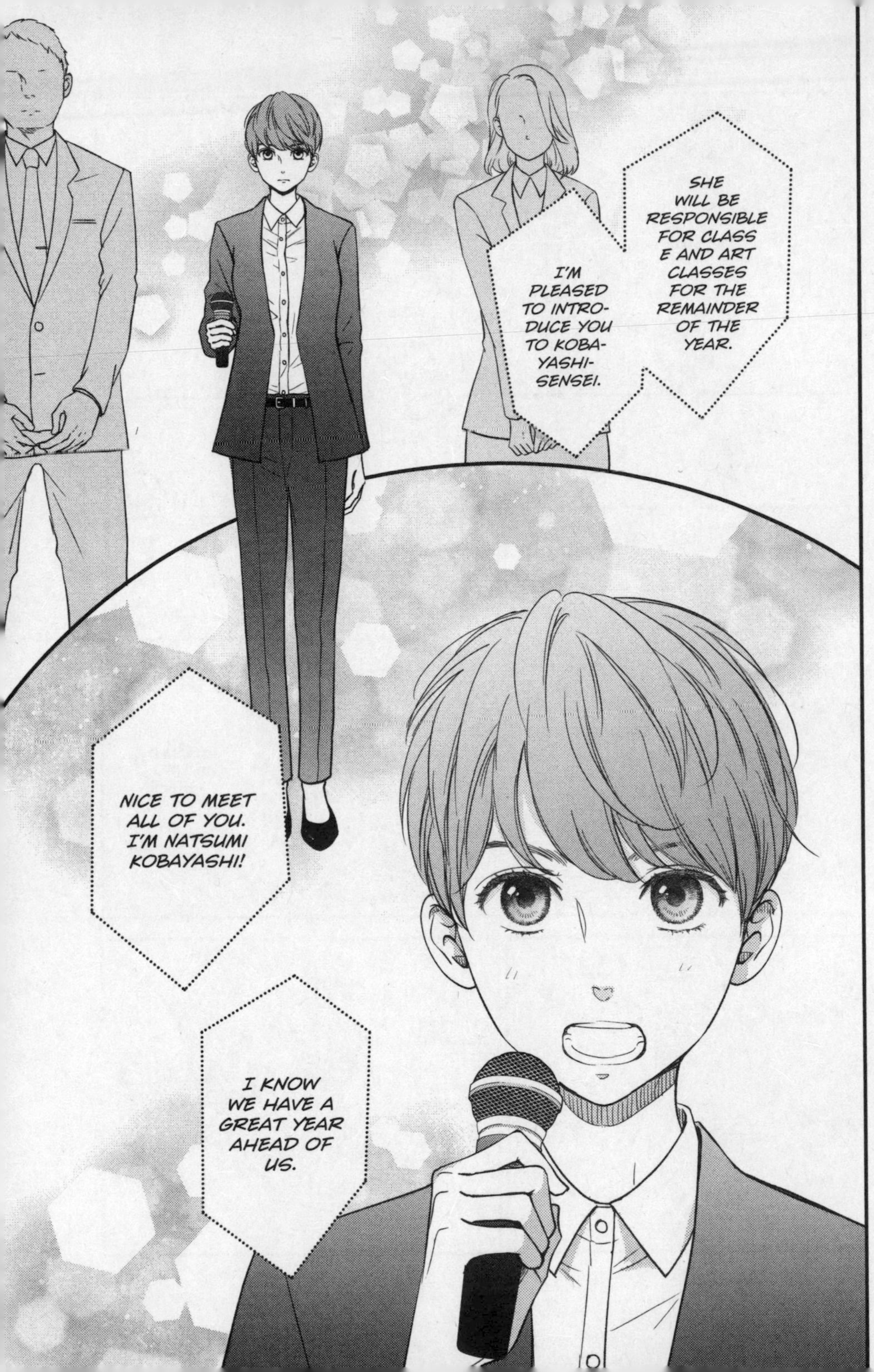

I'M PLEASED TO INTRODUCE YOU TO KOBAYASHI-SENSEI.
SHE WILL BE RESPONSIBLE FOR CLASS E AND ART CLASSES FOR THE REMAINDER OF THE YEAR.
NICE TO MEET ALL OF YOU. I'M NATSUMI KOBAYASHI!
I KNOW WE HAVE A GREAT YEAR AHEAD OF US.

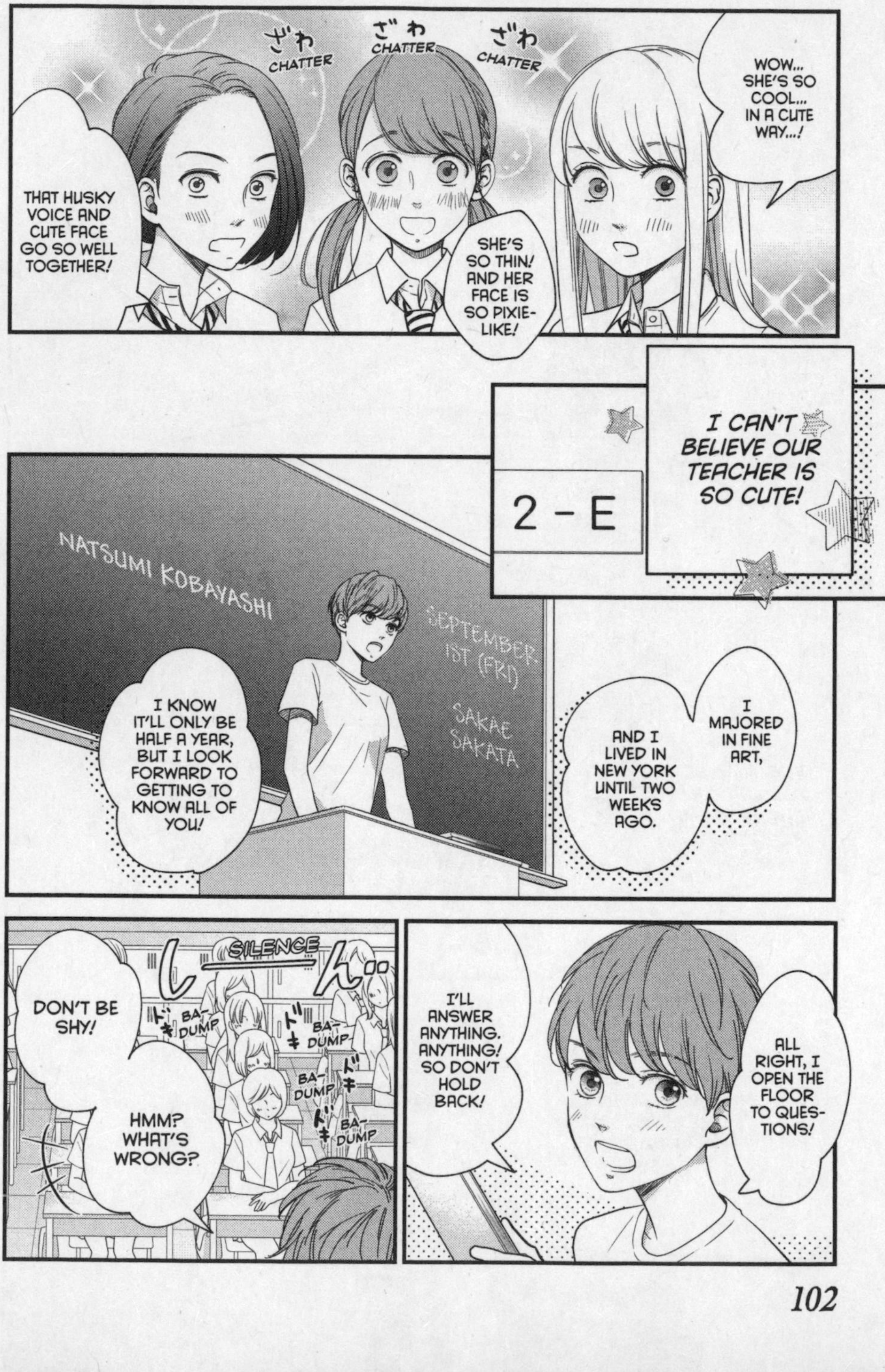
WOW... SHE'S SO COOL... IN A CUTE WAY...!
ざわ CHATTER
ざわ CHATTER
ざわ CHATTER
SHE'S SO THIN! AND HER FACE IS SO PIXIE-LIKE!
THAT HUSKY VOICE AND CUTE FACE GO SO WELL TOGETHER!
I CAN'T BELIEVE OUR TEACHER IS SO CUTE!
2 – E
NATSUMI KOBAYASHI
SEPTEMBER 1ST (FRI)
SAKAE SAKATA
I MAJORED IN FINE ART,
AND I LIVED IN NEW YORK UNTIL TWO WEEKS AGO.
I KNOW IT'LL ONLY BE HALF A YEAR, BUT I LOOK FORWARD TO GETTING TO KNOW ALL OF YOU!
ALL RIGHT, I OPEN THE FLOOR TO QUES-TIONS!
I'LL ANSWER ANYTHING. ANYTHING! SO DON'T HOLD BACK!
し—ん SILENCE
DON'T BE SHY!
ドキ BA-DUMP
ドキ BA-DUMP
ドキ BA-DUMP
ドキ BA-DUMP
HMM? WHAT'S WRONG?

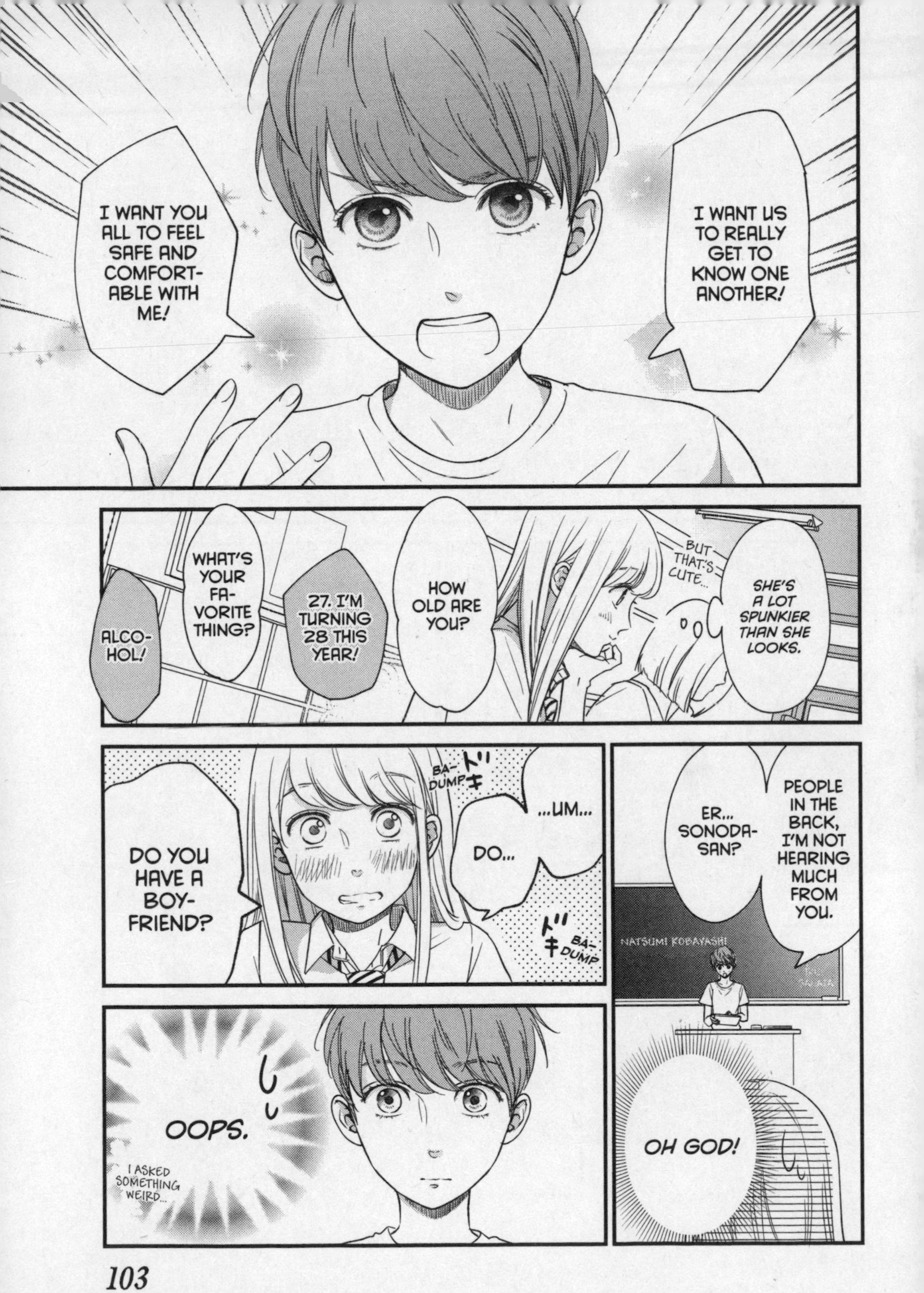
I WANT US TO REALLY GET TO KNOW ONE ANOTHER!
I WANT YOU ALL TO FEEL SAFE AND COMFORTABLE WITH ME!
SHE'S A LOT SPUNKIER THAN SHE LOOKS.
BUT THAT'S CUTE...
HOW OLD ARE YOU?
27. I'M TURNING 28 THIS YEAR!
WHAT'S YOUR FAVORITE THING?
ALCOHOL!
PEOPLE IN THE BACK, I'M NOT HEARING MUCH FROM YOU.
ER... SONODA-SAN?
NATSUMI KOBAYASHI
OH GOD!
BA-DUMP
...UM...
DO...
BA-DUMP
DO YOU HAVE A BOYFRIEND?
OOPS.
I ASKED SOMETHING WEIRD...

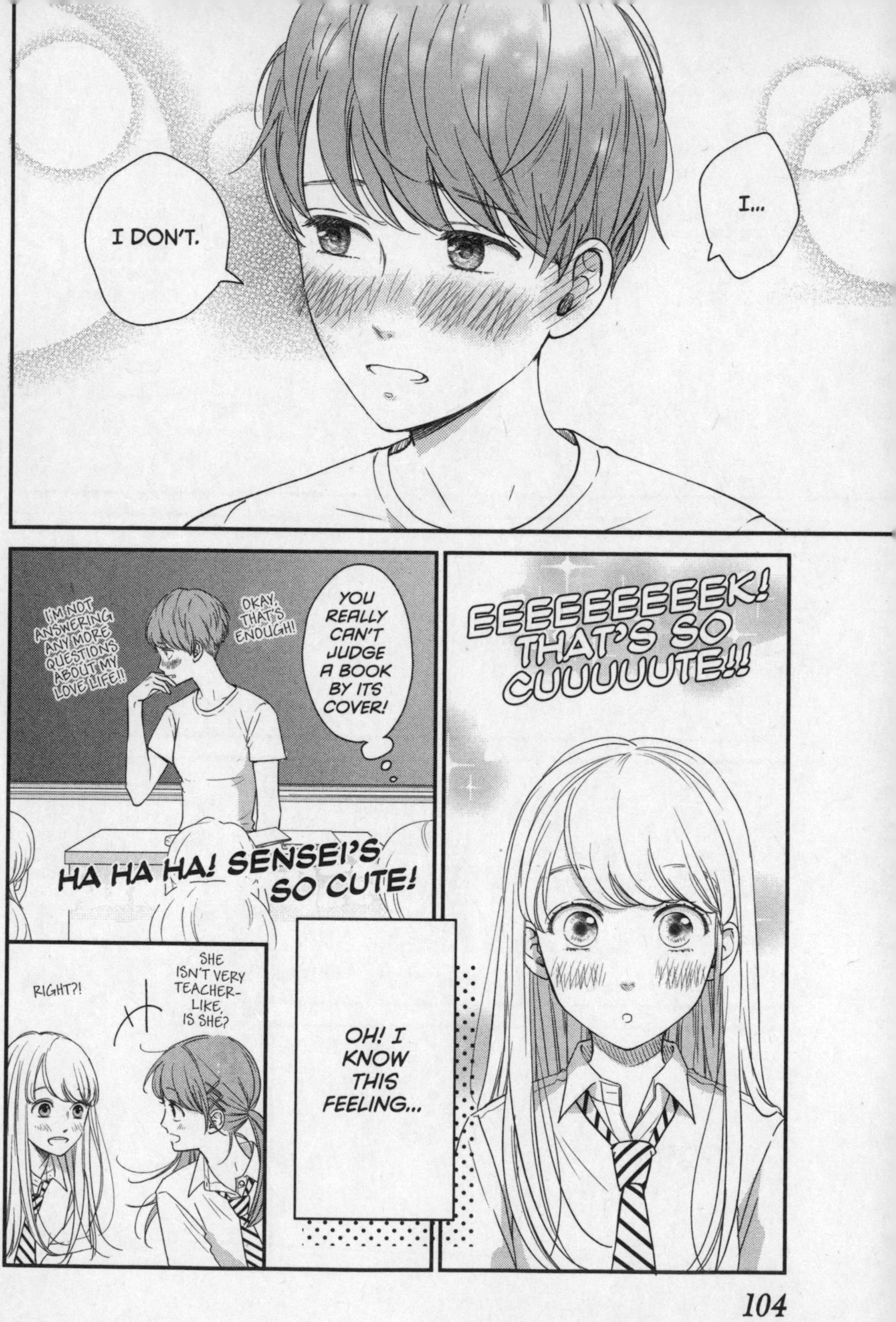
I...
I DON'T.
EEEEEEEEEK! THAT'S SO CUUUUUTE!!
YOU REALLY CAN'T JUDGE A BOOK BY ITS COVER!
OKAY, THAT'S ENOUGH!
I'M NOT ANSWERING ANY MORE QUESTIONS ABOUT MY LOVE LIFE!!
HA HA HA! SENSEI'S SO CUTE!
SHE ISN'T VERY TEACHER-LIKE, IS SHE?
RIGHT?!
OH! I KNOW THIS FEELING...

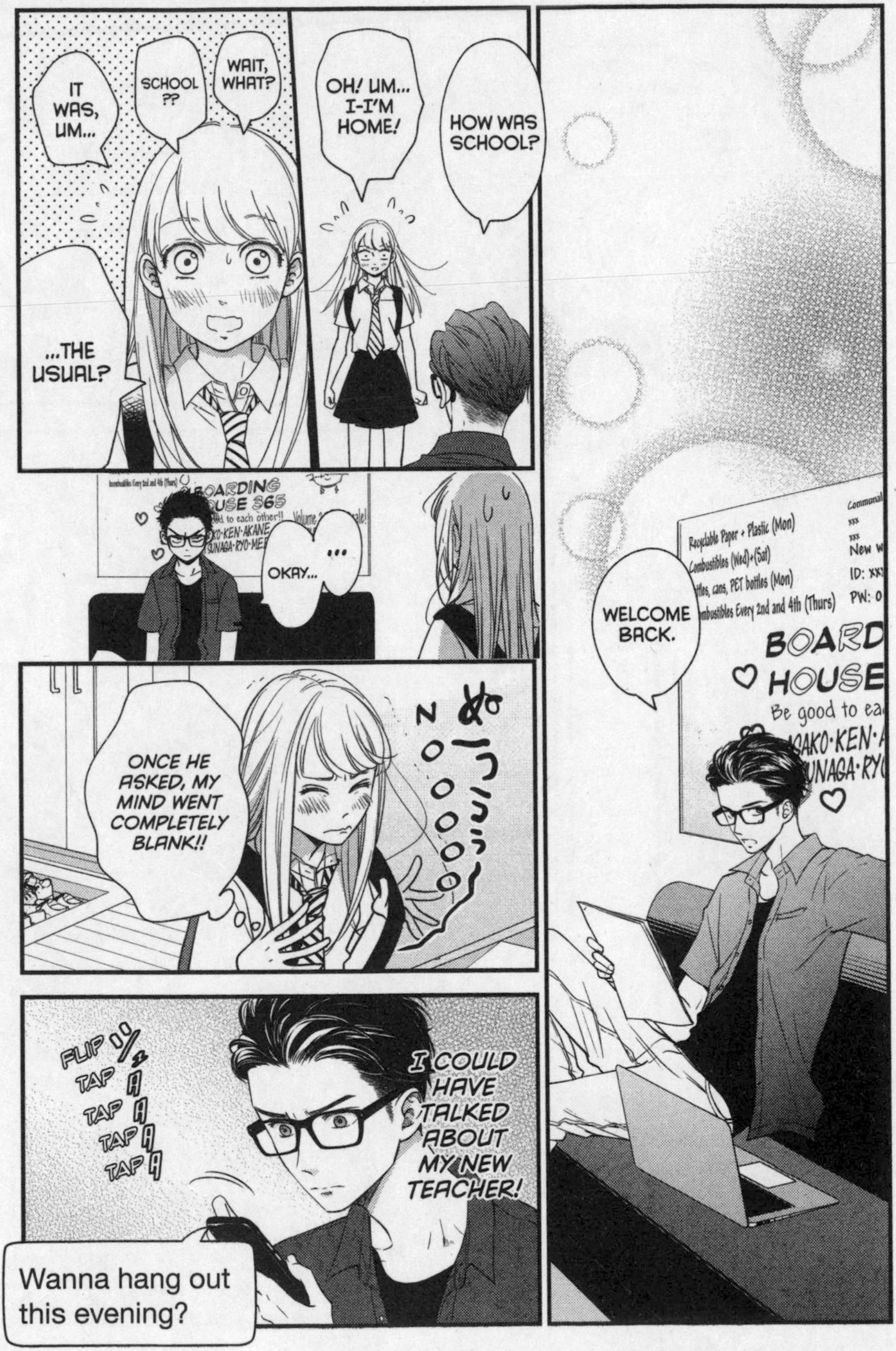
Recyclable Paper + Plastic (Mon)
Combustibles (Wed)+(Sat)
ID:
PW:
WELCOME BACK.
Be good to ea
HOW WAS SCHOOL?
OH! UM... I-I'M HOME!
WAIT, WHAT?
SCHOOL??
IT WAS, UM...
...THE USUAL?
OKAY...
...
ONCE HE ASKED, MY MIND WENT COMPLETELY BLANK!!
ぬーっっ
NOOOOOO
I COULD HAVE TALKED ABOUT MY NEW TEACHER!
FLIP
TAP
TAP
TAP
TAP
Wanna hang out this evening?

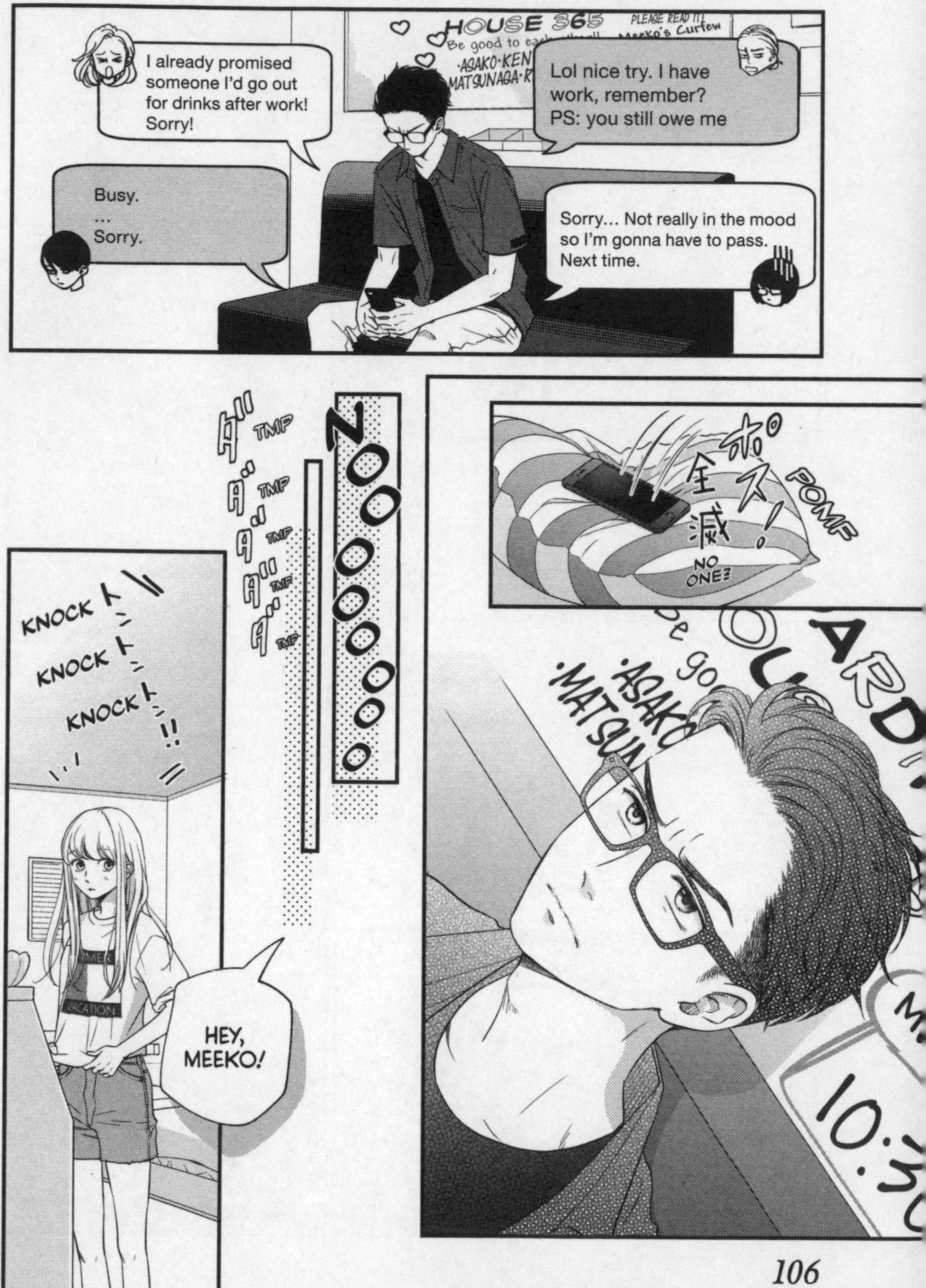

HOUSE 365
PLEASE READ IT! Meeko's Curfew
Be good to each other!!
·ASAKO·KEN
MATSUNAGA·R
Lol nice try. I have work, remember? PS: you still owe me
I already promised someone I'd go out for drinks after work! Sorry!
Sorry... Not really in the mood so I'm gonna have to pass. Next time.
Busy. ... Sorry.
ポス!
POMF
全滅
NO ONE?
ASAKO
MATSUNA
10:30
NOOOOOOOOO
ダ TMP
ダ TMP
ダ TMP
ダ TMP
ダ TMP
KNOCK
KNOCK
KNOCK
HEY, MEEKO!

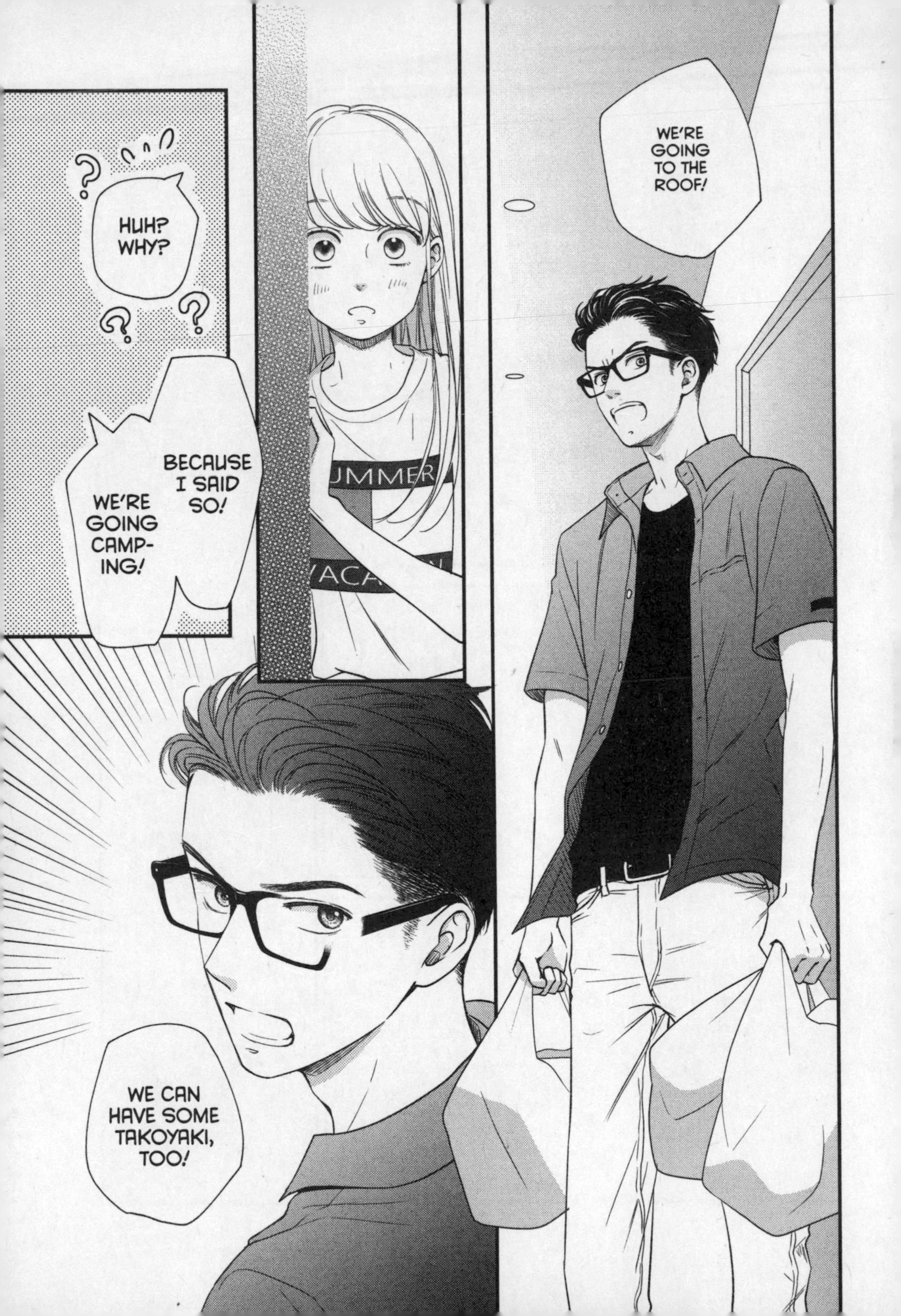
WE'RE GOING TO THE ROOF!
HUH? WHY?
BECAUSE I SAID SO!
WE'RE GOING CAMP-ING!
WE CAN HAVE SOME TAKOYAKI, TOO!

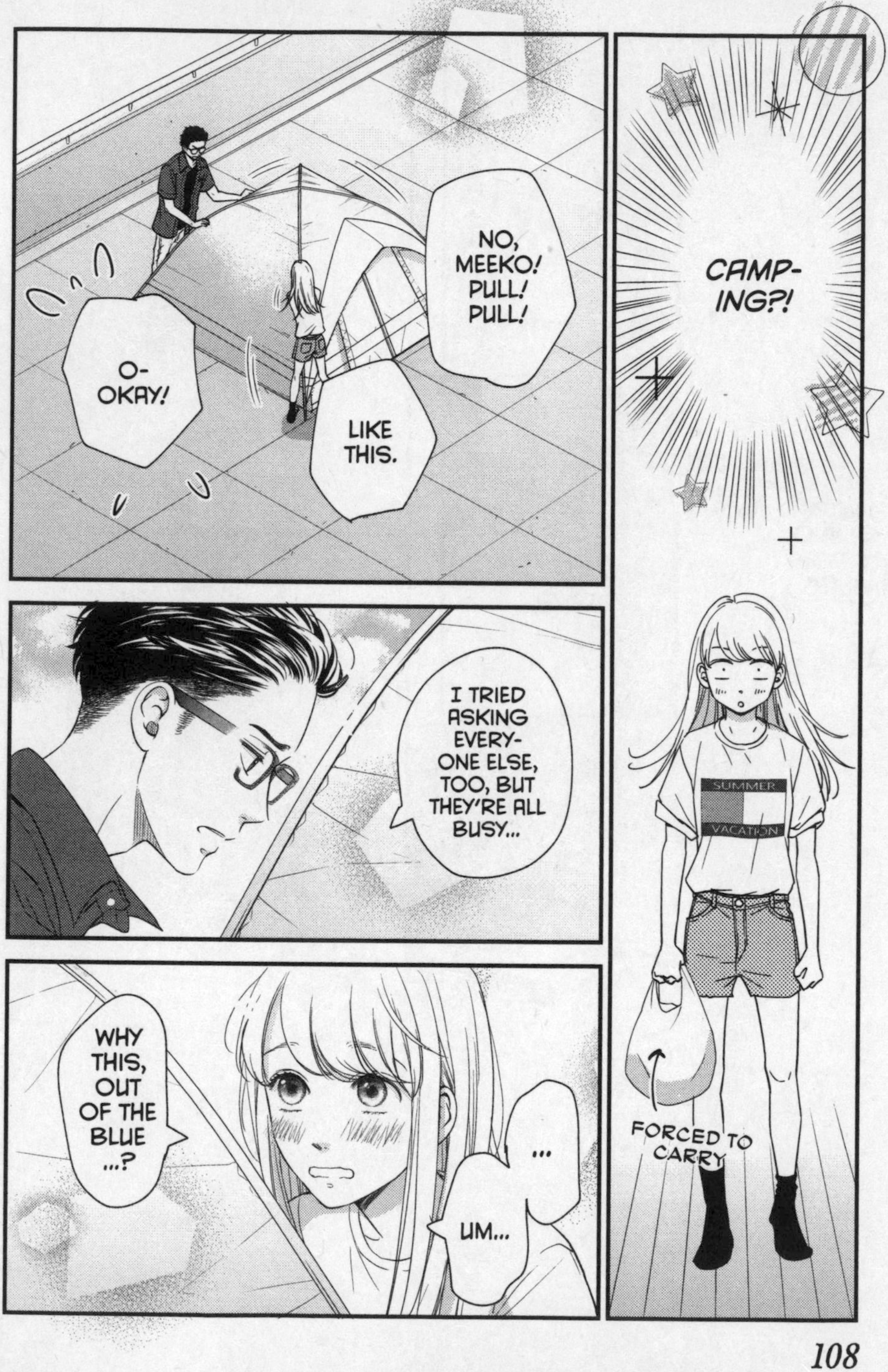
CAMPING?!
FORCED TO CARRY
NO, MEEKO! PULL! PULL!
LIKE THIS.
O-OKAY!
I TRIED ASKING EVERYONE ELSE, TOO, BUT THEY'RE ALL BUSY...
...
UM...
WHY THIS, OUT OF THE BLUE ...?

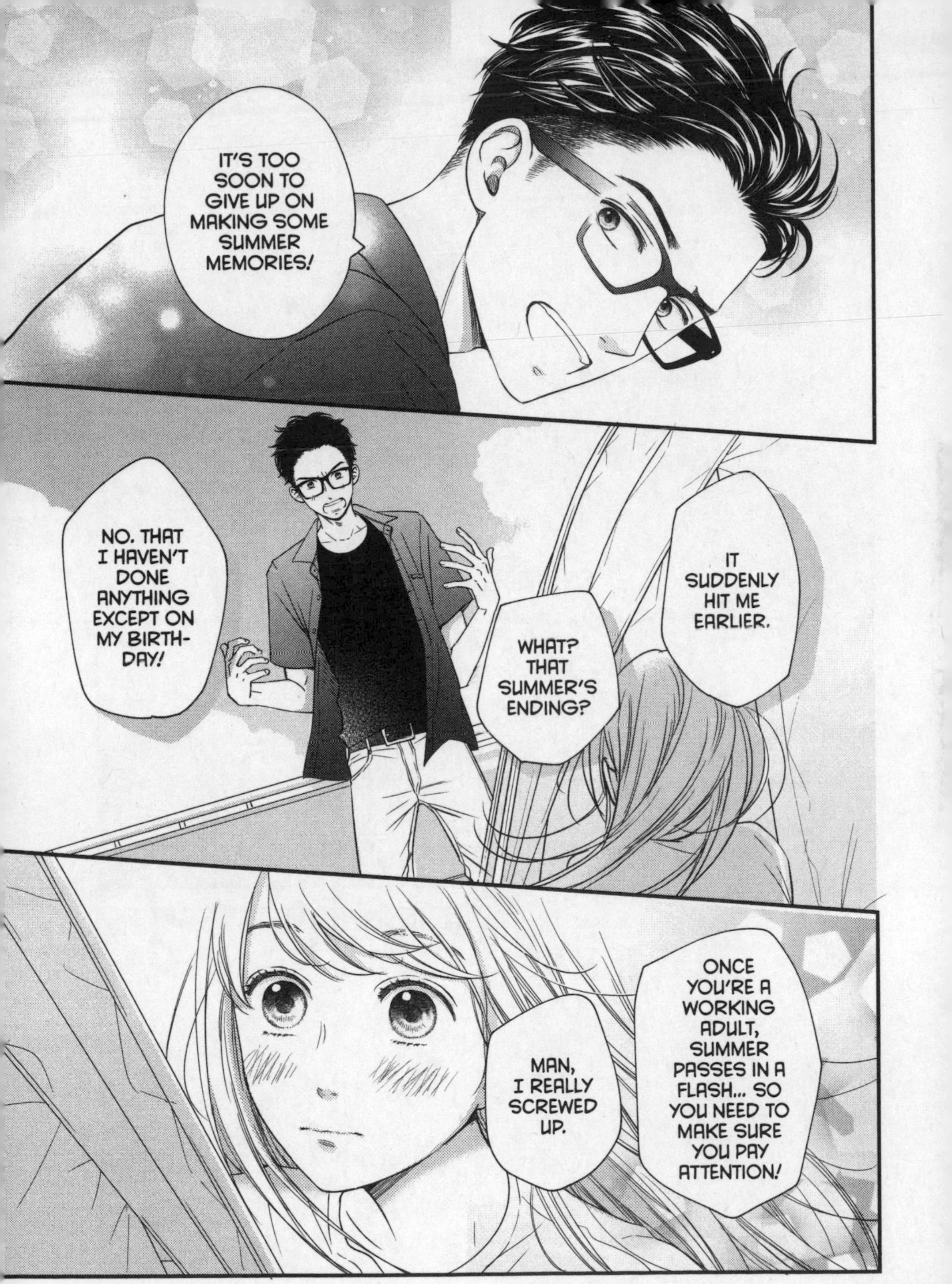
IT'S TOO SOON TO GIVE UP ON MAKING SOME SUMMER MEMORIES!
IT SUDDENLY HIT ME EARLIER.
WHAT? THAT SUMMER'S ENDING?
NO. THAT I HAVEN'T DONE ANYTHING EXCEPT ON MY BIRTH-DAY!
ONCE YOU'RE A WORKING ADULT, SUMMER PASSES IN A FLASH... SO YOU NEED TO MAKE SURE YOU PAY ATTENTION!
MAN, I REALLY SCREWED UP.

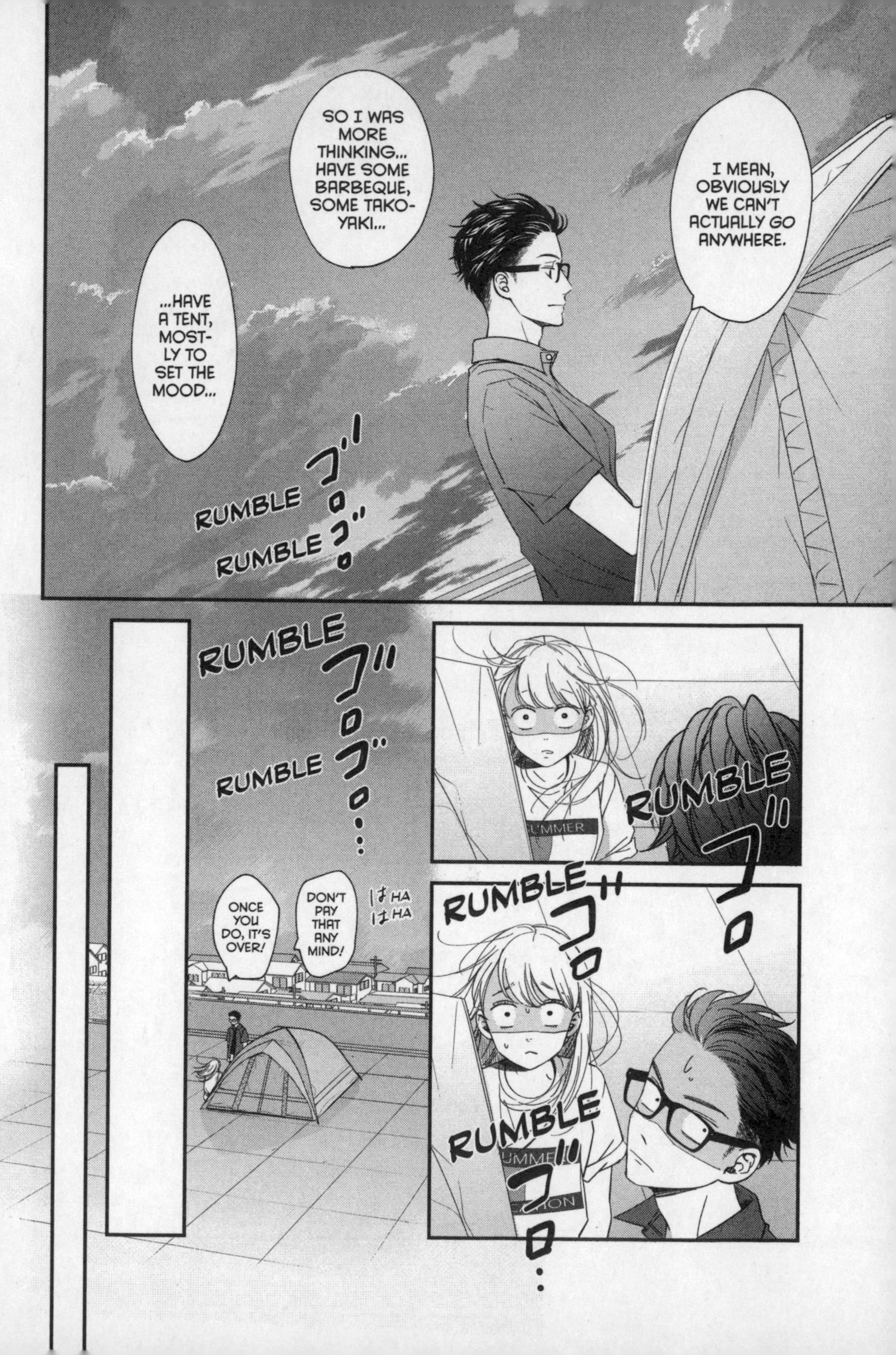
I MEAN, OBVIOUSLY WE CAN'T ACTUALLY GO ANYWHERE.
SO I WAS MORE THINKING... HAVE SOME BARBEQUE, SOME TAKO-YAKI...
...HAVE A TENT, MOSTLY TO SET THE MOOD...
RUMBLE ゴロ
RUMBLE ゴロ
RUMBLE ゴロ
RUMBLE ゴロ
RUMBLE ゴロ...
RUMBLE ゴロ
RUMBLE ゴロ...
は HA
は HA
DON'T PAY THAT ANY MIND!
ONCE YOU DO, IT'S OVER!

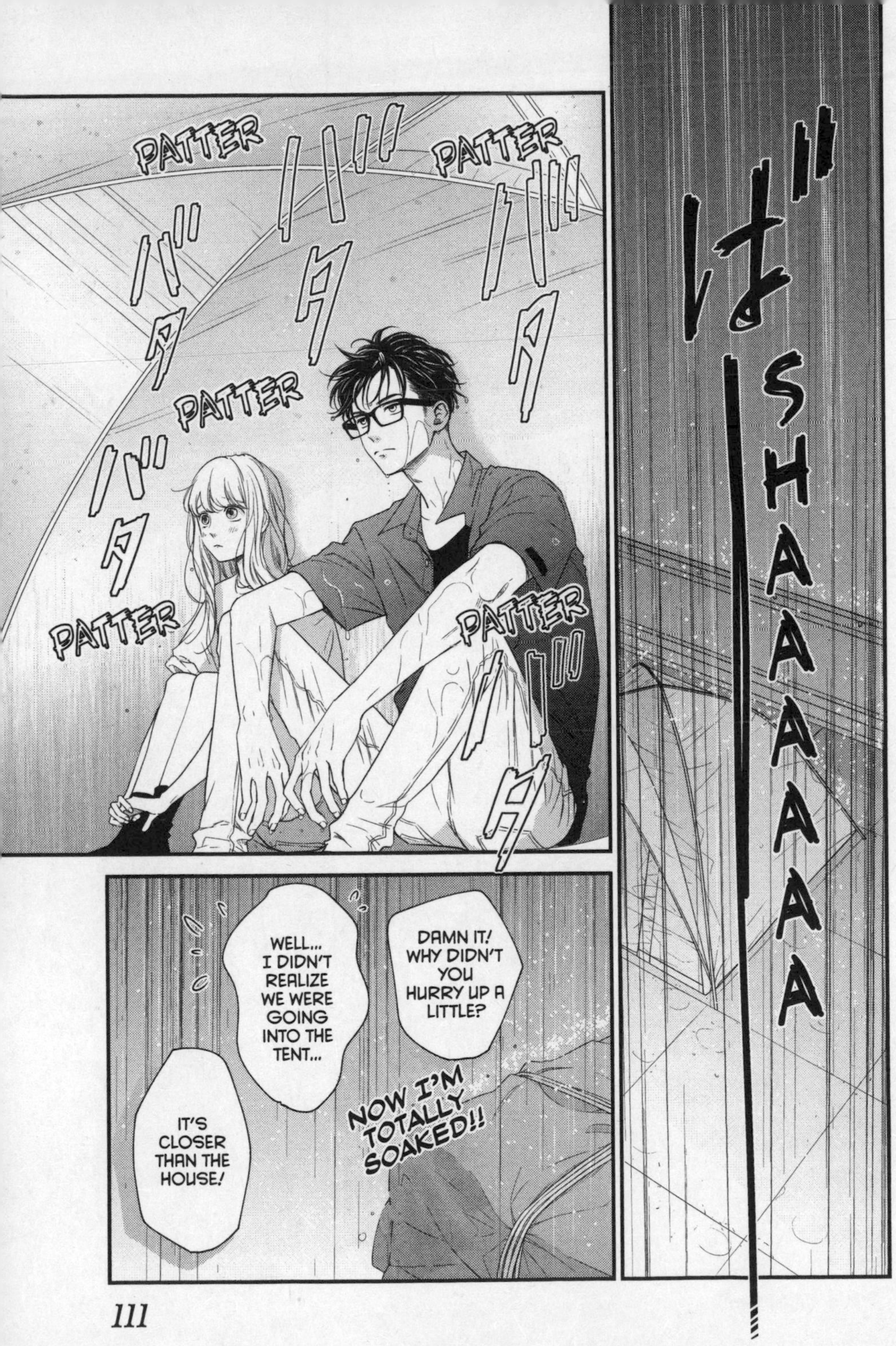
ばー
SHAAAAAA
PATTER
バタ
PATTER
バタ
バタ
PATTER
バタ
PATTER
PATTER
バタ
DAMN IT! WHY DIDN'T YOU HURRY UP A LITTLE?
WELL... I DIDN'T REALIZE WE WERE GOING INTO THE TENT...
NOW I'M TOTALLY SOAKED!!
IT'S CLOSER THAN THE HOUSE!

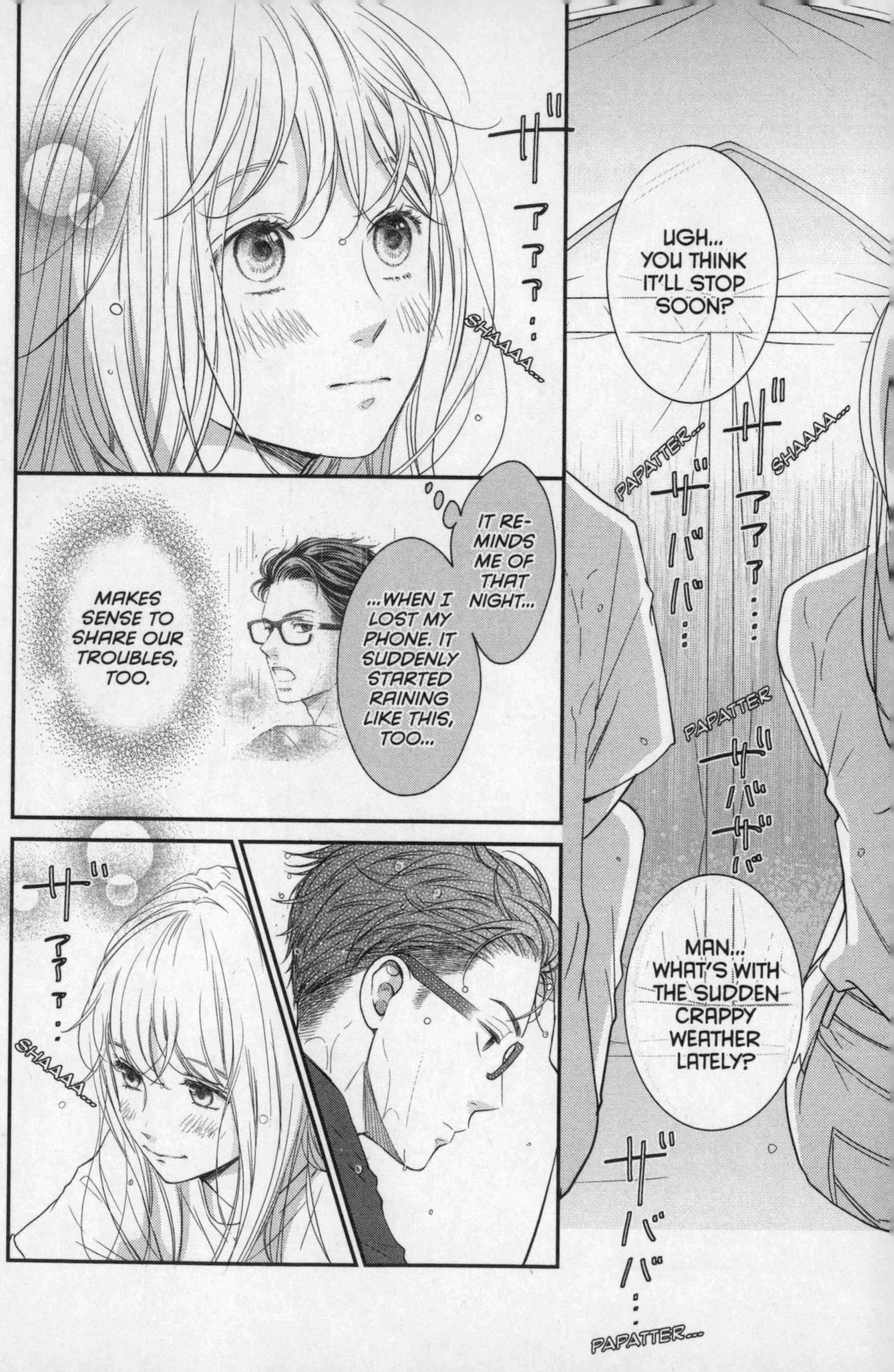
UGH... YOU THINK IT'LL STOP SOON?
ザァァァ…
SHAAAA...
ザババ…
PAPATTER...
ザバザバ
PAPATTER
MAN... WHAT'S WITH THE SUDDEN CRAPPY WEATHER LATELY?
ザババ…
PAPATTER...
ザァァァ…
SHAAAA...
IT RE-MINDS ME OF THAT NIGHT...
...WHEN I LOST MY PHONE. IT SUDDENLY STARTED RAINING LIKE THIS, TOO...
MAKES SENSE TO SHARE OUR TROUBLES, TOO.
ザァァァ…
SHAAAA...

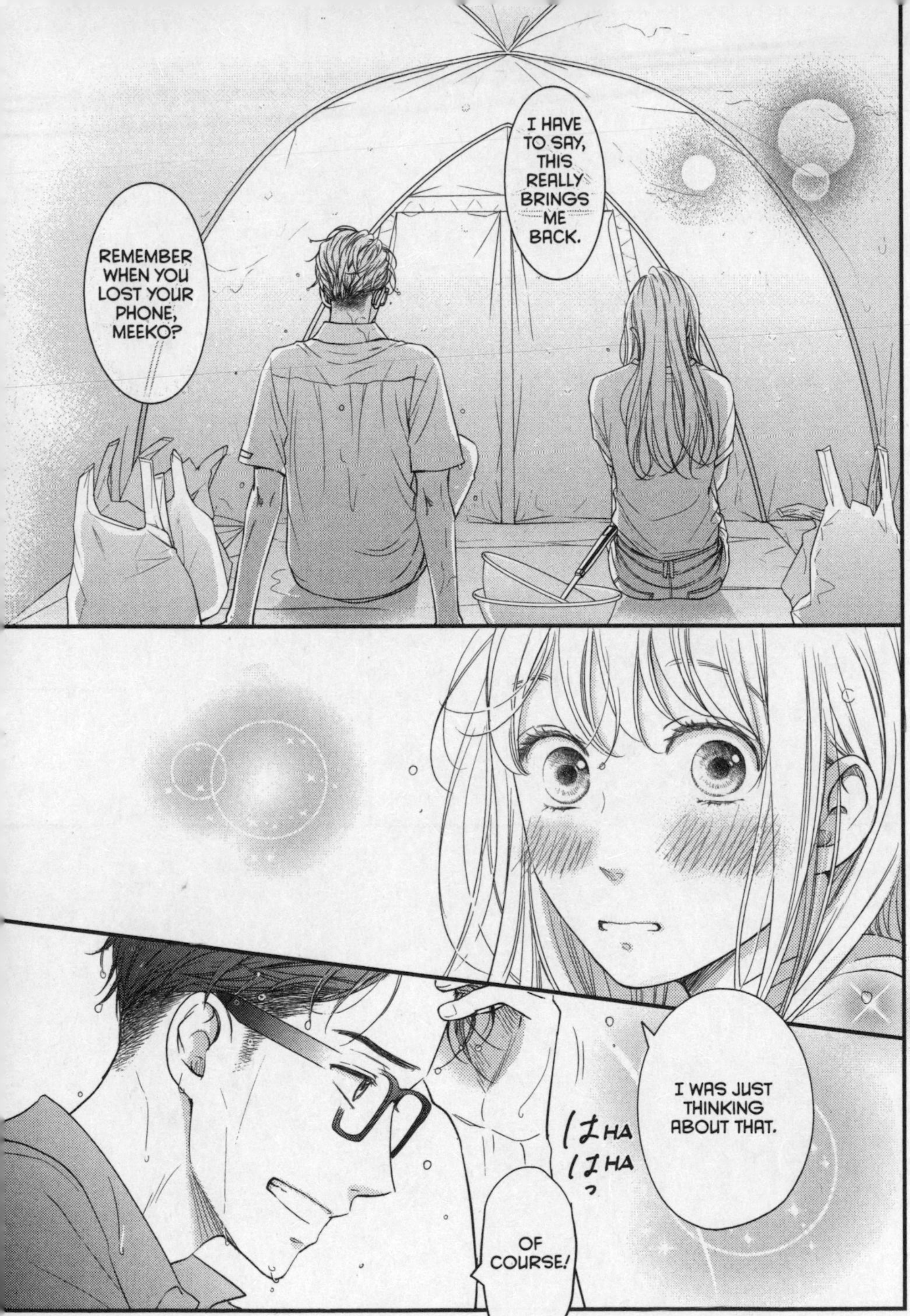
I HAVE TO SAY, THIS REALLY BRINGS ME BACK.
REMEMBER WHEN YOU LOST YOUR PHONE, MEEKO?
I WAS JUST THINKING ABOUT THAT.
はは HA
はは HA
OF COURSE!

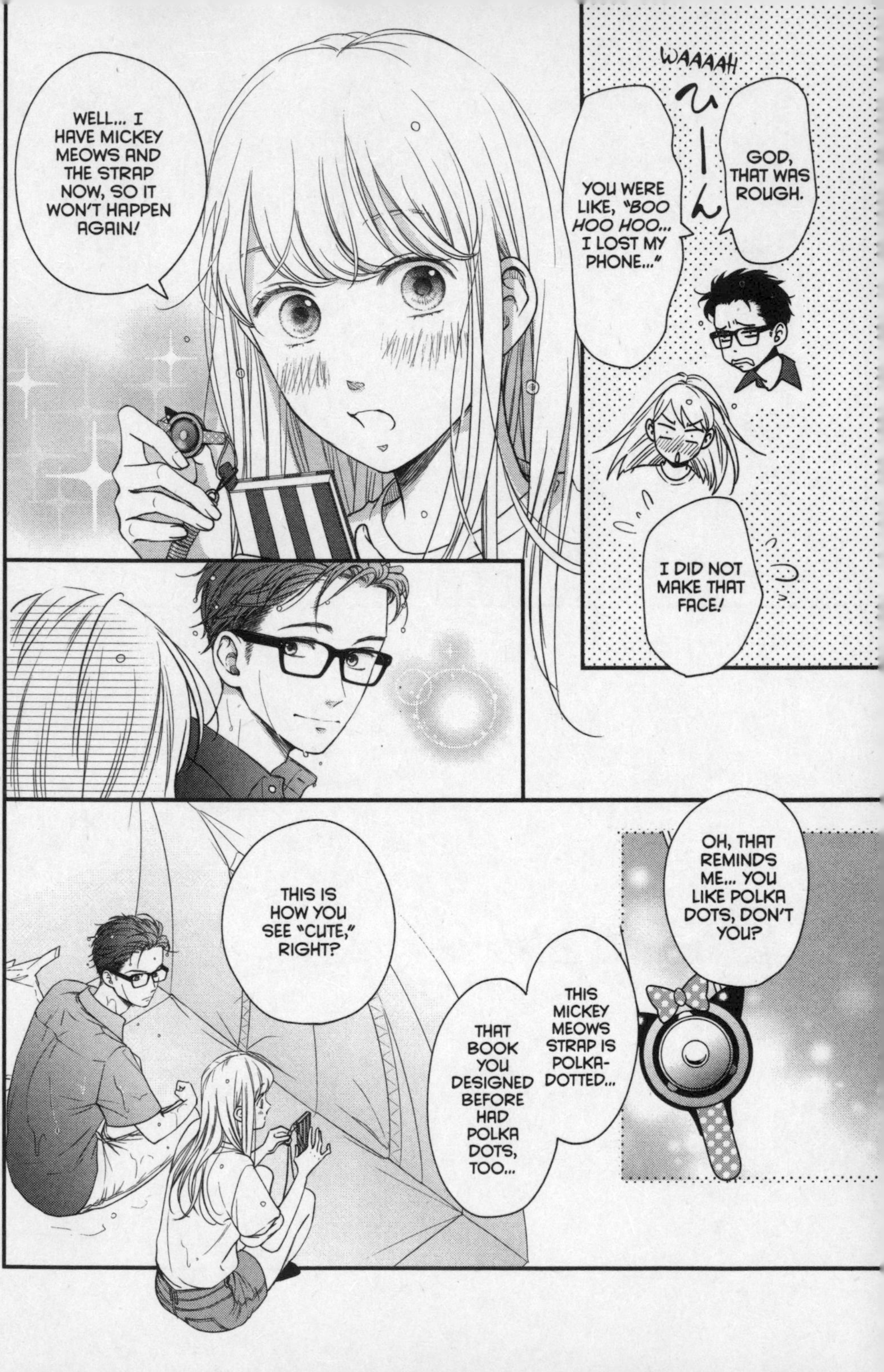
WAAAAH
GOD, THAT WAS ROUGH.
YOU WERE LIKE, "BOO HOO HOO... I LOST MY PHONE..."
I DID NOT MAKE THAT FACE!
WELL... I HAVE MICKEY MEOWS AND THE STRAP NOW, SO IT WON'T HAPPEN AGAIN!
OH, THAT REMINDS ME... YOU LIKE POLKA DOTS, DON'T YOU?
THIS MICKEY MEOWS STRAP IS POLKA-DOTTED...
THAT BOOK YOU DESIGNED BEFORE HAD POLKA DOTS, TOO...
THIS IS HOW YOU SEE "CUTE," RIGHT?

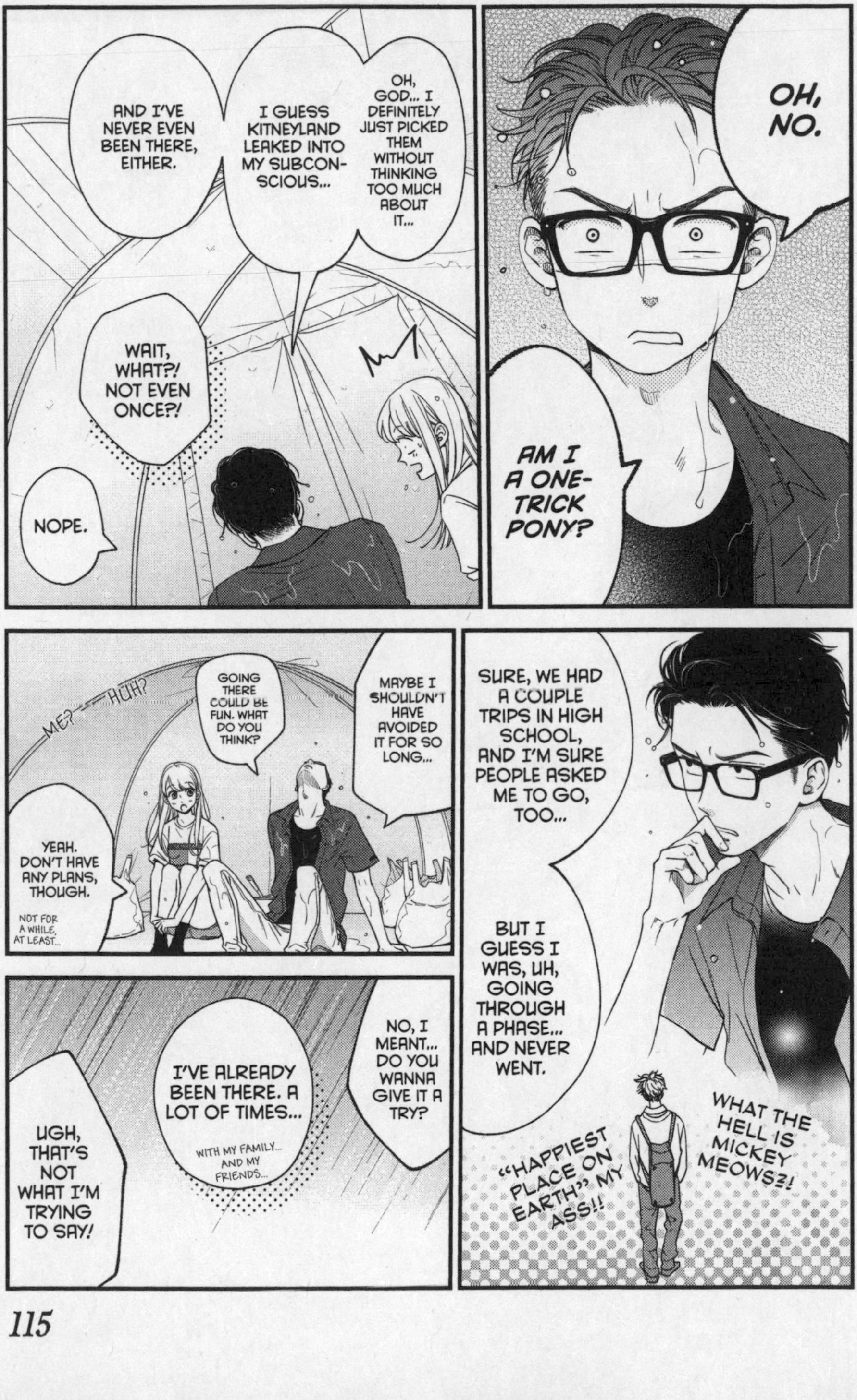
OH, NO.
AM I A ONE-TRICK PONY?
OH, GOD... I DEFINITELY JUST PICKED THEM WITHOUT THINKING TOO MUCH ABOUT IT...
I GUESS KITNEYLAND LEAKED INTO MY SUBCONSCIOUS...
AND I'VE NEVER EVEN BEEN THERE, EITHER.
WAIT, WHAT?! NOT EVEN ONCE?!
NOPE.
SURE, WE HAD A COUPLE TRIPS IN HIGH SCHOOL, AND I'M SURE PEOPLE ASKED ME TO GO, TOO...
BUT I GUESS I WAS, UH, GOING THROUGH A PHASE... AND NEVER WENT.
WHAT THE HELL IS MICKEY MEOWS?!
"HAPPIEST PLACE ON EARTH" MY ASS!!
MAYBE I SHOULDN'T HAVE AVOIDED IT FOR SO LONG...
GOING THERE COULD BE FUN. WHAT DO YOU THINK?
HUH?
ME?
YEAH. DON'T HAVE ANY PLANS, THOUGH.
NOT FOR A WHILE, AT LEAST...
NO, I MEANT... DO YOU WANNA GIVE IT A TRY?
I'VE ALREADY BEEN THERE. A LOT OF TIMES...
WITH MY FAMILY... AND MY FRIENDS...
UGH, THAT'S NOT WHAT I'M TRYING TO SAY!

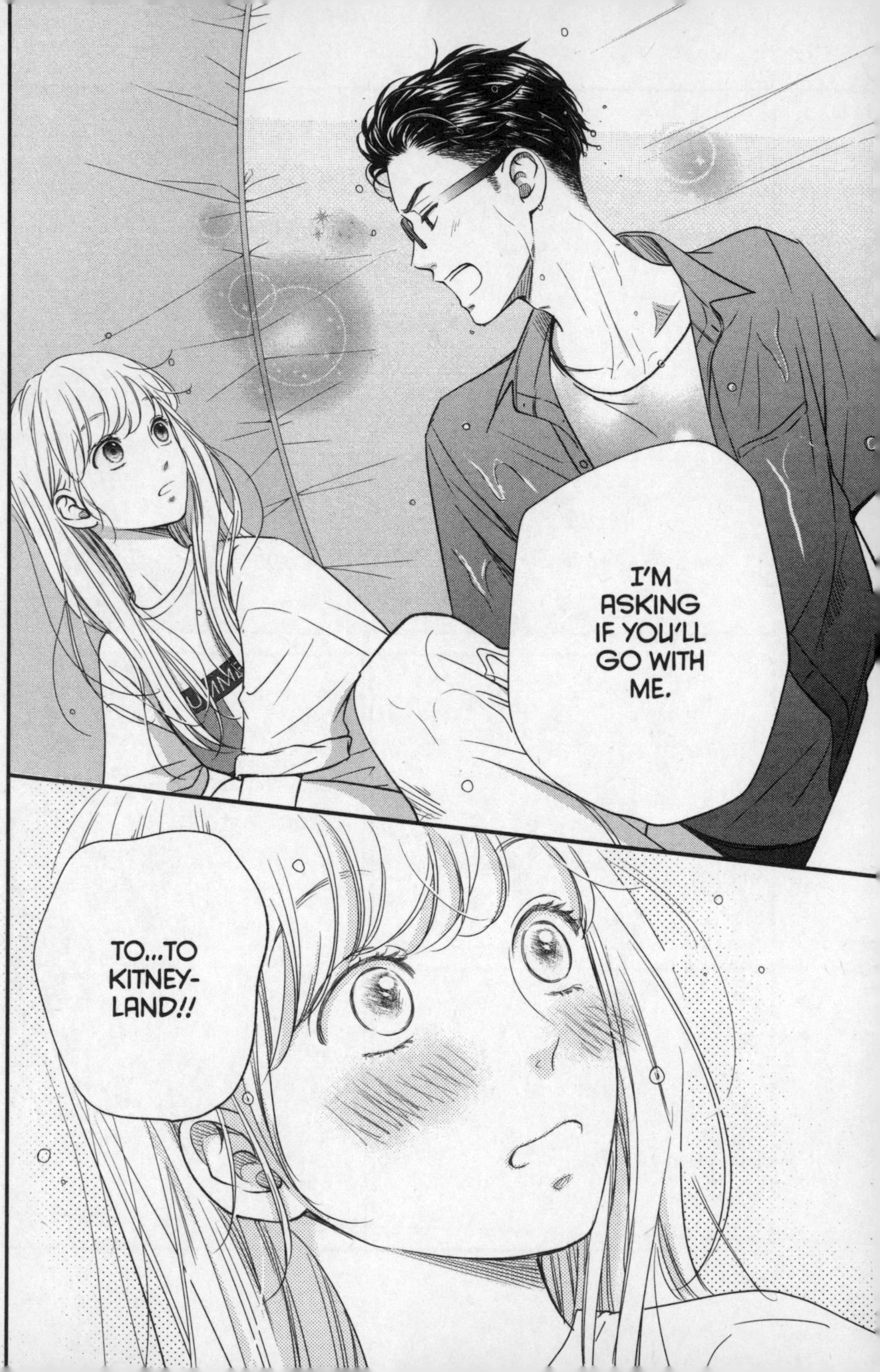
I'M ASKING IF YOU'LL GO WITH ME.
TO...TO KITNEY-LAND!!

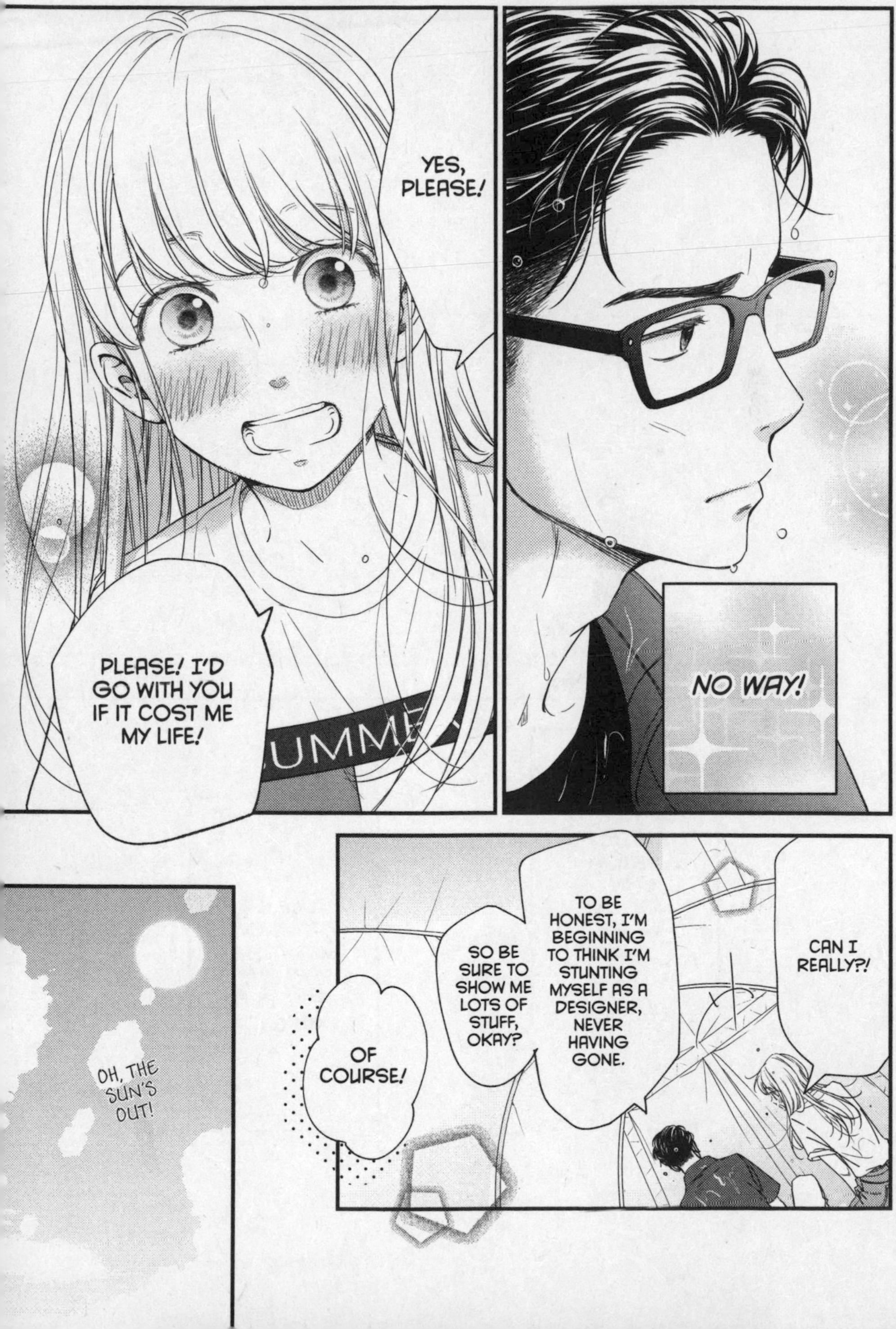
NO WAY!
YES, PLEASE!
PLEASE! I'D GO WITH YOU IF IT COST ME MY LIFE!
CAN I REALLY?!
TO BE HONEST, I'M BEGINNING TO THINK I'M STUNTING MYSELF AS A DESIGNER, NEVER HAVING GONE.
SO BE SURE TO SHOW ME LOTS OF STUFF, OKAY?
OF COURSE!
OH, THE SUN'S OUT!

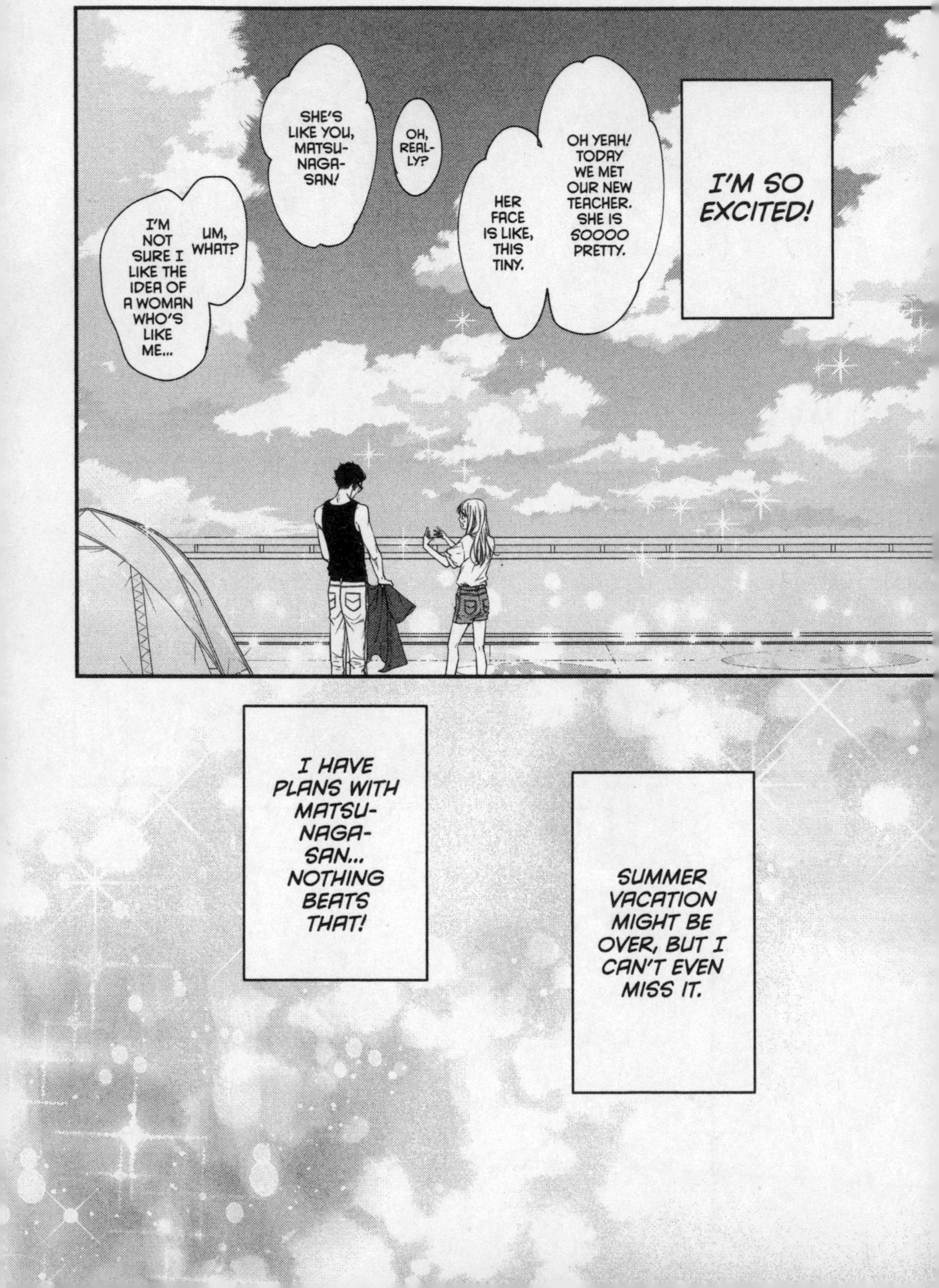
I'M SO EXCITED!
OH YEAH! TODAY WE MET OUR NEW TEACHER. SHE IS SOOOO PRETTY.
HER FACE IS LIKE, THIS TINY.
OH, REALLY?
SHE'S LIKE YOU, MATSUNAGA-SAN!
UM, WHAT?
I'M NOT SURE I LIKE THE IDEA OF A WOMAN WHO'S LIKE ME...
SUMMER VACATION MIGHT BE OVER, BUT I CAN'T EVEN MISS IT.
I HAVE PLANS WITH MATSUNAGA-SAN... NOTHING BEATS THAT!

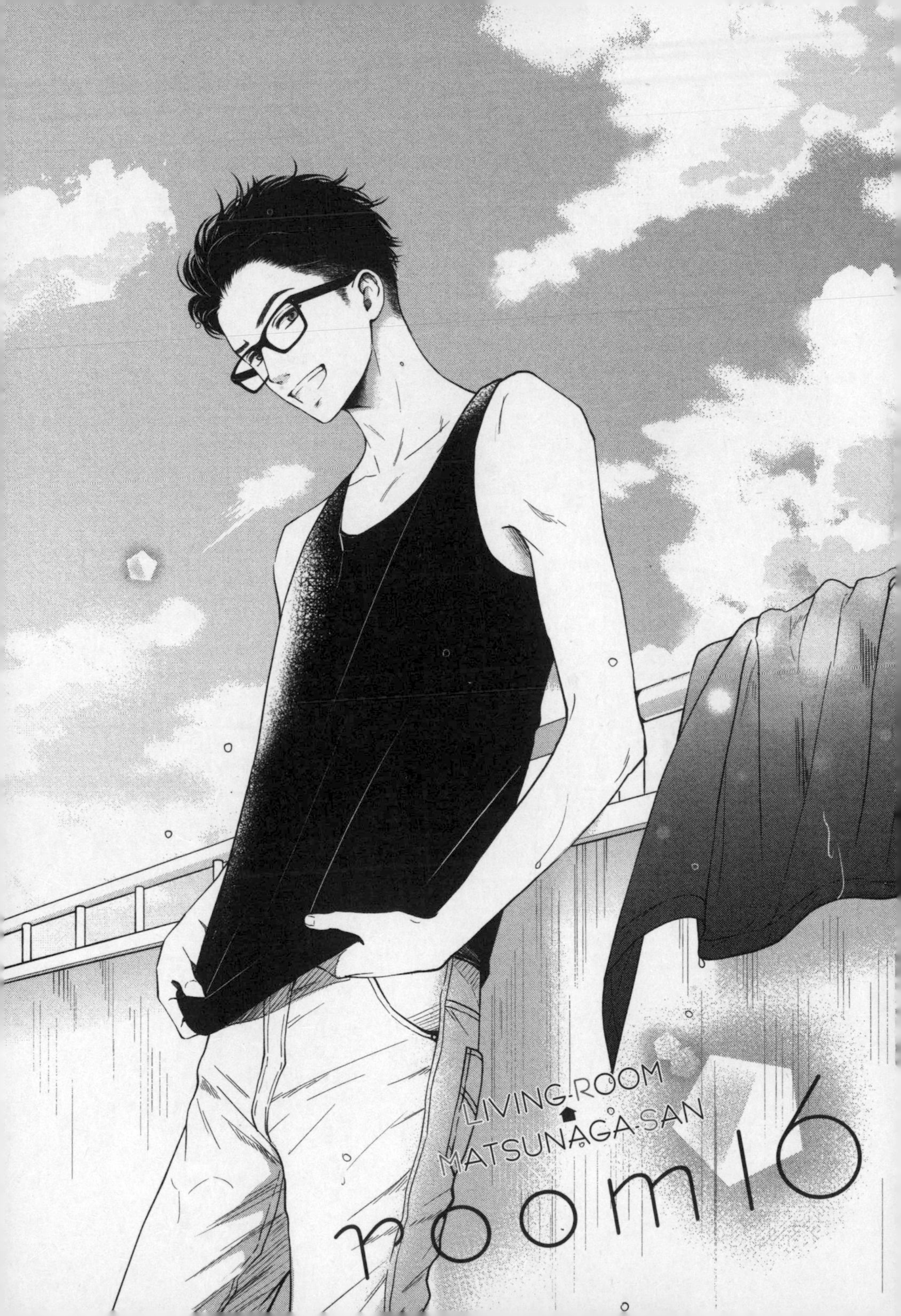
LIVING-ROOM
MATSUNAGA-SAN
room16

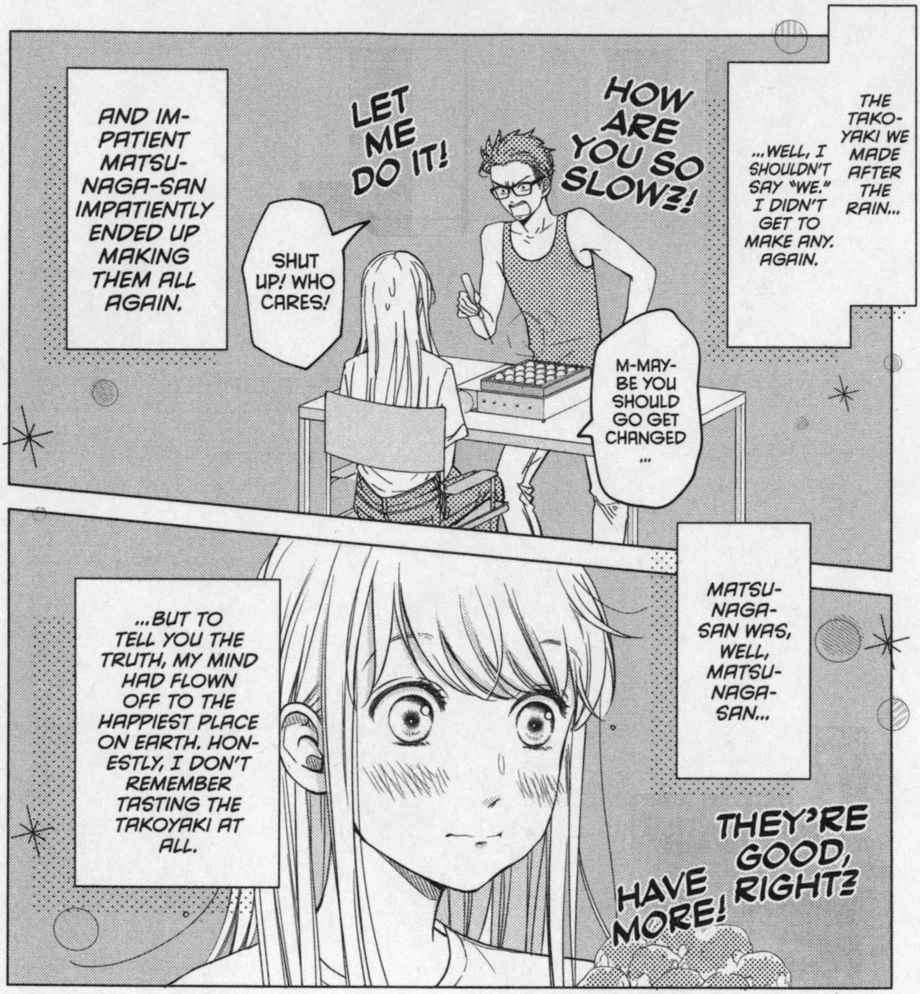
THE TAKO-YAKI WE MADE AFTER THE RAIN...
...WELL, I SHOULDN'T SAY "WE." I DIDN'T GET TO MAKE ANY. AGAIN.
HOW ARE YOU SO SLOW?!
LET ME DO IT!
M-MAY-BE YOU SHOULD GO GET CHANGED ...
SHUT UP! WHO CARES!
AND IM-PATIENT MATSU-NAGA-SAN IMPATIENTLY ENDED UP MAKING THEM ALL AGAIN.
MATSU-NAGA-SAN WAS, WELL, MATSU-NAGA-SAN...
THEY'RE GOOD, RIGHT?
HAVE MORE!
...BUT TO TELL YOU THE TRUTH, MY MIND HAD FLOWN OFF TO THE HAPPIEST PLACE ON EARTH. HON-ESTLY, I DON'T REMEMBER TASTING THE TAKOYAKI AT ALL.

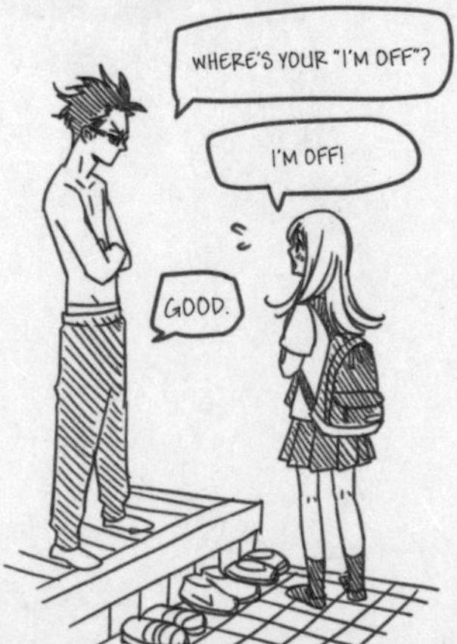
WHERE'S YOUR "I'M OFF"?
I'M OFF!
GOOD.

ASAKO / KENTARO: HA HA HA...

ASAKO: IT'S LIKE THIS EVERY DAY, ISN'T IT?

KENTARO: YOU'RE SUPPOSED TO REPLY "TAKE CARE."

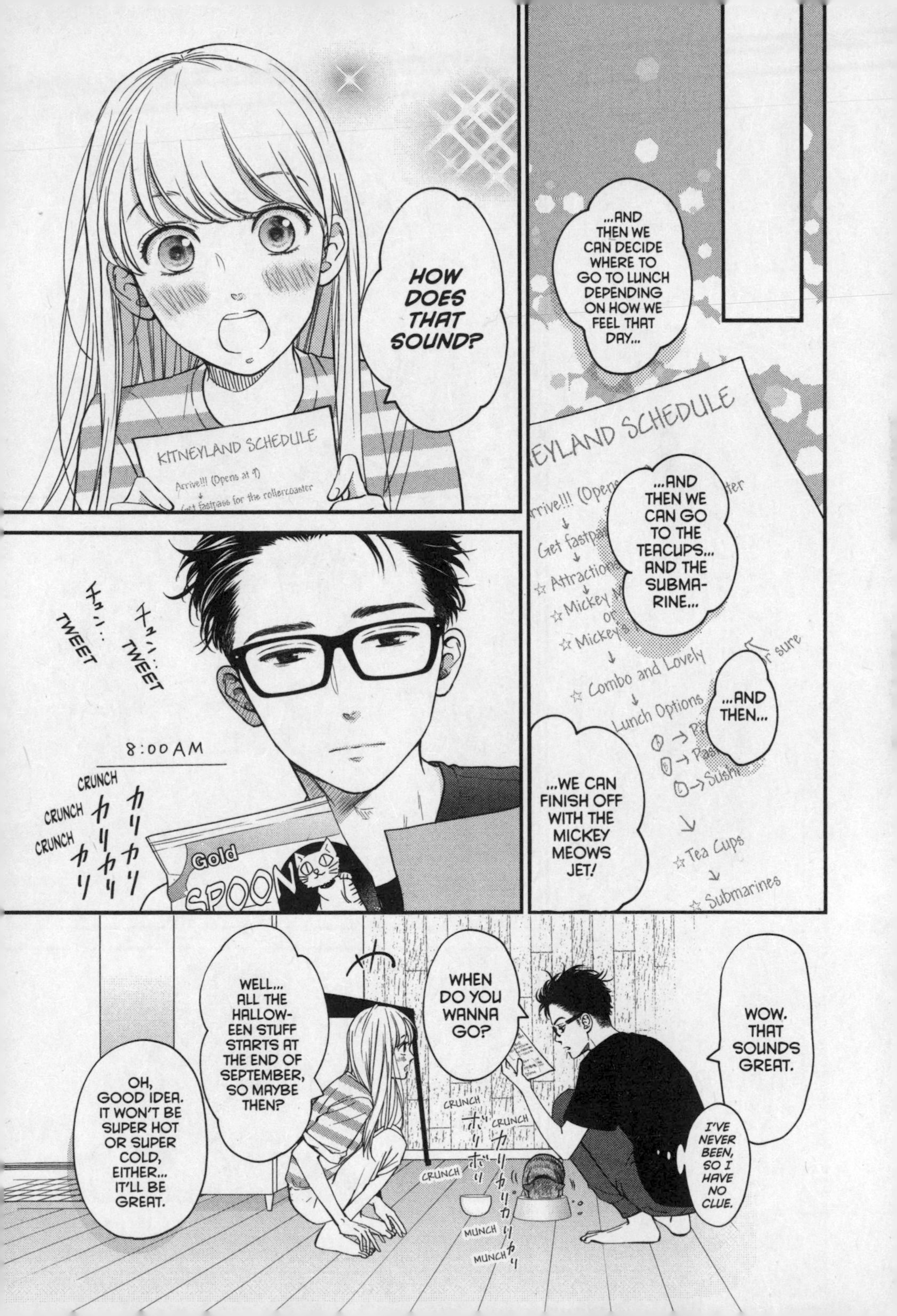
...AND THEN WE CAN DECIDE WHERE TO GO TO LUNCH DEPENDING ON HOW WE FEEL THAT DAY...
EYLAND SCHEDULE
...AND THEN WE CAN GO TO THE TEACUPS... AND THE SUBMARINE...
Combo and Lovely
Lunch Options
Sushi
...AND THEN...
...WE CAN FINISH OFF WITH THE MICKEY MEOWS JET!
Tea Cups
Submarines
HOW DOES THAT SOUND?
KITNEYLAND SCHEDULE
Arrive!!! (Opens at 9)
Get fastpass for the rollercoaster
チュン… TWEET
チュン… TWEET
8:00 AM
カリカリ CRUNCH
カリカリ CRUNCH
カリ CRUNCH
Gold SPOON
WOW. THAT SOUNDS GREAT.
I'VE NEVER BEEN, SO I HAVE NO CLUE.
WHEN DO YOU WANNA GO?
CRUNCH
CRUNCH
MUNCH
MUNCH
WELL... ALL THE HALLOWEEN STUFF STARTS AT THE END OF SEPTEMBER, SO MAYBE THEN?
OH, GOOD IDEA. IT WON'T BE SUPER HOT OR SUPER COLD, EITHER... IT'LL BE GREAT.

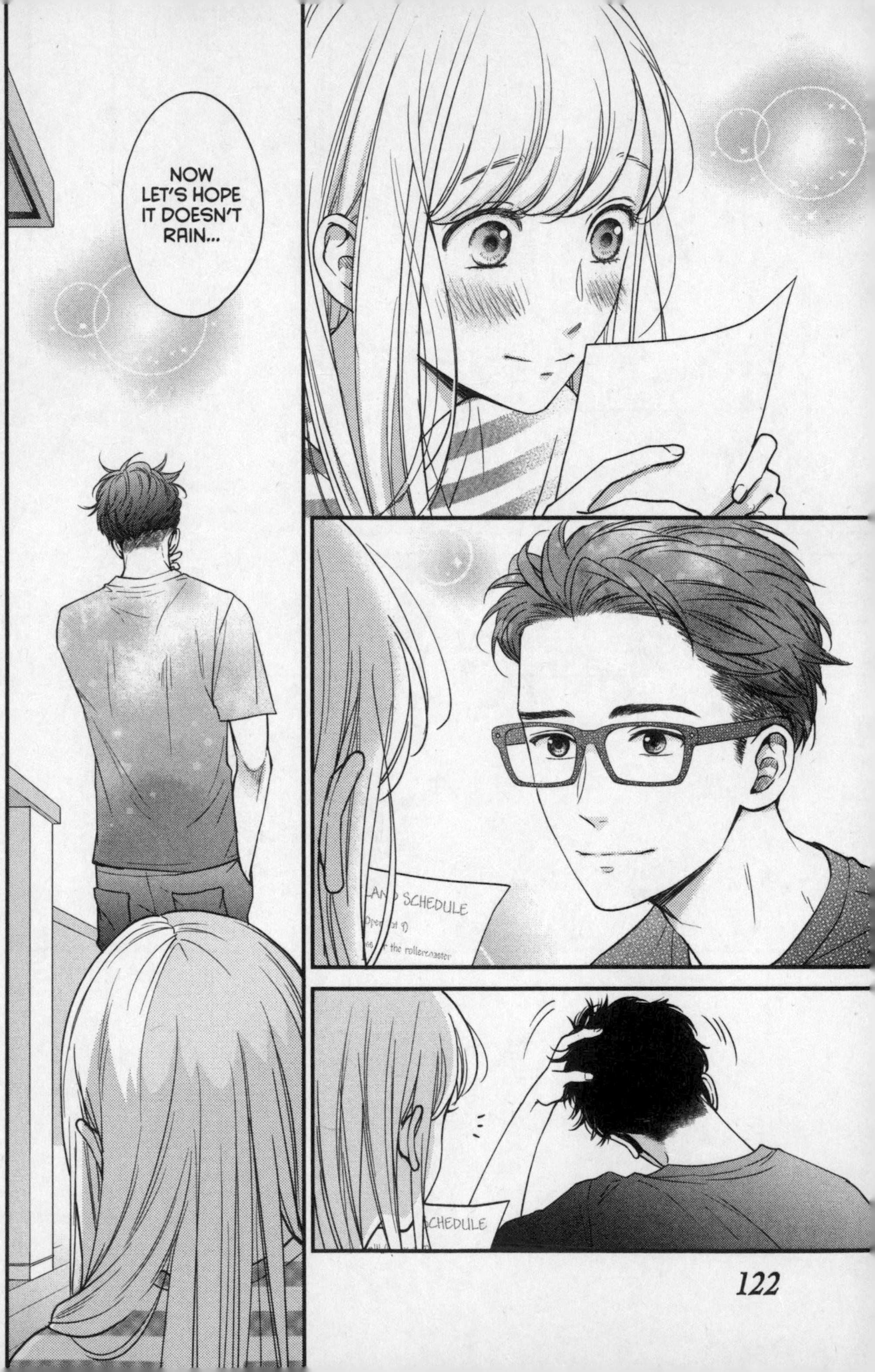
SCHEDULE
the rollercoaster
NOW LET'S HOPE IT DOESN'T RAIN...

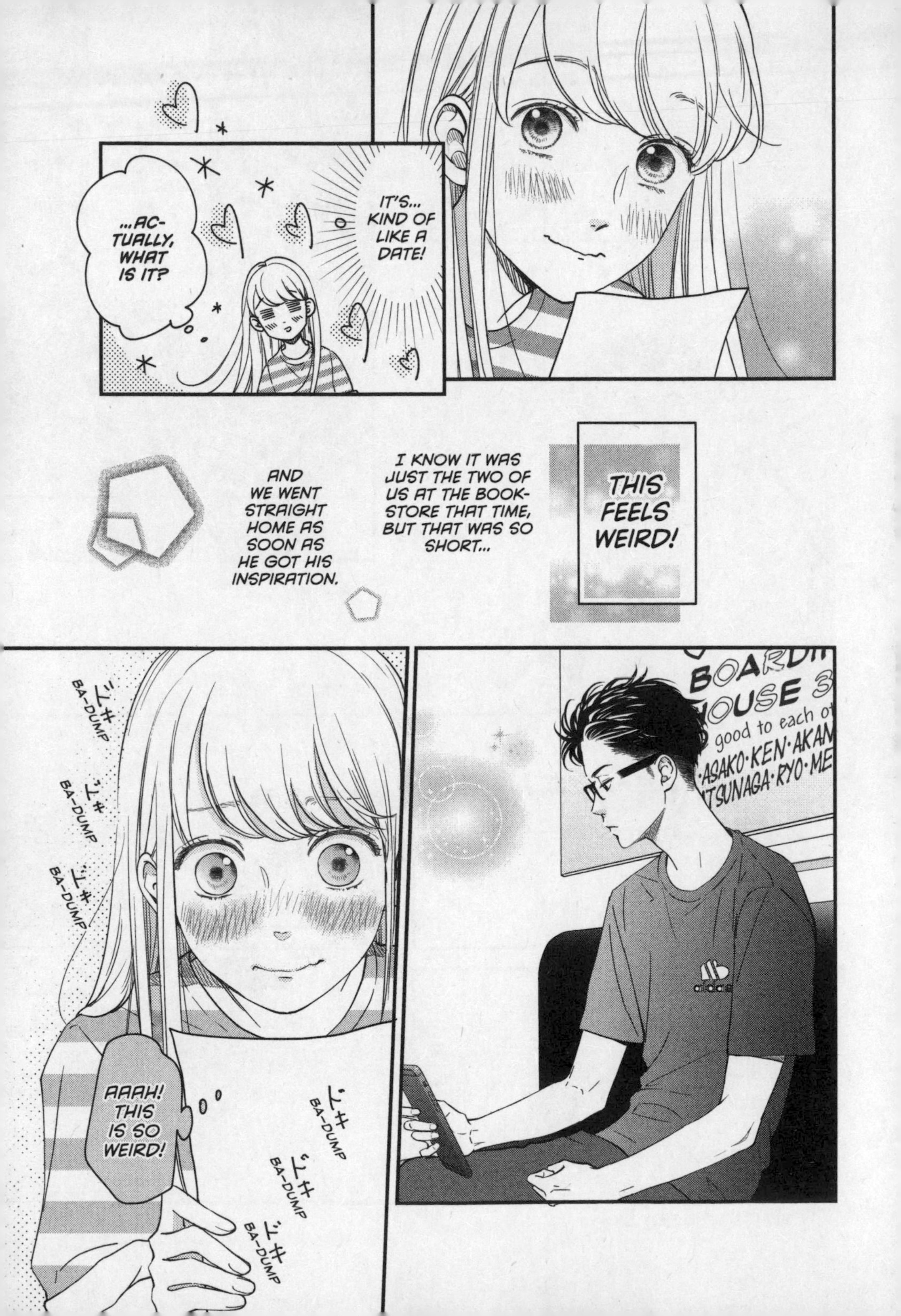
IT'S... KIND OF LIKE A DATE!
...ACTUALLY, WHAT IS IT?
THIS FEELS WEIRD!
I KNOW IT WAS JUST THE TWO OF US AT THE BOOKSTORE THAT TIME, BUT THAT WAS SO SHORT...
AND WE WENT STRAIGHT HOME AS SOON AS HE GOT HIS INSPIRATION.
BOARDI
HOUSE 3
good to each ot
ASAKO·KEN·AKAN
TSUNAGA·RYO·ME
ドキ BA-DUMP
ドキ BA-DUMP
ドキ BA-DUMP
AAAH! THIS IS SO WEIRD!
ドキ BA-DUMP
ドキ BA-DUMP
ドキ BA-DUMP

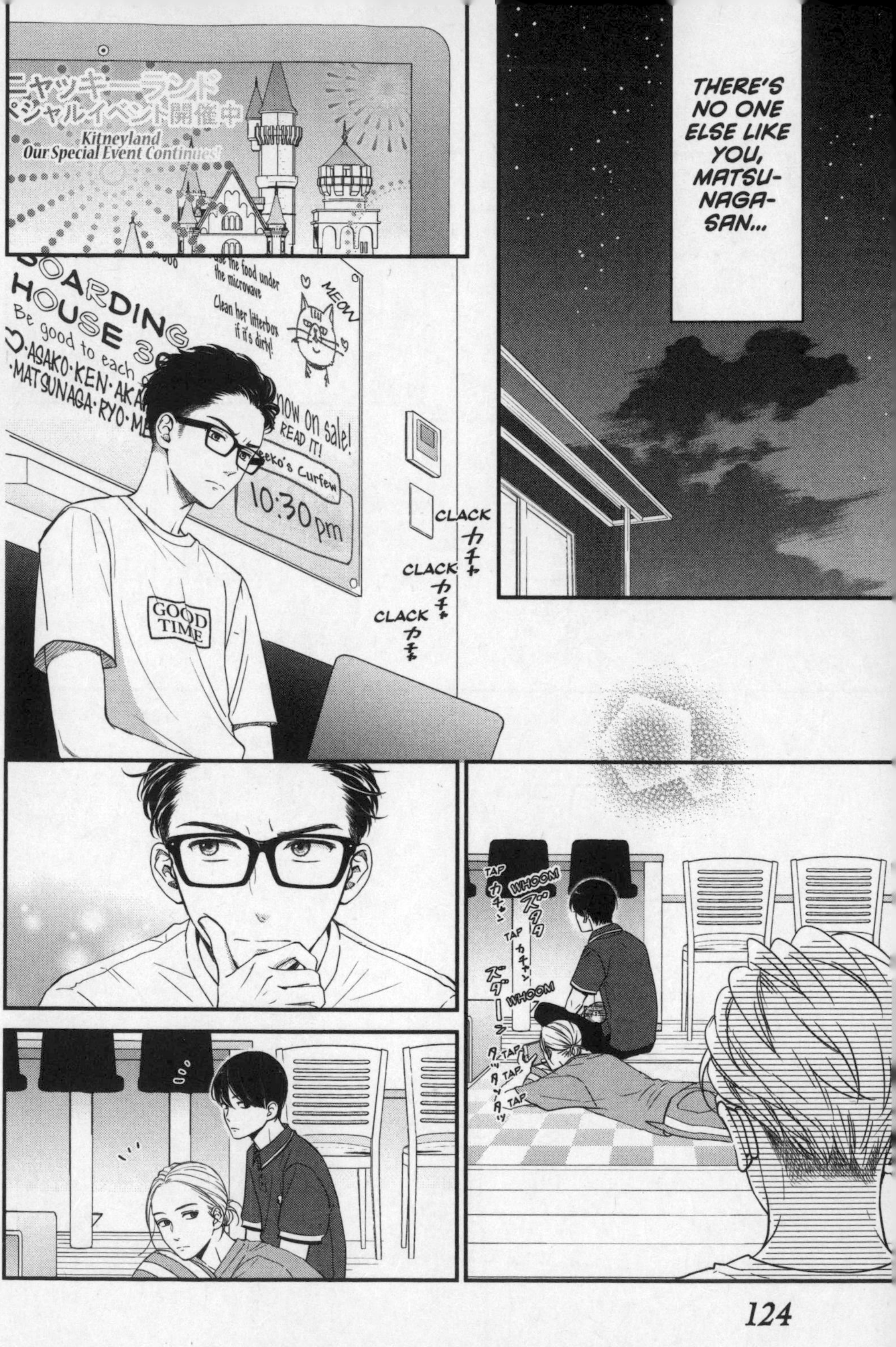

THERE'S NO ONE ELSE LIKE YOU, MATSUNAGA-SAN...
Kitneyland
Our Special Event Continues!
BOARDING HOUSE 3
Be good to each
ASAKO·KEN·AKA
MATSUNAGA·RYO·ME
the food under the microwave
Clean her litterbox if it's dirty!
MEOW
now on sale!
READ IT!
Curfew
10:30 pm
GOOD TIME
CLACK
CLACK
CLACK
TAP
WHOOM
TAP
WHOOM
TAP
TAP
TAP

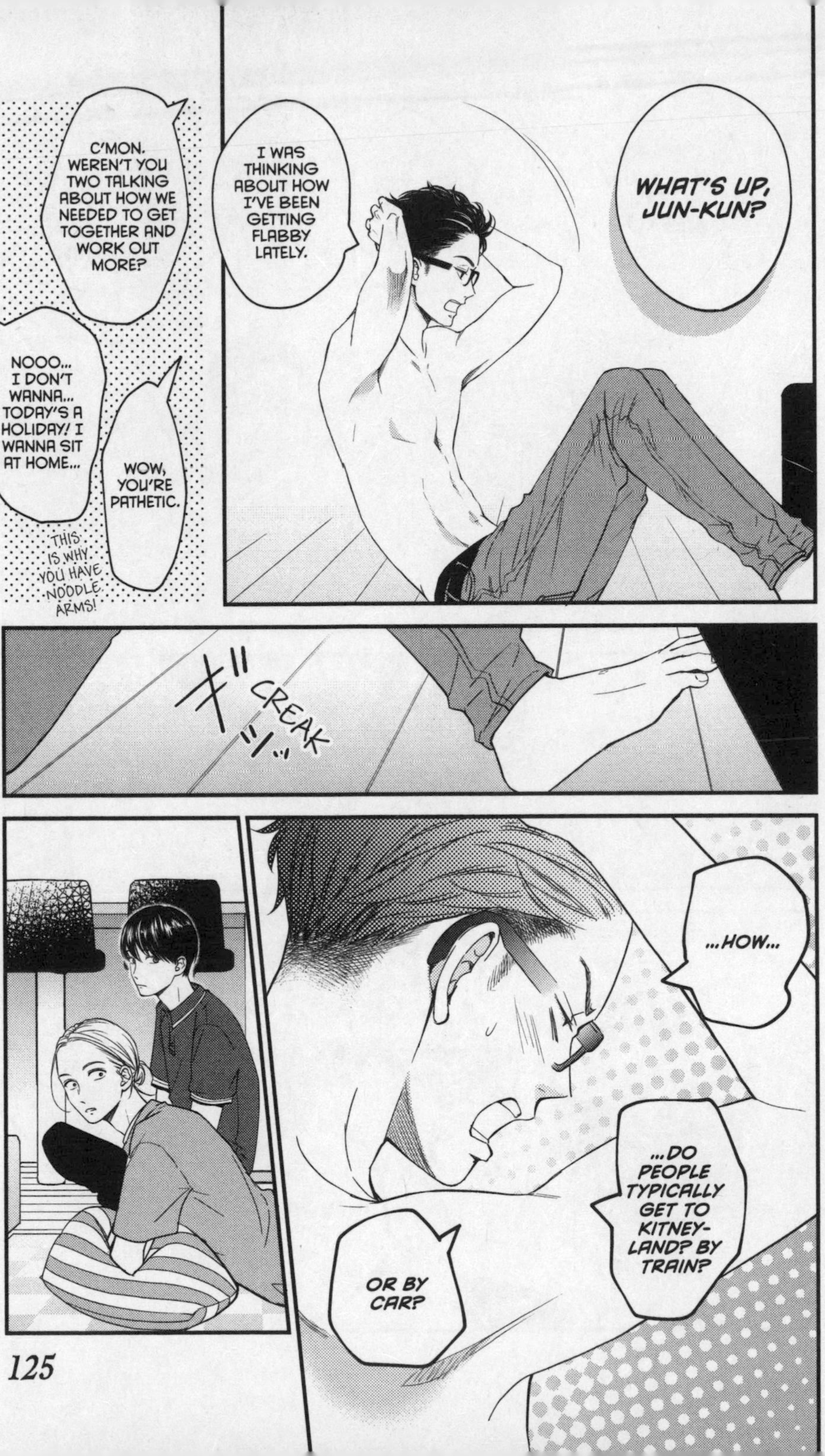
WHAT'S UP, JUN-KUN?
I WAS THINKING ABOUT HOW I'VE BEEN GETTING FLABBY LATELY.
C'MON. WEREN'T YOU TWO TALKING ABOUT HOW WE NEEDED TO GET TOGETHER AND WORK OUT MORE?
NOOO... I DON'T WANNA... TODAY'S A HOLIDAY! I WANNA SIT AT HOME...
WOW, YOU'RE PATHETIC.
THIS IS WHY YOU HAVE NOODLE ARMS!
ギッ
CREAK
...HOW...
...DO PEOPLE TYPICALLY GET TO KITNEY-LAND? BY TRAIN?
OR BY CAR?

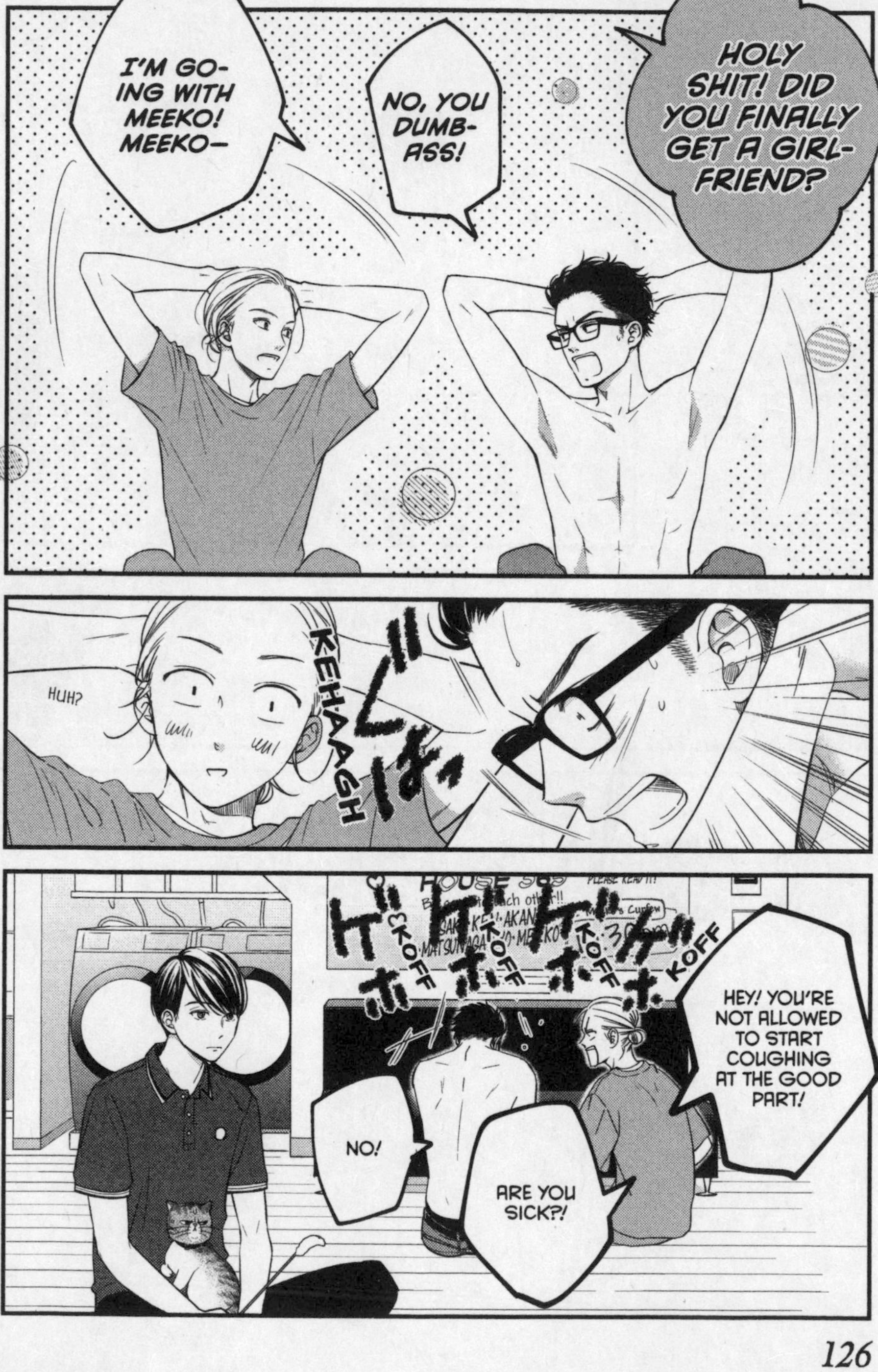
HOLY SHIT! DID YOU FINALLY GET A GIRL-FRIEND?
NO, YOU DUMB-ASS!
I'M GO-ING WITH MEEKO! MEEKO—
KEHAAGH
HUH?
KOFF KOFF KOFF KOFF
HEY! YOU'RE NOT ALLOWED TO START COUGHING AT THE GOOD PART!
NO!
ARE YOU SICK?!

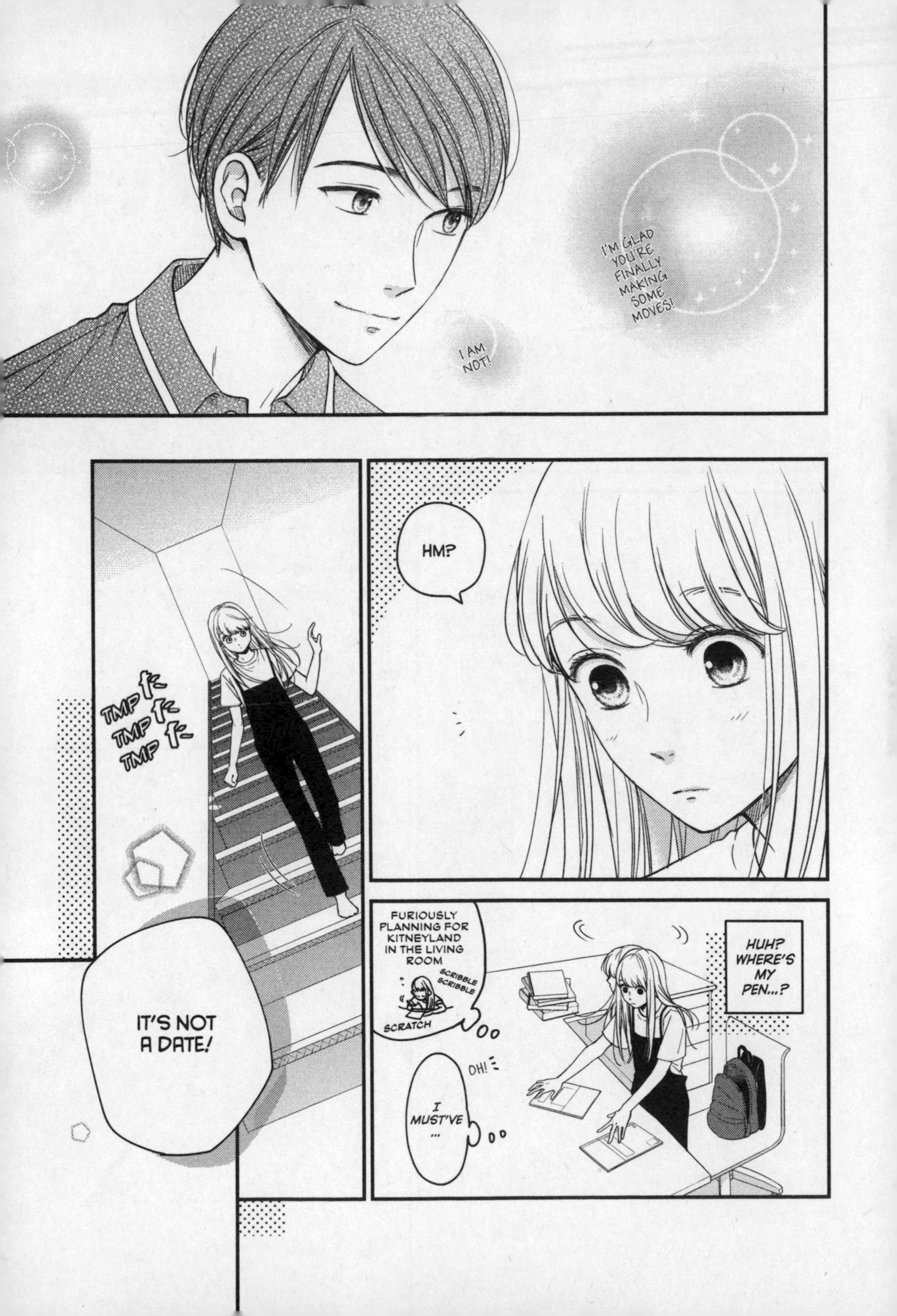
I'M GLAD YOU'RE FINALLY MAKING SOME MOVES!
I AM NOT!
HM?
HUH? WHERE'S MY PEN...?
FURIOUSLY PLANNING FOR KITNEYLAND IN THE LIVING ROOM
SCRIBBLE SCRIBBLE
SCRATCH
OH!
I MUST'VE ...
TMP TMP TMP
IT'S NOT A DATE!

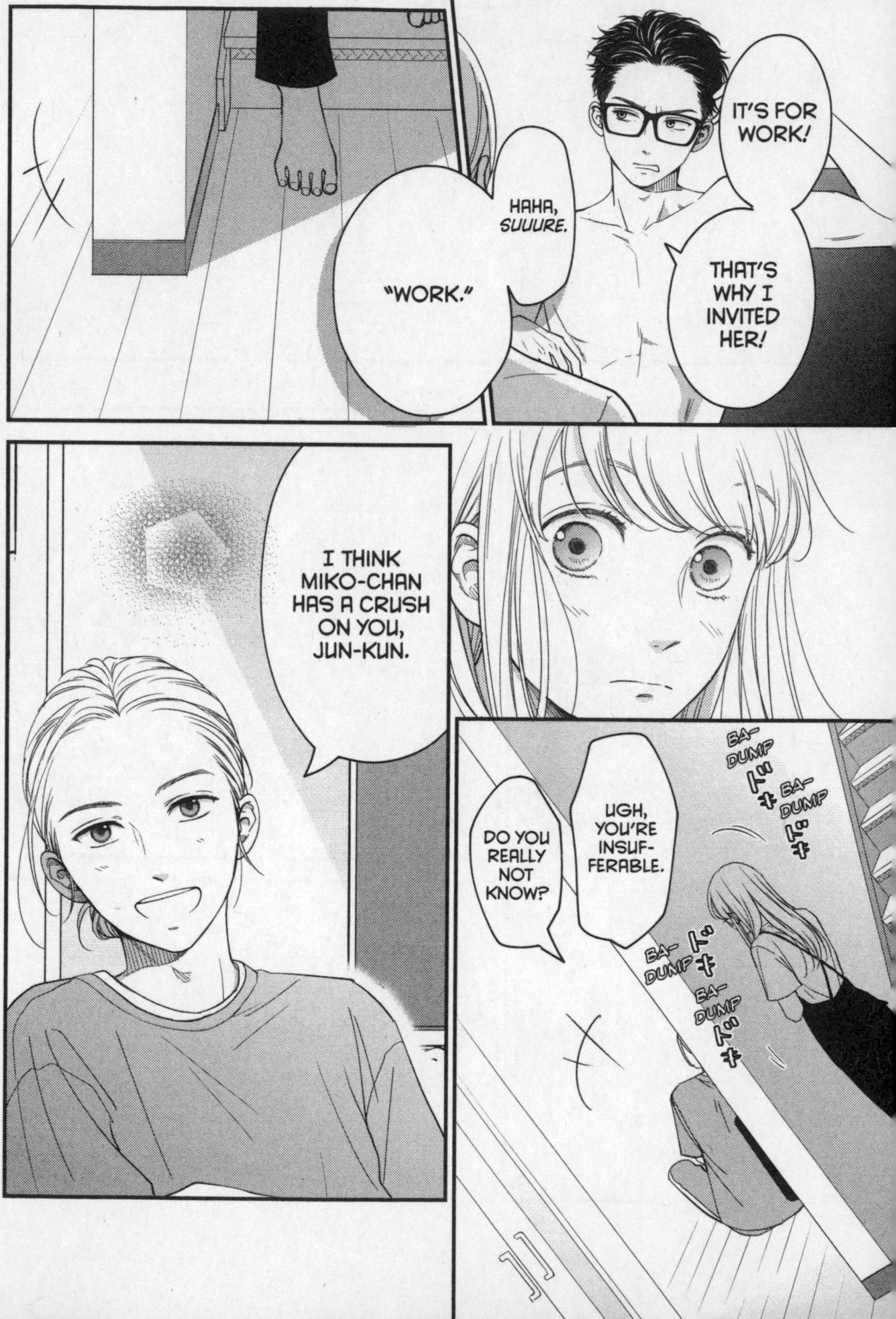
IT'S FOR WORK!
THAT'S WHY I INVITED HER!
HAHA, SUUURE.
"WORK."
BA-DUMP ドキ
BA-DUMP ドキ
UGH, YOU'RE INSUF-FERABLE.
DO YOU REALLY NOT KNOW?
BA-DUMP ドキ
BA-DUMP ドキ
I THINK MIKO-CHAN HAS A CRUSH ON YOU, JUN-KUN.

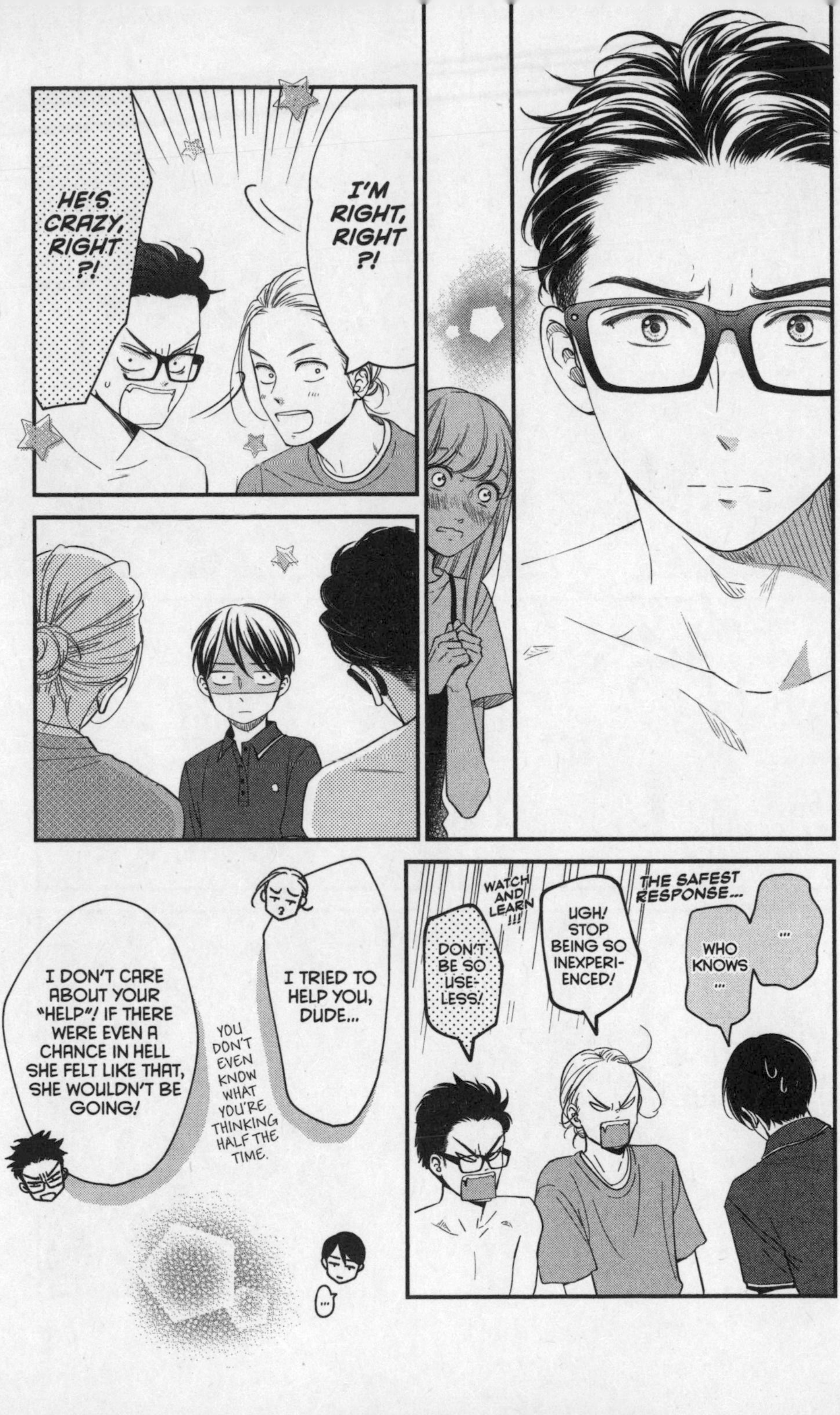
I'M RIGHT, RIGHT?!
HE'S CRAZY, RIGHT?!
THE SAFEST RESPONSE...
...
WHO KNOWS ...
UGH! STOP BEING SO INEXPERIENCED!
WATCH AND LEARN!!!
DON'T BE SO USELESS!
I TRIED TO HELP YOU, DUDE...
YOU DON'T EVEN KNOW WHAT YOU'RE THINKING HALF THE TIME.
I DON'T CARE ABOUT YOUR "HELP"! IF THERE WERE EVEN A CHANCE IN HELL SHE FELT LIKE THAT, SHE WOULDN'T BE GOING!
...

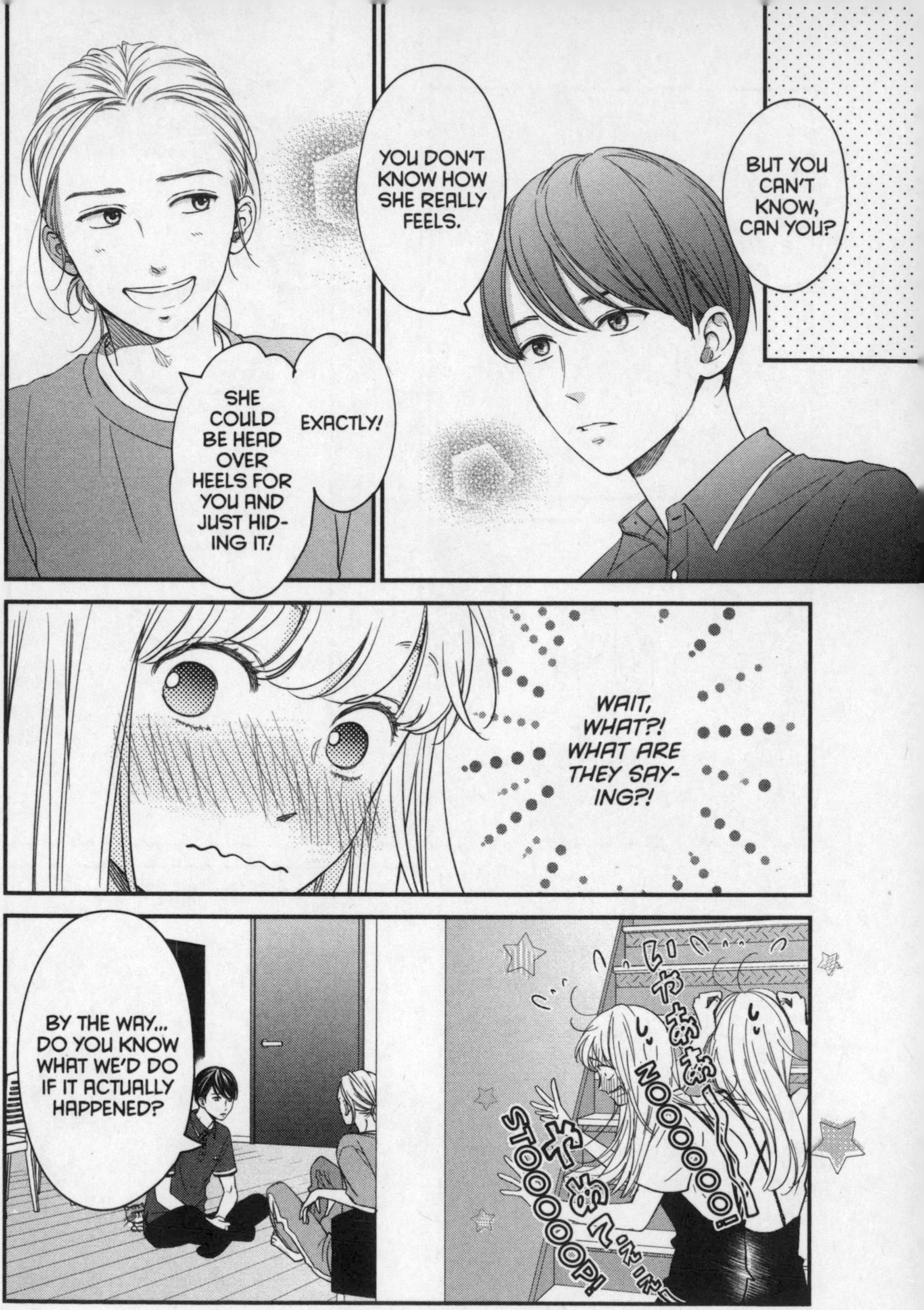
BUT YOU CAN'T KNOW, CAN YOU?
YOU DON'T KNOW HOW SHE REALLY FEELS.
EXACTLY!
SHE COULD BE HEAD OVER HEELS FOR YOU AND JUST HIDING IT!
WAIT, WHAT?! WHAT ARE THEY SAYING?!
NOOOOOO!
STOOOOOP!
BY THE WAY... DO YOU KNOW WHAT WE'D DO IF IT ACTUALLY HAPPENED?

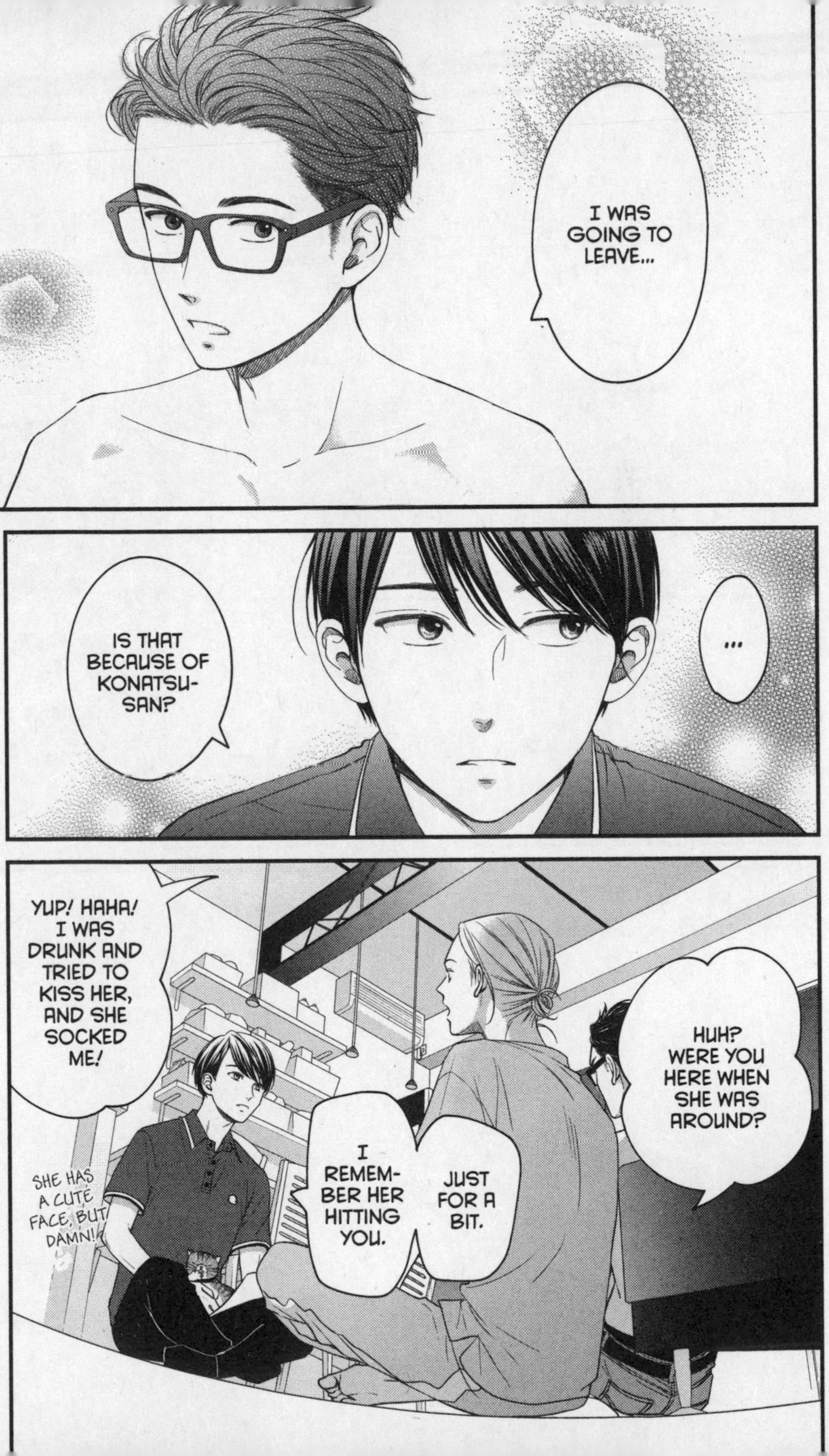
I WAS GOING TO LEAVE...
...
IS THAT BECAUSE OF KONATSU-SAN?
YUP! HAHA! I WAS DRUNK AND TRIED TO KISS HER, AND SHE SOCKED ME!
HUH? WERE YOU HERE WHEN SHE WAS AROUND?
JUST FOR A BIT.
I REMEMBER HER HITTING YOU.
SHE HAS A CUTE FACE, BUT DAMN!

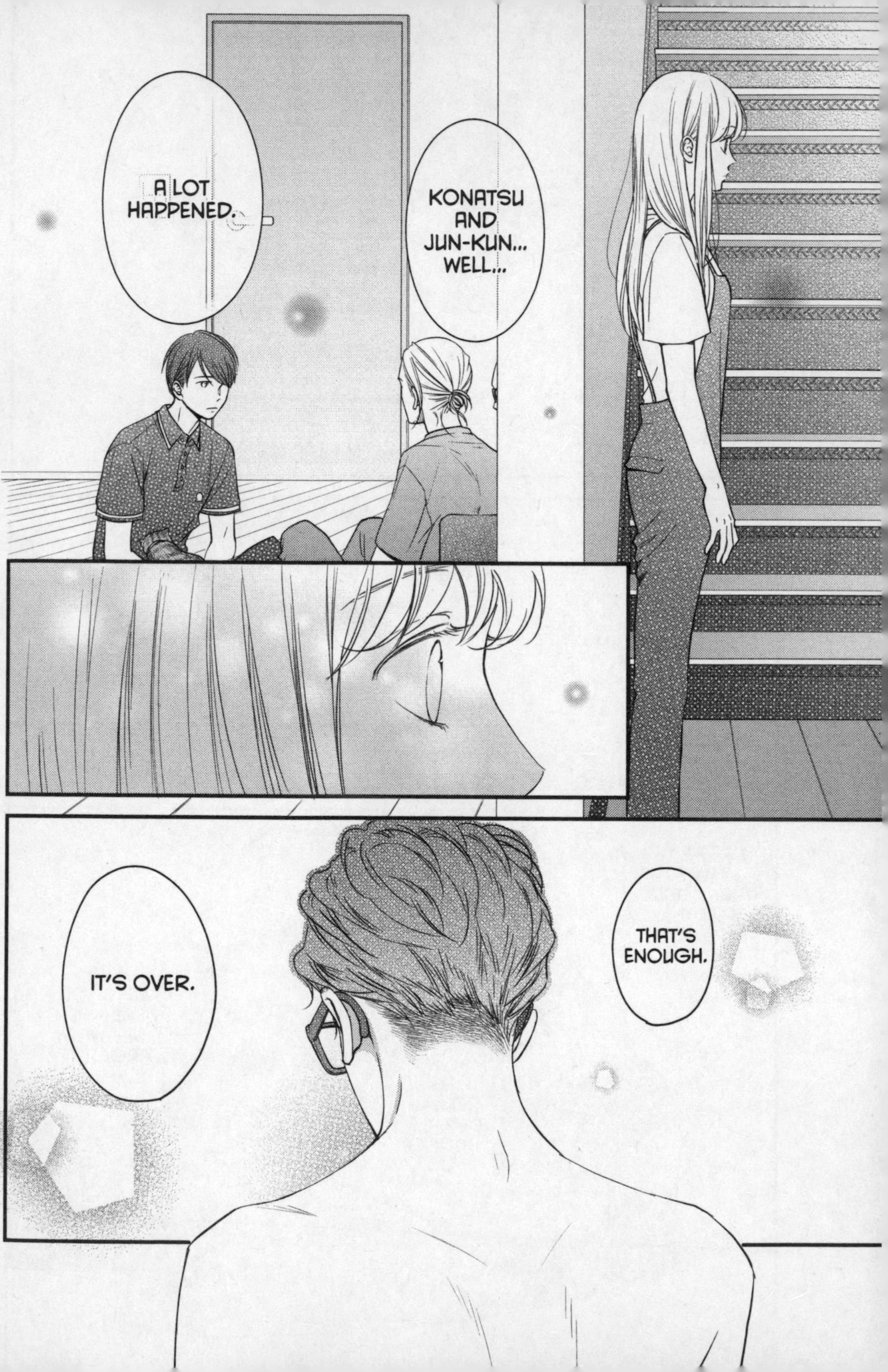
KONATSU AND JUN-KUN... WELL...
A LOT HAPPENED.
THAT'S ENOUGH.
IT'S OVER.

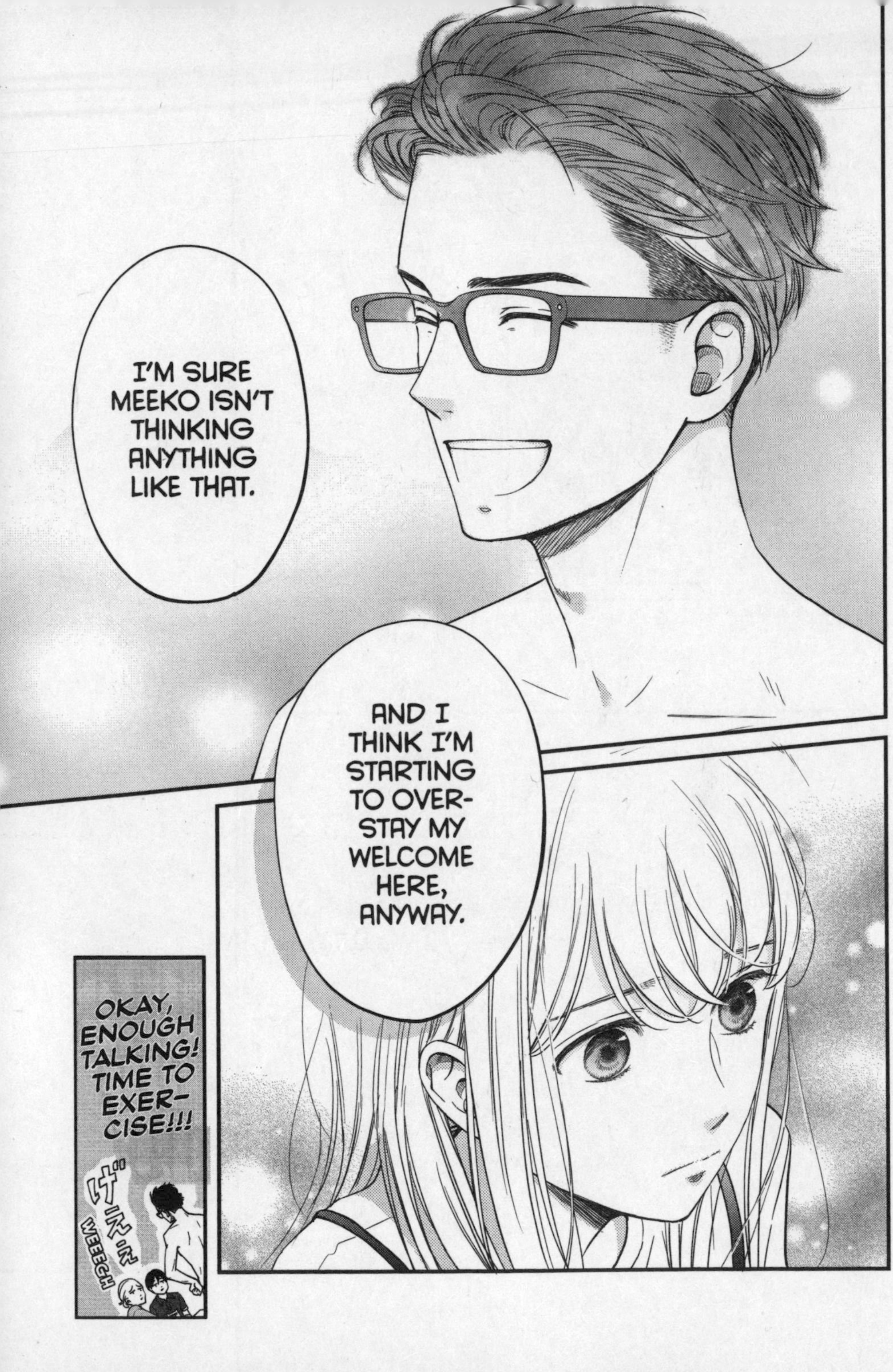
I'M SURE MEEKO ISN'T THINKING ANYTHING LIKE THAT.
AND I THINK I'M STARTING TO OVER-STAY MY WELCOME HERE, ANYWAY.
OKAY, ENOUGH TALKING! TIME TO EXER-CISE!!!
げぇぇ
WEEECH

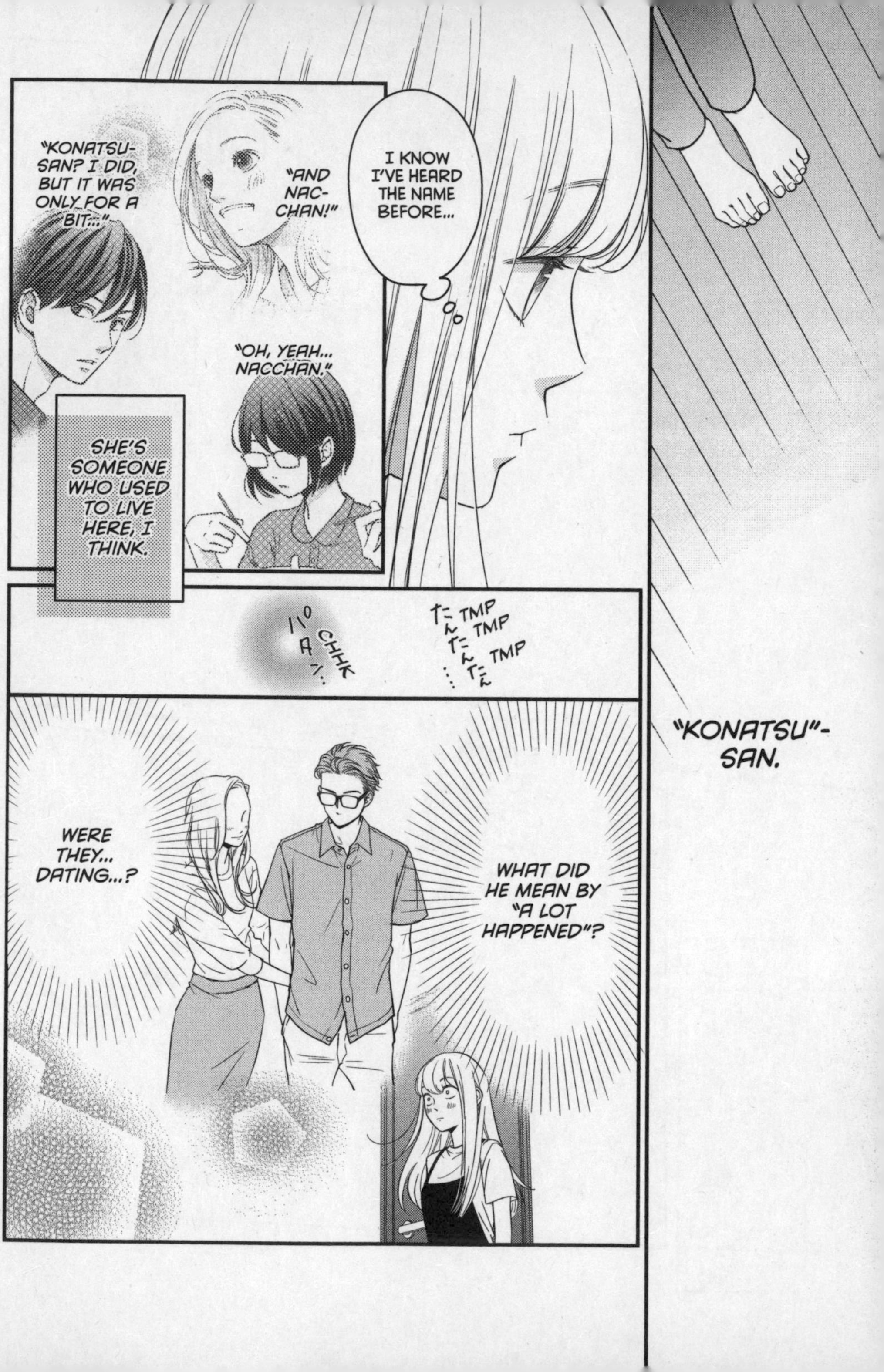
"KONATSU"-SAN.
I KNOW I'VE HEARD THE NAME BEFORE...
"AND NAC-CHAN!"
"KONATSU-SAN? I DID, BUT IT WAS ONLY FOR A BIT..."
"OH, YEAH... NACCHAN."
SHE'S SOMEONE WHO USED TO LIVE HERE, I THINK.
TMP TMP TMP
CHIK
WHAT DID HE MEAN BY "A LOT HAPPENED"?
WERE THEY... DATING...?

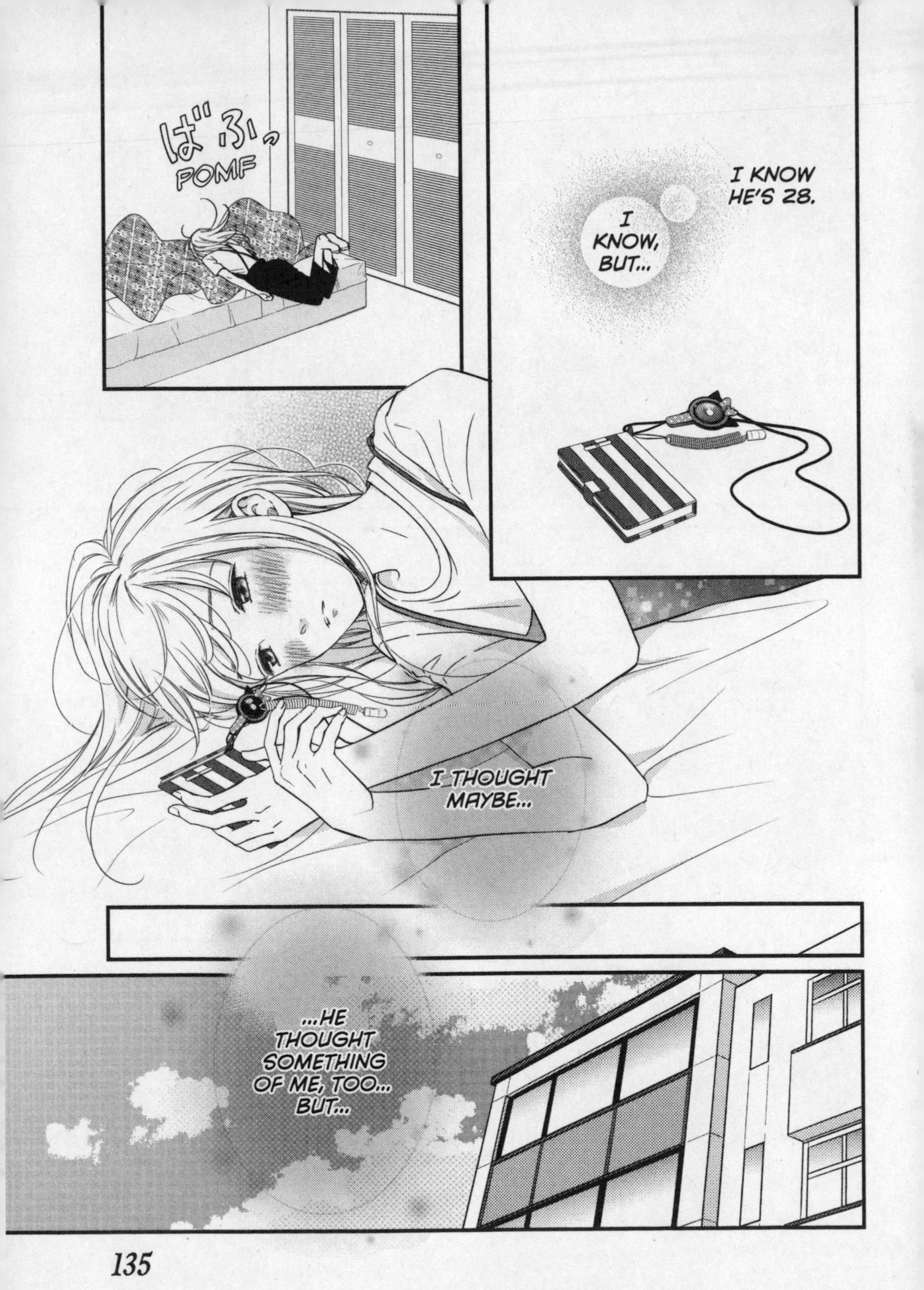
I KNOW HE'S 28.
I KNOW, BUT...
ばふっ
POMF
I THOUGHT MAYBE...
...HE THOUGHT SOMETHING OF ME, TOO... BUT...

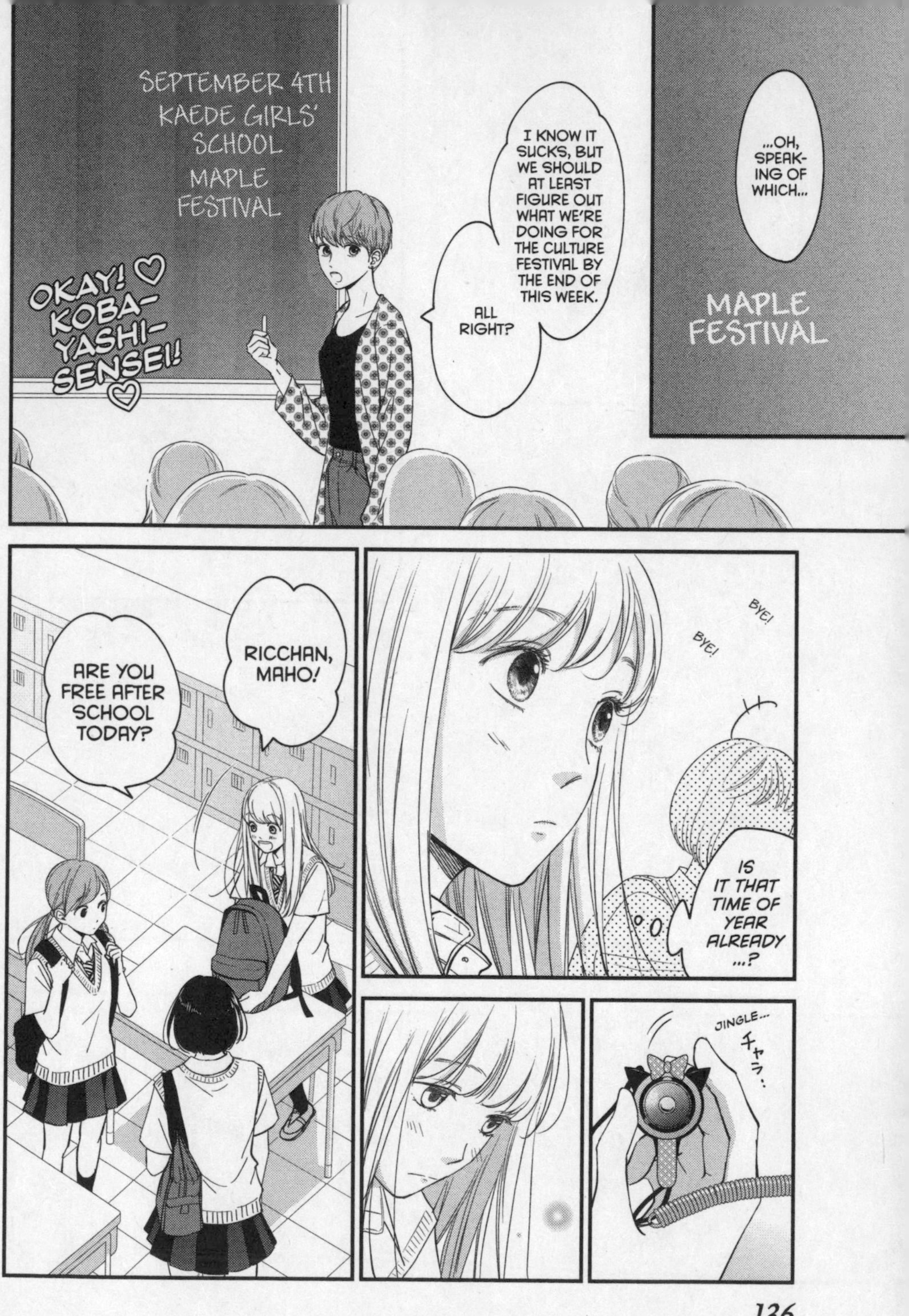
...OH, SPEAK-ING OF WHICH...
MAPLE FESTIVAL
SEPTEMBER 4TH KAEDE GIRLS' SCHOOL MAPLE FESTIVAL
I KNOW IT SUCKS, BUT WE SHOULD AT LEAST FIGURE OUT WHAT WE'RE DOING FOR THE CULTURE FESTIVAL BY THE END OF THIS WEEK.
ALL RIGHT?
OKAY! KOBA-YASHI-SENSEI!
BYE!
BYE!
IS IT THAT TIME OF YEAR ALREADY ...?
JINGLE...
チャラ・・
RICCHAN, MAHO!
ARE YOU FREE AFTER SCHOOL TODAY?

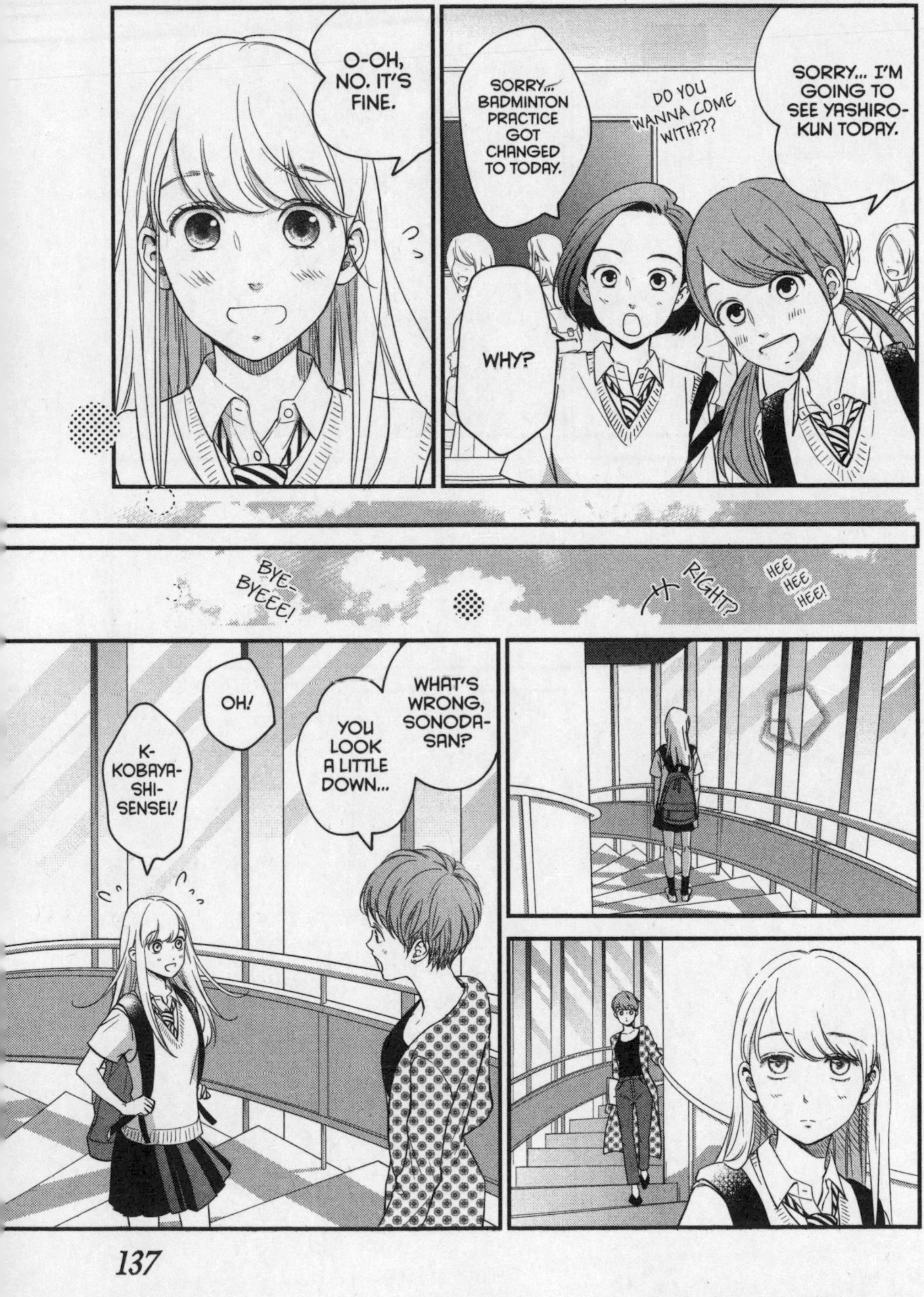
SORRY... I'M GOING TO SEE YASHIRO-KUN TODAY.
DO YOU WANNA COME WITH???
SORRY... BADMINTON PRACTICE GOT CHANGED TO TODAY.
WHY?
O-OH, NO. IT'S FINE.
HEE HEE HEE!
RIGHT?
BYE-BYEEE!
WHAT'S WRONG, SONODA-SAN?
YOU LOOK A LITTLE DOWN...
OH!
K-KOBAYASHI-SENSEI!

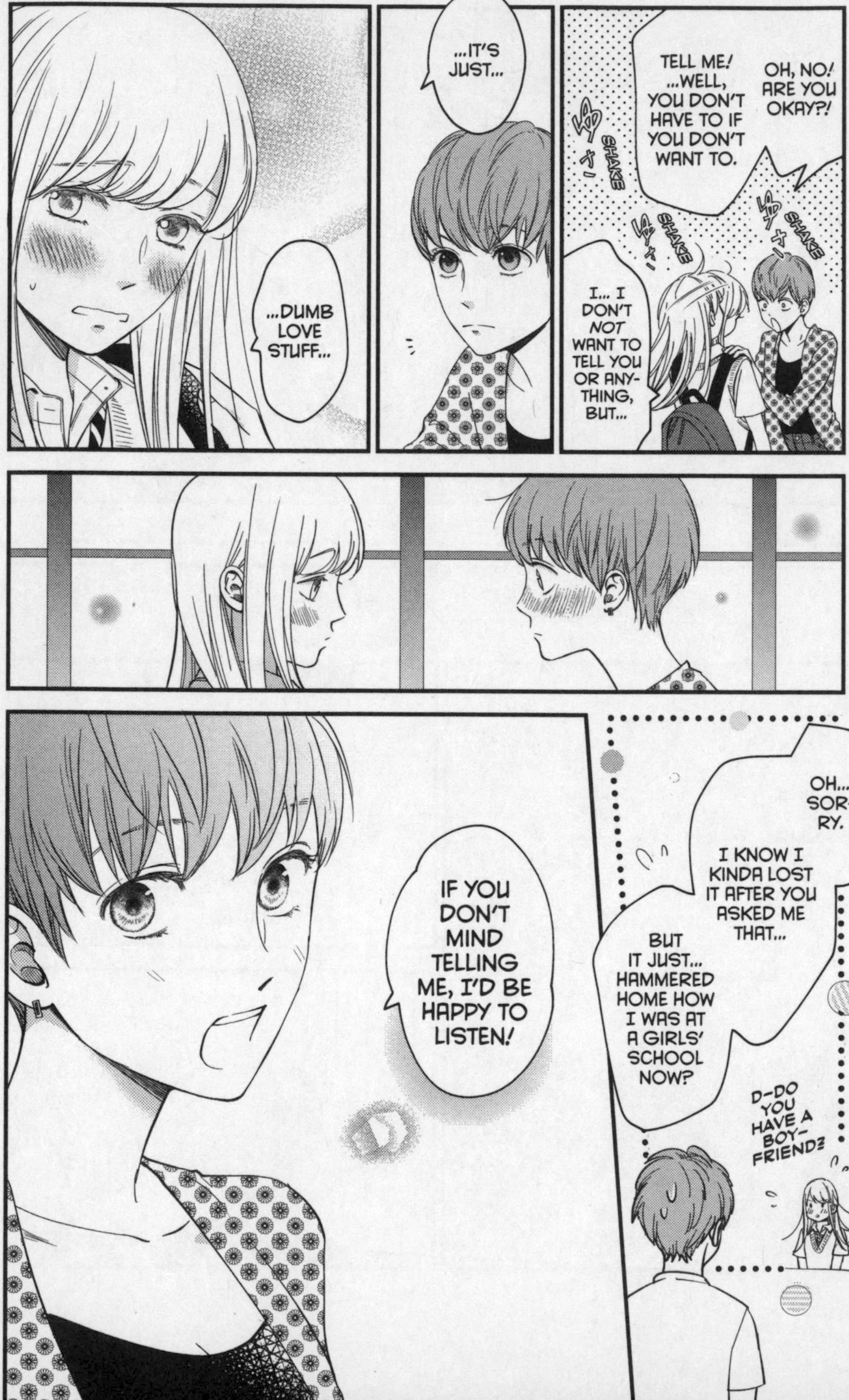
OH, NO! ARE YOU OKAY?!
TELL ME! ...WELL, YOU DON'T HAVE TO IF YOU DON'T WANT TO.
SHAKE
SHAKE
SHAKE
I... I DON'T *NOT* WANT TO TELL YOU OR ANYTHING, BUT...
...IT'S JUST...
...DUMB LOVE STUFF...
OH... SORRY.
I KNOW I KINDA LOST IT AFTER YOU ASKED ME THAT...
BUT IT JUST... HAMMERED HOME HOW I WAS AT A GIRLS' SCHOOL NOW?
D-DO YOU HAVE A BOY-FRIEND?
IF YOU DON'T MIND TELLING ME, I'D BE HAPPY TO LISTEN!

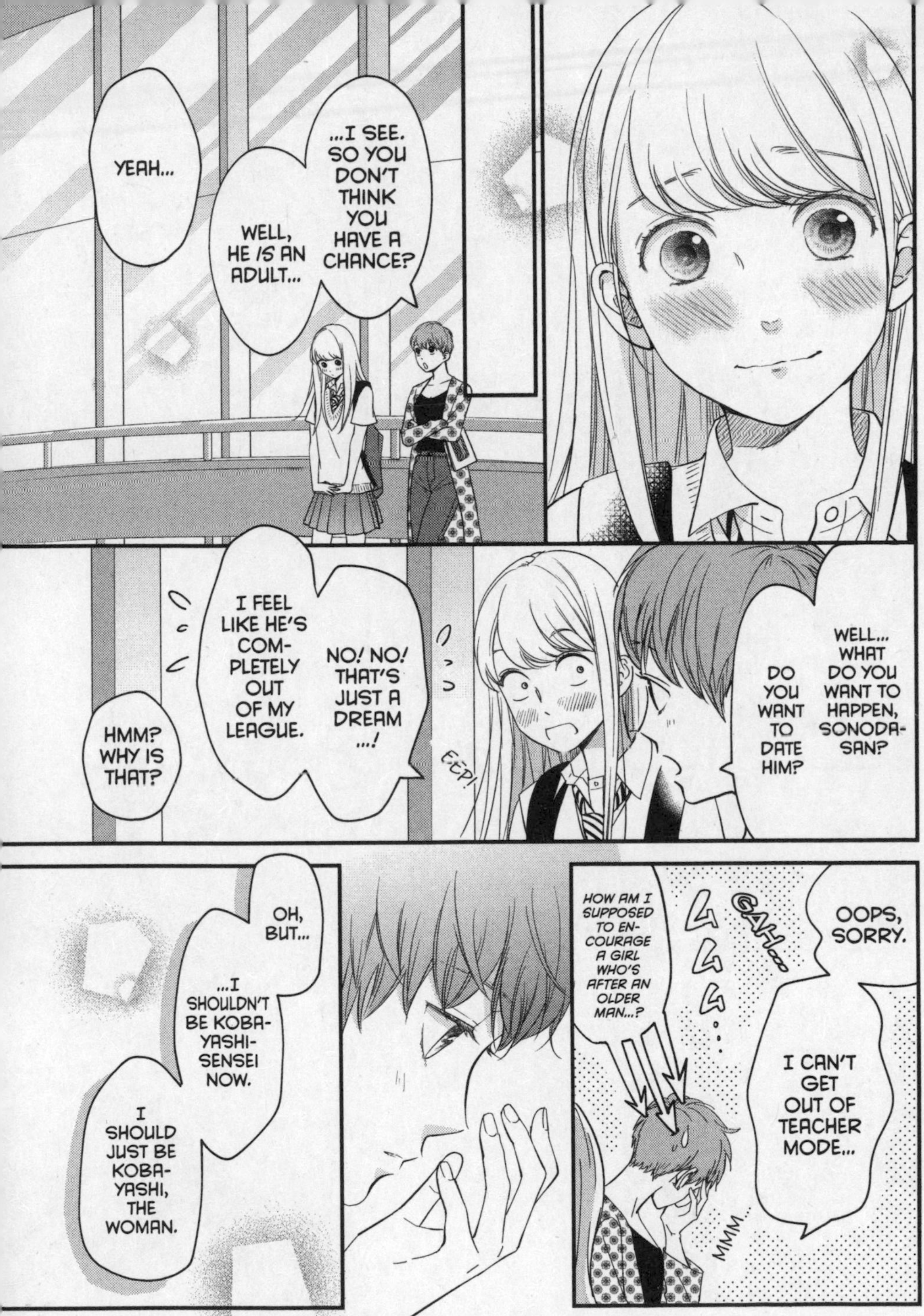
...I SEE. SO YOU DON'T THINK YOU HAVE A CHANCE?
YEAH...
WELL, HE *IS* AN ADULT...
WELL... WHAT DO YOU WANT TO HAPPEN, SONODA-SAN?
DO YOU WANT TO DATE HIM?
EEP!
NO! NO! THAT'S JUST A DREAM...!
I FEEL LIKE HE'S COM-PLETELY OUT OF MY LEAGUE.
HMM? WHY IS THAT?
OOPS, SORRY.
GAH...
HOW AM I SUPPOSED TO EN-COURAGE A GIRL WHO'S AFTER AN OLDER MAN...?
I CAN'T GET OUT OF TEACHER MODE...
MMM...
OH, BUT...
...I SHOULDN'T BE KOBA-YASHI-SENSEI NOW.
I SHOULD JUST BE KOBA-YASHI, THE WOMAN.

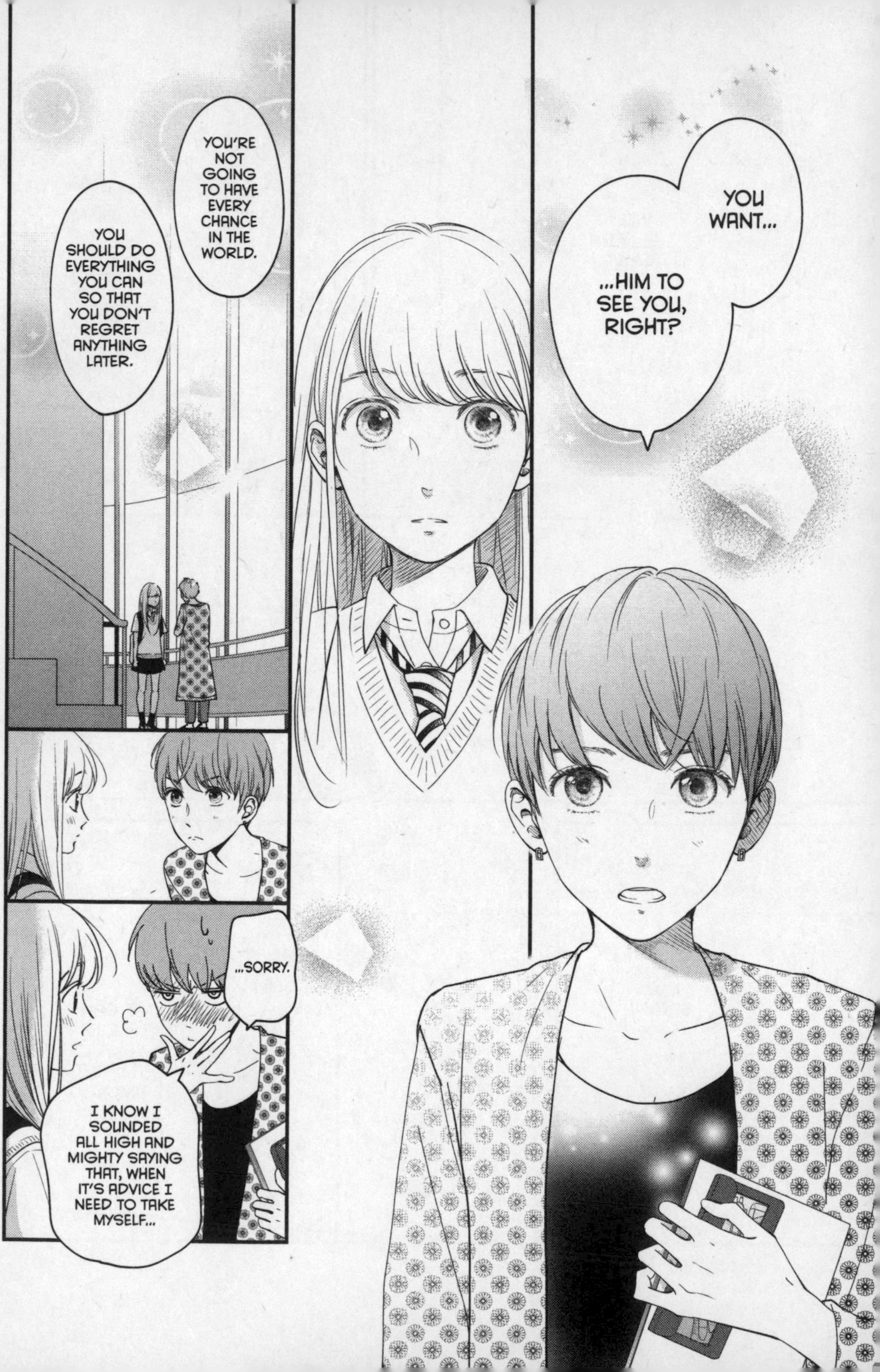
YOU WANT...
...HIM TO SEE YOU, RIGHT?
YOU'RE NOT GOING TO HAVE EVERY CHANCE IN THE WORLD.
YOU SHOULD DO EVERYTHING YOU CAN SO THAT YOU DON'T REGRET ANYTHING LATER.
...SORRY.
I KNOW I SOUNDED ALL HIGH AND MIGHTY SAYING THAT, WHEN IT'S ADVICE I NEED TO TAKE MYSELF...

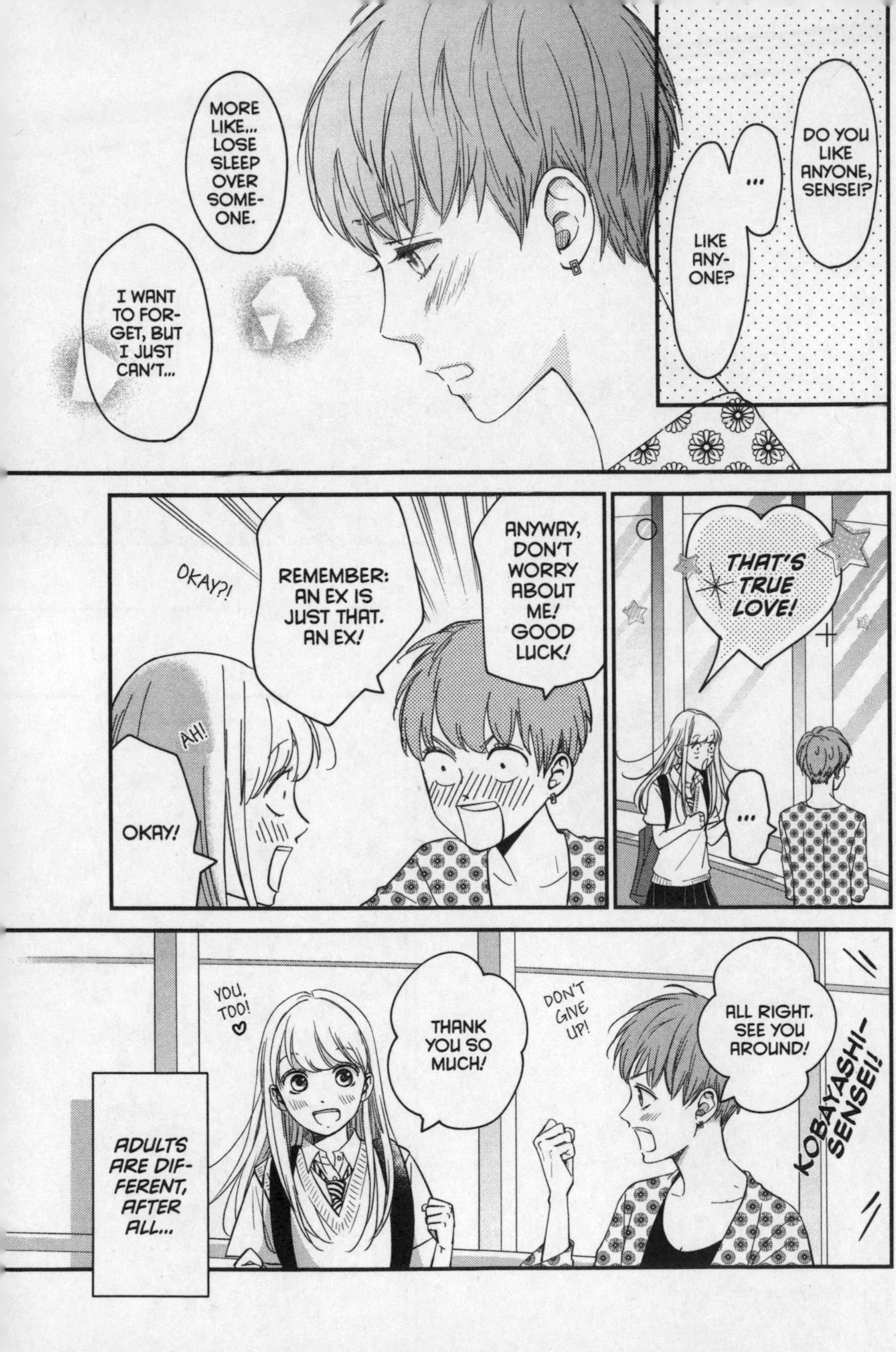
DO YOU LIKE ANYONE, SENSEI?
... LIKE ANYONE?
MORE LIKE... LOSE SLEEP OVER SOME-ONE.
I WANT TO FOR-GET, BUT I JUST CAN'T...
THAT'S TRUE LOVE!
...
ANYWAY, DON'T WORRY ABOUT ME! GOOD LUCK!
REMEMBER: AN EX IS JUST THAT. AN EX!
OKAY?!
AH!
OKAY!
KOBAYASHI-SENSEI!
ALL RIGHT. SEE YOU AROUND!
DON'T GIVE UP!
THANK YOU SO MUCH!
YOU, TOO!
ADULTS ARE DIF-FERENT, AFTER ALL...

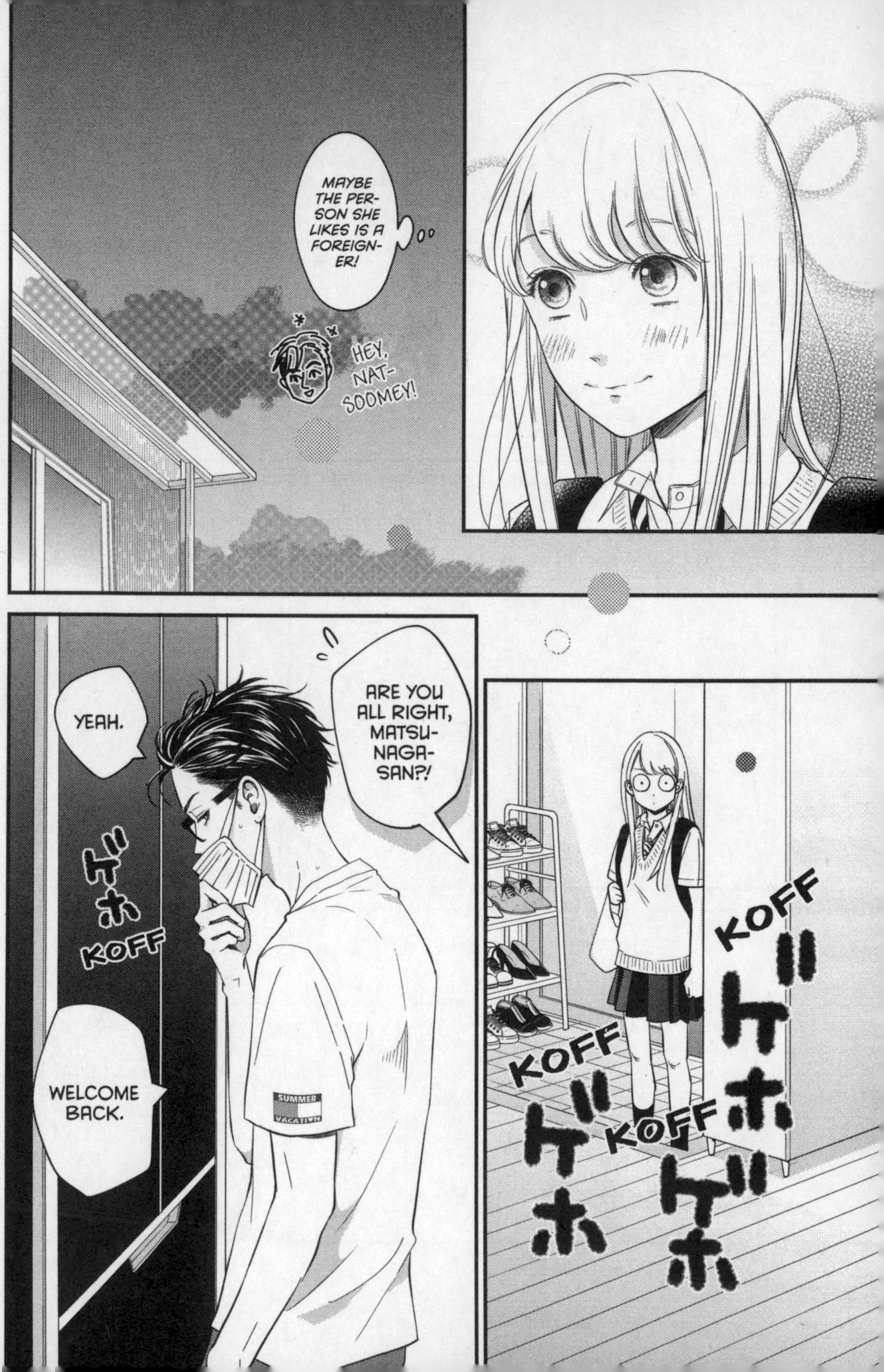
MAYBE THE PERSON SHE LIKES IS A FOREIGNER!
HEY, NAT-SOOMEY!
KOFF
ゲホ
KOFF
ゲホ
KOFF
ゲホ
ARE YOU ALL RIGHT, MATSUNAGA-SAN?!
YEAH.
ゲホ
KOFF
WELCOME BACK.
SUMMER VACATION

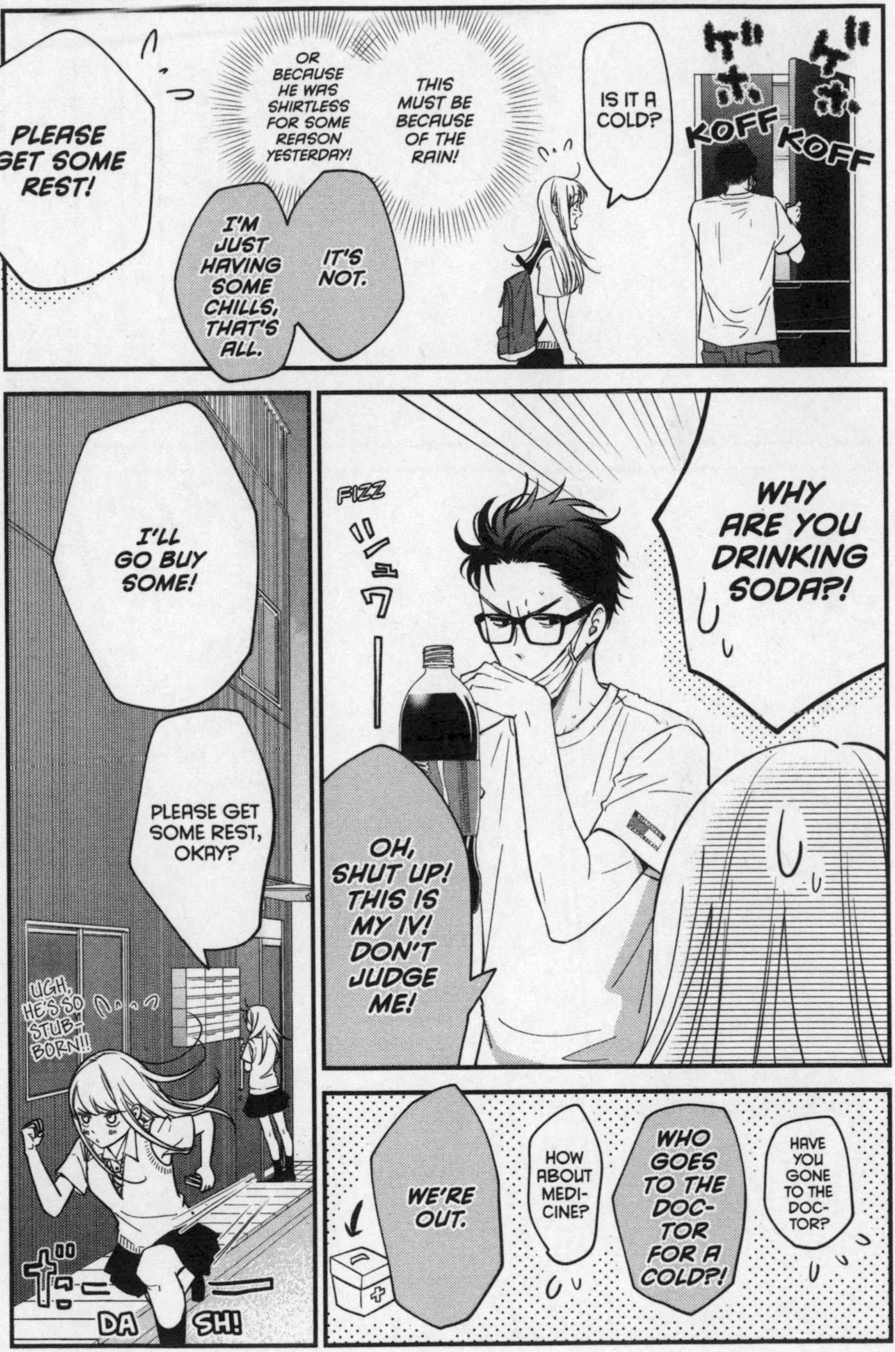
ゲホ ゲホ
KOFF KOFF
IS IT A COLD?
THIS MUST BE BECAUSE OF THE RAIN!
OR BECAUSE HE WAS SHIRTLESS FOR SOME REASON YESTERDAY!
IT'S NOT.
I'M JUST HAVING SOME CHILLS, THAT'S ALL.
PLEASE GET SOME REST!
WHY ARE YOU DRINKING SODA?!
FIZZ
シュワー
OH, SHUT UP! THIS IS MY IV! DON'T JUDGE ME!
HAVE YOU GONE TO THE DOCTOR?
WHO GOES TO THE DOCTOR FOR A COLD?!
HOW ABOUT MEDICINE?
WE'RE OUT.
I'LL GO BUY SOME!
PLEASE GET SOME REST, OKAY?
UGH, HE'S SO STUBBORN!!
ダーッ
DASH!

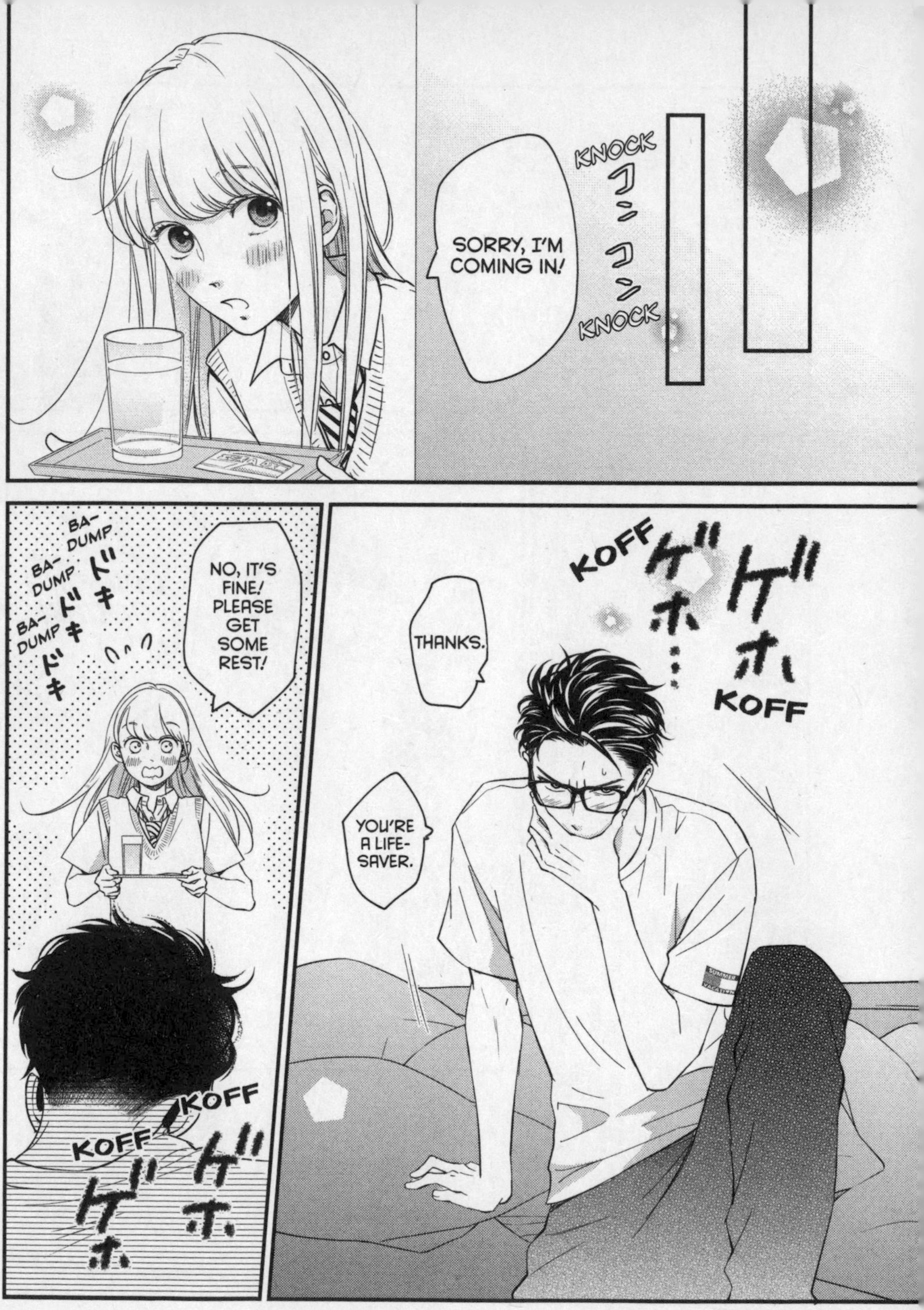
KNOCK
コン
コン
KNOCK
SORRY, I'M COMING IN!
KOFF
ゲホ…
ゲホ
KOFF
THANKS.
YOU'RE A LIFE-SAVER.
BA-DUMP
BA-DUMP
BA-DUMP
ドキ
ドキ
ドキ
NO, IT'S FINE! PLEASE GET SOME REST!
KOFF
KOFF
ゲホ
ゲホ

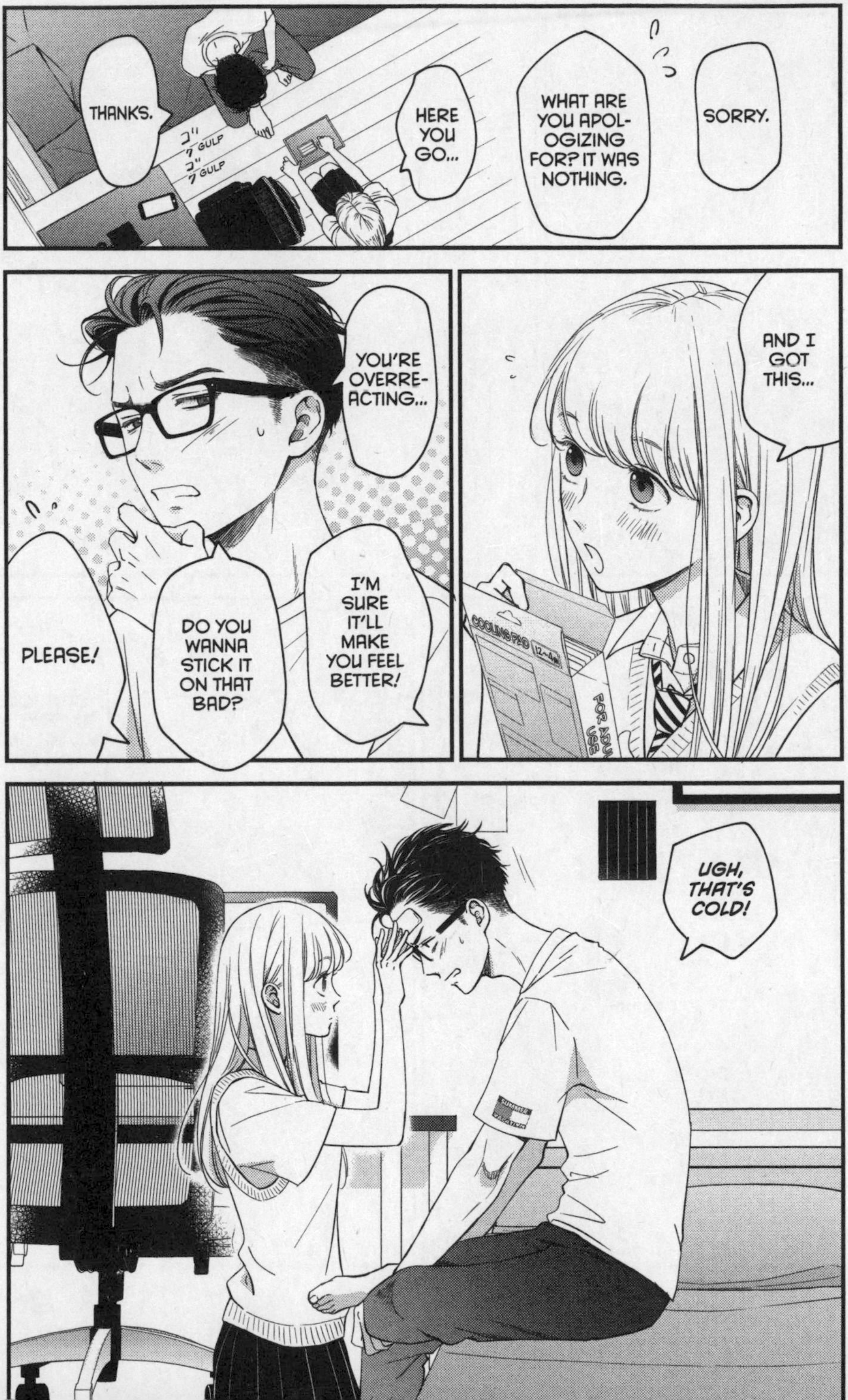
SORRY.
WHAT ARE YOU APOLOGIZING FOR? IT WAS NOTHING.
HERE YOU GO...
GULP
GULP
THANKS.
AND I GOT THIS...
COOLING PAD
YOU'RE OVERREACTING...
I'M SURE IT'LL MAKE YOU FEEL BETTER!
DO YOU WANNA STICK IT ON THAT BAD?
PLEASE!
UGH, THAT'S COLD!

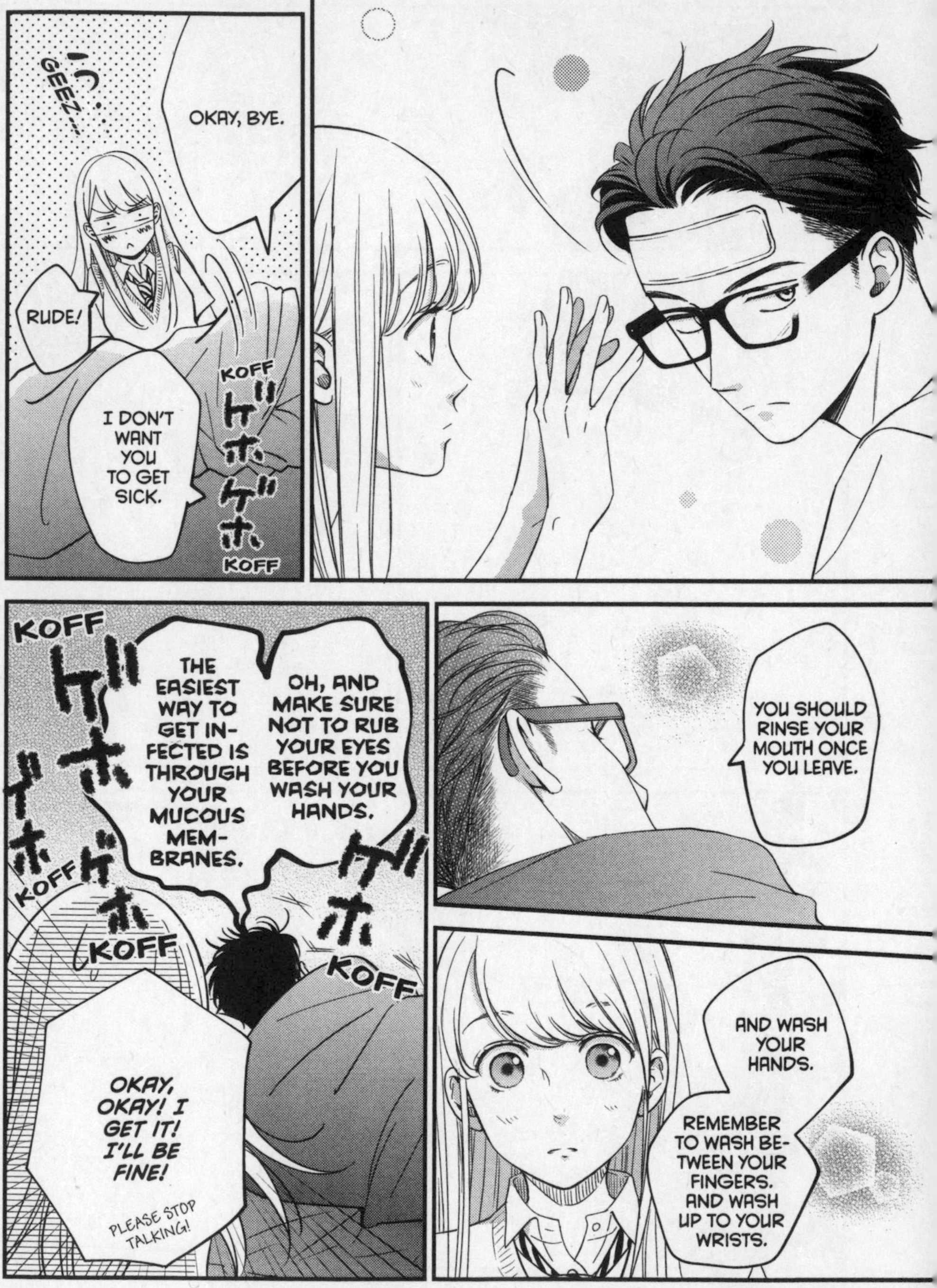
OKAY, BYE.
GEEZ...
RUDE!
KOFF
ゲホゲホ
KOFF
I DON'T WANT YOU TO GET SICK.
YOU SHOULD RINSE YOUR MOUTH ONCE YOU LEAVE.
AND WASH YOUR HANDS.
REMEMBER TO WASH BE-TWEEN YOUR FINGERS. AND WASH UP TO YOUR WRISTS.
OH, AND MAKE SURE NOT TO RUB YOUR EYES BEFORE YOU WASH YOUR HANDS.
THE EASIEST WAY TO GET IN-FECTED IS THROUGH YOUR MUCOUS MEM-BRANES.
KOFF
ゲホ
ゲホ
KOFF
KOFF
ゲホ
KOFF
OKAY, OKAY! I GET IT! I'LL BE FINE!
PLEASE STOP TALKING!

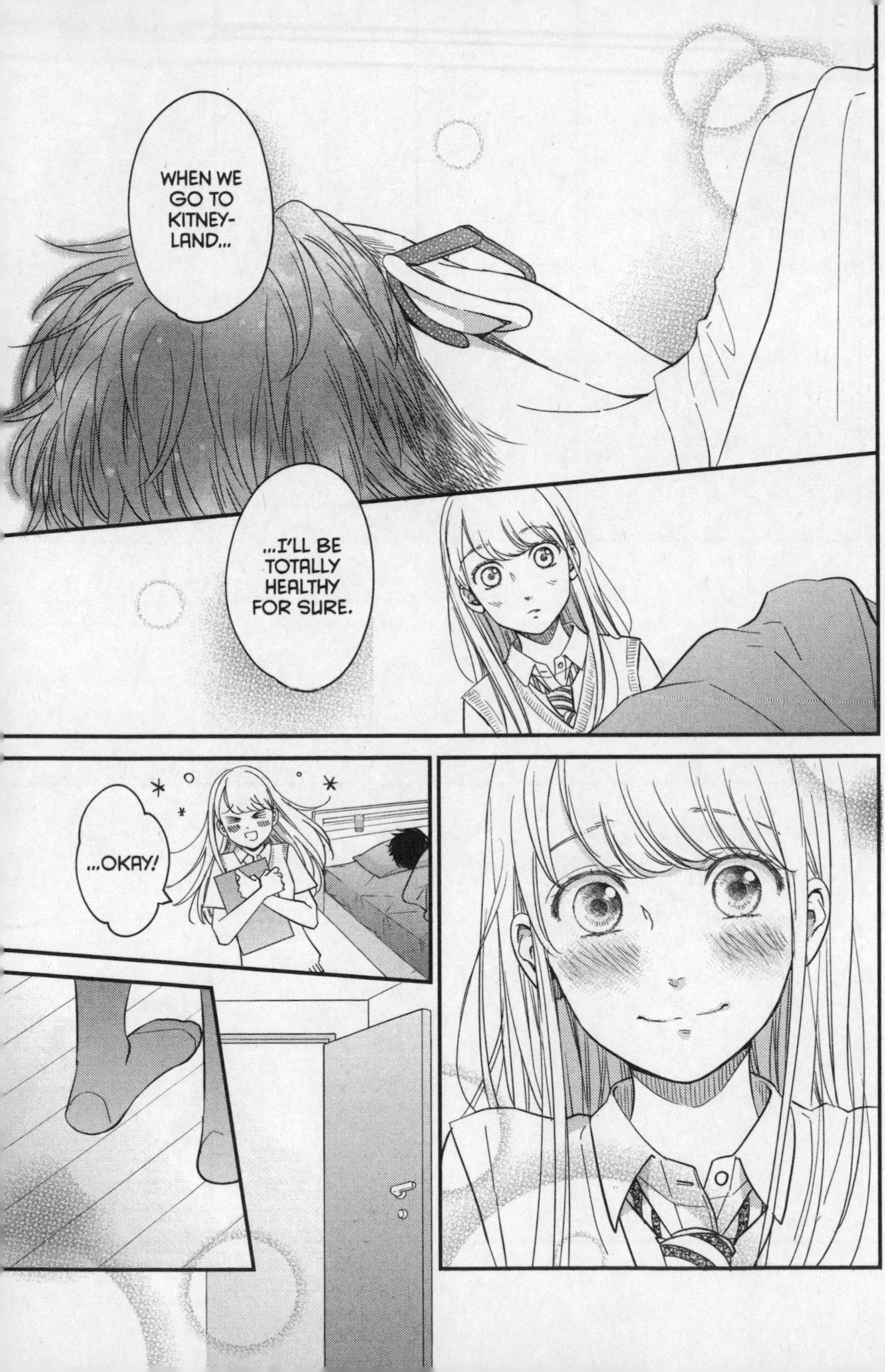
WHEN WE GO TO KITNEY-LAND...
...I'LL BE TOTALLY HEALTHY FOR SURE.
...OKAY!

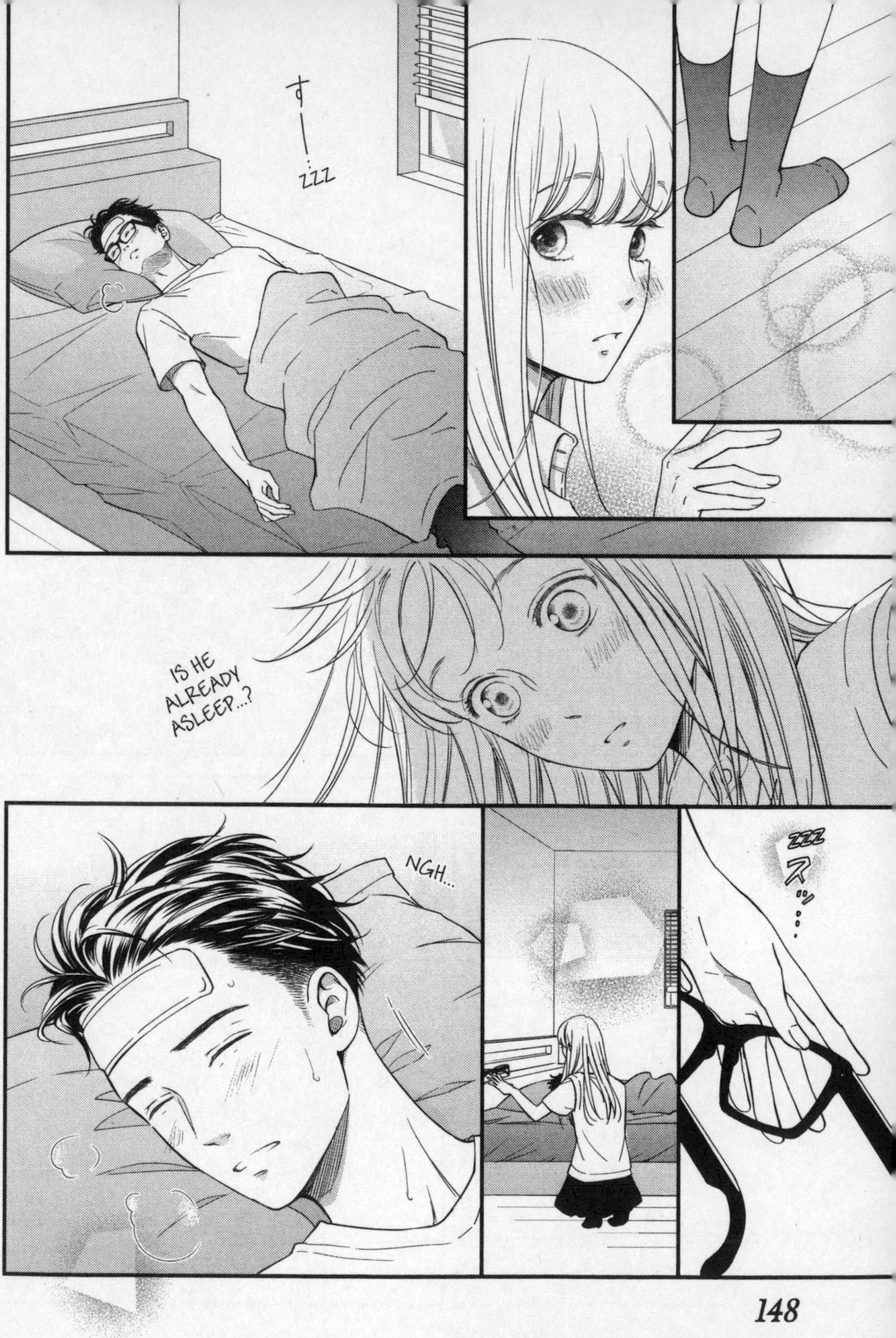
すー…
zzz
IS HE ALREADY ASLEEP...?
zzz
スッ…
NGH...

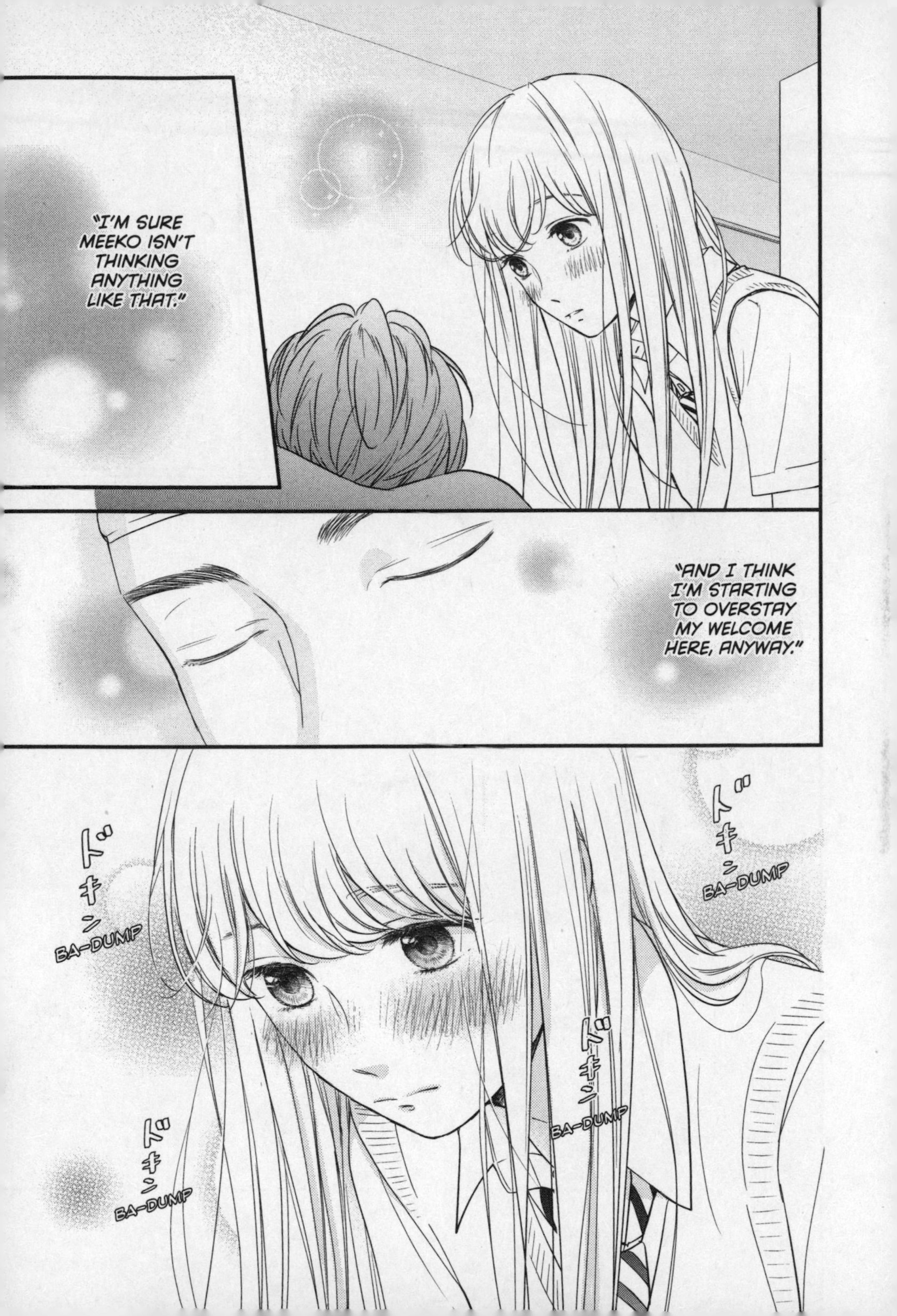
"I'M SURE MEEKO ISN'T THINKING ANYTHING LIKE THAT."
"AND I THINK I'M STARTING TO OVERSTAY MY WELCOME HERE, ANYWAY."
ドキン
BA-DUMP
ドキン
BA-DUMP
ドキン
BA-DUMP
ドキン
BA-DUMP

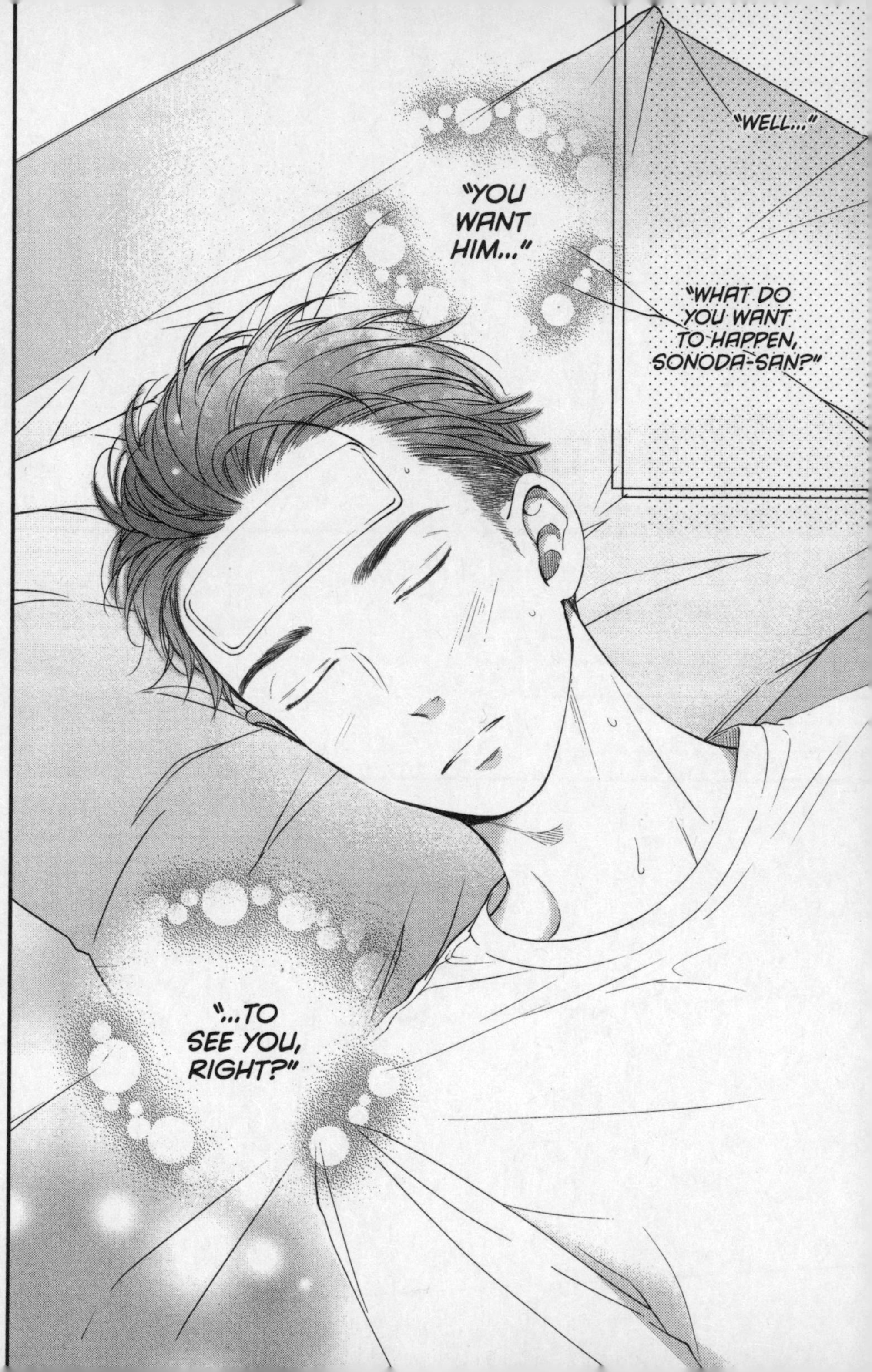
"WELL..."
"WHAT DO YOU WANT TO HAPPEN, SONODA-SAN?"
"YOU WANT HIM..."
"...TO SEE YOU, RIGHT?"

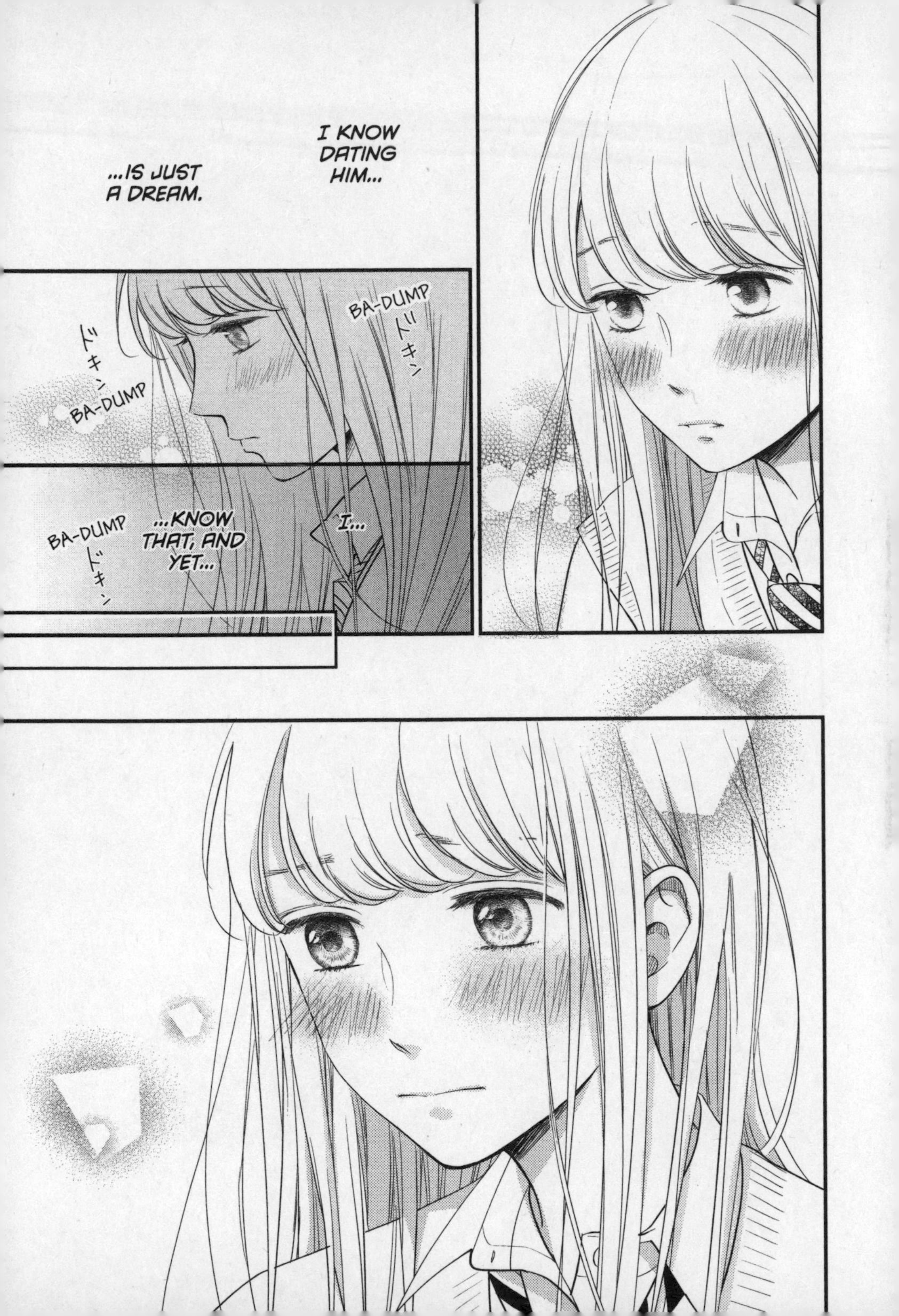
I KNOW DATING HIM...
...IS JUST A DREAM.
BA-DUMP ドキン
ドキン BA-DUMP
I...
...KNOW THAT, AND YET...
BA-DUMP ドキン

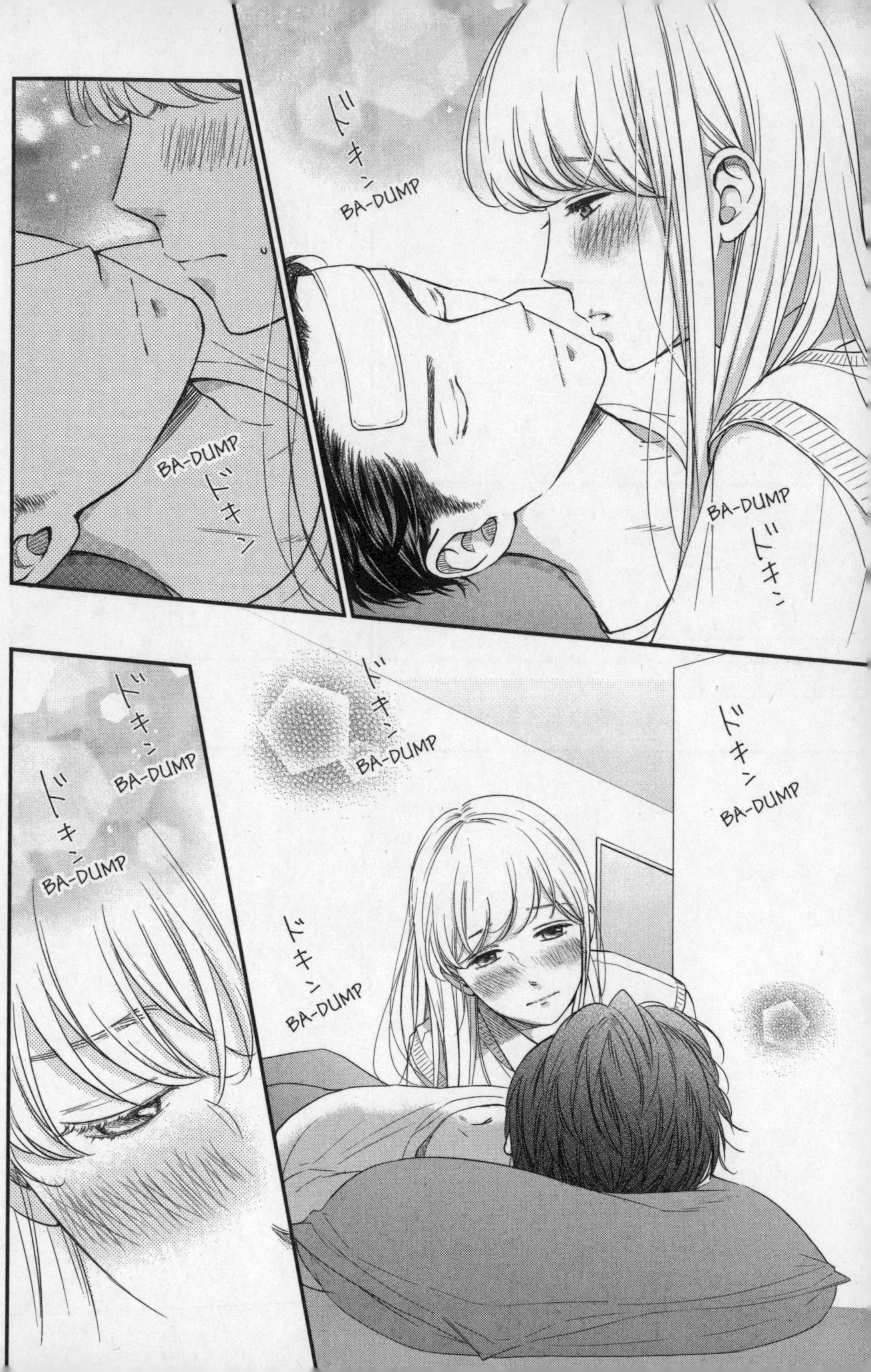
ドキン
BA-DUMP
BA-DUMP
ドキン
BA-DUMP
ドキン
ドキン
BA-DUMP
ドキン
BA-DUMP
ドキン
BA-DUMP
ドキン
BA-DUMP
ドキン
BA-DUMP

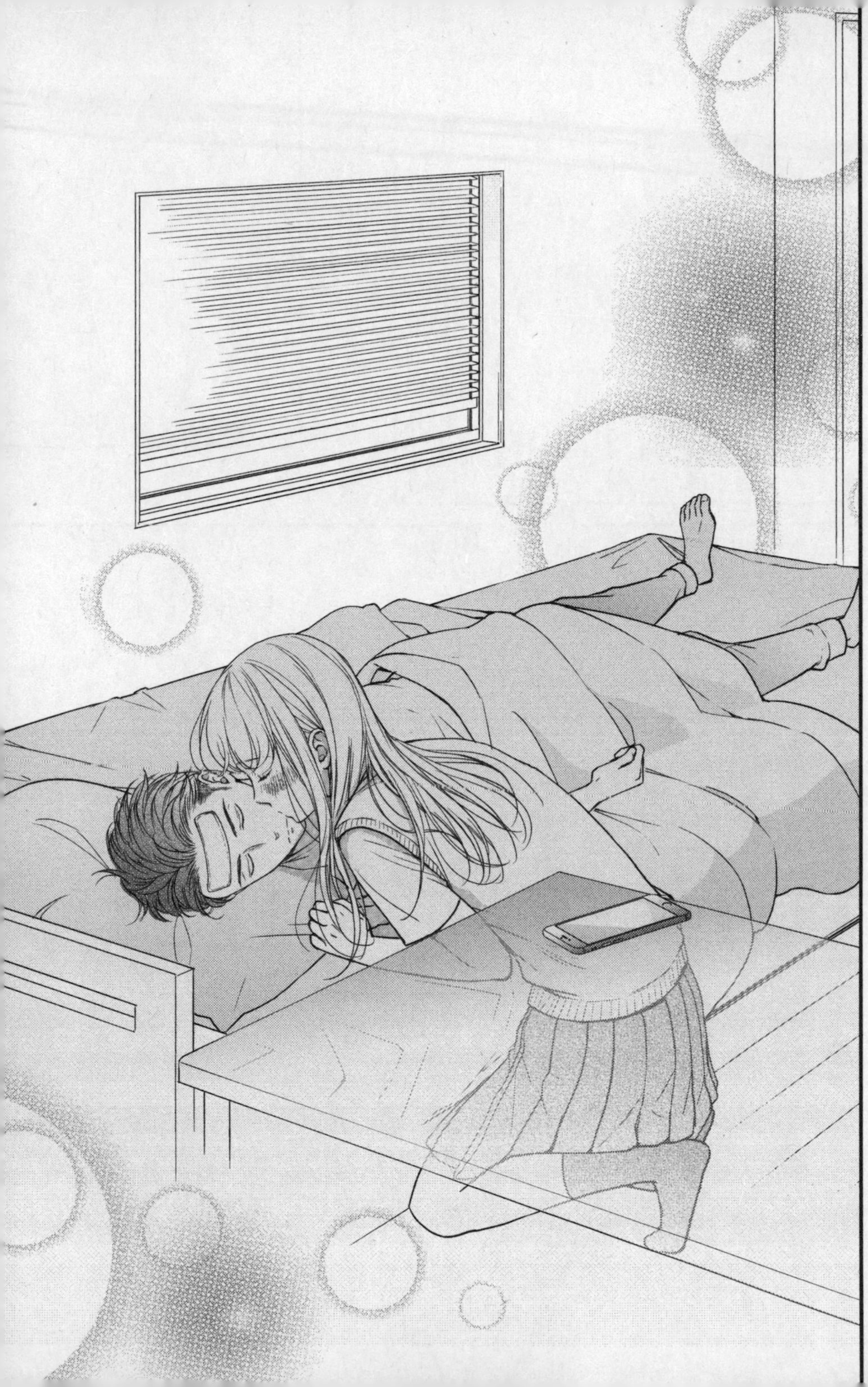

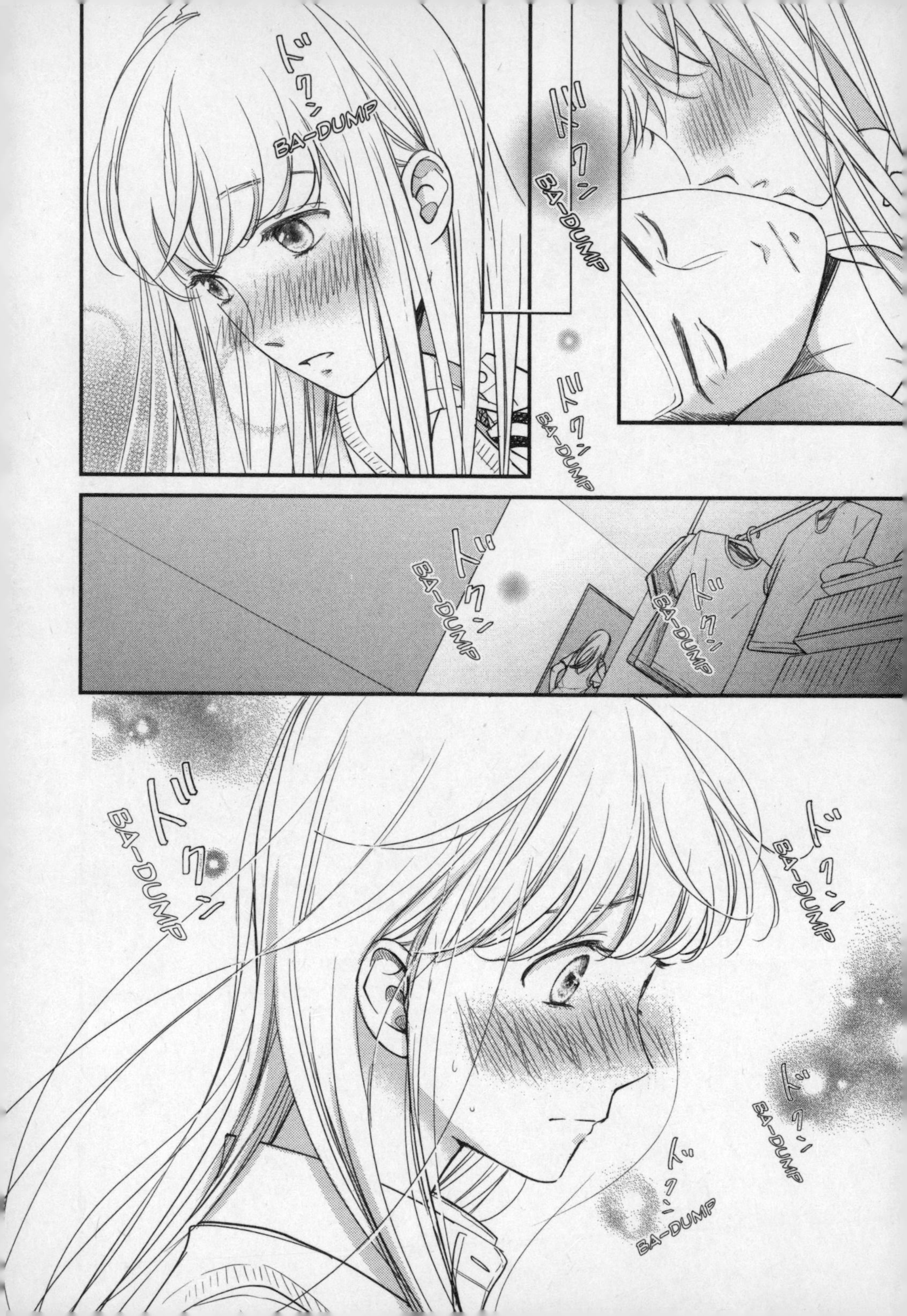
BA-DUMP
BA-DUMP
BA-DUMP
BA-DUMP
BA-DUMP
BA-DUMP
BA-DUMP
BA-DUMP
BA-DUMP

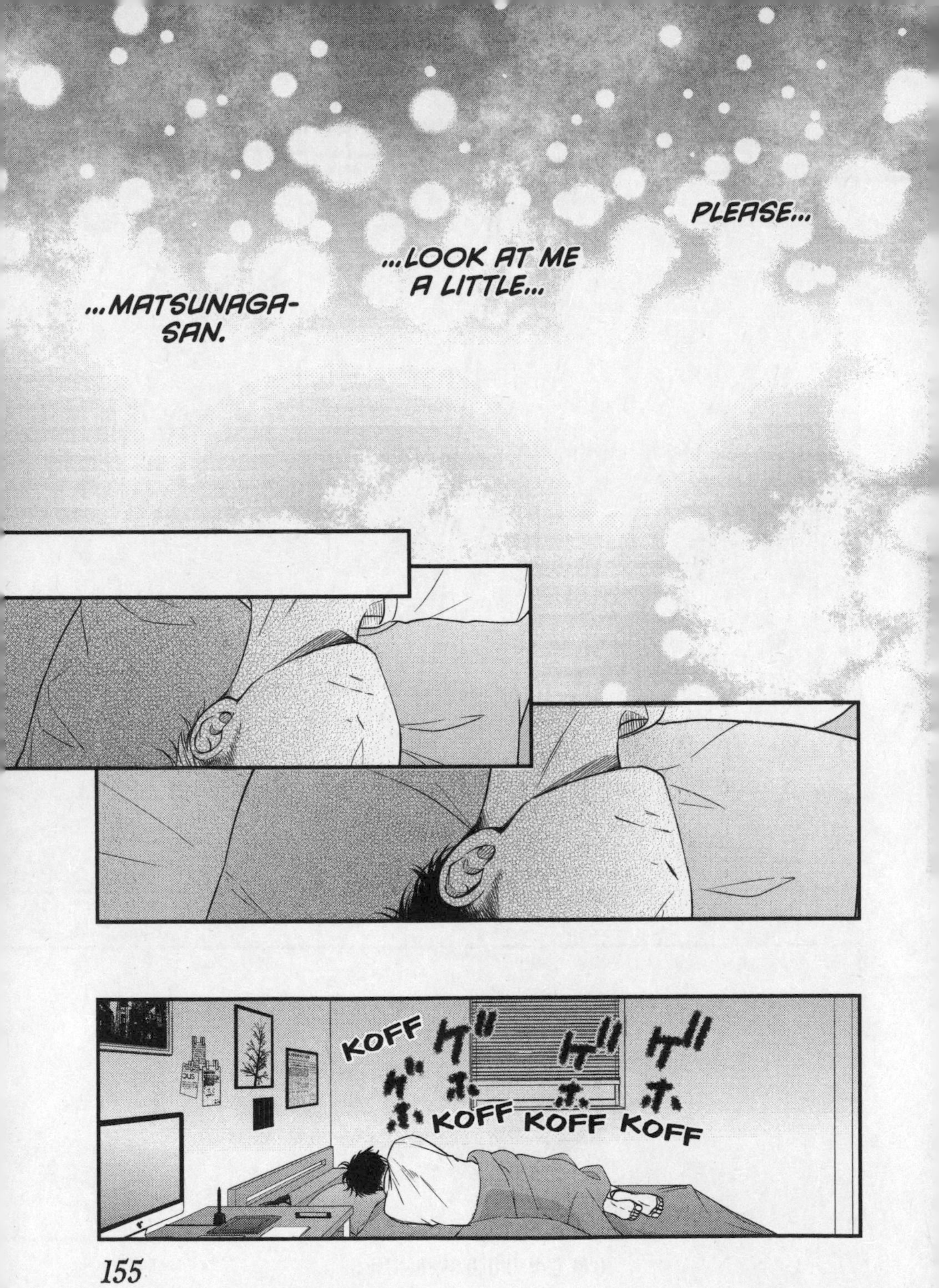
PLEASE...
...LOOK AT ME A LITTLE...
...MATSUNAGA-SAN.
ゲホ
KOFF
ゲホ
KOFF
ゲホ
KOFF
ゲホ
KOFF

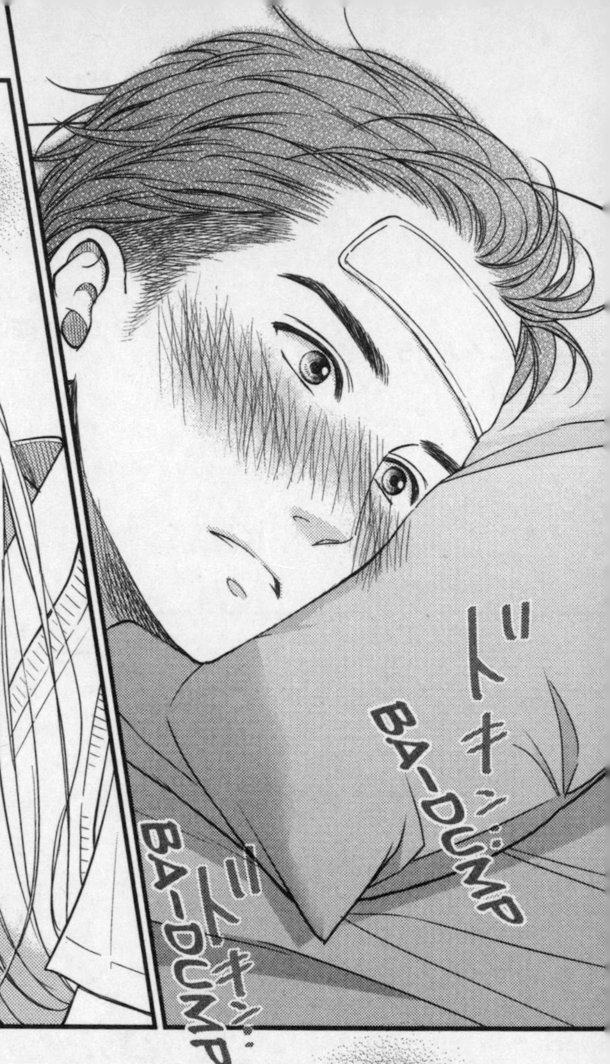
ドキン
BA-DUMP
ドキン
BA-DUMP

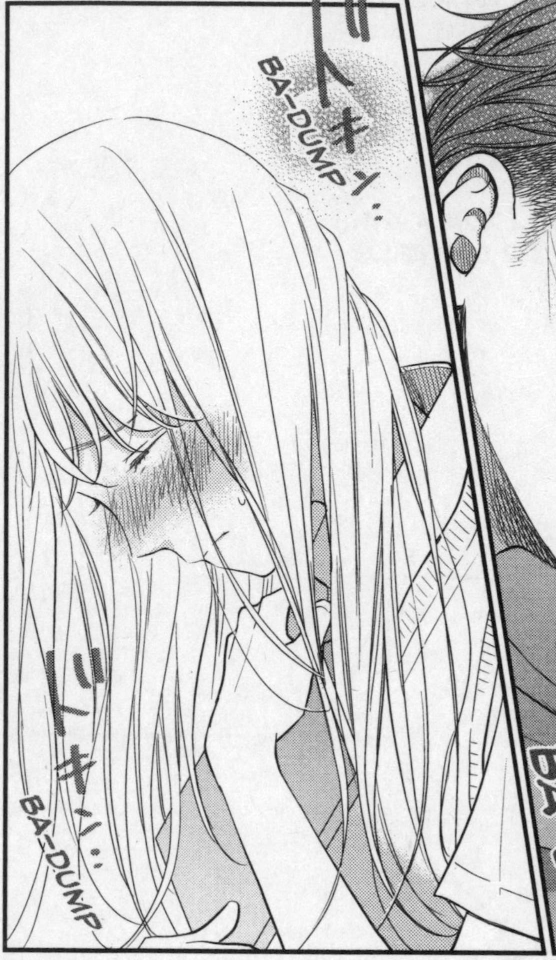
ドキッ
BA-DUMP..
ドキッ
BA-DUMP

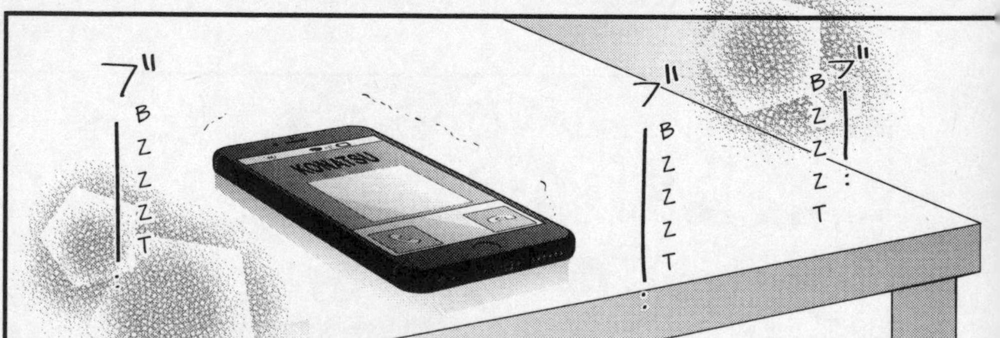
ブー
BZZZT..
ブー
BZZZT..
ブー
BZZZT..

TO BE CONTINUED IN VOLUME 5

AFTERWORD

THANKS FOR READING *LIVING-ROOM MATSUNAGA-SAN!*

WOW! I CAN'T BELIEVE IT! VOLUME 4 ALREADY! I FEEL LIKE I STARTED YESTERDAY...

PLUS, THE NEXT CHAPTER (ROOM 17) IS GOING TO BE THE COVER FEATURE!! I CAN'T BELIEVE IT!!

AND MY SHORT STORY COLLECTION *TOMODACHI NO UTA* IS GOING ON SALE AT THE SAME TIME!!

(...I THINK I MAY DIE TOMORROW...)

BUT!! ANYWAY!! IT'S ALL THANKS TO YOU, MY READERS, THAT ALL THIS AMAZING STUFF COULD HAPPEN!! I REALLY, TRULY AM IN YOUR DEBT!!

I'M GOING TO DO MY BEST TO KEEP PUTTING OUT EXCITING STORIES, CHAPTER BY CHAPTER, SO PLEASE LOOK FORWARD TO IT!!!!

> I FOUND ALL MY DESIGN DRAFTS OF MATSUNAGA-SAN!!!
> (I DIDN'T THROW THEM OUT AFTER ALL!!!!!) I WENT THROUGH A LOT OF DIFFERENT CHOICES. WHICH IS YOUR FAVORITE?

UNDERCUT

ENDED UP GOING WITH THIS!

THIS BECAME KEN-CHAN.

KEN

NO FACIAL HAIR NOW

THIS IS WHAT WOULD HAPPEN IF YOU PUT THEM ALL TOGETHER

SEE YOU AGAIN IN VOLUME 5!!

SPECIAL THANKS

EDITOR KITAHARA, EVERYONE IN THE DESSERT EDITORIAL DEPARTMENT, THE DESIGNERS, EVERYONE AT THE PRINTER

MY ASSISTANTS (EI AND SAKATA), MY FRIENDS AND FAMILY

...AND MY READERS! THANK YOU ALL SO MUCH!! ♡♡♡